桂　　正和

Masakazu Katsura

About the title: *I"s* is meant to be the plural form of I, and I felt it would make for a catchy title. Even if you force yourself to read it in the plural form, I heard some people might read it as "Ice," but that sounded too cold so I changed it to "zu." If it's with an apostrophe, it may seem like it's 'I's', but then that wasn't totally the effect I was going for. So I put a sonant mark on the S to make it sound like "zu." [Be sure you pronounce it this way: "ai-zu."—*ed*.] Words are hard.

When Masakazu Katsura was a high school student, he entered a story he had drawn into a manga contest in hopes of winning money to buy a stereo. He won the contest and was soon published in the immensely popular weekly manga anthology magazine WEEKLY SHONEN JUMP. Katsura was quickly propelled into manga-artist stardom and his subsequent comic series, WINGMAN, VIDEO GIRL AI, DNA2, and SHADOW LADY are perennial fan favorites. *I"s*, which began publication in 1997 and ran for 15 volumes, also inspired an original video series. Katsura lives in Tokyo and possesses an extensive collection of Batman memorabilia.

I"s

VOL. 1: IORI
The SHONEN JUMP ADVANCED Graphic Novel Edition

STORY AND ART BY
MASAKAZU KATSURA

English Adaptation/Lance Caselman
Translation/Joe Yamazaki
Touch-up Art & Lettering/Freeman Wong
Design/Hidemi Sahara
Editor/Kit Fox

Managing Editor/Frances E. Wall
Editorial Director/Elizabeth Kawasaki
VP & Editor in Chief/Yumi Hoashi
Sr. Director of Acquisitions/Rika Inouye
Sr. VP of Marketing/Liza Coppola
Exec. VP of Sales & Marketing/John Easum
Publisher/Hyoe Narita

I"S © 1997 by Masakazu Katsura. All rights reserved. First published in Japan in 1997 by SHUEISHA Inc., Tokyo. English translation rights in the United States of America and Canada arranged by SHUEISHA Inc. Some scenes containing nudity have been modified from the original Japanese edition. The stories, characters and incidents mentioned in this publication are entirely fictional.

Printed in the U.S.A.

Published by VIZ Media, LLC
P.O. Box 77010
San Francisco, CA 94107

SHONEN JUMP ADVANCED Graphic Novel Edition
10 9 8 7 6 5 4 3 2
First printing, March 2005
Second printing, September 2006

www.viz.com

PARENTAL ADVISORY
I"S is rated T+ for Older Teen and is recommended for ages 16 and up. It contains harsh language and sexual situations.

THE WORLD'S MOST CUTTING-EDGE MANGA

SHONEN JUMP ADVANCED
www.shonenjump.com

SHONEN JUMP ADVANCED GRAPHIC NOVEL

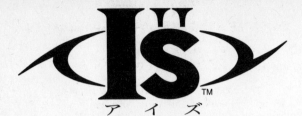

I"s™

アイズ

Vol. 1
IORI

STORY & ART BY
MASAKAZU KATSURA

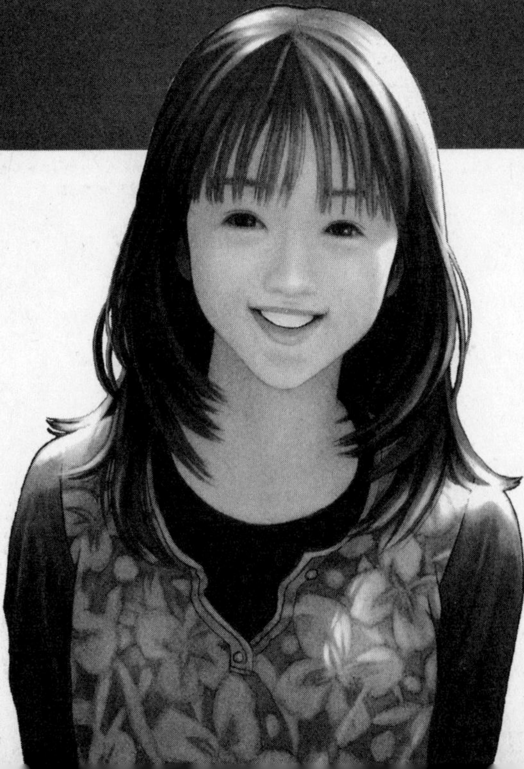

I"s
アイズ
Vol. 1

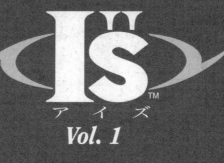

CONTENTS

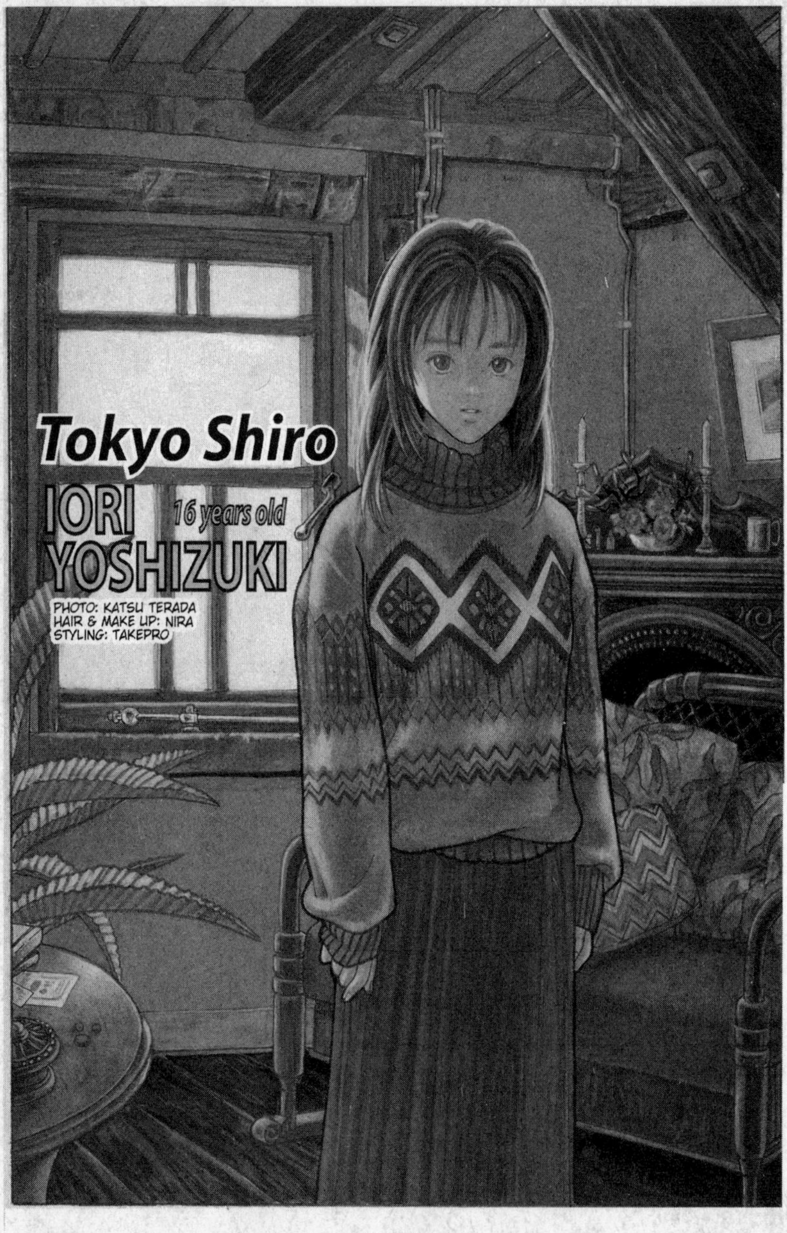
Tokyo Shiro
IORI YOSHIZUKI
16 years old
PHOTO: KATSU TERADA
HAIR & MAKE UP: NIRA
STYLING: TAKEPRO

Chapter 1: The Approach

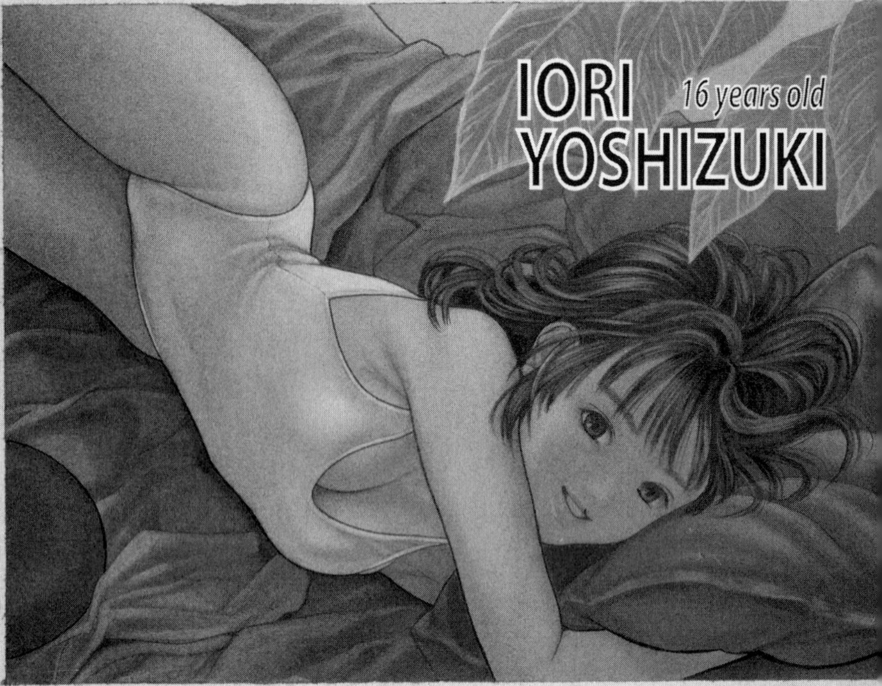
IORI YOSHIZUKI
16 years old

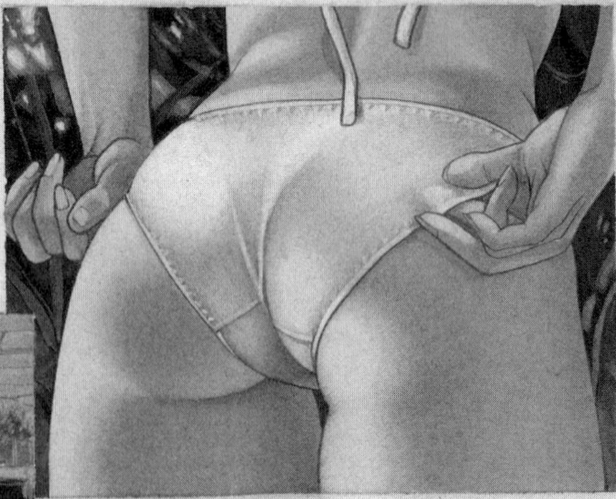

IORI IS A MEMBER OF HER HIGH SCHOOL'S DRAMA CLUB. THOUGH NORMALLY SHY, SHE TRANSFORMS ON STAGE...

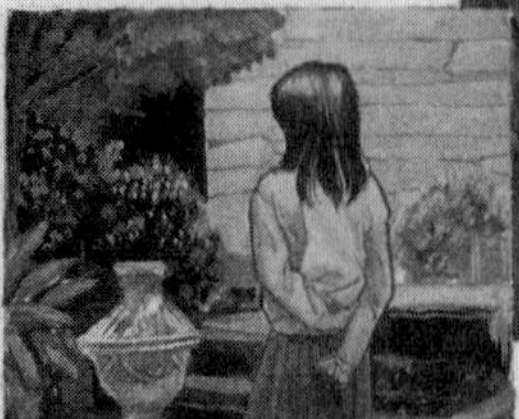

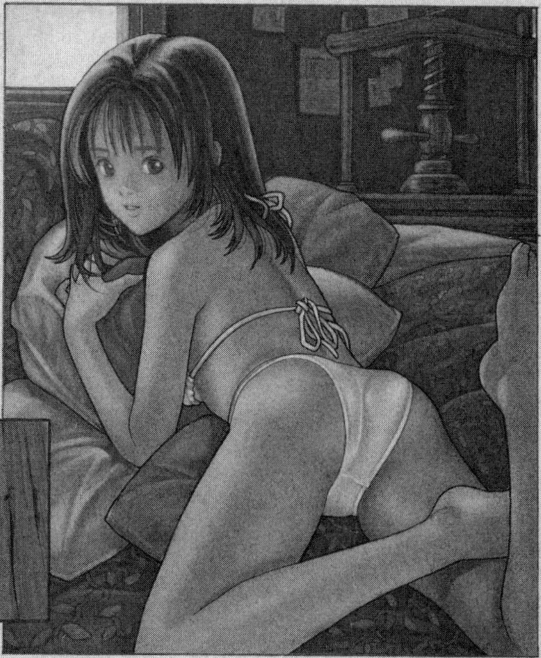

"IT'S FUN PRETENDING TO BE DIFFERENT PEOPLE." SURPRISINGLY, IORI DOES NOT DREAM OF BEING A FILM STAR OR A SINGER. HER PASSION IS FOR THE CRAFT OF ACTING.

IORI YOSHIZUKI *16 years old*

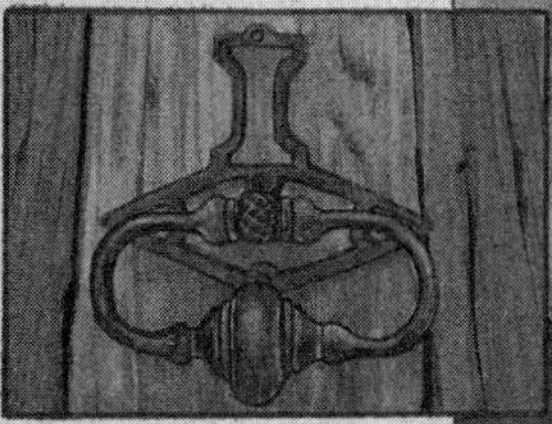

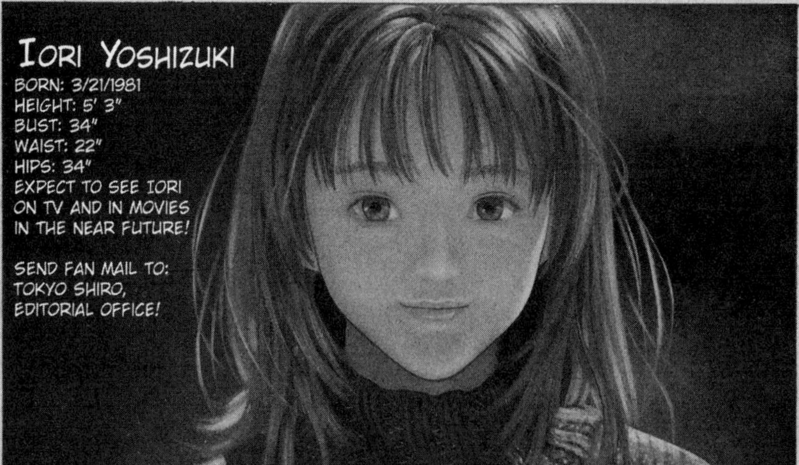
IORI YOSHIZUKI
BORN: 3/21/1981
HEIGHT: 5' 3"
BUST: 34"
WAIST: 22"
HIPS: 34"
EXPECT TO SEE IORI ON TV AND IN MOVIES IN THE NEAR FUTURE!
SEND FAN MAIL TO: TOKYO SHIRO, EDITORIAL OFFICE!

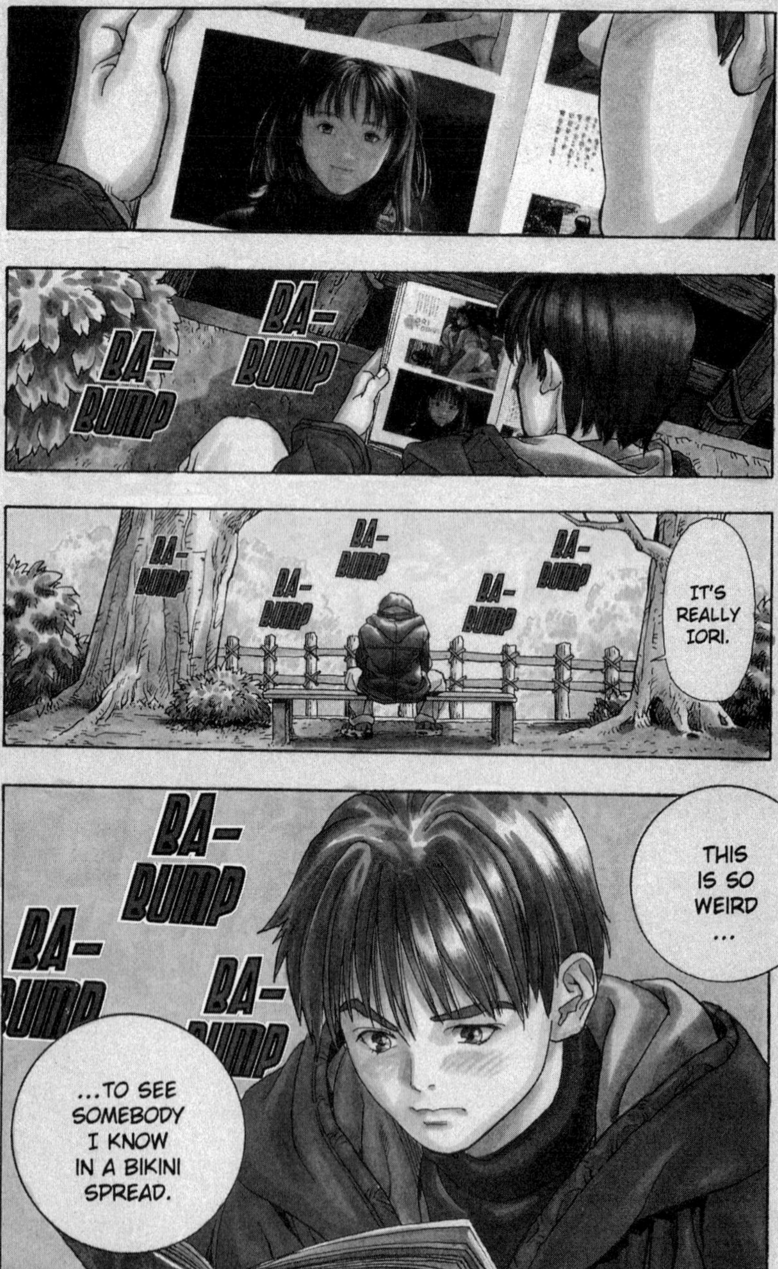
BA-BUMP
BA-BUMP
BA-BUMP
BA-BUMP
BA-BUMP
BA-BUMP
BA-BUMP
IT'S REALLY IORI.
THIS IS SO WEIRD ...
BA-BUMP
BA-
BA-
...TO SEE SOMEBODY I KNOW IN A BIKINI SPREAD.

I"s

アイズ

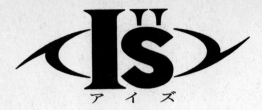

Chapter 1: The Approach

IS

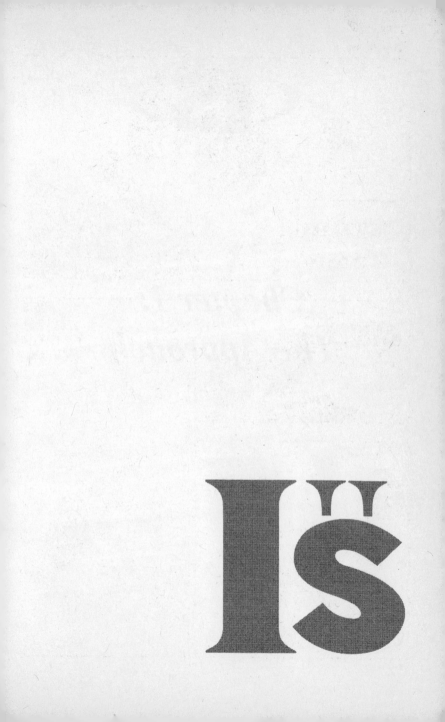

READ THIS WAY

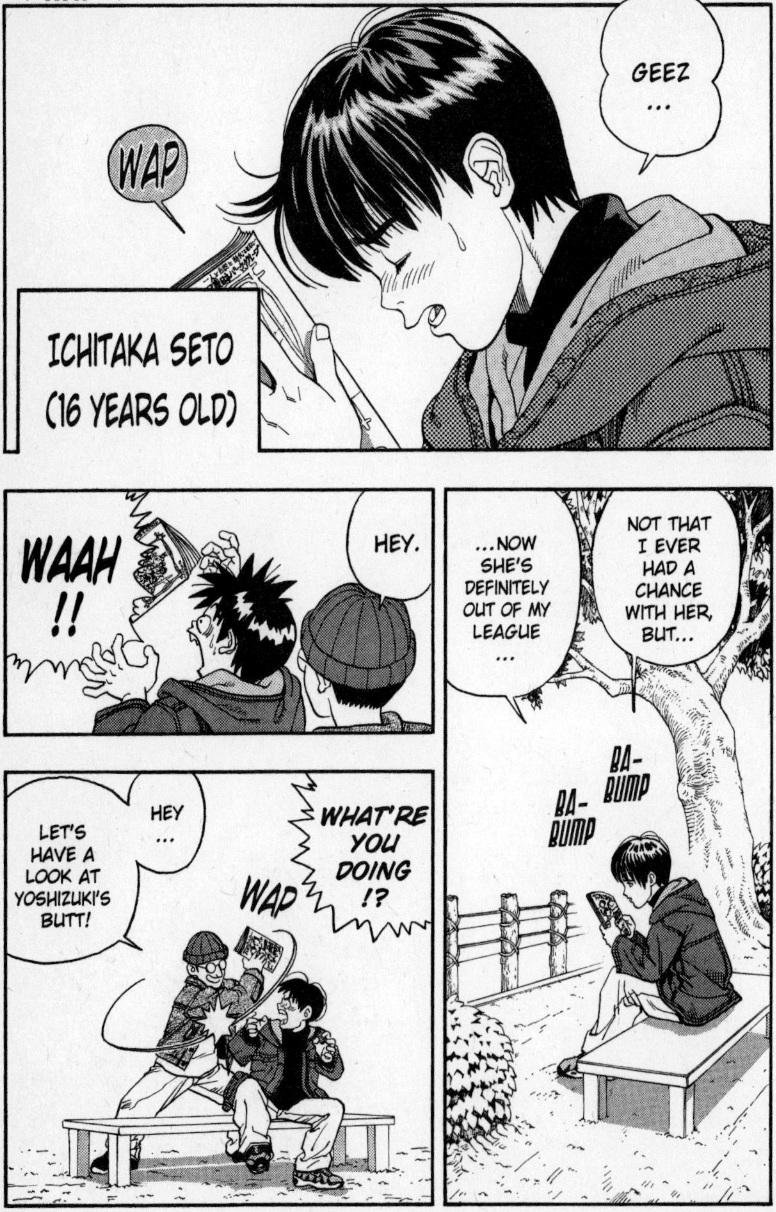
GEEZ ...
WAP
ICHITAKA SETO (16 YEARS OLD)
NOT THAT I EVER HAD A CHANCE WITH HER, BUT...
...NOW SHE'S DEFINITELY OUT OF MY LEAGUE ...
BA-BUMP
BA-BUMP
HEY.
WAAH !!
HEY ...
LET'S HAVE A LOOK AT YOSHIZUKI'S BUTT!
WHAT'RE YOU DOING !?
WAP

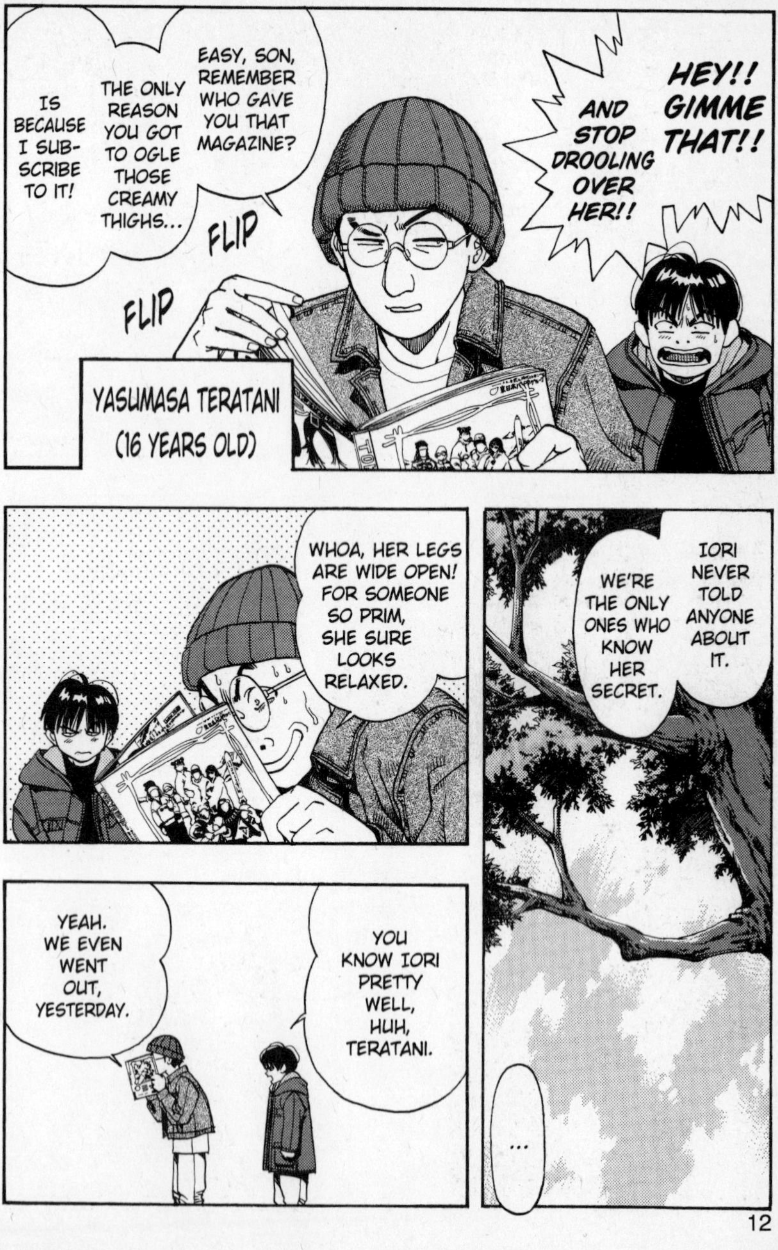
HEY!! GIMME THAT!!
AND STOP DROOLING OVER HER!!
EASY, SON, REMEMBER WHO GAVE YOU THAT MAGAZINE?
THE ONLY REASON YOU GOT TO OGLE THOSE CREAMY THIGHS...
IS BECAUSE I SUB-SCRIBE TO IT!
FLIP
FLIP
YASUMASA TERATANI
(16 YEARS OLD)
IORI NEVER TOLD ANYONE ABOUT IT.
WE'RE THE ONLY ONES WHO KNOW HER SECRET.
...
WHOA, HER LEGS ARE WIDE OPEN! FOR SOMEONE SO PRIM, SHE SURE LOOKS RELAXED.
YOU KNOW IORI PRETTY WELL, HUH, TERATANI.
YEAH. WE EVEN WENT OUT, YESTERDAY.

READ THIS WAY

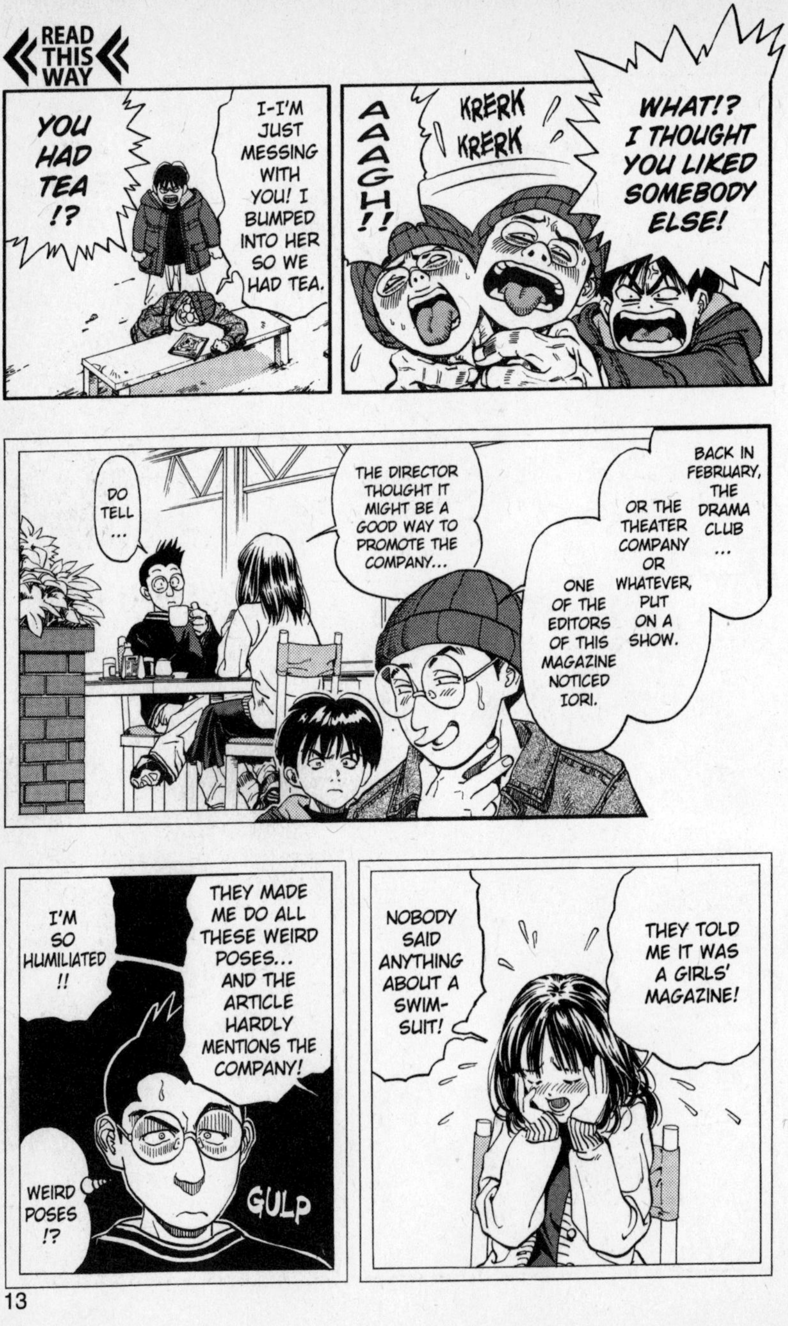
WHAT!? I THOUGHT YOU LIKED SOMEBODY ELSE!
KRERK KRERK
AAAGH!!
I-I'M JUST MESSING WITH YOU! I BUMPED INTO HER SO WE HAD TEA.
YOU HAD TEA !?
BACK IN FEBRUARY, THE DRAMA CLUB ... OR THE THEATER COMPANY OR WHATEVER, PUT ON A SHOW.
ONE OF THE EDITORS OF THIS MAGAZINE NOTICED IORI.
THE DIRECTOR THOUGHT IT MIGHT BE A GOOD WAY TO PROMOTE THE COMPANY...
DO TELL ...
THEY TOLD ME IT WAS A GIRLS' MAGAZINE!
NOBODY SAID ANYTHING ABOUT A SWIM-SUIT!
THEY MADE ME DO ALL THESE WEIRD POSES... AND THE ARTICLE HARDLY MENTIONS THE COMPANY!
I'M SO HUMILIATED !!
GULP
WEIRD POSES !?

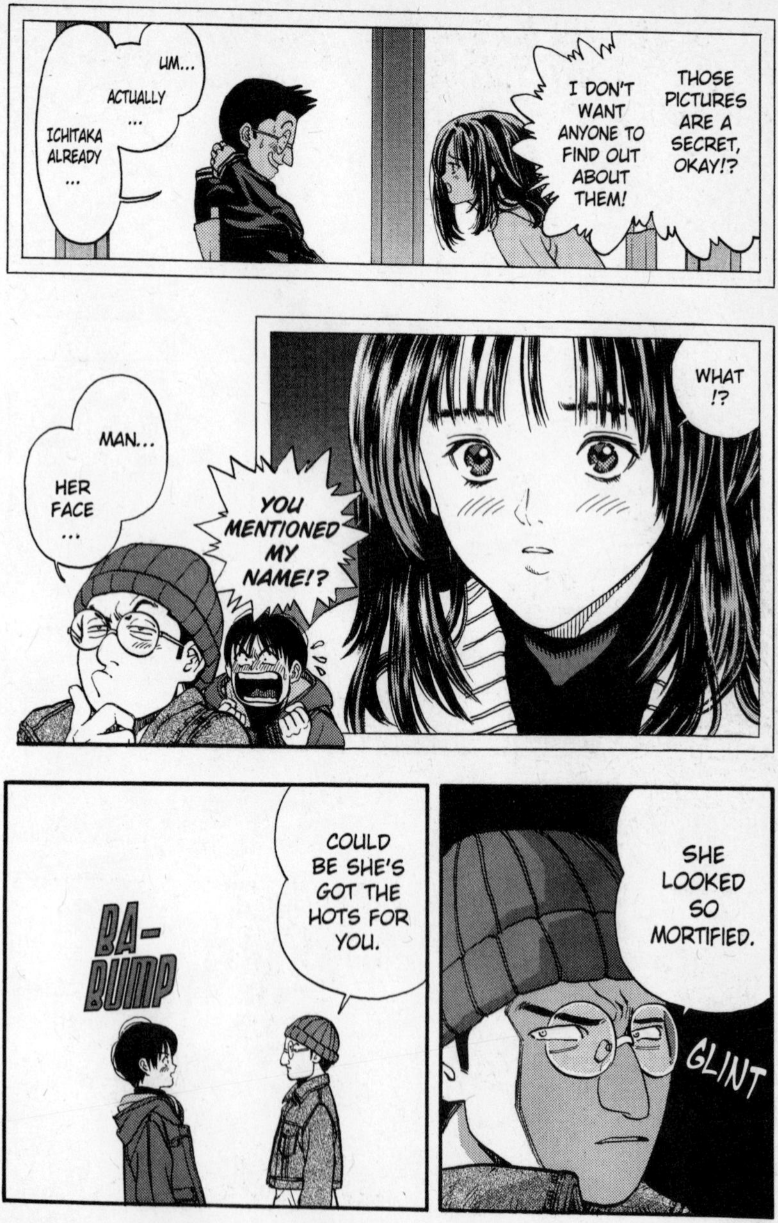
THOSE PICTURES ARE A SECRET, OKAY!?
I DON'T WANT ANYONE TO FIND OUT ABOUT THEM!
UM... ACTUALLY ... ICHITAKA ALREADY ...
WHAT !?
YOU MENTIONED MY NAME!?
MAN... HER FACE ...
SHE LOOKED SO MORTIFIED.
GLINT
COULD BE SHE'S GOT THE HOTS FOR YOU.
BA-BUMP

READ THIS WAY

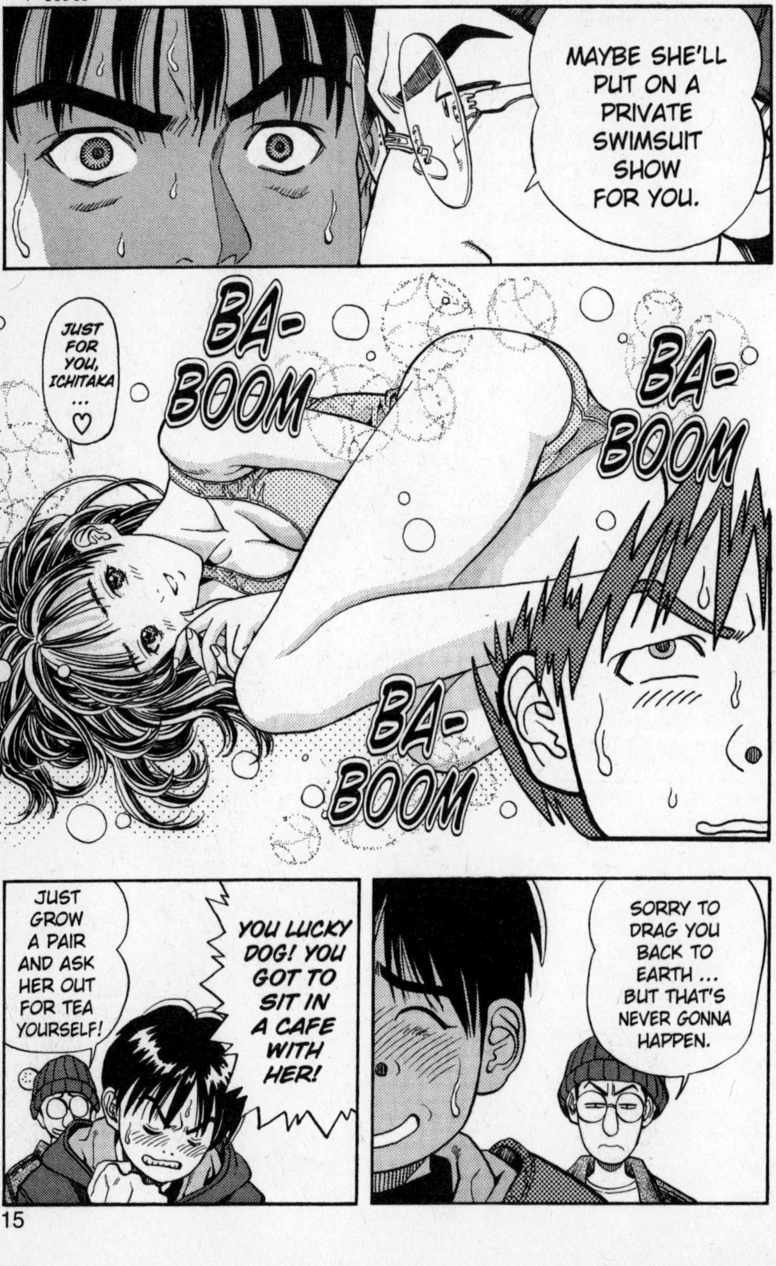
MAYBE SHE'LL PUT ON A PRIVATE SWIMSUIT SHOW FOR YOU.
BA-BOOM
BA-BOOM
JUST FOR YOU, ICHITAKA ... ♡
BA-BOOM
SORRY TO DRAG YOU BACK TO EARTH ... BUT THAT'S NEVER GONNA HAPPEN.
YOU LUCKY DOG! YOU GOT TO SIT IN A CAFE WITH HER!
JUST GROW A PAIR AND ASK HER OUT FOR TEA YOURSELF!

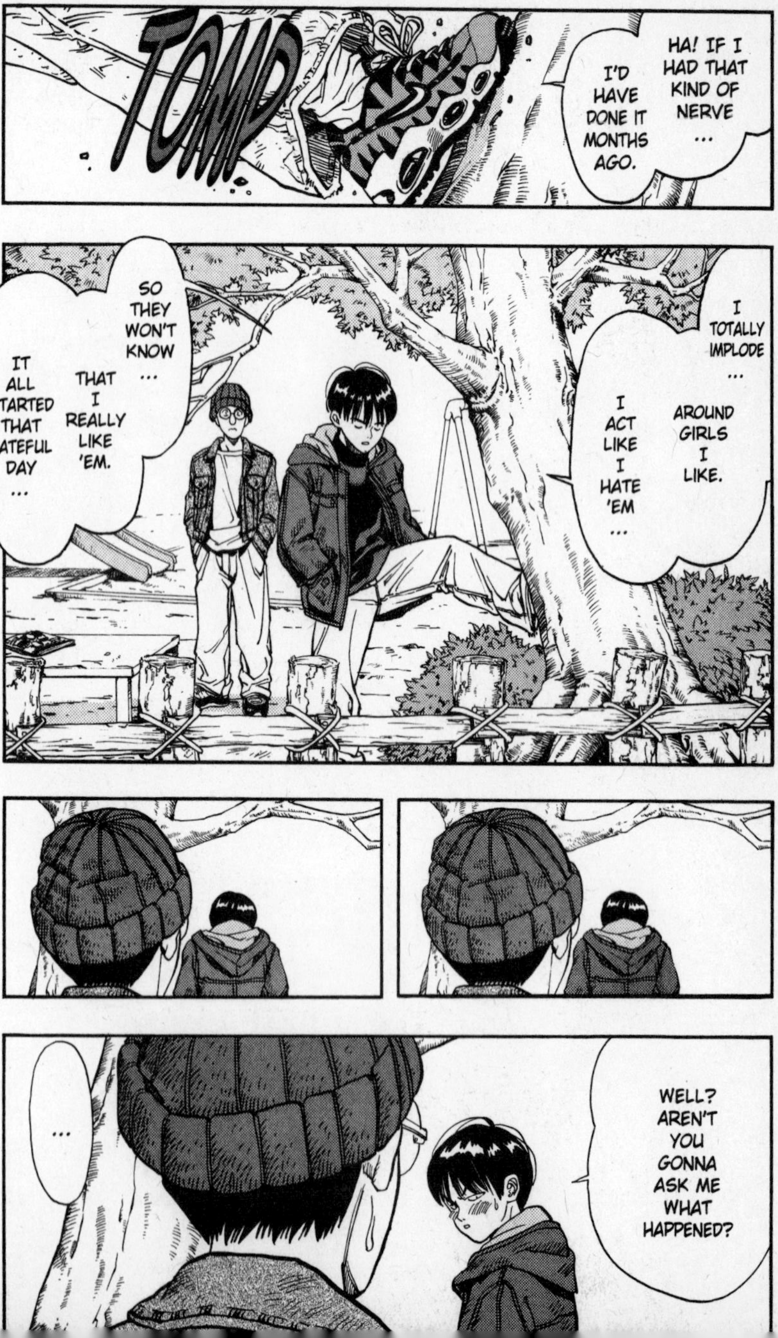
HA! IF I HAD THAT KIND OF NERVE ...
I'D HAVE DONE IT MONTHS AGO.
TOMP
I TOTALLY IMPLODE ...
AROUND GIRLS I LIKE.
I ACT LIKE I HATE 'EM ...
SO THEY WON'T KNOW ...
THAT I REALLY LIKE 'EM.
IT ALL STARTED THAT FATEFUL DAY ...
WELL? AREN'T YOU GONNA ASK ME WHAT HAPPENED?
...

READ THIS WAY

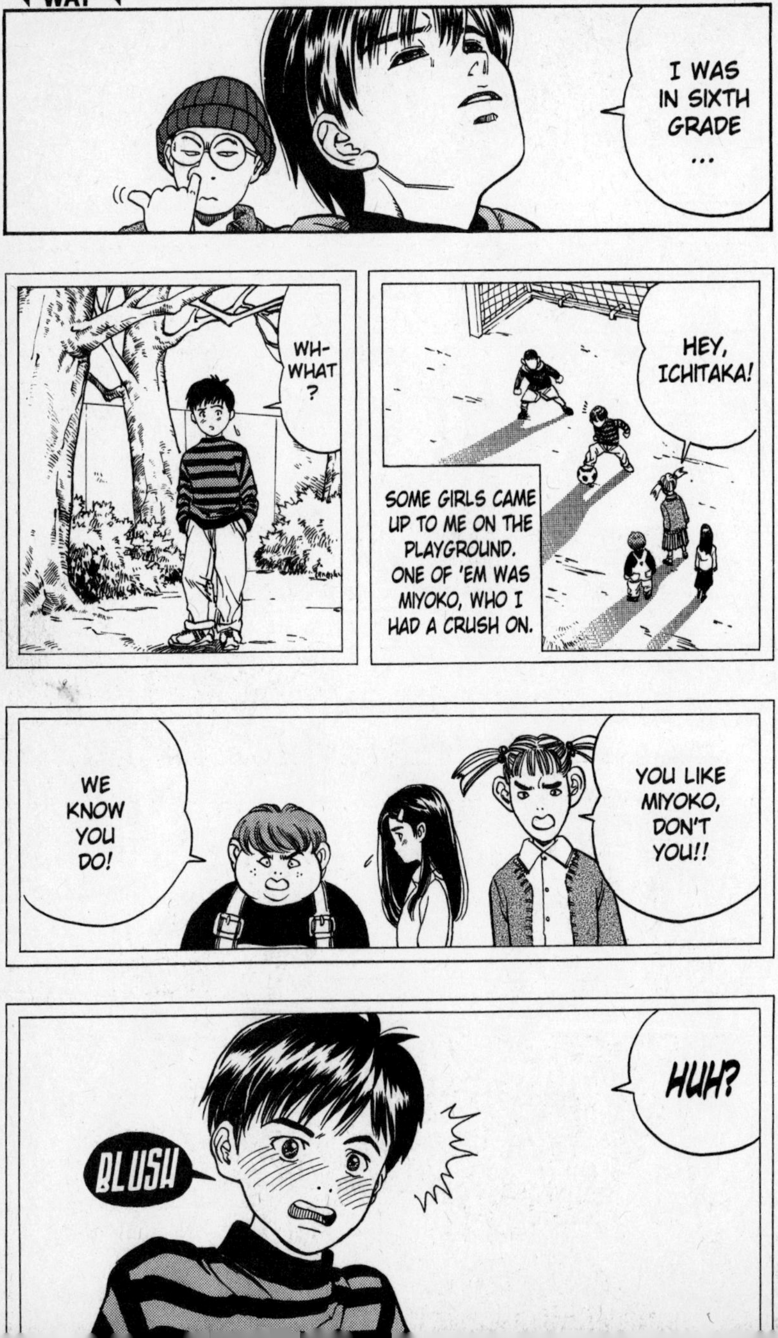
I WAS IN SIXTH GRADE ...
HEY, ICHITAKA!
SOME GIRLS CAME UP TO ME ON THE PLAYGROUND. ONE OF 'EM WAS MIYOKO, WHO I HAD A CRUSH ON.
WH-WHAT?
YOU LIKE MIYOKO, DON'T YOU!!
WE KNOW YOU DO!
HUH?
BLUSH

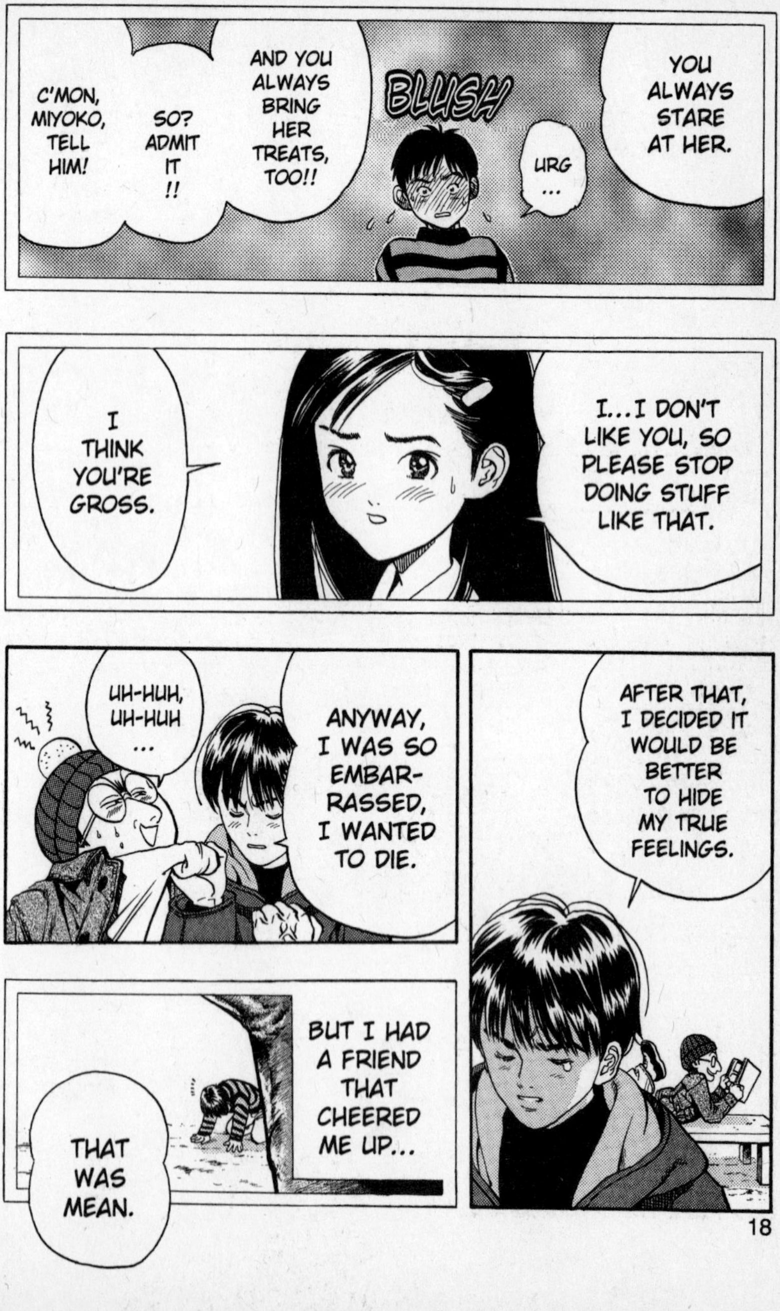
YOU ALWAYS STARE AT HER.
URG ...
BLUSH
AND YOU ALWAYS BRING HER TREATS, TOO!!
SO? ADMIT IT !!
C'MON, MIYOKO, TELL HIM!
I...I DON'T LIKE YOU, SO PLEASE STOP DOING STUFF LIKE THAT.
I THINK YOU'RE GROSS.
AFTER THAT, I DECIDED IT WOULD BE BETTER TO HIDE MY TRUE FEELINGS.
ANYWAY, I WAS SO EMBAR-RASSED, I WANTED TO DIE.
UH-HUH, UH-HUH ...
BUT I HAD A FRIEND THAT CHEERED ME UP...
THAT WAS MEAN.

READ THIS WAY

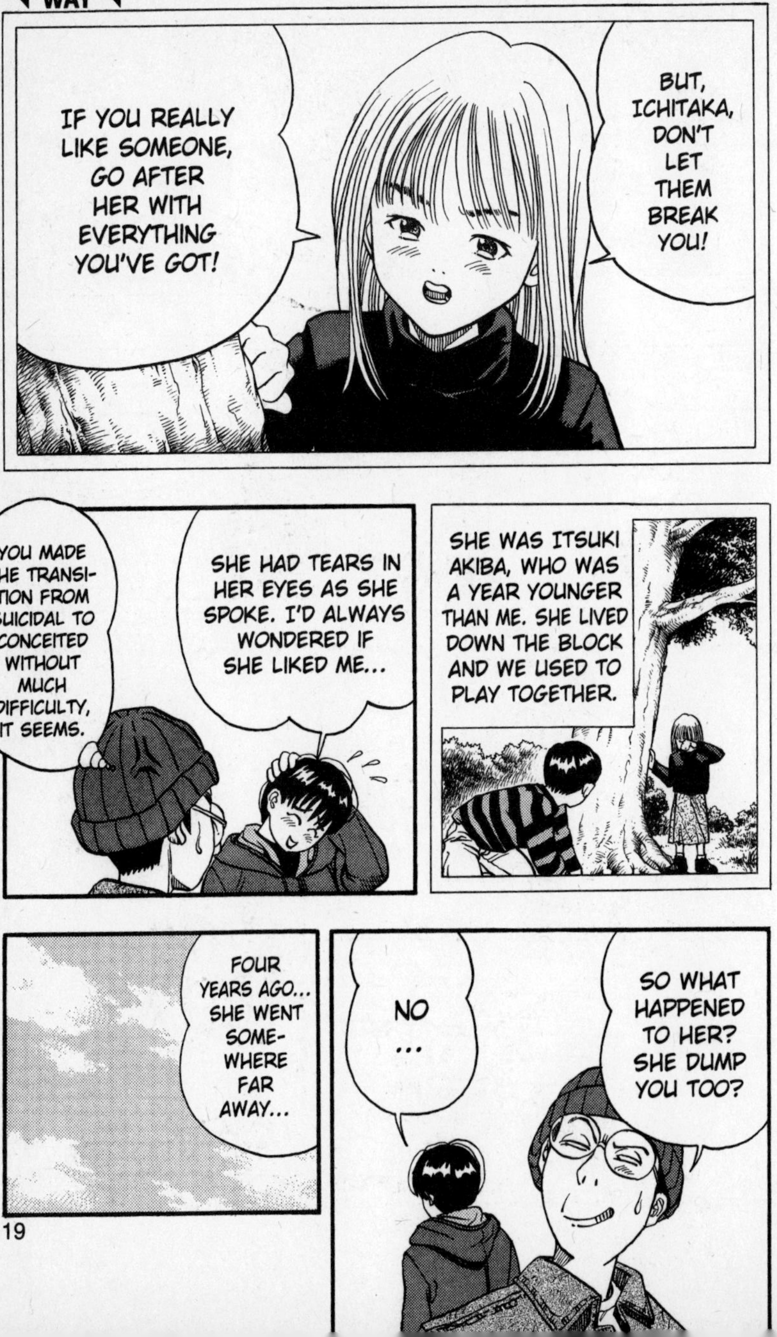
IF YOU REALLY LIKE SOMEONE, GO AFTER HER WITH EVERYTHING YOU'VE GOT!
BUT, ICHITAKA, DON'T LET THEM BREAK YOU!
SHE WAS ITSUKI AKIBA, WHO WAS A YEAR YOUNGER THAN ME. SHE LIVED DOWN THE BLOCK AND WE USED TO PLAY TOGETHER.
SHE HAD TEARS IN HER EYES AS SHE SPOKE. I'D ALWAYS WONDERED IF SHE LIKED ME...
YOU MADE THE TRANSITION FROM SUICIDAL TO CONCEITED WITHOUT MUCH DIFFICULTY, IT SEEMS.
SO WHAT HAPPENED TO HER? SHE DUMP YOU TOO?
NO ...
FOUR YEARS AGO... SHE WENT SOMEWHERE FAR AWAY...

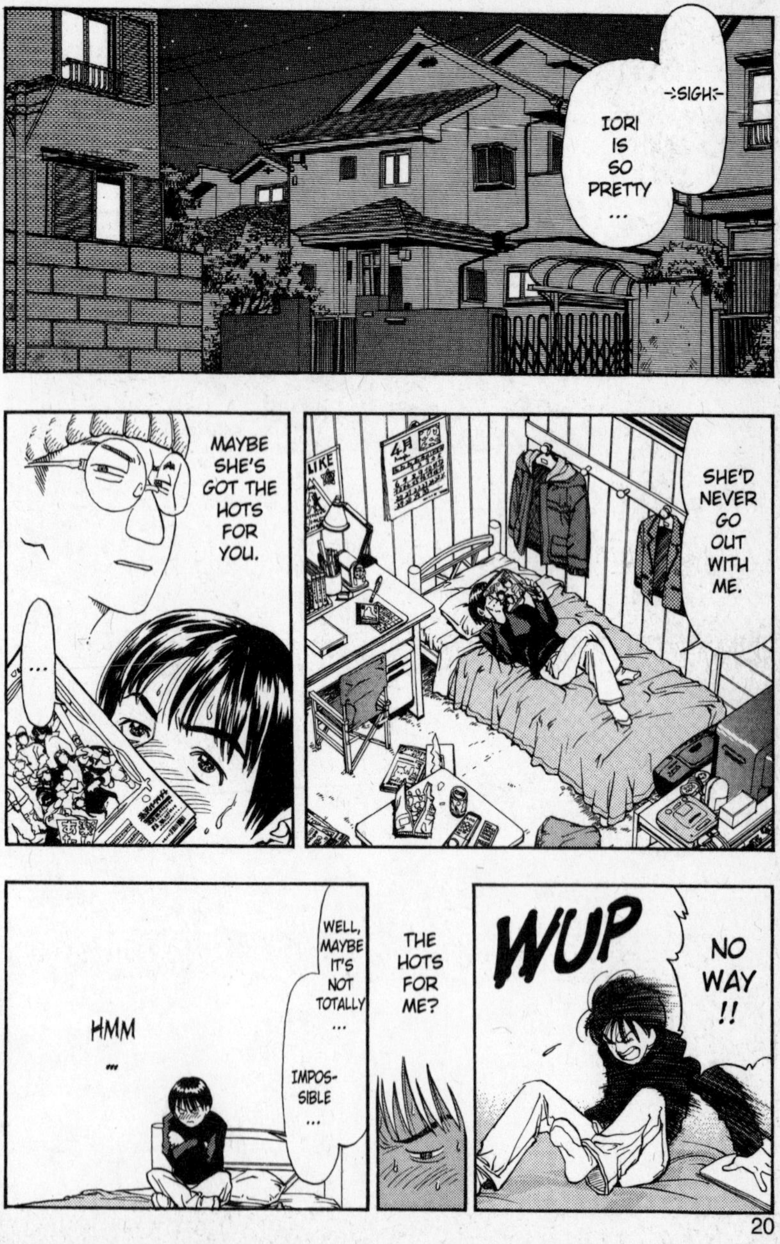
-SIGH-
IORI IS SO PRETTY ...
SHE'D NEVER GO OUT WITH ME.
MAYBE SHE'S GOT THE HOTS FOR YOU.
...
WUP
NO WAY !!
THE HOTS FOR ME?
WELL, MAYBE IT'S NOT TOTALLY ...
IMPOS-SIBLE ...
HMM ...

READ THIS WAY

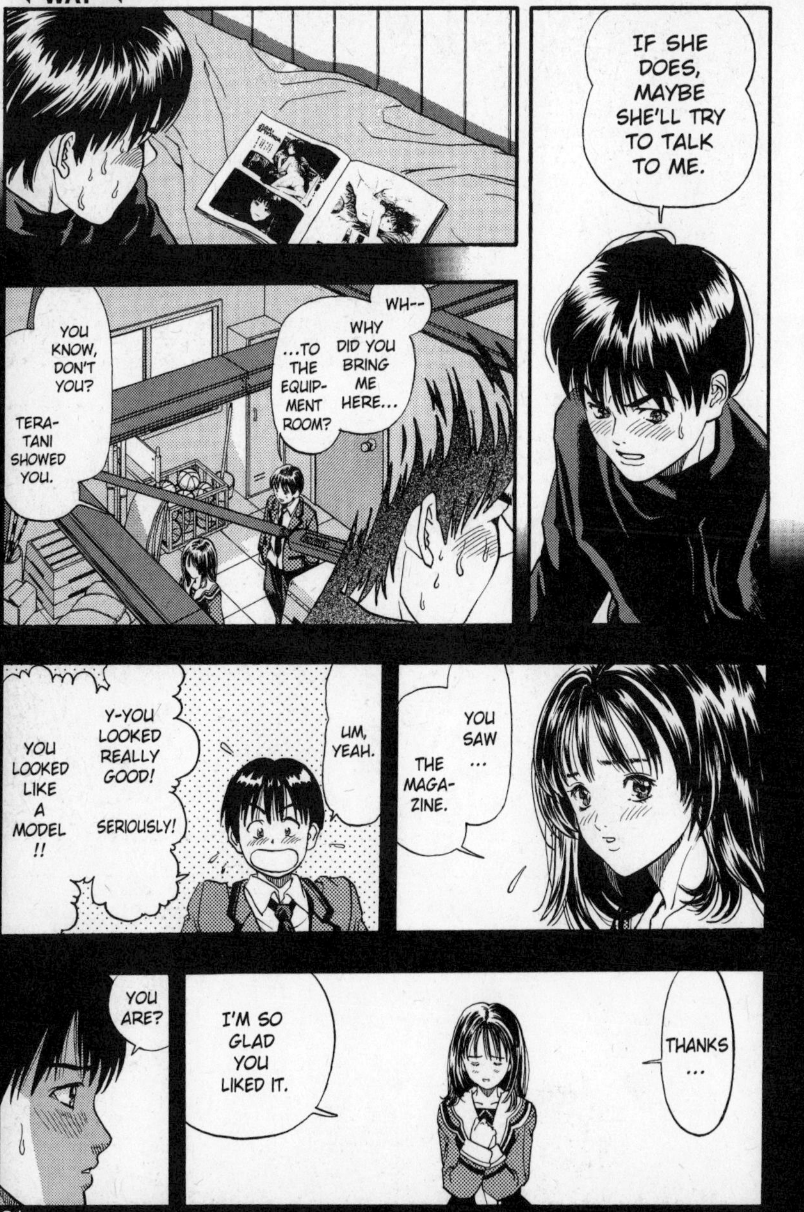

IF SHE DOES, MAYBE SHE'LL TRY TO TALK TO ME.
WH-- WHY DID YOU BRING ME HERE...
...TO THE EQUIPMENT ROOM?
YOU KNOW, DON'T YOU?
TERA-TANI SHOWED YOU.
YOU SAW ...
THE MAGAZINE.
UM, YEAH.
Y-YOU LOOKED REALLY GOOD!
SERIOUSLY!
YOU LOOKED LIKE A MODEL !!
THANKS ...
I'M SO GLAD YOU LIKED IT.
YOU ARE?

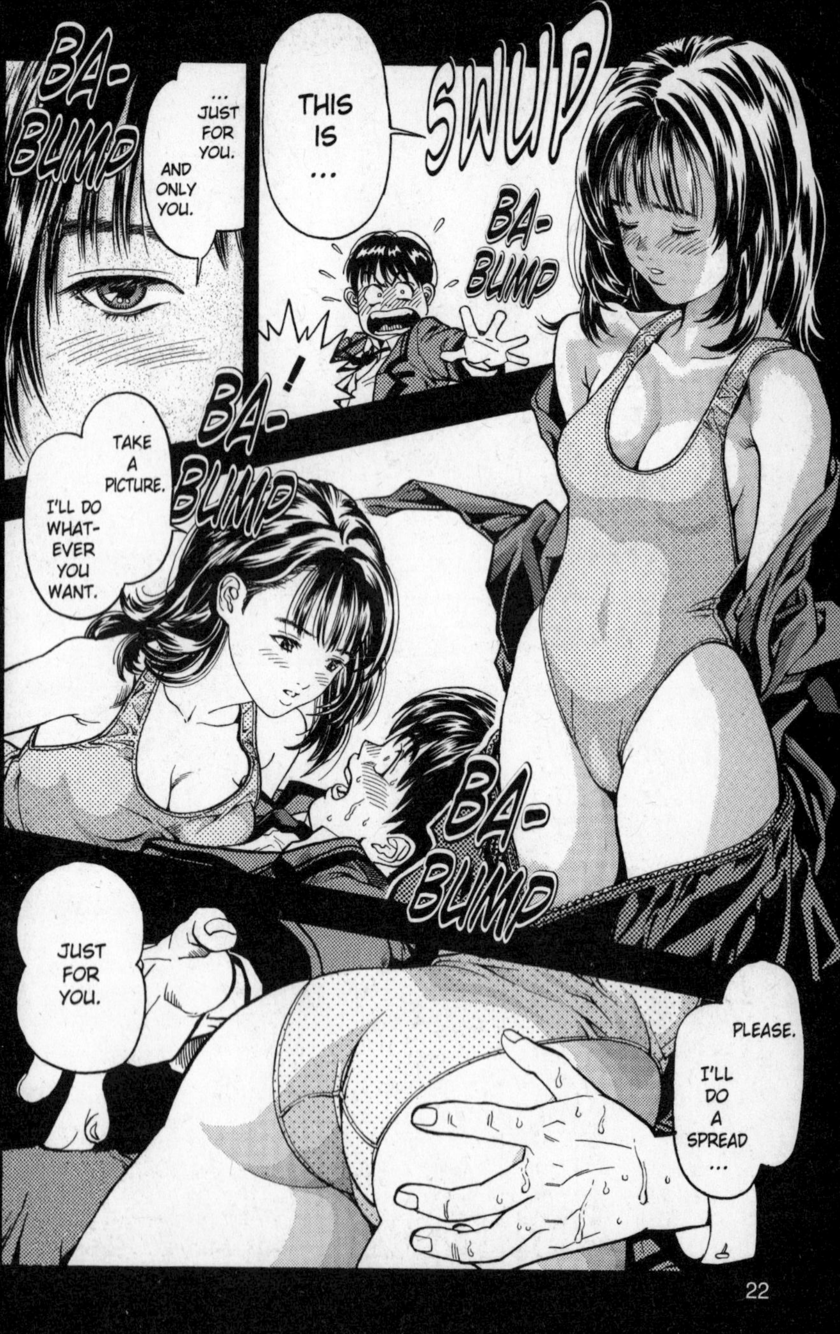
SWUD
BA-BUMP
THIS IS ...
!
BA-BUMP
... JUST FOR YOU.
AND ONLY YOU.
BA-BUMP
TAKE A PICTURE.
I'LL DO WHAT-EVER YOU WANT.
BA-BUMP
PLEASE.
I'LL DO A SPREAD ...
JUST FOR YOU.

READ THIS WAY

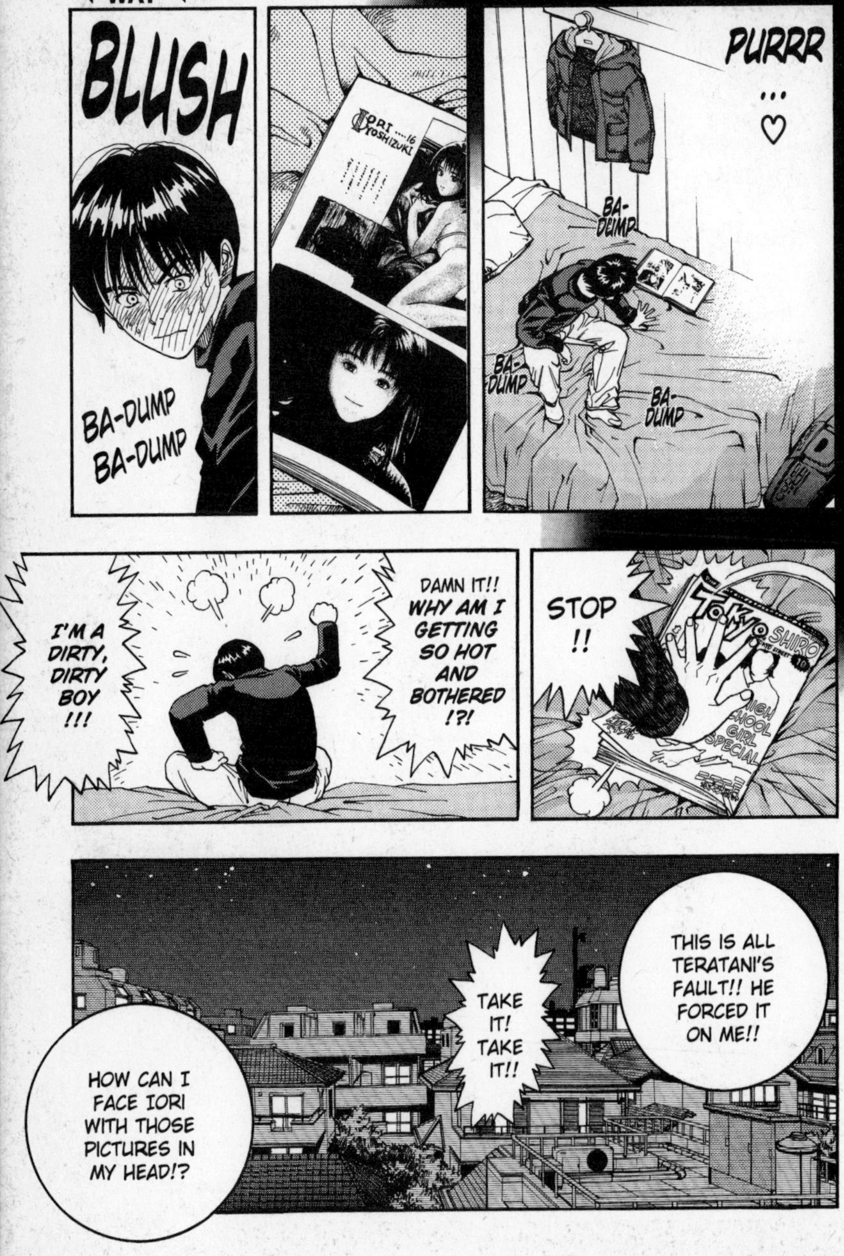
PURRR
... ♡
BA-DEIMP
BA-DUMP
BA-DUMP
IORI ....16 YOSHIZUKI
BLUSH
BA-DUMP BA-DUMP
STOP !!
SHIRO
GIRL SPECIAL
DAMN IT!! WHY AM I GETTING SO HOT AND BOTHERED !?!
I'M A DIRTY, DIRTY BOY !!!
THIS IS ALL TERATANI'S FAULT!! HE FORCED IT ON ME!!
TAKE IT! TAKE IT!!
HOW CAN I FACE IORI WITH THOSE PICTURES IN MY HEAD!?

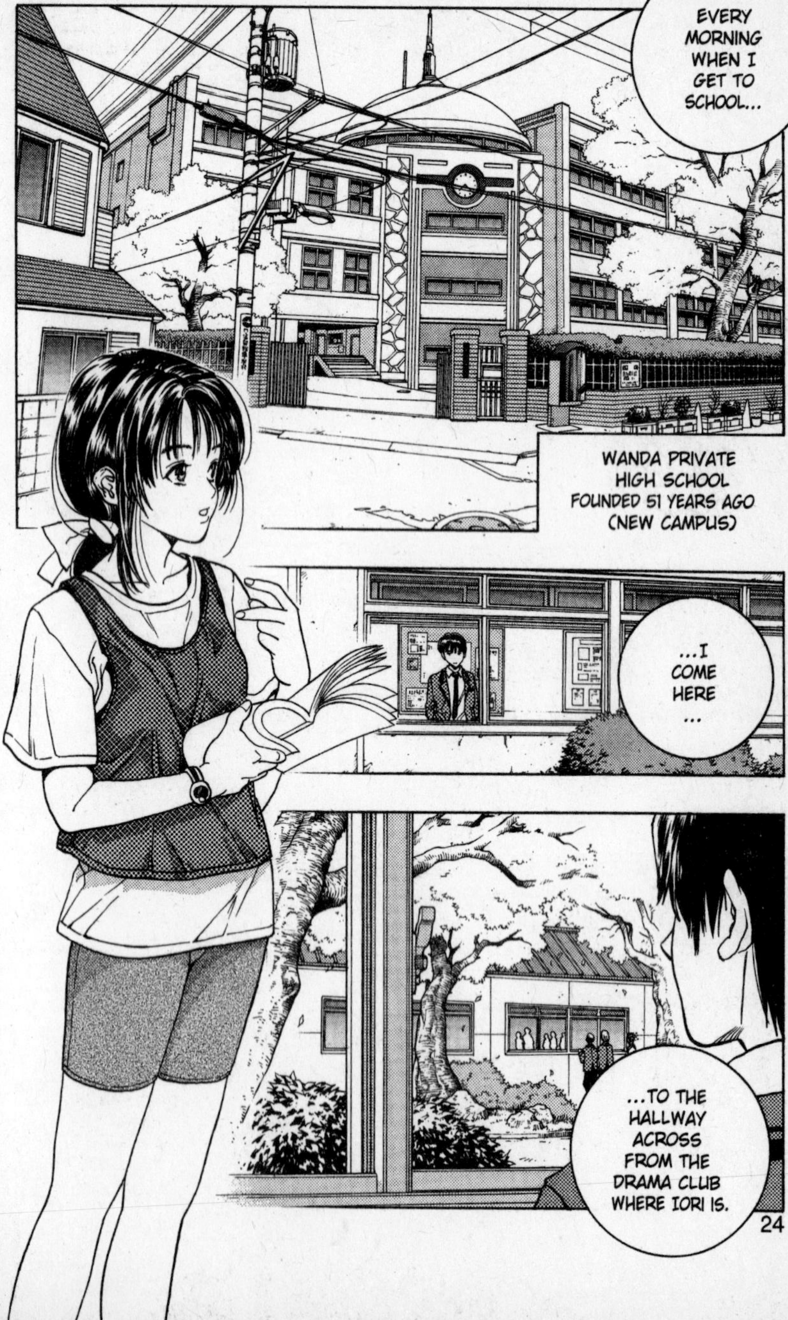
EVERY MORNING WHEN I GET TO SCHOOL...
WANDA PRIVATE HIGH SCHOOL FOUNDED 51 YEARS AGO (NEW CAMPUS)
...I COME HERE ...
...TO THE HALLWAY ACROSS FROM THE DRAMA CLUB WHERE IORI IS.

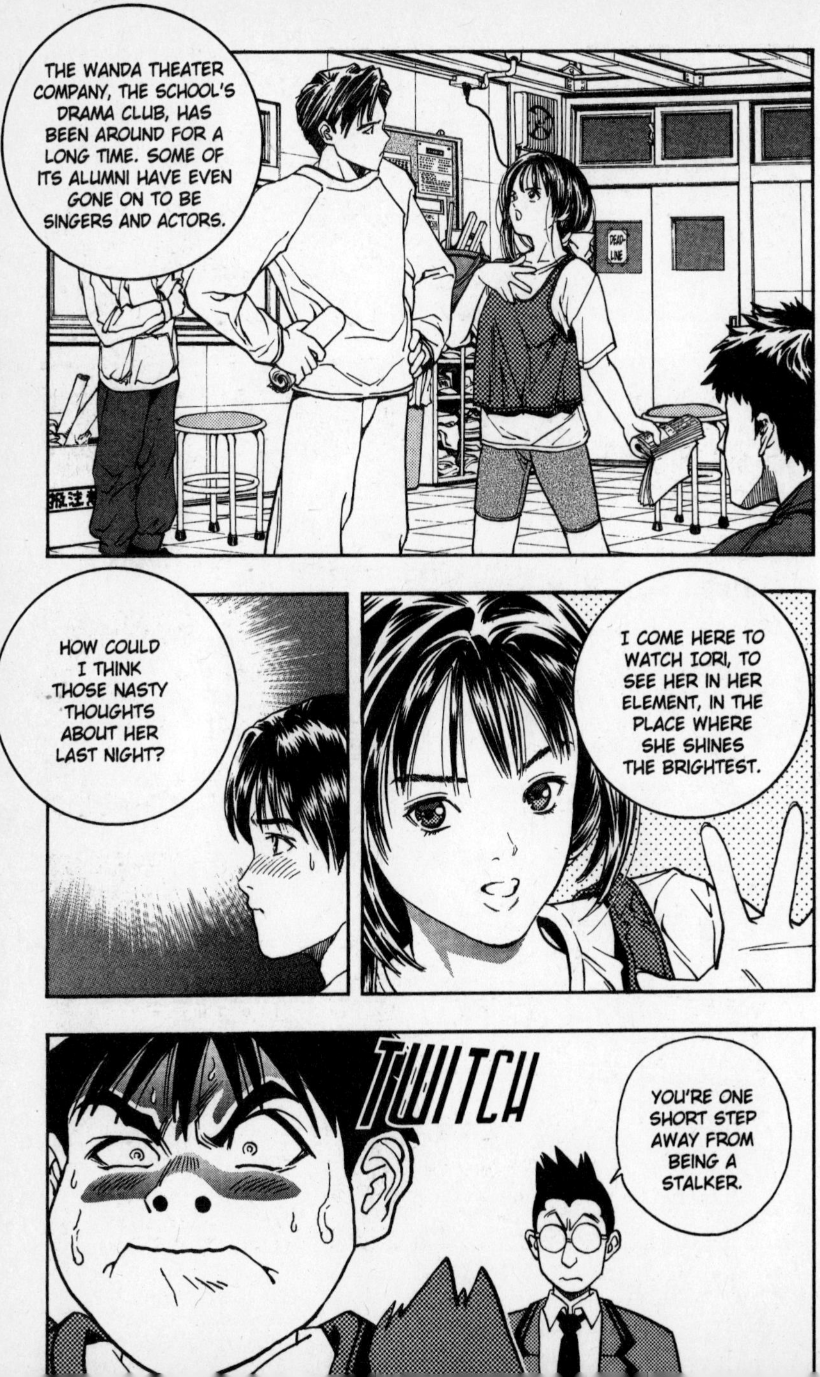
THE WANDA THEATER COMPANY, THE SCHOOL'S DRAMA CLUB, HAS BEEN AROUND FOR A LONG TIME. SOME OF ITS ALUMNI HAVE EVEN GONE ON TO BE SINGERS AND ACTORS.
I COME HERE TO WATCH IORI, TO SEE HER IN HER ELEMENT, IN THE PLACE WHERE SHE SHINES THE BRIGHTEST.
HOW COULD I THINK THOSE NASTY THOUGHTS ABOUT HER LAST NIGHT?
YOU'RE ONE SHORT STEP AWAY FROM BEING A STALKER.
TWITCH

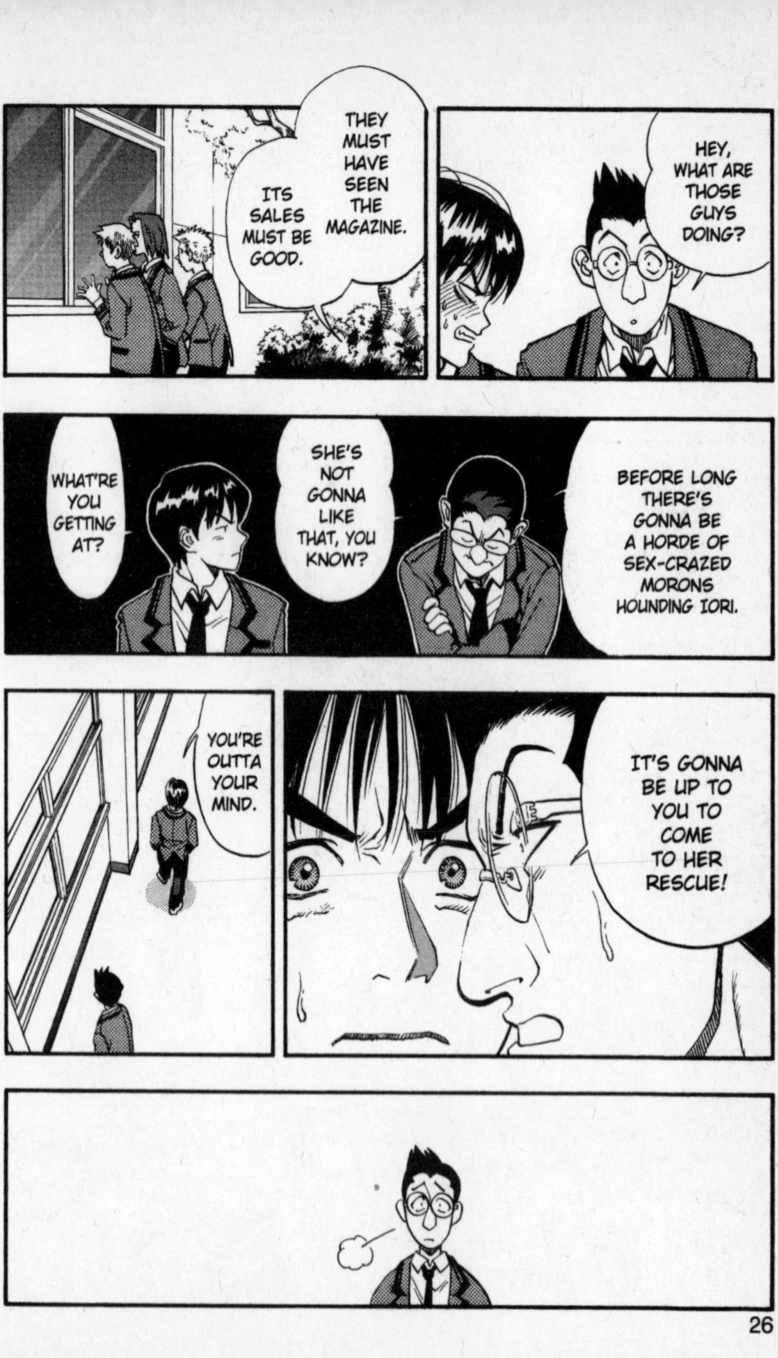
HEY, WHAT ARE THOSE GUYS DOING?
THEY MUST HAVE SEEN THE MAGAZINE.
ITS SALES MUST BE GOOD.
BEFORE LONG THERE'S GONNA BE A HORDE OF SEX-CRAZED MORONS HOUNDING IORI.
SHE'S NOT GONNA LIKE THAT, YOU KNOW?
WHAT'RE YOU GETTING AT?
IT'S GONNA BE UP TO YOU TO COME TO HER RESCUE!
YOU'RE OUTTA YOUR MIND.

READ THIS WAY

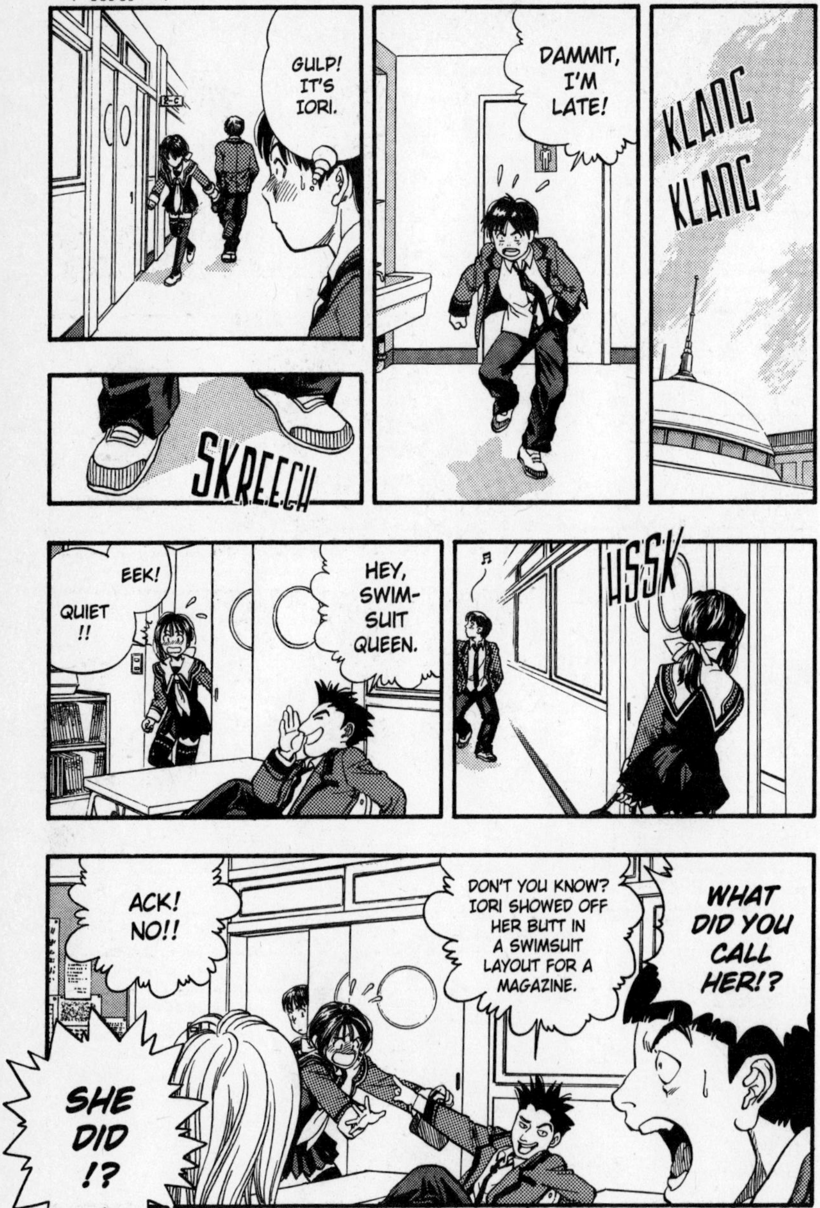
KLANG
KLANG
DAMMIT, I'M LATE!
GULP! IT'S IORI.
SKREECH
HSSK
HEY, SWIM-SUIT QUEEN.
EEK!
QUIET!!
WHAT DID YOU CALL HER!?
DON'T YOU KNOW? IORI SHOWED OFF HER BUTT IN A SWIMSUIT LAYOUT FOR A MAGAZINE.
ACK! NO!!
SHE DID!?

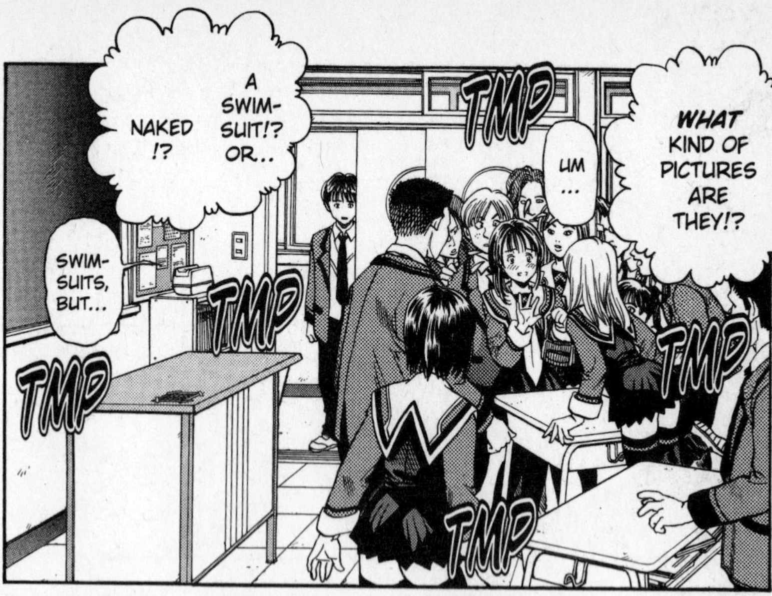
WHAT KIND OF PICTURES ARE THEY!?
UM ...
TMP
A SWIM-SUIT!? OR...
NAKED !?
SWIM-SUITS, BUT...
TMP
TMP
TMP
TMP

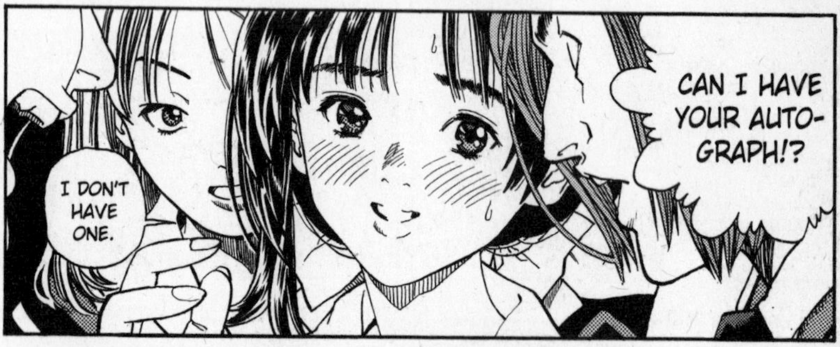
CAN I HAVE YOUR AUTO-GRAPH!?
I DON'T HAVE ONE.

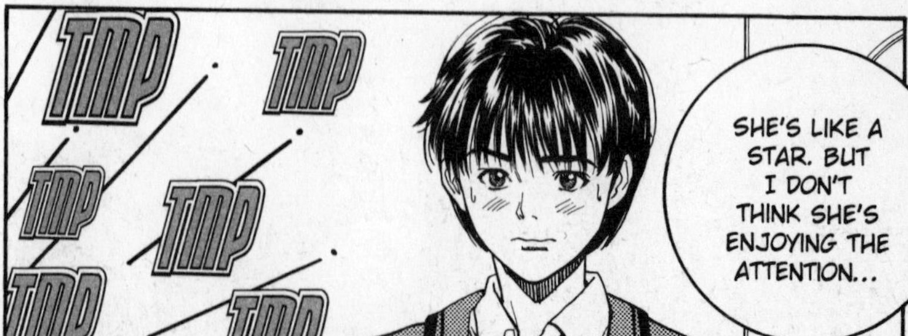
SHE'S LIKE A STAR. BUT I DON'T THINK SHE'S ENJOYING THE ATTENTION...
TMP
TMP
TMP
TMP
TMP
TMP

READ THIS WAY

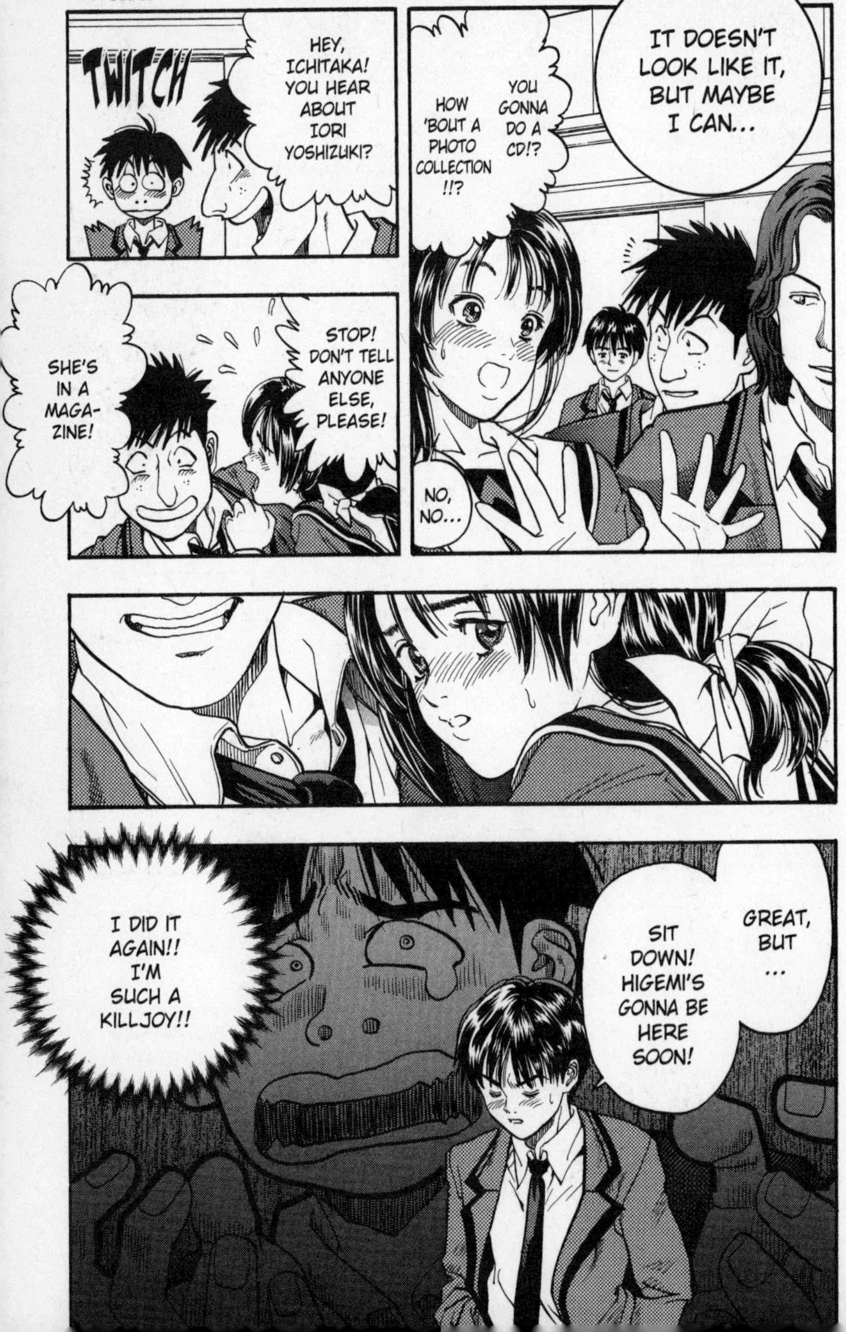

IT DOESN'T LOOK LIKE IT, BUT MAYBE I CAN...
YOU GONNA DO A CD!?
HOW 'BOUT A PHOTO COLLECTION !!?
NO, NO...
HEY, ICHITAKA! YOU HEAR ABOUT IORI YOSHIZUKI?
TWITCH
STOP! DON'T TELL ANYONE ELSE, PLEASE!
SHE'S IN A MAGA-ZINE!
GREAT, BUT ...
SIT DOWN! HIGEMI'S GONNA BE HERE SOON!
I DID IT AGAIN!! I'M SUCH A KILLJOY!!

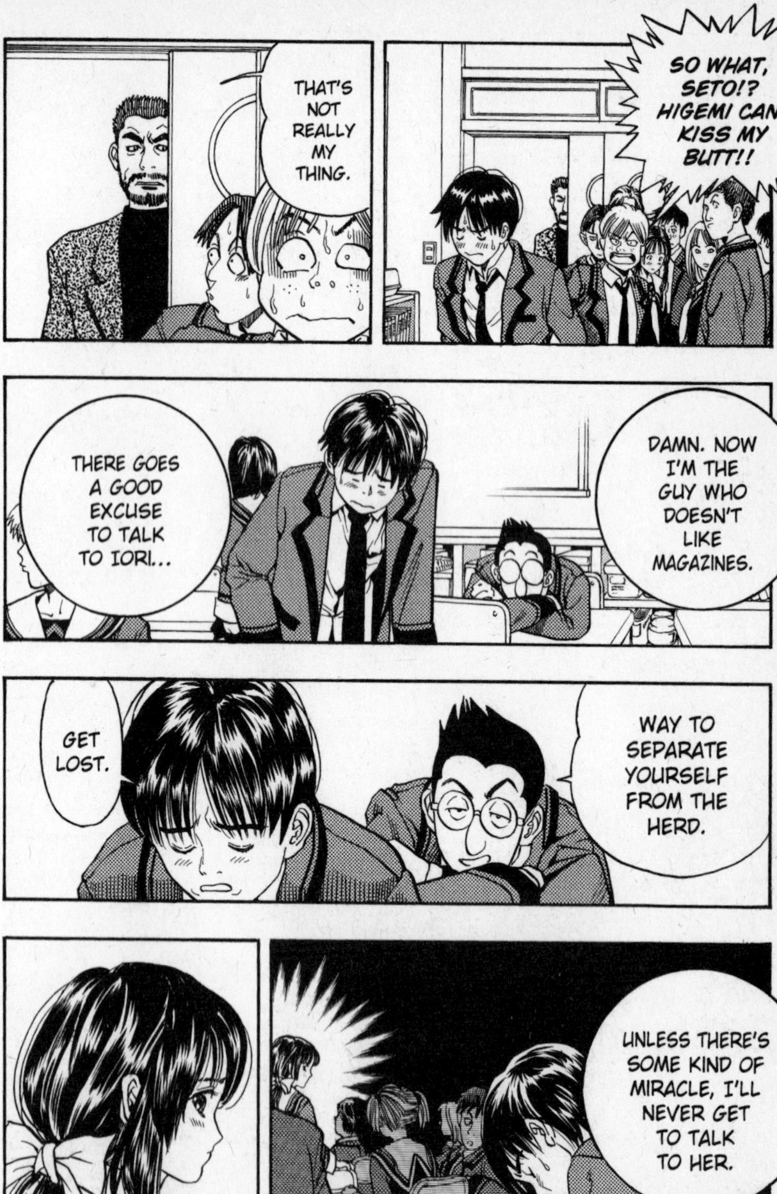
SO WHAT, SETO!? HIGEMI CAN KISS MY BUTT!!
THAT'S NOT REALLY MY THING.
DAMN. NOW I'M THE GUY WHO DOESN'T LIKE MAGAZINES.
THERE GOES A GOOD EXCUSE TO TALK TO IORI...
WAY TO SEPARATE YOURSELF FROM THE HERD.
GET LOST.
UNLESS THERE'S SOME KIND OF MIRACLE, I'LL NEVER GET TO TALK TO HER.

READ THIS WAY

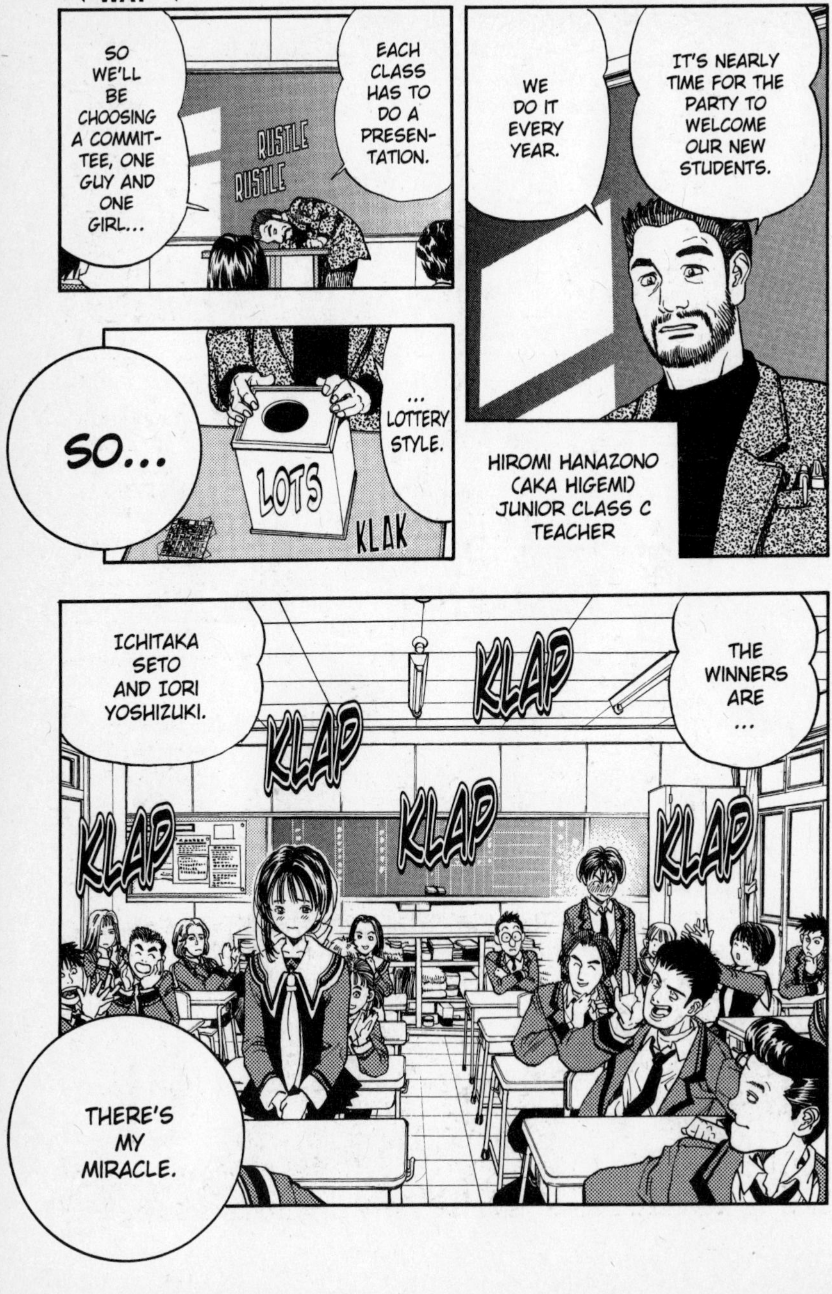
IT'S NEARLY TIME FOR THE PARTY TO WELCOME OUR NEW STUDENTS.
WE DO IT EVERY YEAR.
HIROMI HANAZONO (AKA HIGEMI) JUNIOR CLASS C TEACHER
EACH CLASS HAS TO DO A PRESENTATION.
SO WE'LL BE CHOOSING A COMMITTEE, ONE GUY AND ONE GIRL...
RUSTLE
RUSTLE
...LOTTERY STYLE.
LOTS
KLAK
SO...
THE WINNERS ARE...
ICHITAKA SETO AND IORI YOSHIZUKI.
KLAP
KLAP
KLAP
KLAP
KLAP
THERE'S MY MIRACLE.

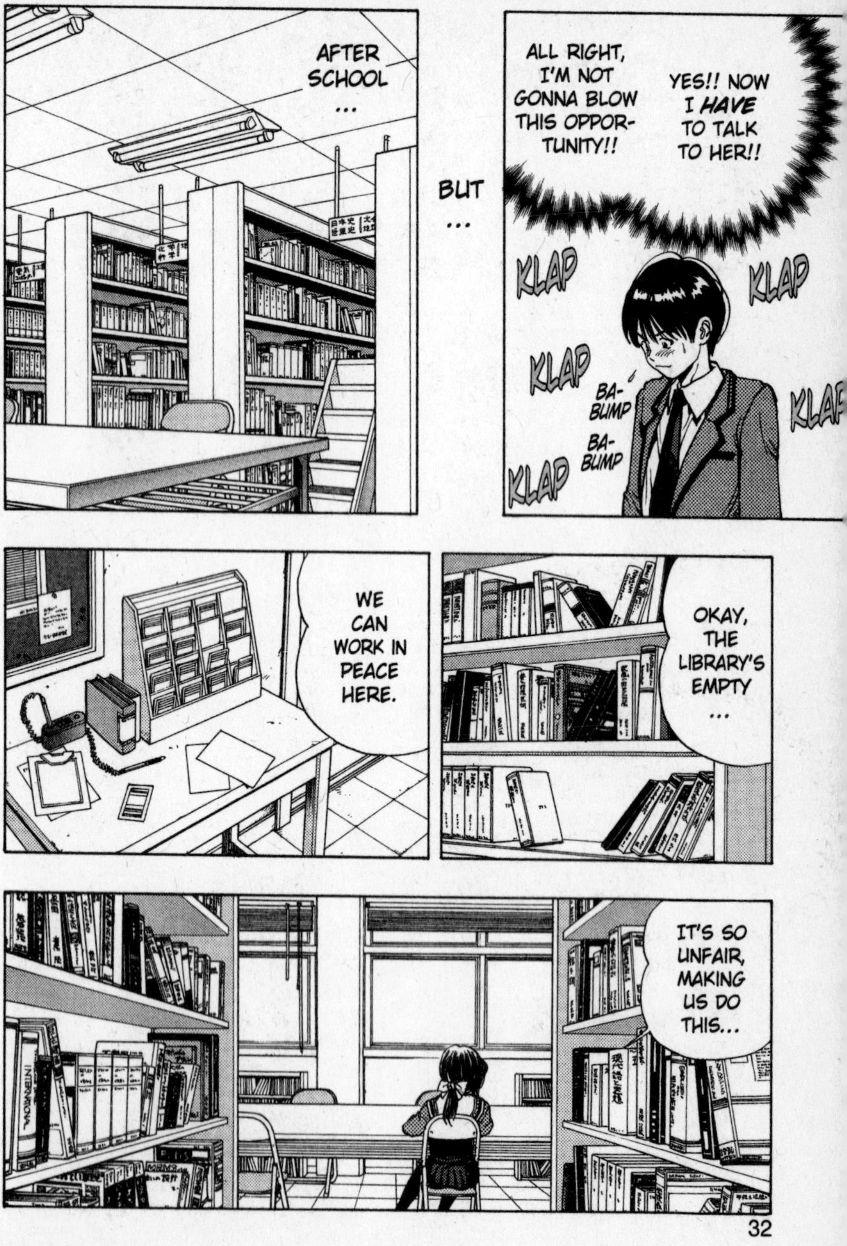
YES!! NOW I *HAVE* TO TALK TO HER!!
ALL RIGHT, I'M NOT GONNA BLOW THIS OPPORTUNITY!!
KLAP
KLAP
KLAP
BA-BUMP
BA-BUMP
KLAP
KLAP
AFTER SCHOOL ...
BUT ...
OKAY, THE LIBRARY'S EMPTY ...
WE CAN WORK IN PEACE HERE.
IT'S SO UNFAIR, MAKING US DO THIS...

READ THIS WAY

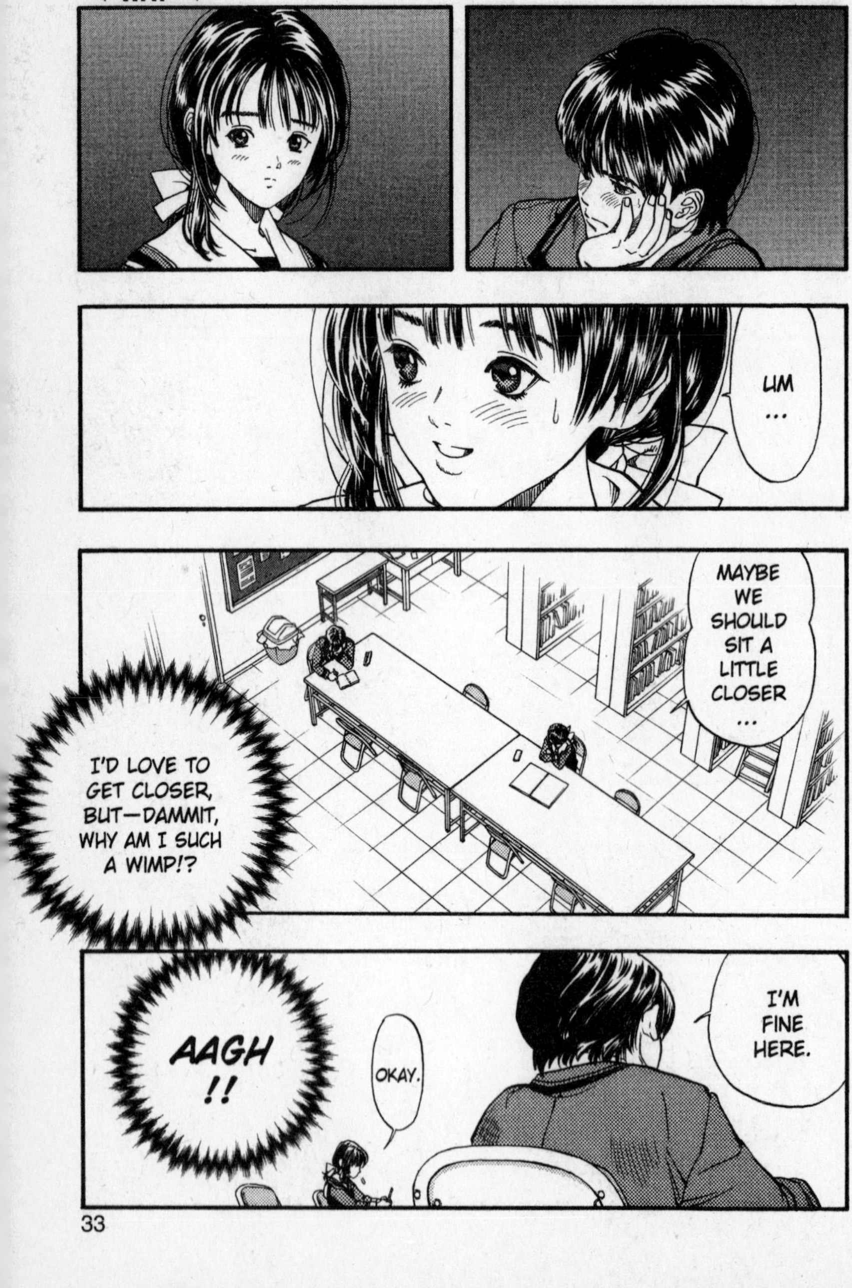
UM ...
MAYBE WE SHOULD SIT A LITTLE CLOSER ...
I'D LOVE TO GET CLOSER, BUT—DAMMIT, WHY AM I SUCH A WIMP!?
I'M FINE HERE.
OKAY.
AAGH !!

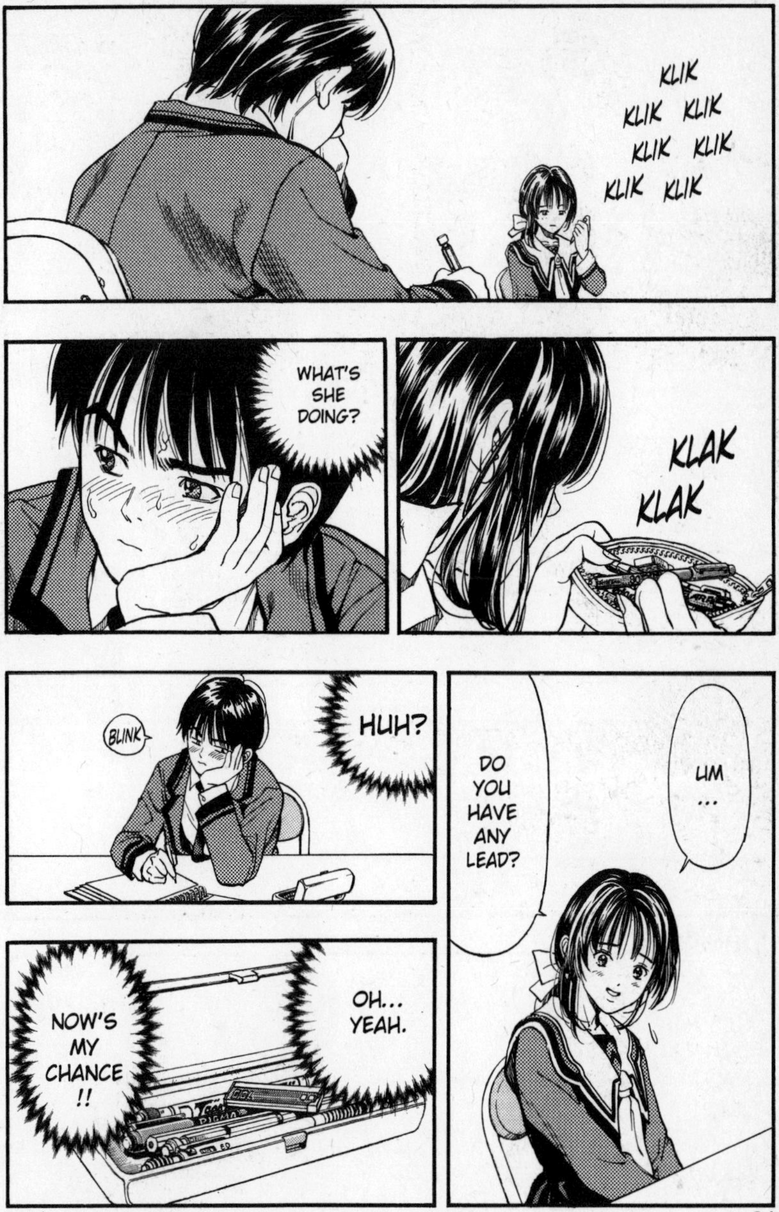
KLIK
KLIK KLIK
KLIK KLIK
KLIK KLIK
KLAK
KLAK
WHAT'S SHE DOING?
UM ...
DO YOU HAVE ANY LEAD?
HUH?
BLINK
OH... YEAH.
NOW'S MY CHANCE !!

READ THIS WAY

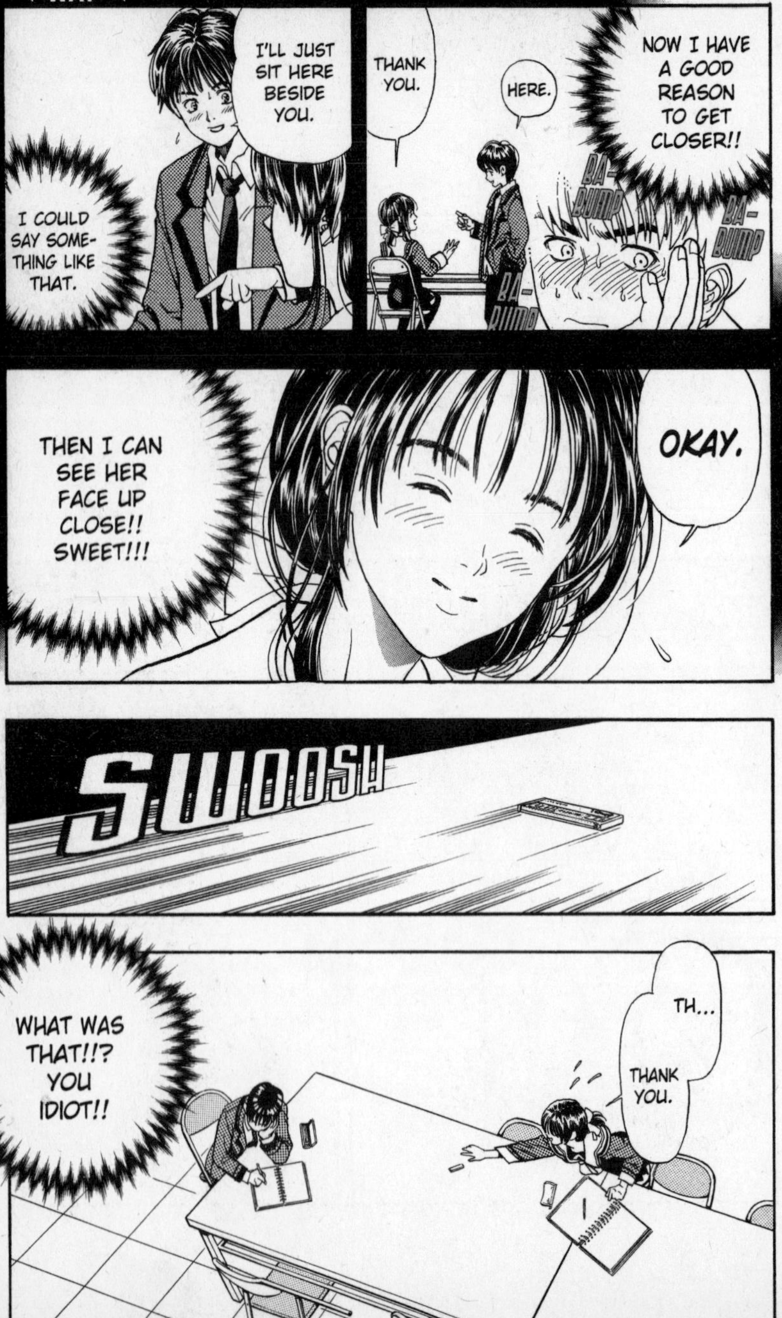
NOW I HAVE A GOOD REASON TO GET CLOSER!!
BA-BUMP
BA-BUMP
BA-BUMP
HERE.
THANK YOU.
I'LL JUST SIT HERE BESIDE YOU.
I COULD SAY SOME-THING LIKE THAT.
OKAY.
THEN I CAN SEE HER FACE UP CLOSE!! SWEET!!!
SWOOSH
TH...
THANK YOU.
WHAT WAS THAT!!? YOU IDIOT!!

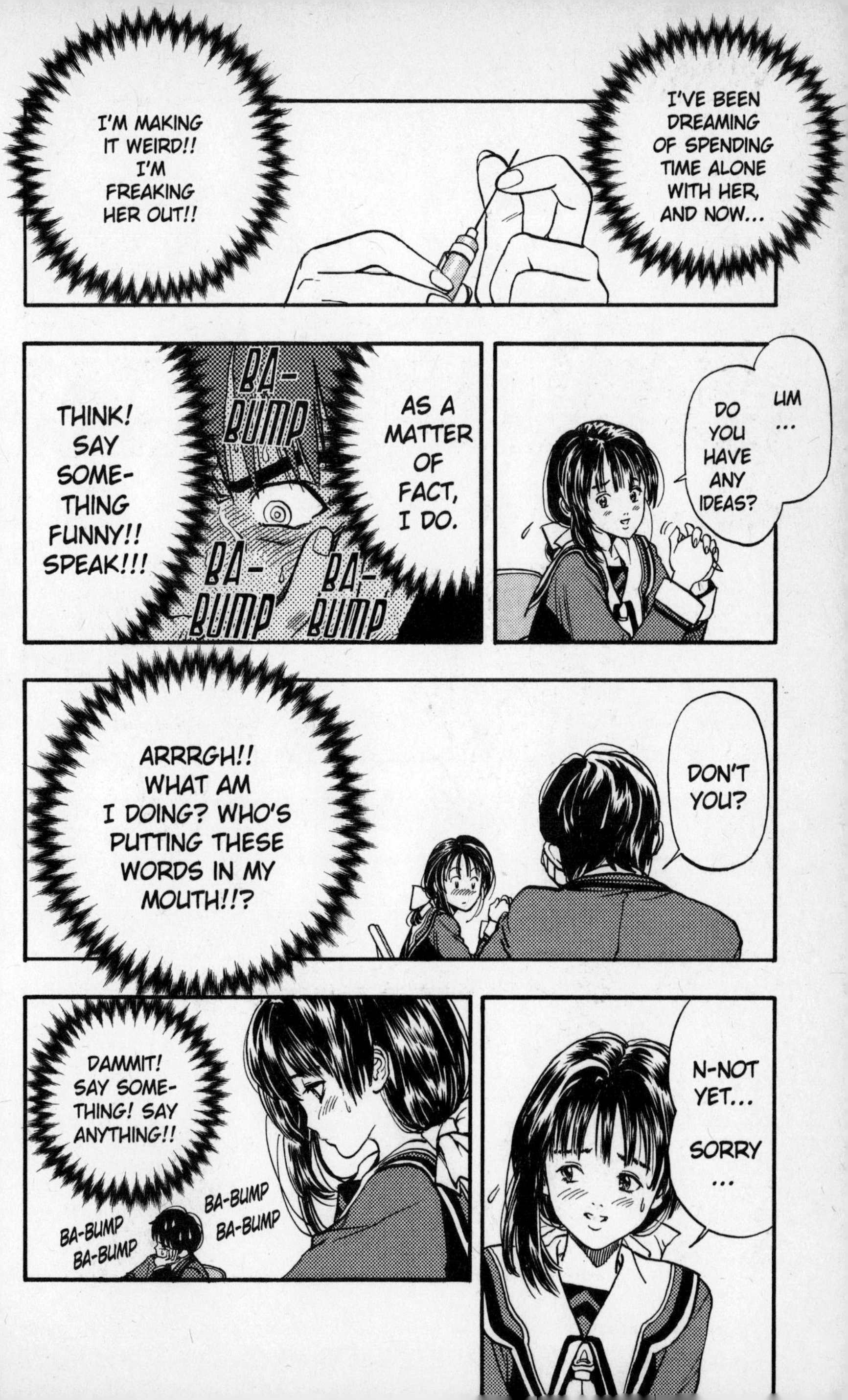
I'VE BEEN DREAMING OF SPENDING TIME ALONE WITH HER, AND NOW...
I'M MAKING IT WEIRD!! I'M FREAKING HER OUT!!
UM ...
DO YOU HAVE ANY IDEAS?
AS A MATTER OF FACT, I DO.
BA-BUMP
BA-BUMP
BA-BUMP
THINK! SAY SOME-THING FUNNY!! SPEAK!!!
DON'T YOU?
ARRRGH!! WHAT AM I DOING? WHO'S PUTTING THESE WORDS IN MY MOUTH!!?
N-NOT YET...
SORRY ...
DAMMIT! SAY SOME-THING! SAY ANYTHING!!
BA-BUMP BA-BUMP
BA-BUMP BA-BUMP

READ THIS WAY

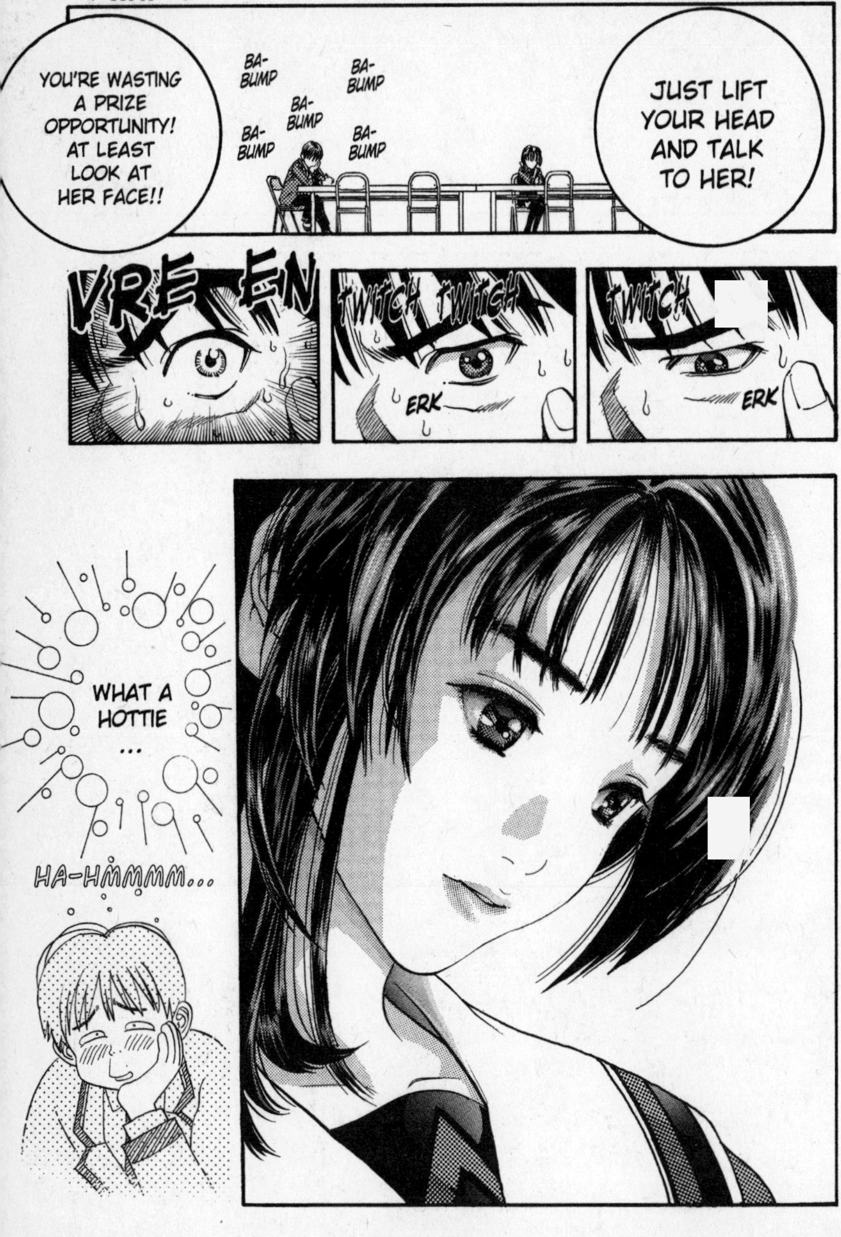
JUST LIFT YOUR HEAD AND TALK TO HER!
BA-BUMP
BA-BUMP
BA-BUMP
BA-BUMP
BA-BUMP
YOU'RE WASTING A PRIZE OPPORTUNITY! AT LEAST LOOK AT HER FACE!!
TWITCH
ERK
TWITCH TWITCH
ERK
VRE EN
WHAT A HOTTIE ...
HA-HMMMM...

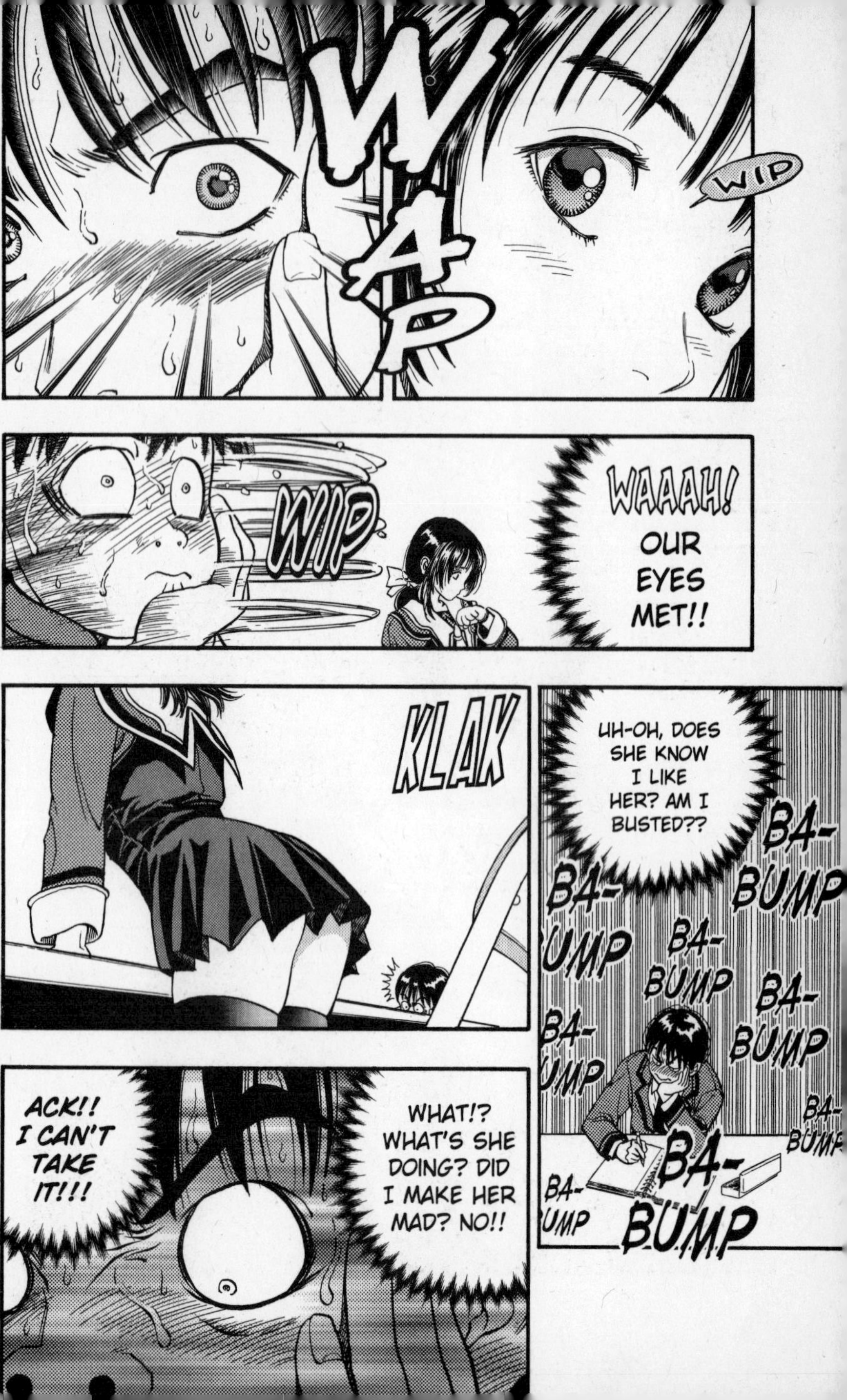
WIP
WHAP
WAAAH! OUR EYES MET!!
WIP
UH-OH, DOES SHE KNOW I LIKE HER? AM I BUSTED??
BA-BUMP
BA-BUMP
BA-BUMP
BA-BUMP
BA-BUMP
BA-BUMP
BA-BUMP
BA-BUMP
KLAK
WHAT!? WHAT'S SHE DOING? DID I MAKE HER MAD? NO!!
ACK!! I CAN'T TAKE IT!!!

READ THIS WAY

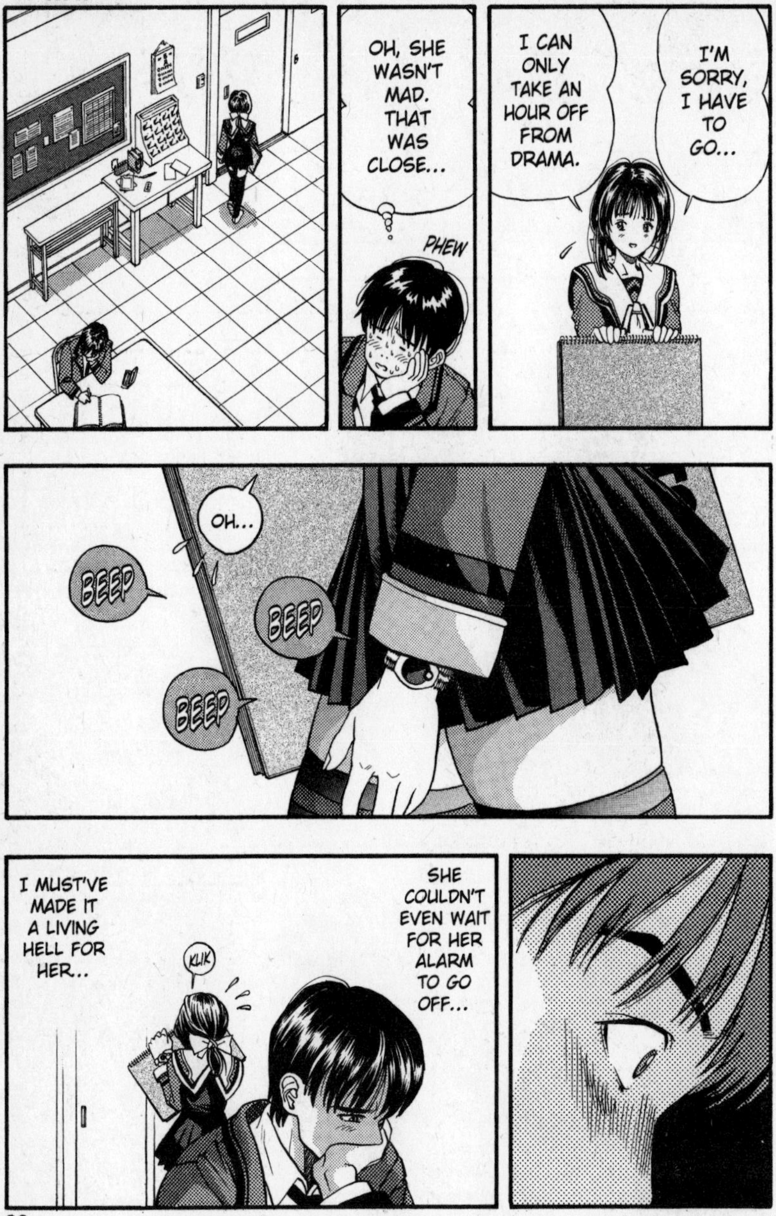
I'M SORRY, I HAVE TO GO...
I CAN ONLY TAKE AN HOUR OFF FROM DRAMA.
OH, SHE WASN'T MAD. THAT WAS CLOSE...
PHEW
OH...
BEEP
BEEP
BEEP
SHE COULDN'T EVEN WAIT FOR HER ALARM TO GO OFF...
KLIK
I MUST'VE MADE IT A LIVING HELL FOR HER...

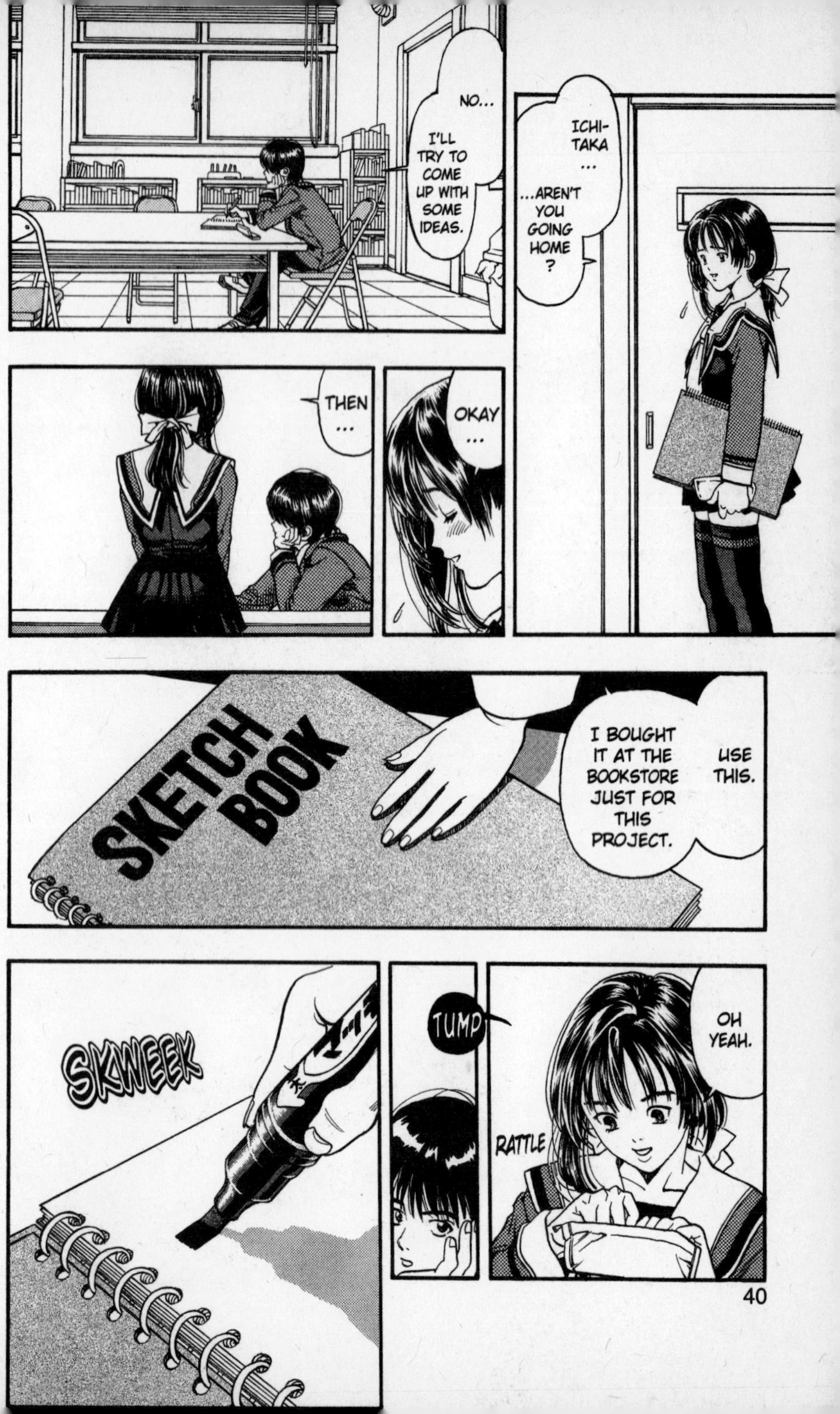
ICHI-TAKA ...
...AREN'T YOU GOING HOME ?
NO...
I'LL TRY TO COME UP WITH SOME IDEAS.
OKAY ...
THEN ...
USE THIS.
I BOUGHT IT AT THE BOOKSTORE JUST FOR THIS PROJECT.
SKETCH BOOK
OH YEAH.
RATTLE
TUMP
SKWEEK

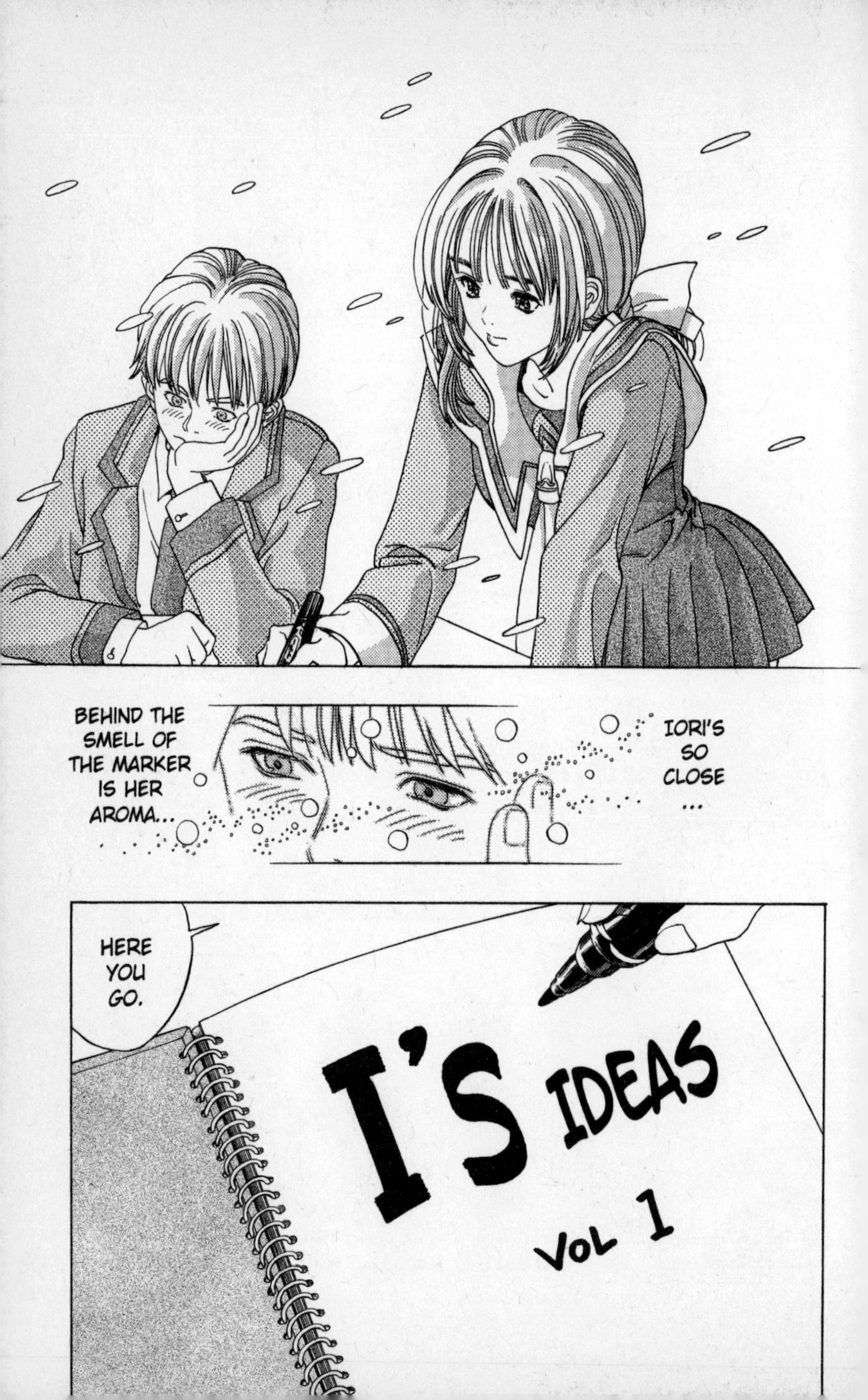
IORI'S SO CLOSE ...
BEHIND THE SMELL OF THE MARKER IS HER AROMA...
HERE YOU GO.
I'S IDEAS
VOL 1

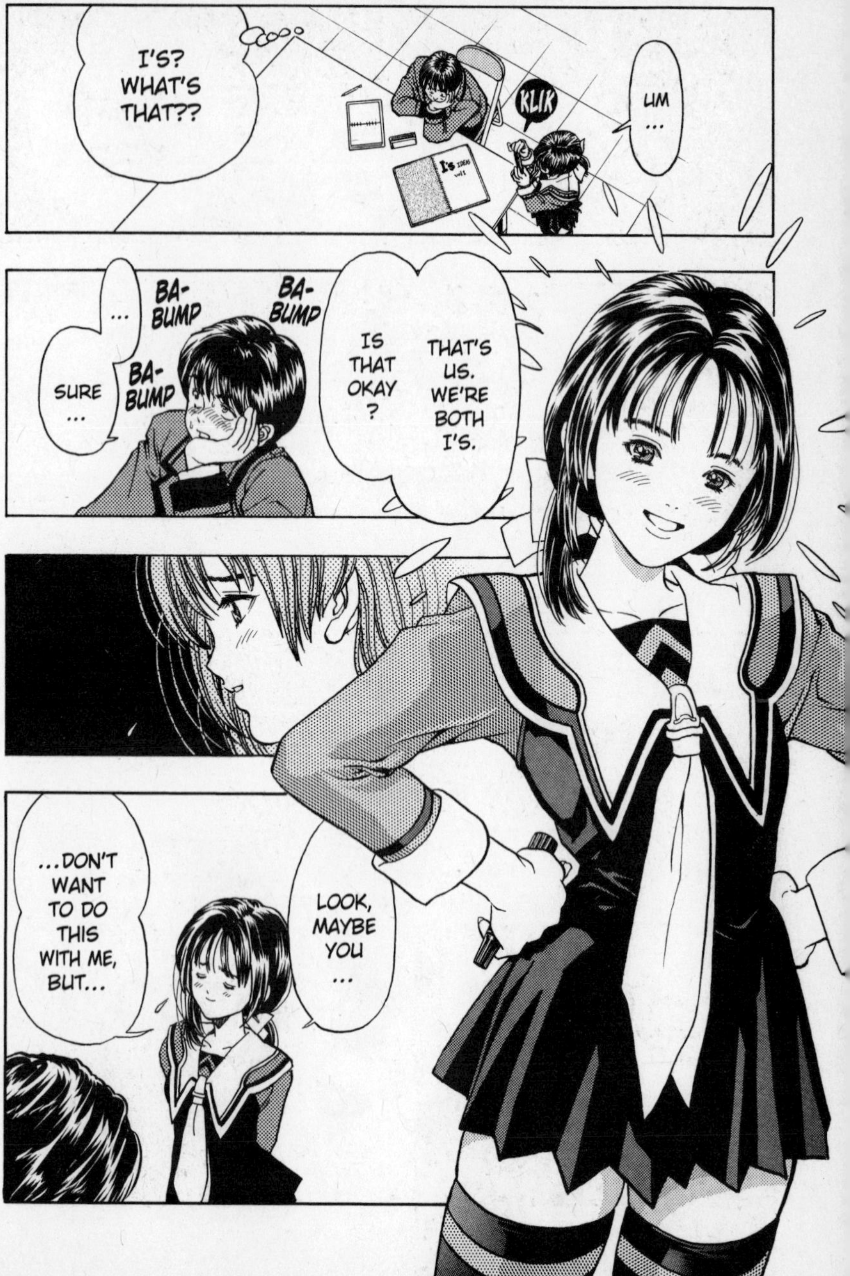
UM ...
KLIK
I'S? WHAT'S THAT??
THAT'S US. WE'RE BOTH I'S.
IS THAT OKAY ?
BA-BUMP
BA-BUMP
BA-BUMP
... SURE ...
LOOK, MAYBE YOU ...
...DON'T WANT TO DO THIS WITH ME, BUT...

READ THIS WAY

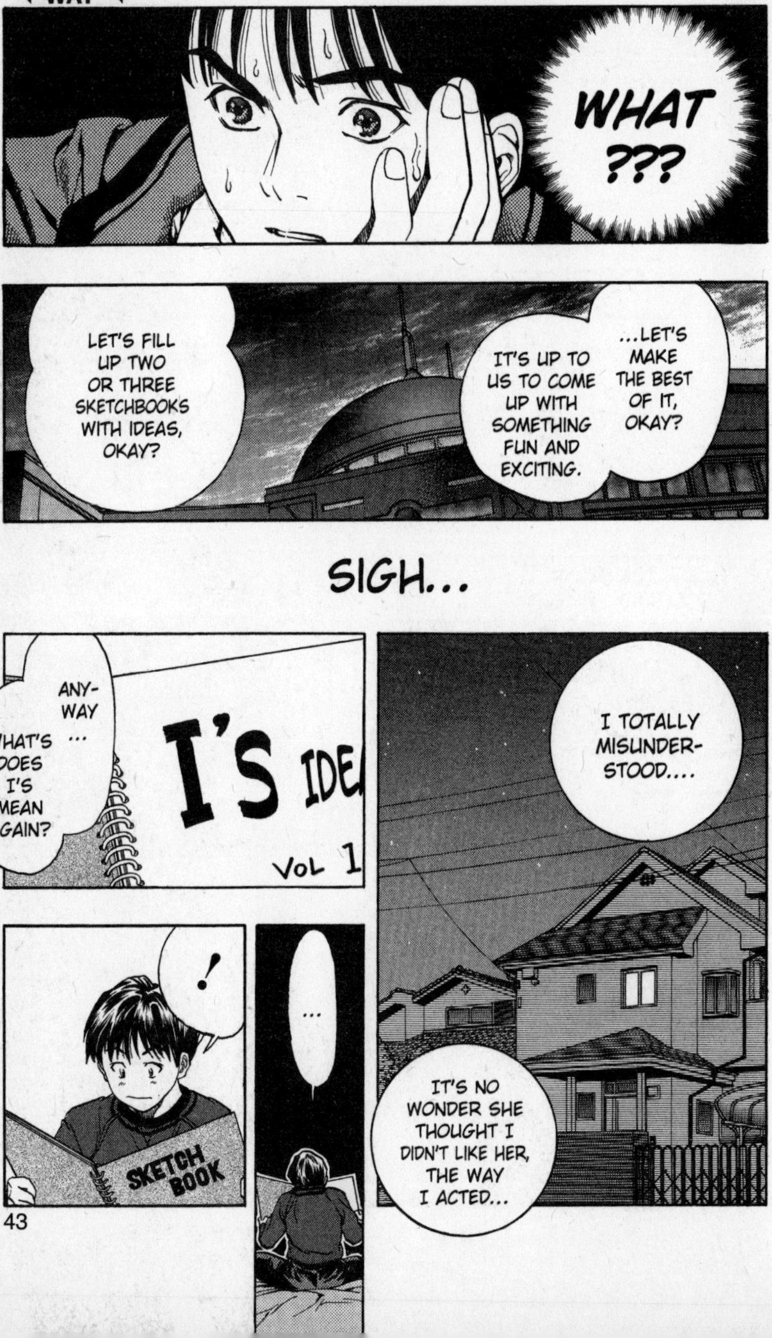
WHAT ???
...LET'S MAKE THE BEST OF IT, OKAY?
IT'S UP TO US TO COME UP WITH SOMETHING FUN AND EXCITING.
LET'S FILL UP TWO OR THREE SKETCHBOOKS WITH IDEAS, OKAY?
SIGH...
I TOTALLY MISUNDER-STOOD....
IT'S NO WONDER SHE THOUGHT I DIDN'T LIKE HER, THE WAY I ACTED...
ANY-WAY ...
WHAT'S DOES I'S MEAN AGAIN?
I'S IDE
VOL 1
...
!
SKETCH BOOK

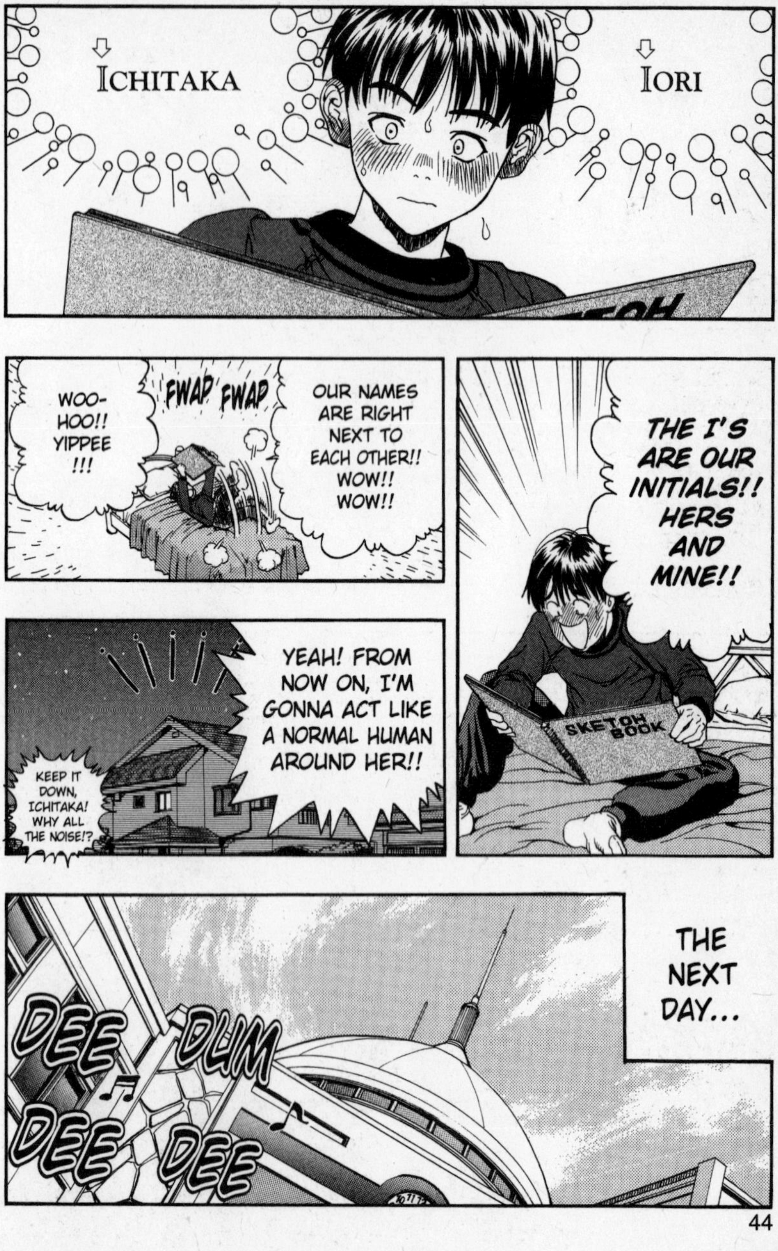
IORI
ICHITAKA
THE I'S ARE OUR INITIALS!! HERS AND MINE!!
OUR NAMES ARE RIGHT NEXT TO EACH OTHER!! WOW!! WOW!!
FWAP FWAP
WOO-HOO!! YIPPEE!!!
YEAH! FROM NOW ON, I'M GONNA ACT LIKE A NORMAL HUMAN AROUND HER!!
KEEP IT DOWN, ICHITAKA! WHY ALL THE NOISE!?
THE NEXT DAY...
DEE DUM
DEE DEE

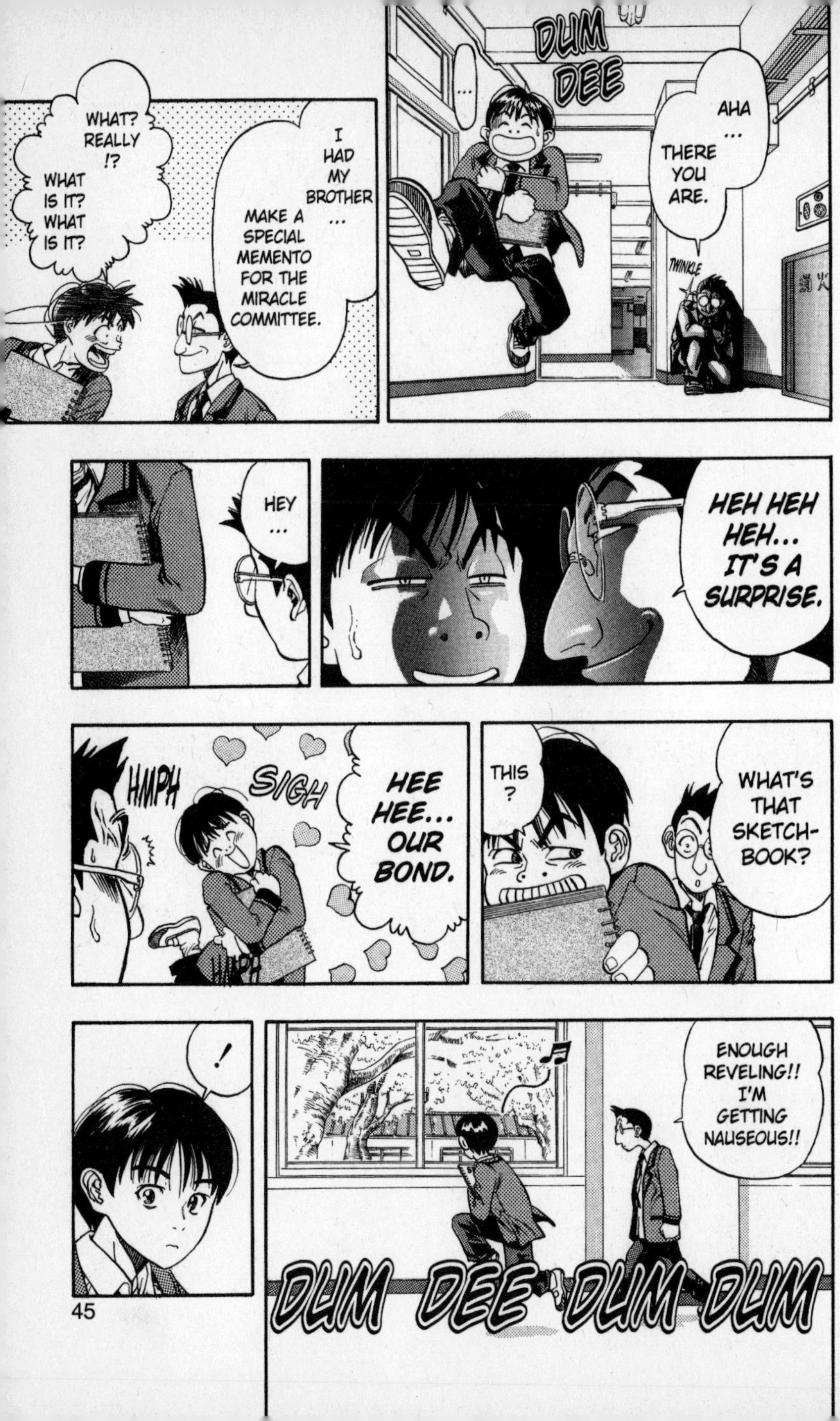
DUM DEE
...
AHA ... THERE YOU ARE.
TWINKLE
I HAD MY BROTHER ... MAKE A SPECIAL MEMENTO FOR THE MIRACLE COMMITTEE.
WHAT? REALLY !?
WHAT IS IT? WHAT IS IT?
HEH HEH HEH... IT'S A SURPRISE.
HEY ...
WHAT'S THAT SKETCH-BOOK?
THIS ?
HEE HEE... OUR BOND.
SIGH
HMPH
ENOUGH REVELING!! I'M GETTING NAUSEOUS!!
DUM DEE DUM DUM
!

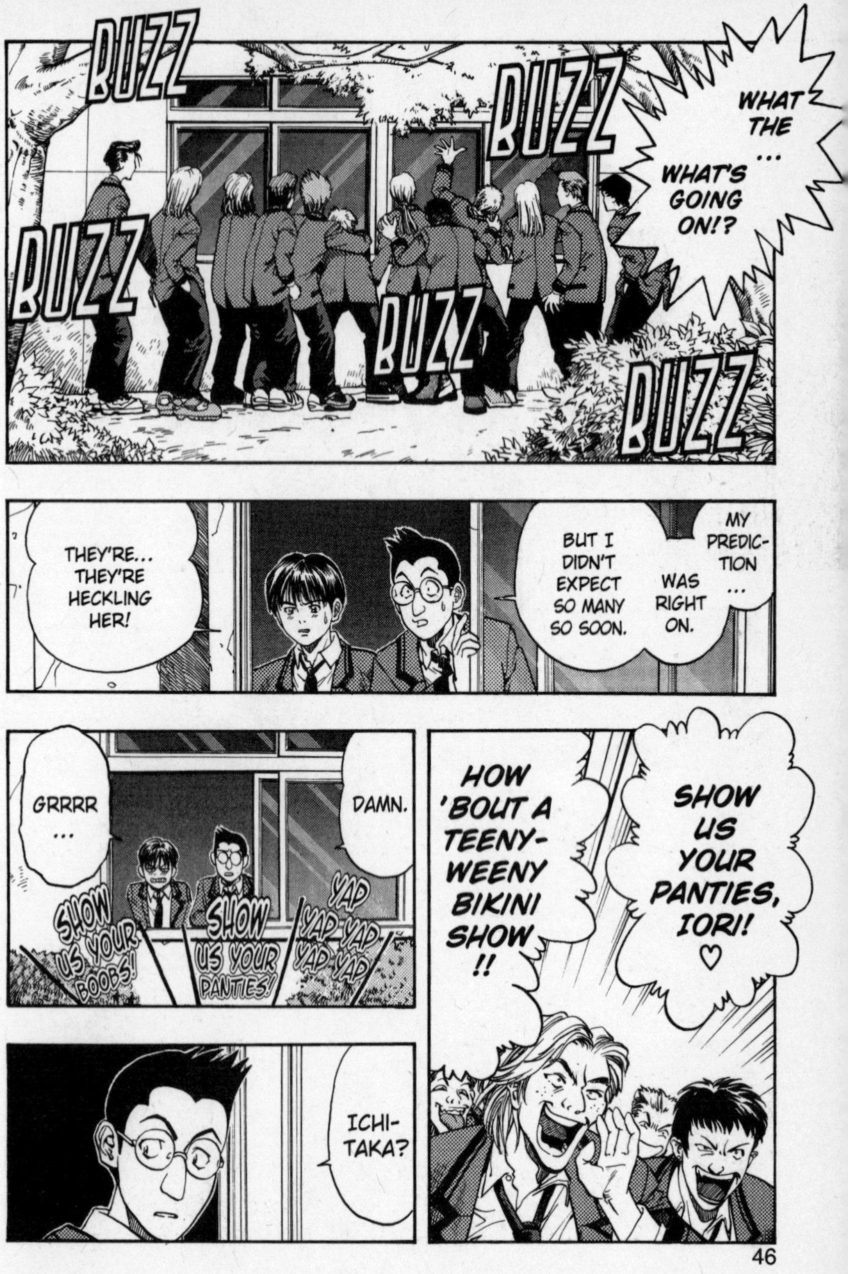
BUZZ
BUZZ
WHAT THE ...
WHAT'S GOING ON!?
BUZZ
BUZZ
BUZZ
MY PREDICTION ...
WAS RIGHT ON.
BUT I DIDN'T EXPECT SO MANY SO SOON.
THEY'RE... THEY'RE HECKLING HER!
SHOW US YOUR PANTIES, IORI! ♡
HOW 'BOUT A TEENY-WEENY BIKINI SHOW !!
DAMN.
GRRRR ...
YAP YAP YAP YAP YAP
SHOW US YOUR PANTIES!
SHOW US YOUR BOOBS!
ICHI-TAKA?

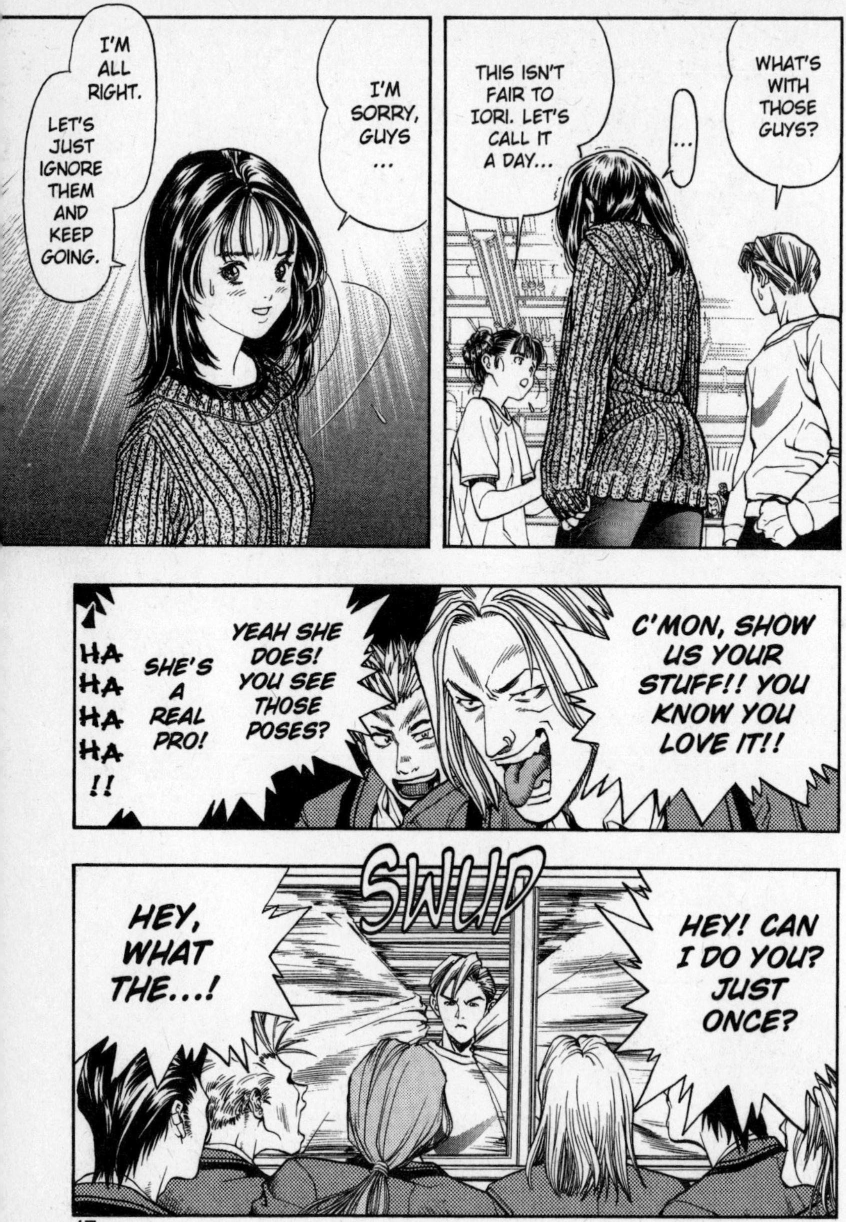
WHAT'S WITH THOSE GUYS?
...
THIS ISN'T FAIR TO IORI. LET'S CALL IT A DAY...
I'M SORRY, GUYS ...
I'M ALL RIGHT.
LET'S JUST IGNORE THEM AND KEEP GOING.
C'MON, SHOW US YOUR STUFF!! YOU KNOW YOU LOVE IT!!
YEAH SHE DOES! YOU SEE THOSE POSES?
SHE'S A REAL PRO!
HA HA HA HA !!
SWUP
HEY! CAN I DO YOU? JUST ONCE?
HEY, WHAT THE...!

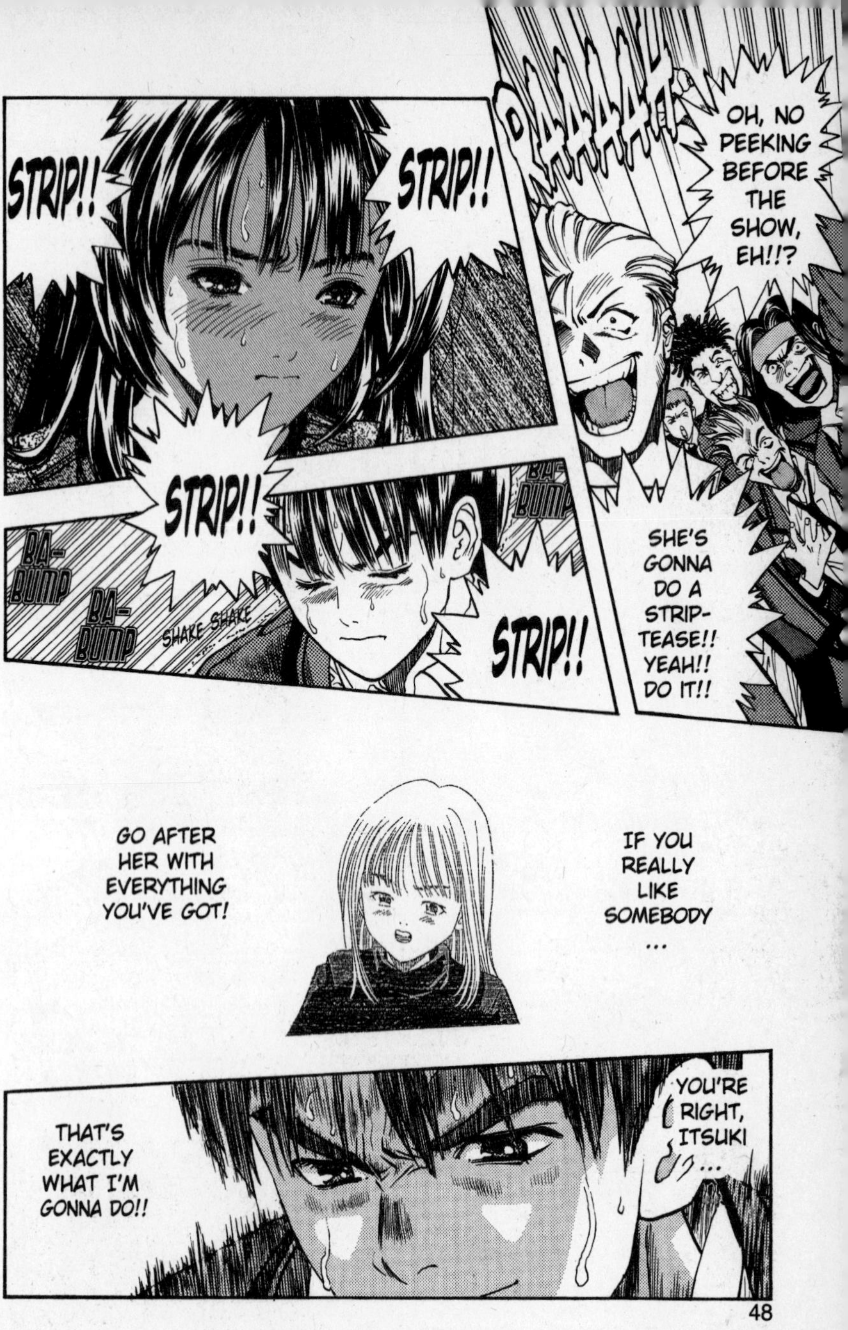

OH, NO PEEKING BEFORE THE SHOW, EH!!?
SHE'S GONNA DO A STRIP-TEASE!! YEAH!! DO IT!!
STRIP!!
STRIP!!
BA-BUMP
STRIP!!
STRIP!!
BA-BUMP
BA-BUMP
SHAKE SHAKE
IF YOU REALLY LIKE SOMEBODY ...
GO AFTER HER WITH EVERYTHING YOU'VE GOT!
YOU'RE RIGHT, ITSUKI ...
THAT'S EXACTLY WHAT I'M GONNA DO!!

READ THIS WAY

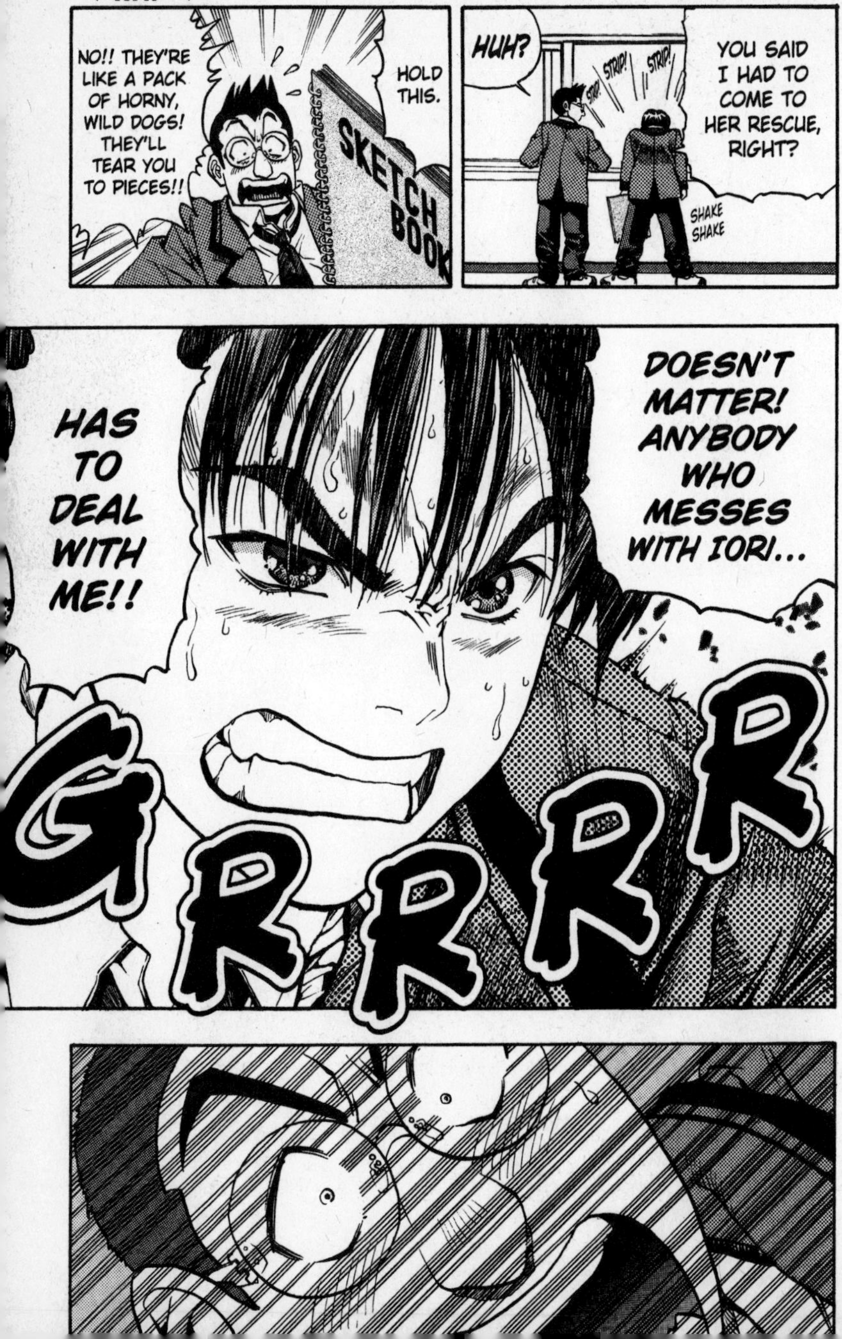
YOU SAID I HAD TO COME TO HER RESCUE, RIGHT?
STRIP!
STRIP!
STRIP!
SHAKE SHAKE
HUH?
HOLD THIS.
NO!! THEY'RE LIKE A PACK OF HORNY, WILD DOGS! THEY'LL TEAR YOU TO PIECES!!
SKETCH BOOK
DOESN'T MATTER! ANYBODY WHO MESSES WITH IORI...
HAS TO DEAL WITH ME!!
GRRRR

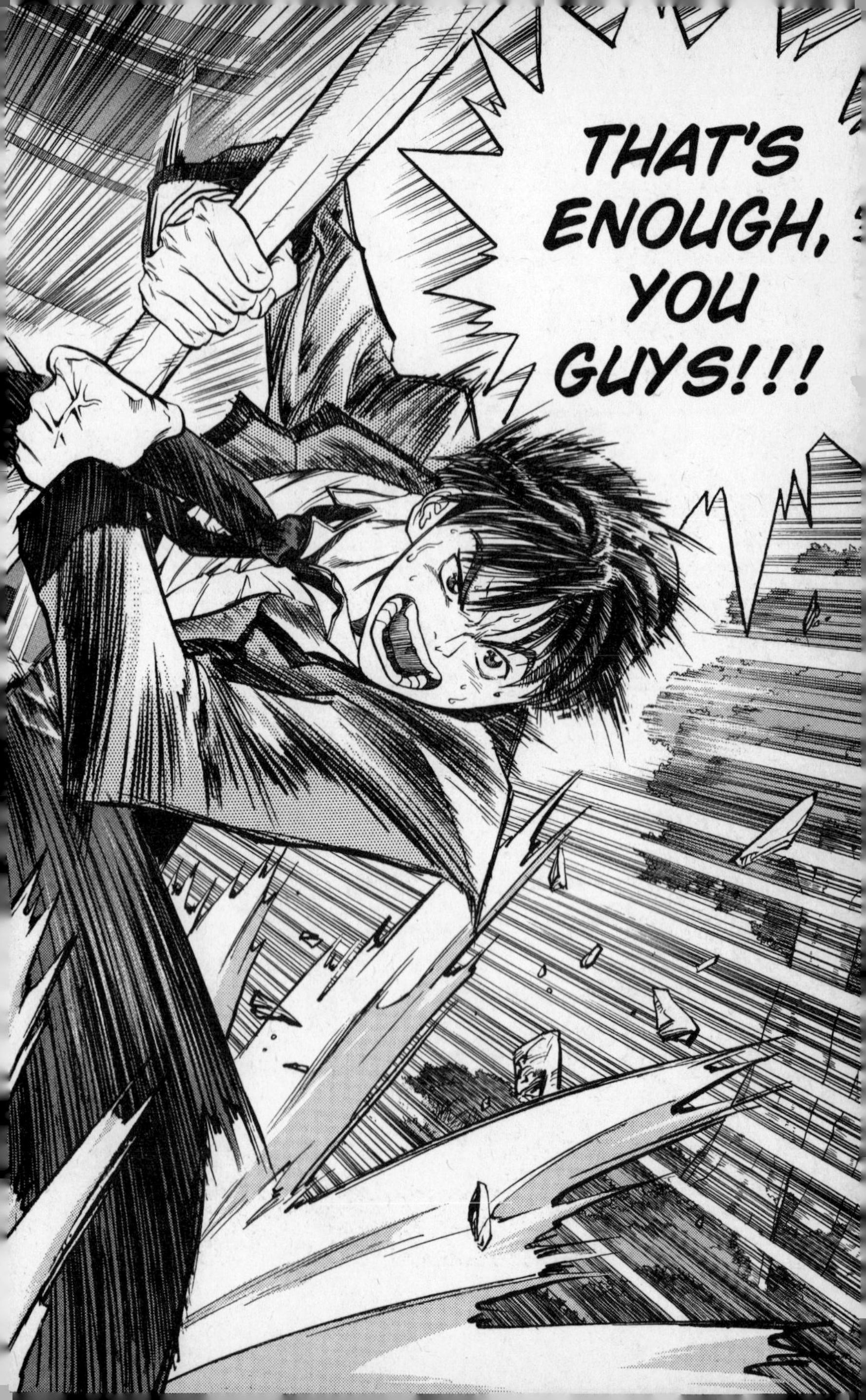
THAT'S ENOUGH, YOU GUYS!!!

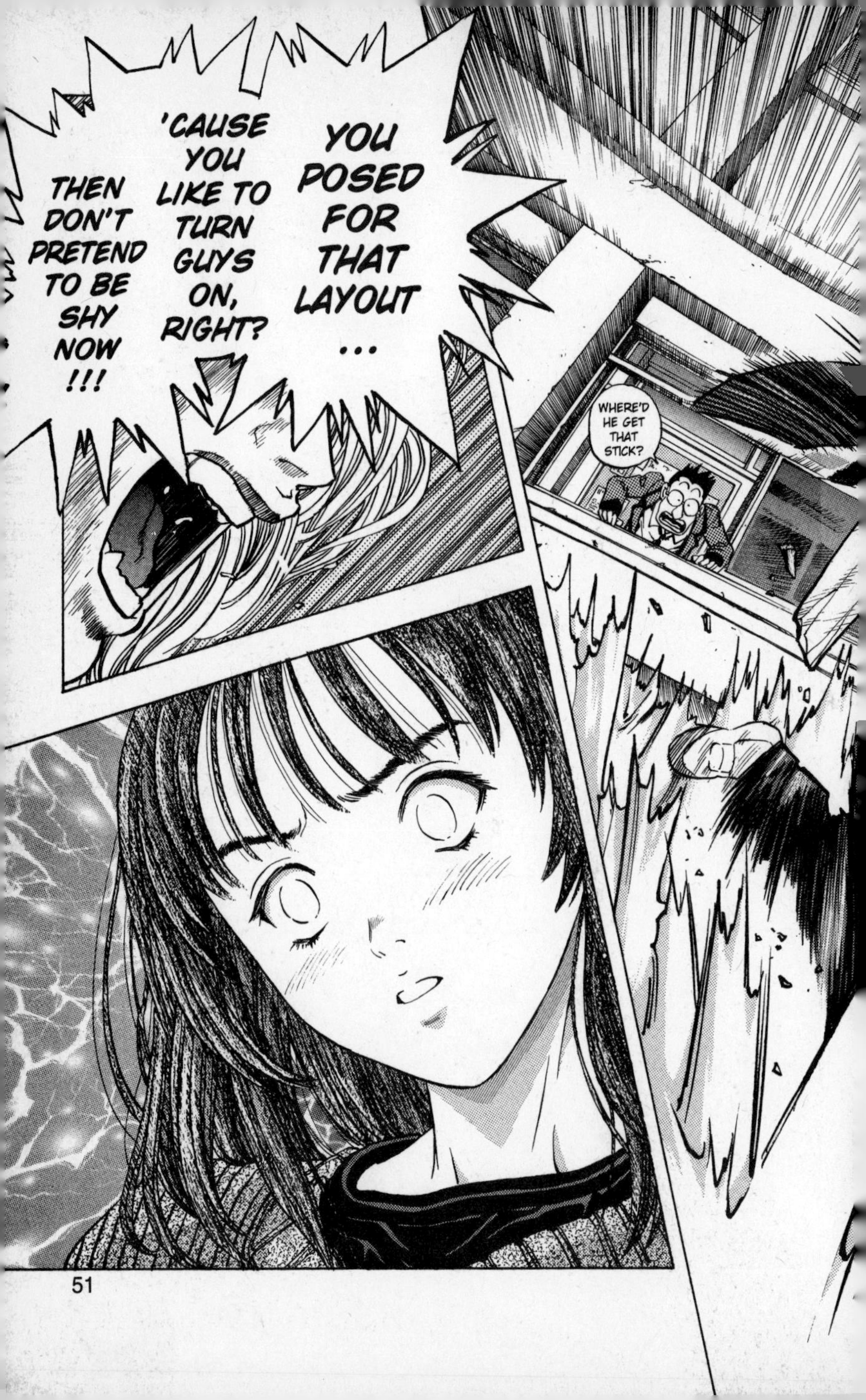
YOU POSED FOR THAT LAYOUT...
'CAUSE YOU LIKE TO TURN GUYS ON, RIGHT?
THEN DON'T PRETEND TO BE SHY NOW!!!
WHERE'D HE GET THAT STICK?

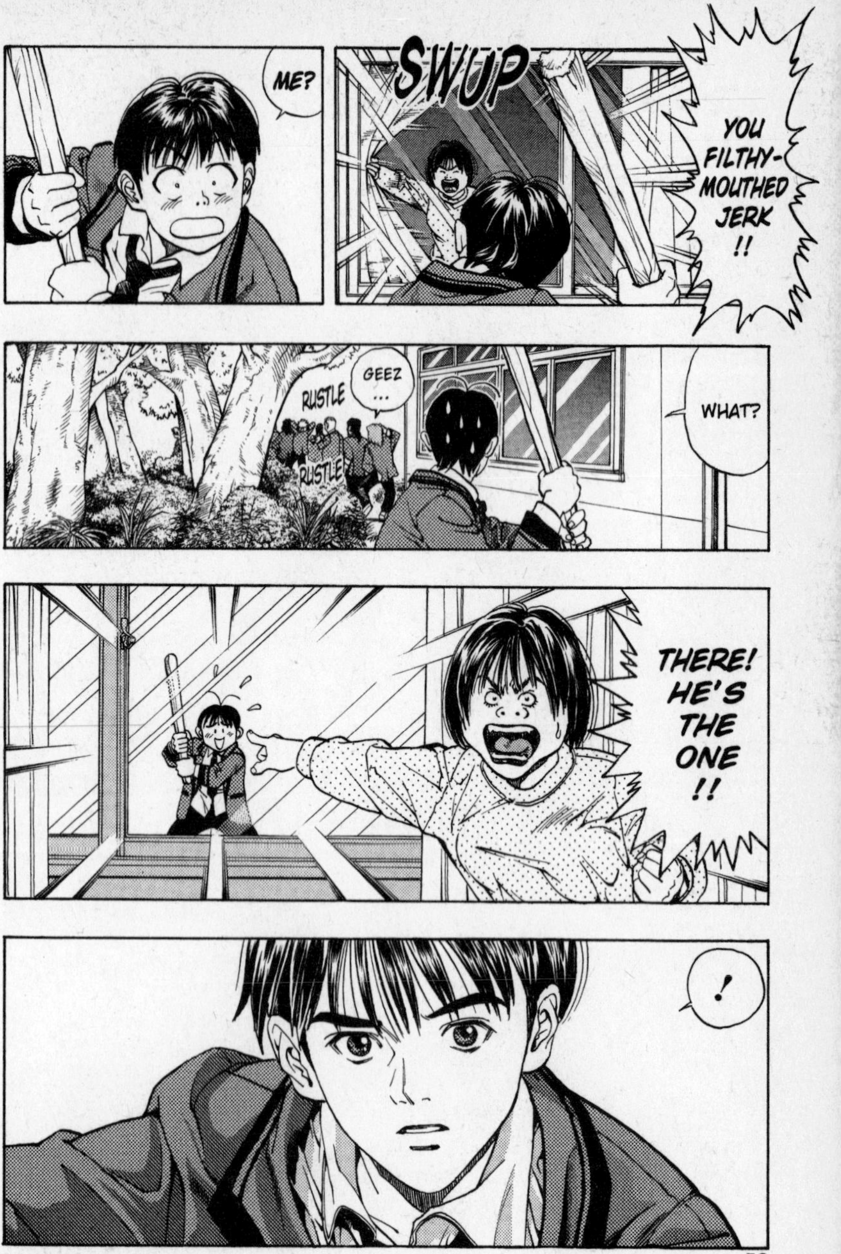
SWUP
YOU FILTHY-MOUTHED JERK !!
ME?
WHAT?
GEEZ ...
RUSTLE
RUSTLE
THERE! HE'S THE ONE !!
!

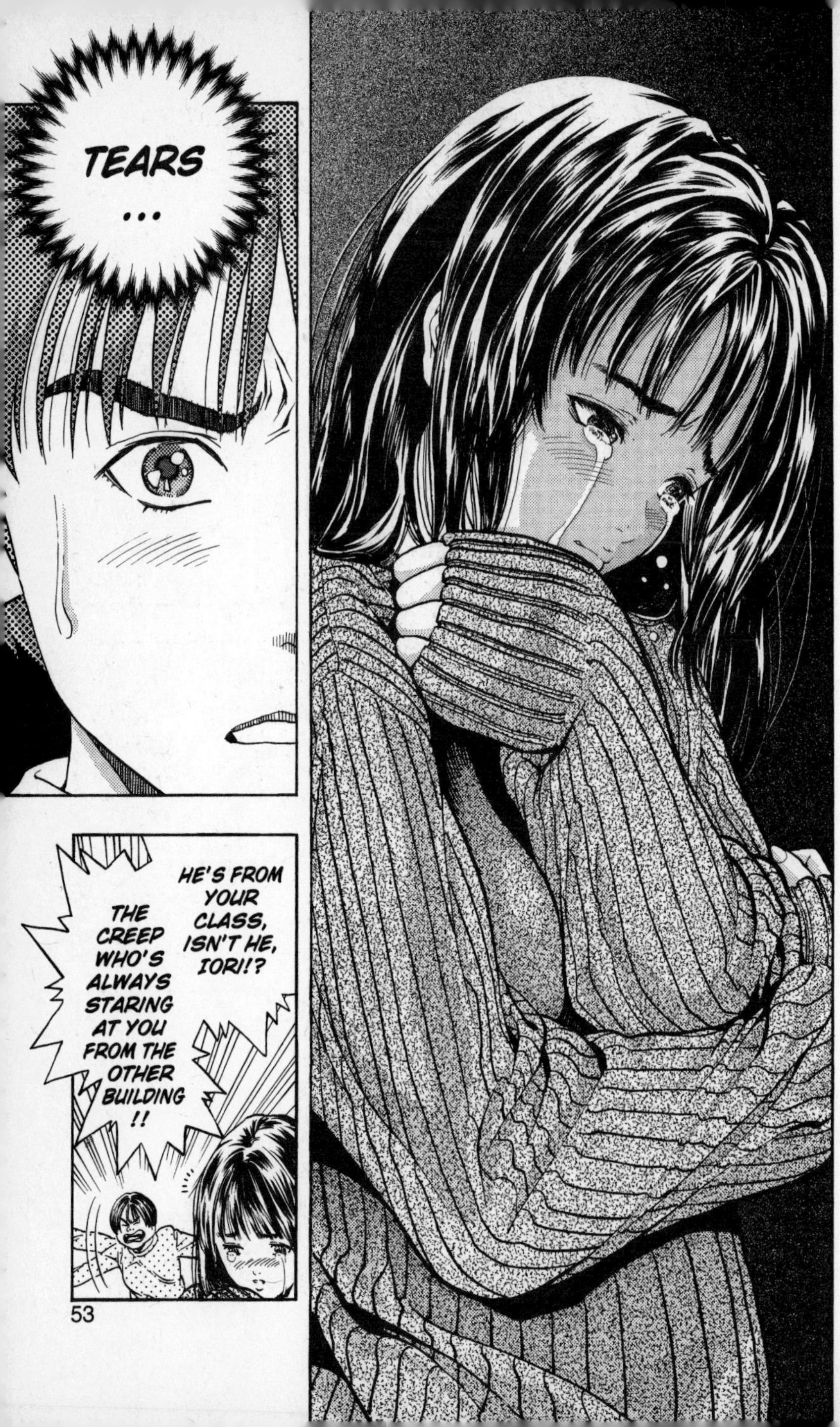
TEARS ...
HE'S FROM YOUR CLASS, ISN'T HE, IORI!?
THE CREEP WHO'S ALWAYS STARING AT YOU FROM THE OTHER BUILDING!!

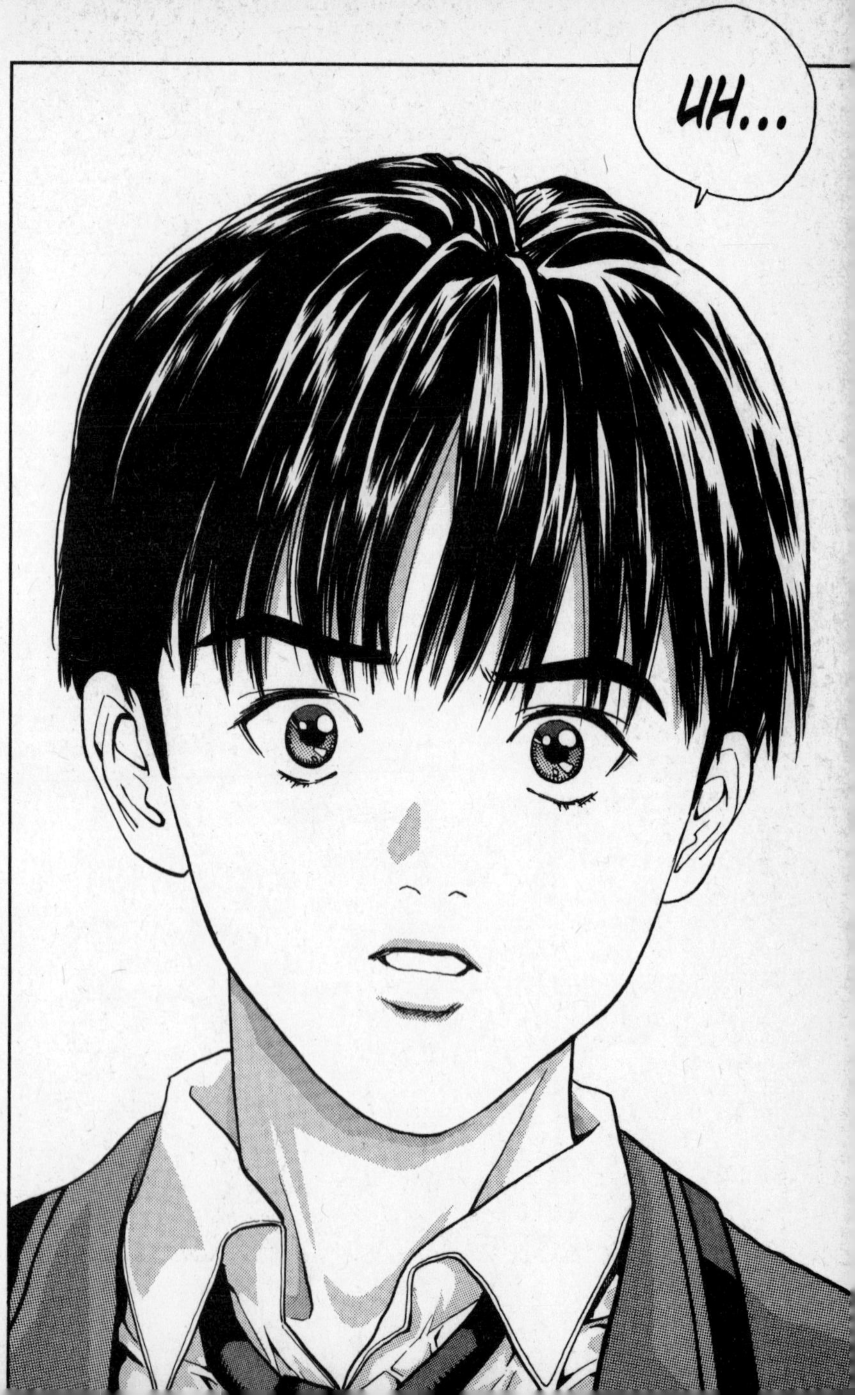
UH...

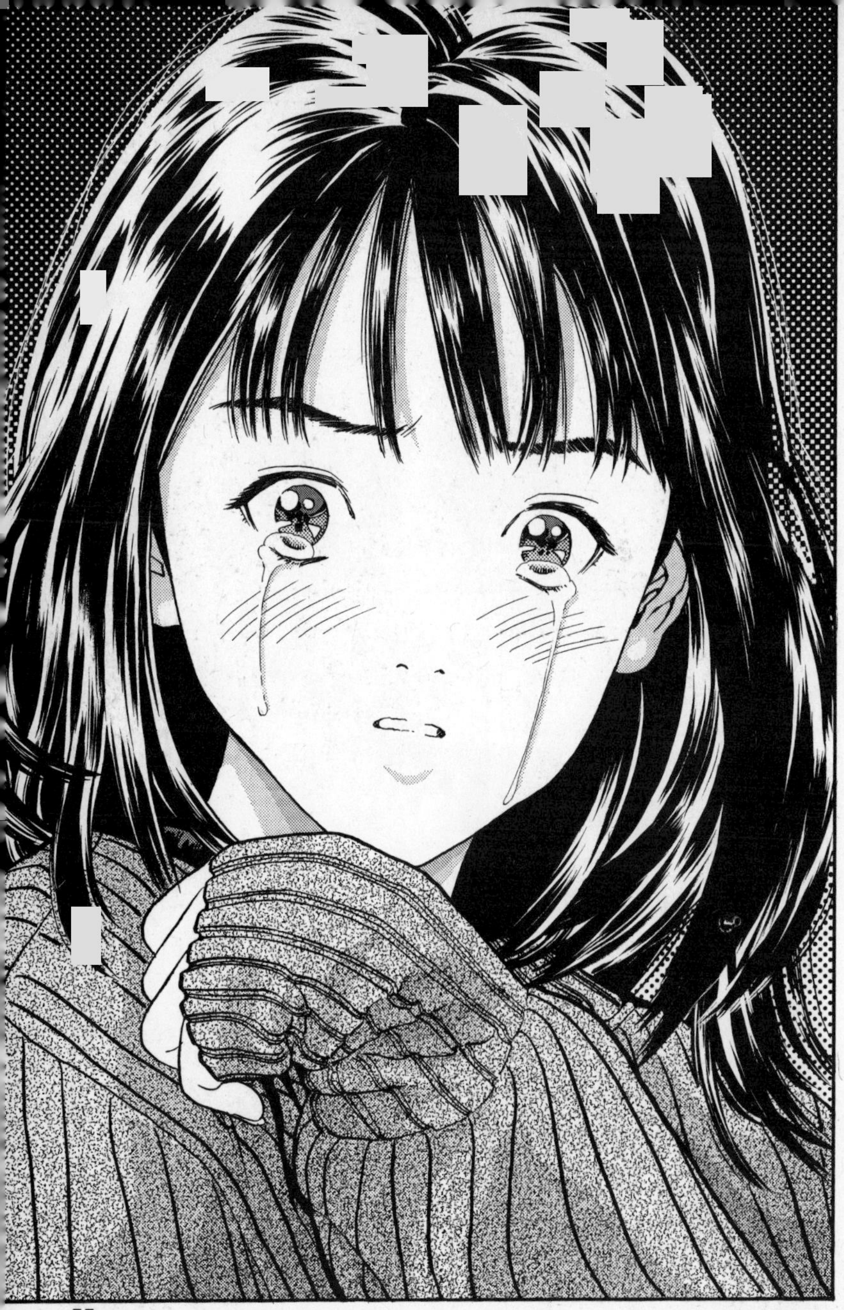

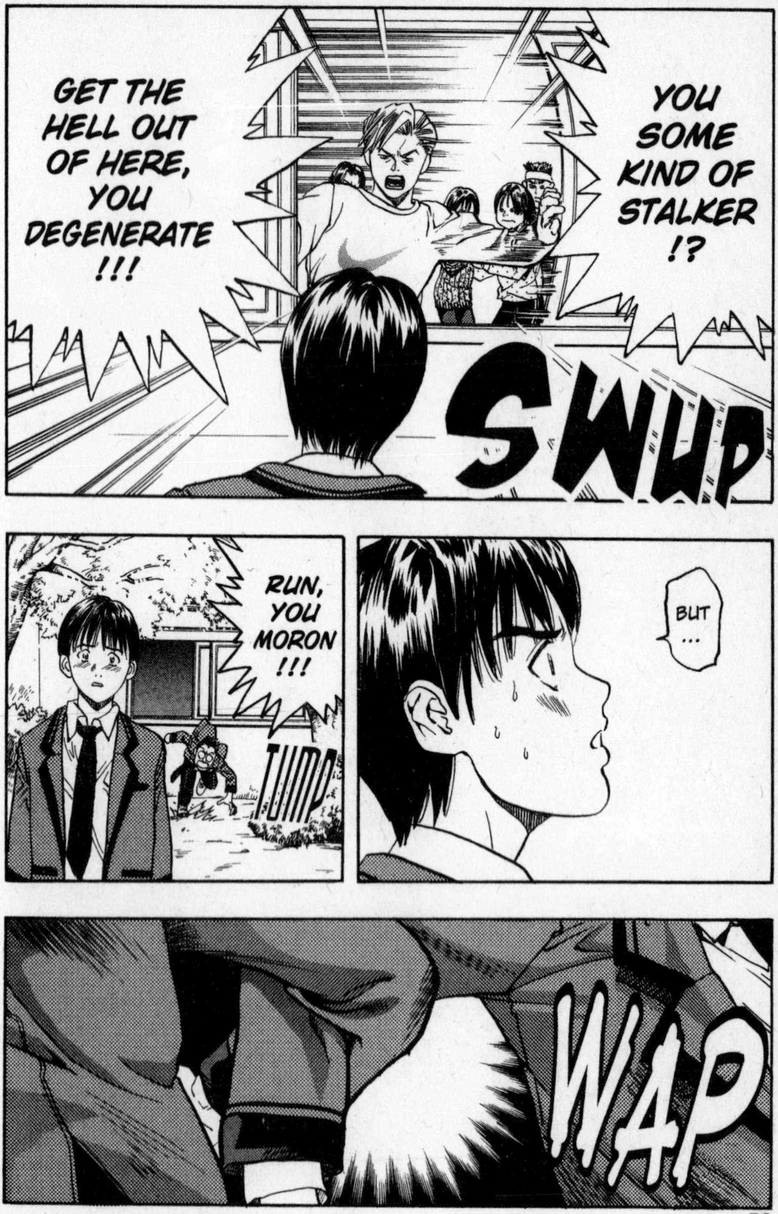
YOU SOME KIND OF STALKER !?
GET THE HELL OUT OF HERE, YOU DEGENERATE !!!
SWUP
BUT ...
RUN, YOU MORON !!!
TUMP
WAP

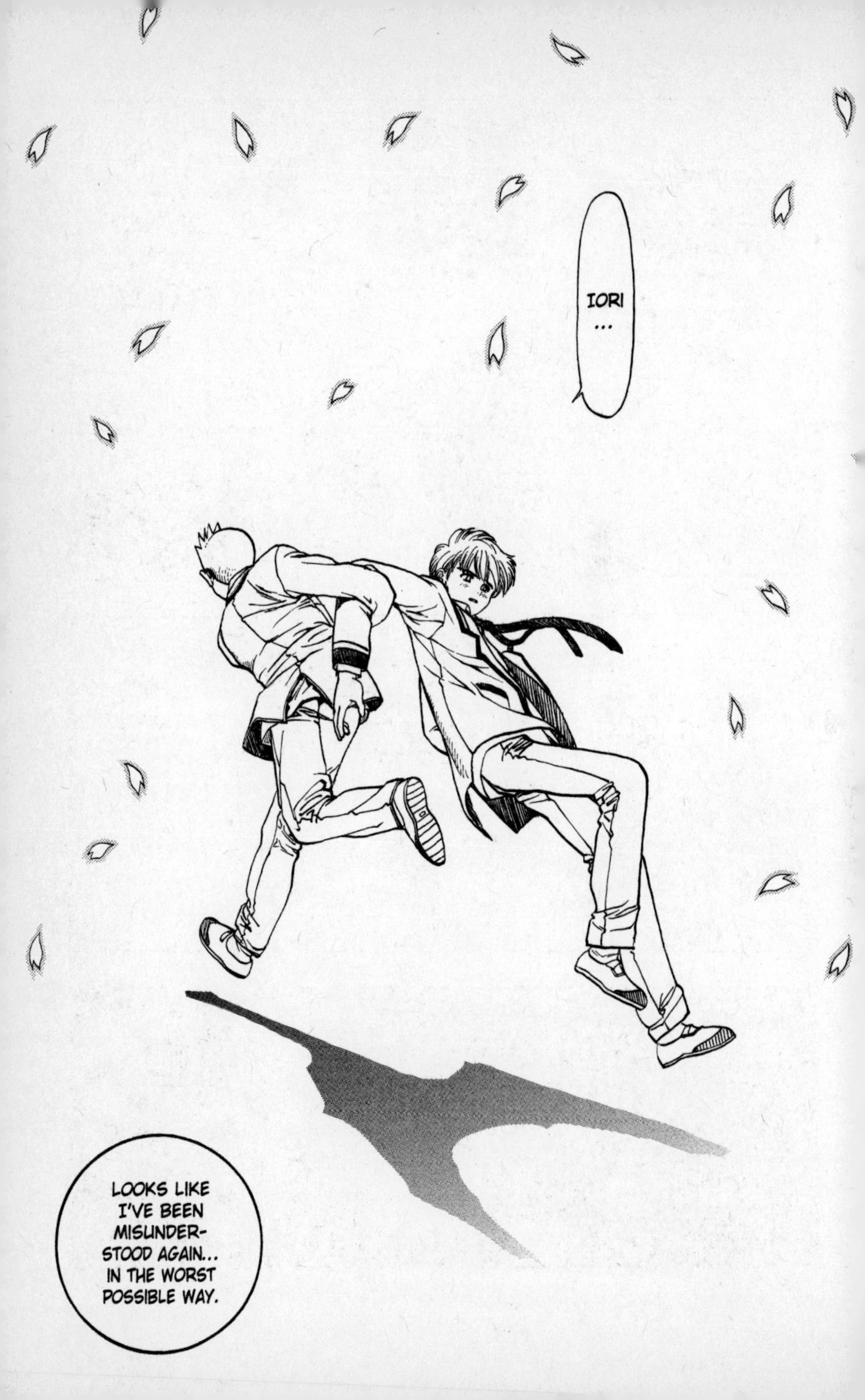
IORI
...
LOOKS LIKE
I'VE BEEN
MISUNDER-
STOOD AGAIN...
IN THE WORST
POSSIBLE WAY.

I"s
アイズ

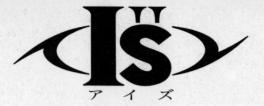

Chapter 2:
An Angry Wind

READ THIS WAY

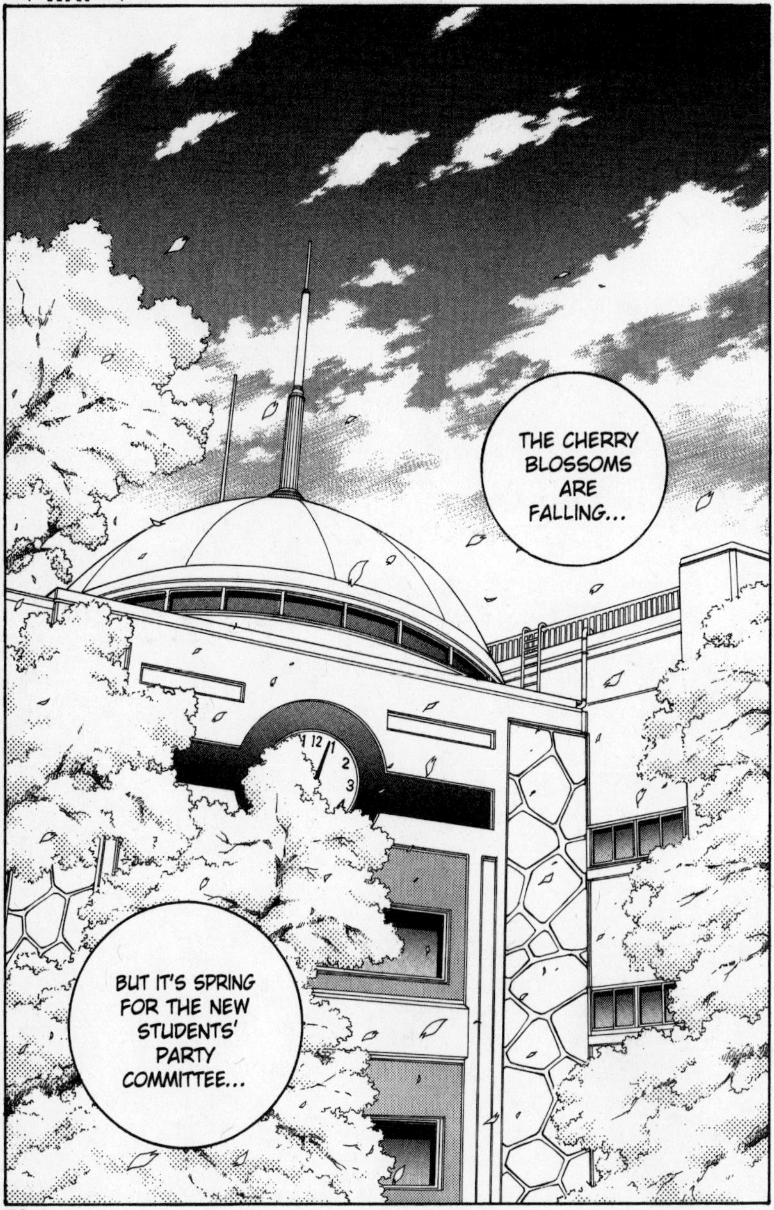
THE CHERRY BLOSSOMS ARE FALLING...
BUT IT'S SPRING FOR THE NEW STUDENTS' PARTY COMMITTEE...

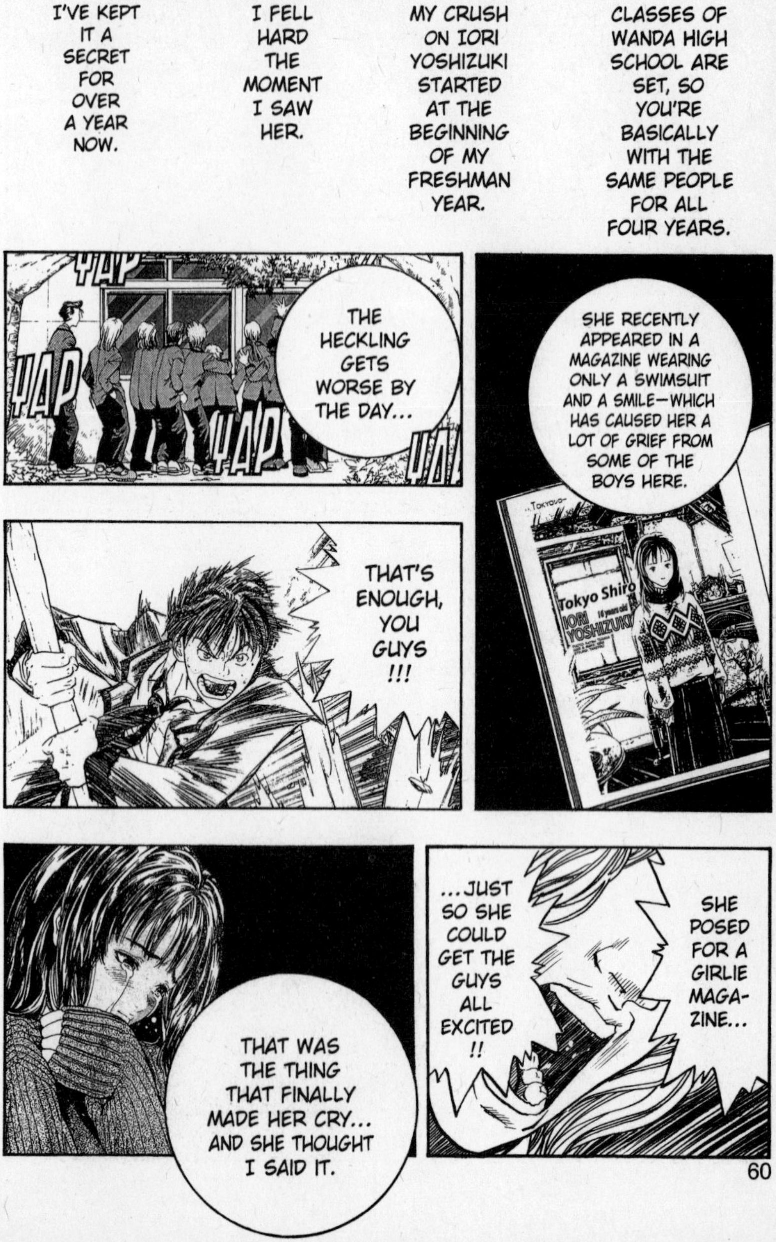
CLASSES OF WANDA HIGH SCHOOL ARE SET, SO YOU'RE BASICALLY WITH THE SAME PEOPLE FOR ALL FOUR YEARS.
MY CRUSH ON IORI YOSHIZUKI STARTED AT THE BEGINNING OF MY FRESHMAN YEAR.
I FELL HARD THE MOMENT I SAW HER.
I'VE KEPT IT A SECRET FOR OVER A YEAR NOW.
SHE RECENTLY APPEARED IN A MAGAZINE WEARING ONLY A SWIMSUIT AND A SMILE—WHICH HAS CAUSED HER A LOT OF GRIEF FROM SOME OF THE BOYS HERE.
Tokyo Shiro
IORI YOSHIZUKI
YAP
YAP
THE HECKLING GETS WORSE BY THE DAY...
YAP
THAT'S ENOUGH, YOU GUYS !!!
SHE POSED FOR A GIRLIE MAGA-ZINE...
...JUST SO SHE COULD GET THE GUYS ALL EXCITED !!
THAT WAS THE THING THAT FINALLY MADE HER CRY... AND SHE THOUGHT I SAID IT.

READ THIS WAY

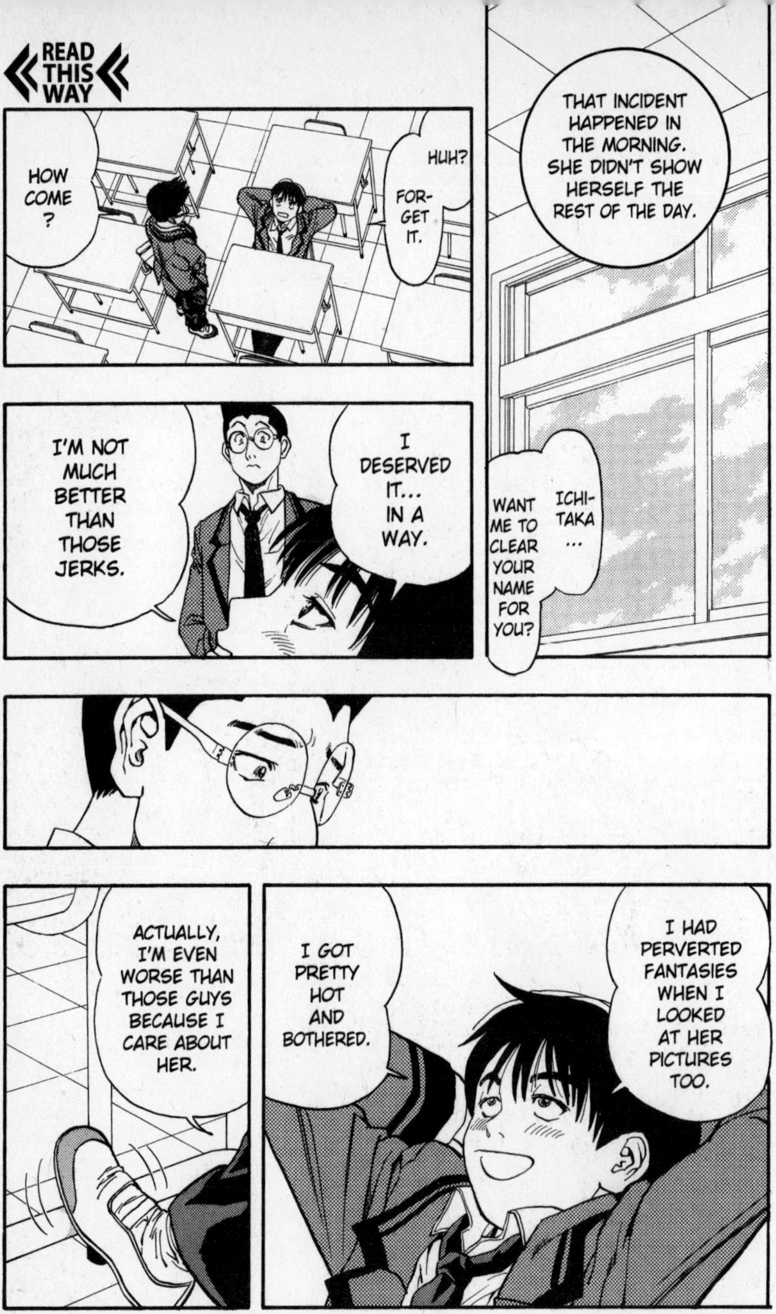
THAT INCIDENT HAPPENED IN THE MORNING. SHE DIDN'T SHOW HERSELF THE REST OF THE DAY.
ICHI-TAKA...
WANT ME TO CLEAR YOUR NAME FOR YOU?
HUH?
FOR-GET IT.
HOW COME?
I DESERVED IT... IN A WAY.
I'M NOT MUCH BETTER THAN THOSE JERKS.
I HAD PERVERTED FANTASIES WHEN I LOOKED AT HER PICTURES TOO.
I GOT PRETTY HOT AND BOTHERED.
ACTUALLY, I'M EVEN WORSE THAN THOSE GUYS BECAUSE I CARE ABOUT HER.

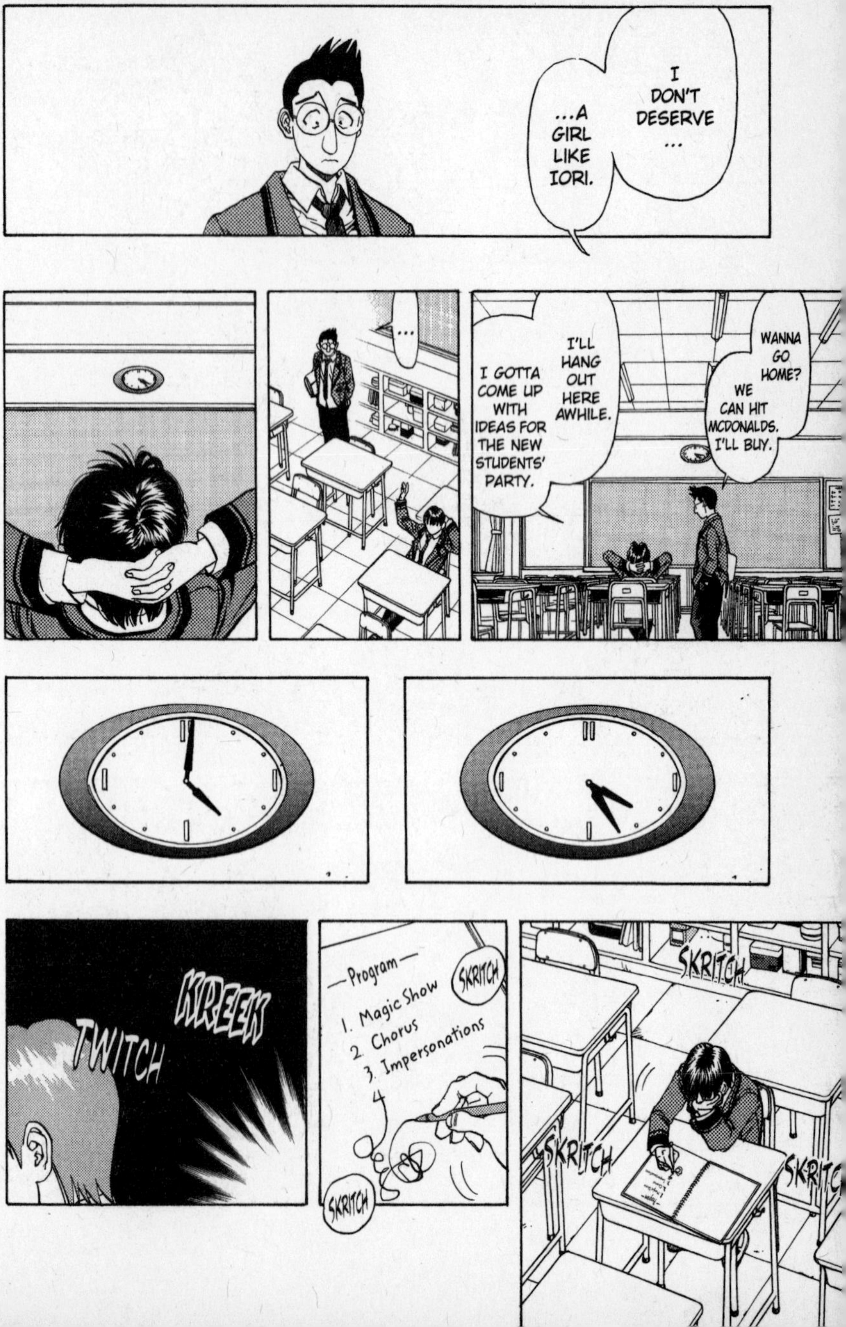
I DON'T DESERVE ...
...A GIRL LIKE IORI.
WANNA GO HOME? WE CAN HIT MCDONALDS. I'LL BUY.
I'LL HANG OUT HERE AWHILE.
I GOTTA COME UP WITH IDEAS FOR THE NEW STUDENTS' PARTY.
...
SKRITCH
SKRITCH
SKRITCH
—Program—
1. Magic Show
2. Chorus
3. Impersonations
4
SKRITCH
SKRITCH
KIREEK
TWITCH

READ THIS WAY

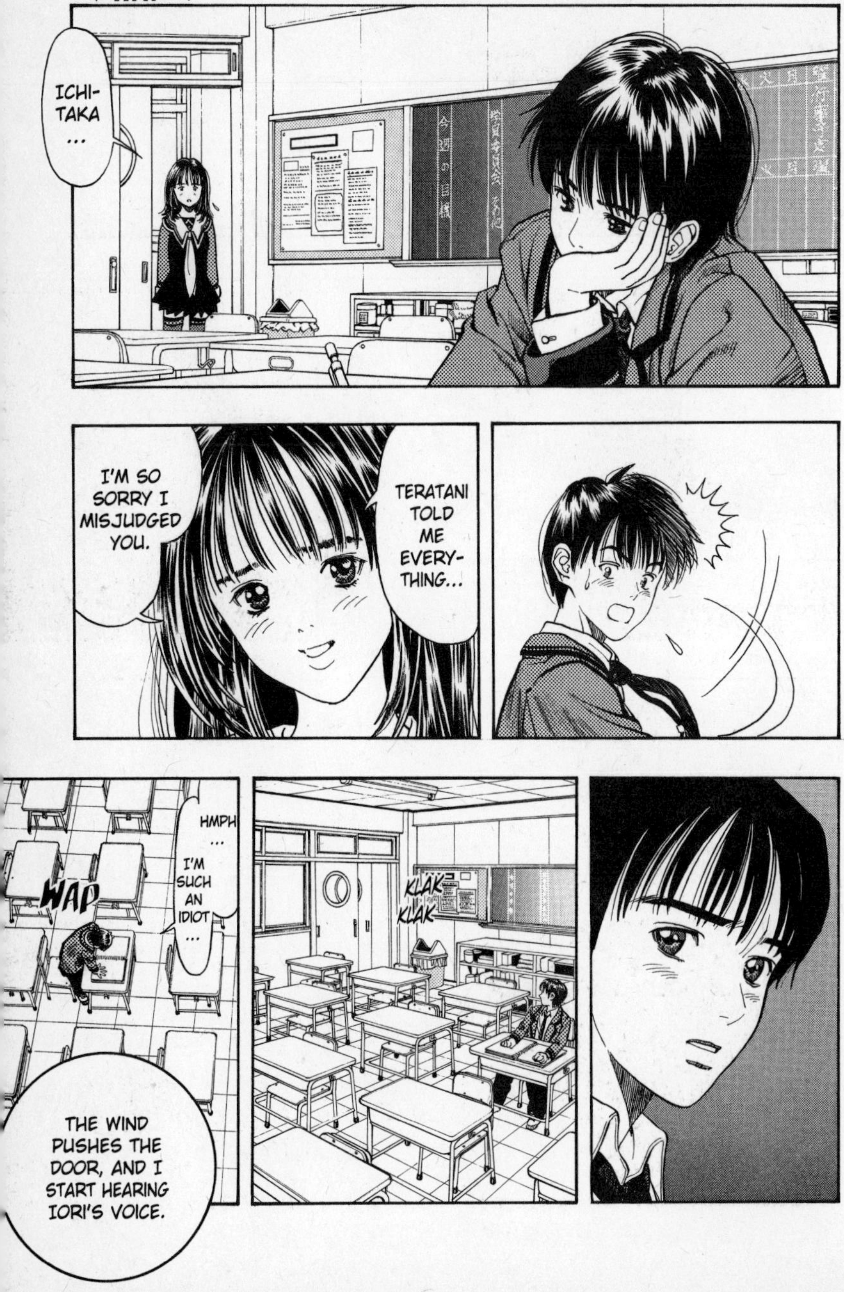
ICHI-TAKA ...
TERATANI TOLD ME EVERYTHING...
I'M SO SORRY I MISJUDGED YOU.
KLAK KLAK
HMPH ... I'M SUCH AN IDIOT ...
WAP
THE WIND PUSHES THE DOOR, AND I START HEARING IORI'S VOICE.

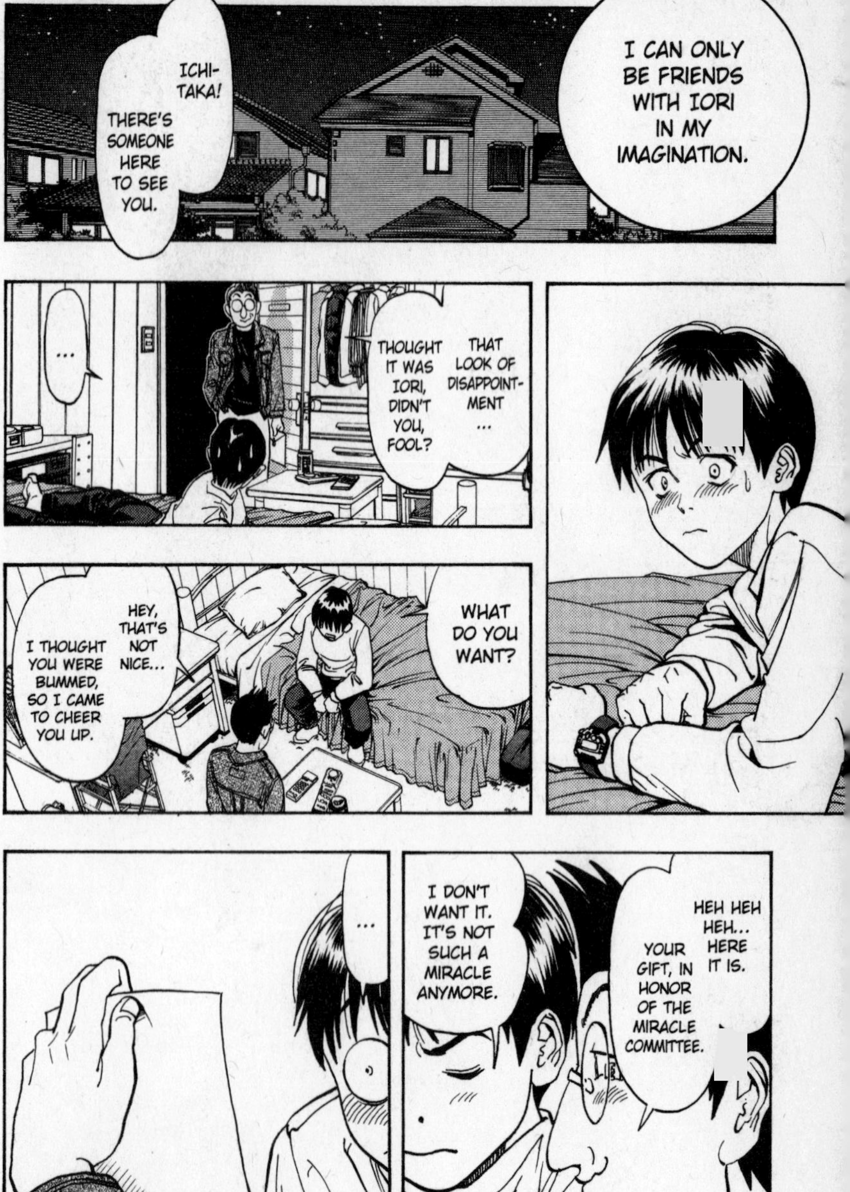
I CAN ONLY BE FRIENDS WITH IORI IN MY IMAGINATION.
ICHI-TAKA!
THERE'S SOMEONE HERE TO SEE YOU.
THAT LOOK OF DISAPPOINT-MENT ...
THOUGHT IT WAS IORI, DIDN'T YOU, FOOL?
...
WHAT DO YOU WANT?
HEY, THAT'S NOT NICE...
I THOUGHT YOU WERE BUMMED, SO I CAME TO CHEER YOU UP.
HEH HEH HEH... HERE IT IS.
YOUR GIFT, IN HONOR OF THE MIRACLE COMMITTEE.
I DON'T WANT IT. IT'S NOT SUCH A MIRACLE ANYMORE.
...

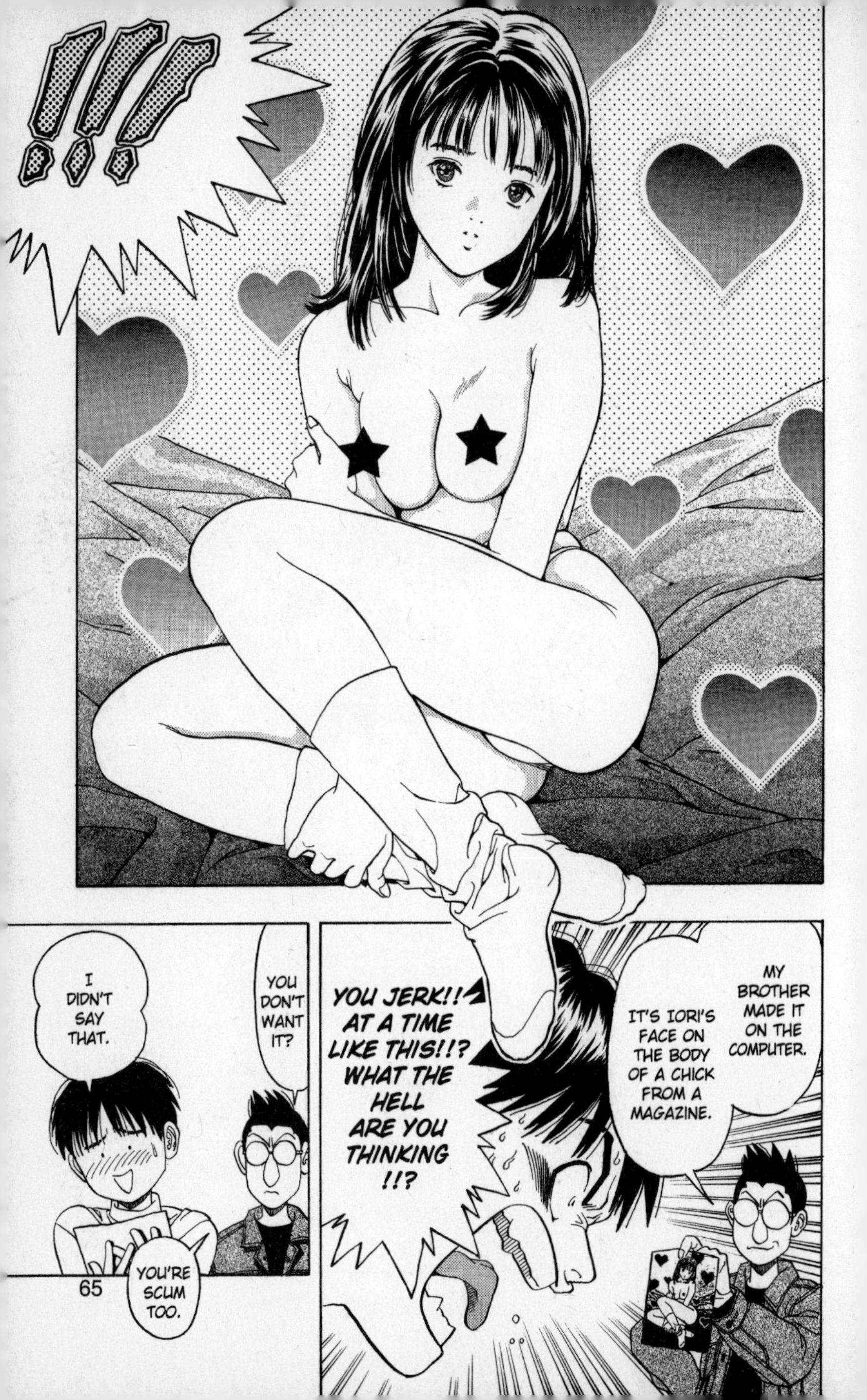
!!!
MY BROTHER MADE IT ON THE COMPUTER.
IT'S IORI'S FACE ON THE BODY OF A CHICK FROM A MAGAZINE.
YOU JERK!! AT A TIME LIKE THIS!!? WHAT THE HELL ARE YOU THINKING!!?
YOU DON'T WANT IT?
I DIDN'T SAY THAT.
YOU'RE SCUM TOO.

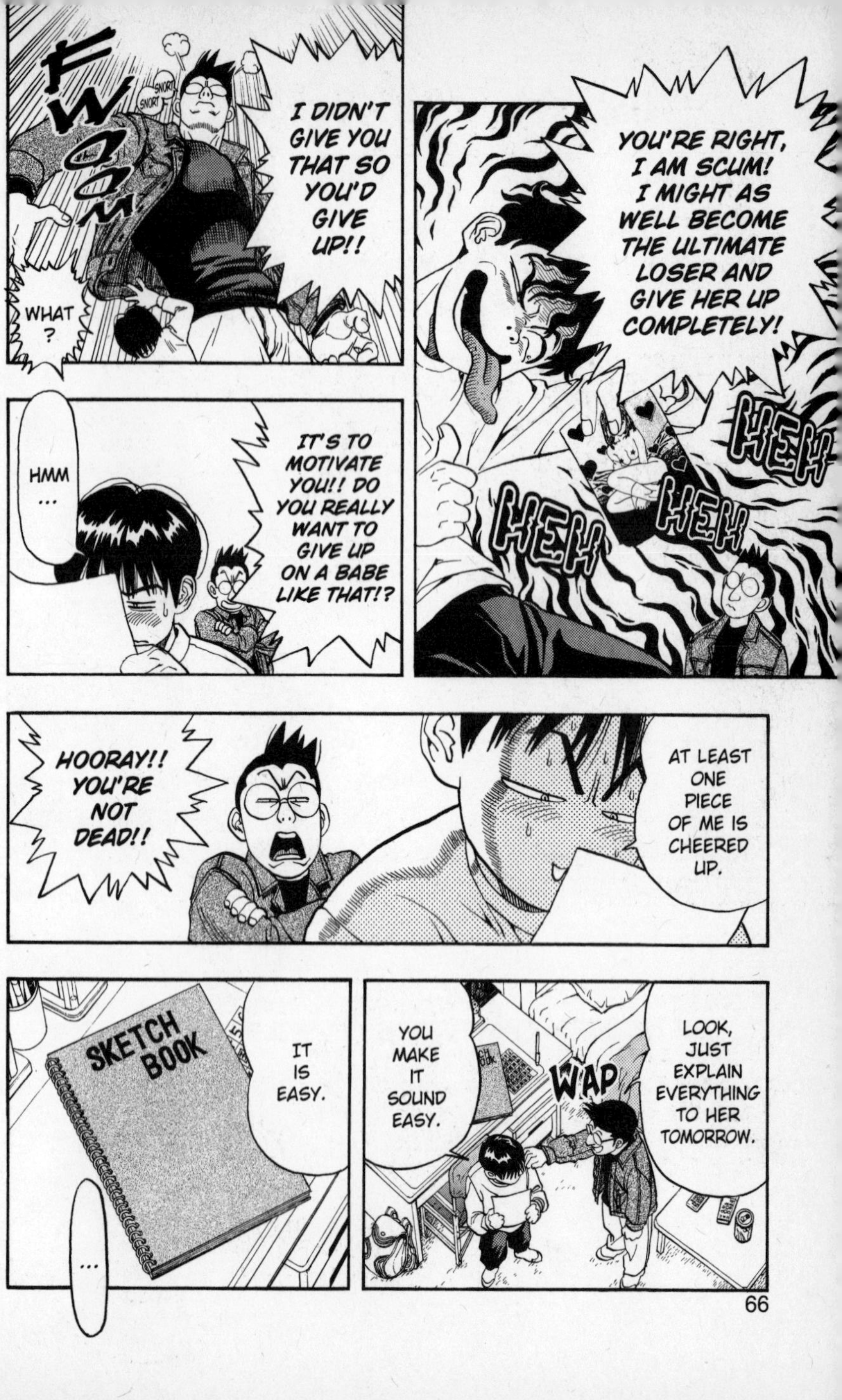
YOU'RE RIGHT, I AM SCUM! I MIGHT AS WELL BECOME THE ULTIMATE LOSER AND GIVE HER UP COMPLETELY!
HEH
HEH
HEH
I DIDN'T GIVE YOU THAT SO YOU'D GIVE UP!!
SNORT
SNORT
FWOOM
WHAT?
IT'S TO MOTIVATE YOU!! DO YOU REALLY WANT TO GIVE UP ON A BABE LIKE THAT!?
HMM...
AT LEAST ONE PIECE OF ME IS CHEERED UP.
HOORAY!! YOU'RE NOT DEAD!!
LOOK, JUST EXPLAIN EVERYTHING TO HER TOMORROW.
WAP
YOU MAKE IT SOUND EASY.
IT IS EASY.
SKETCH BOOK
...

READ THIS WAY

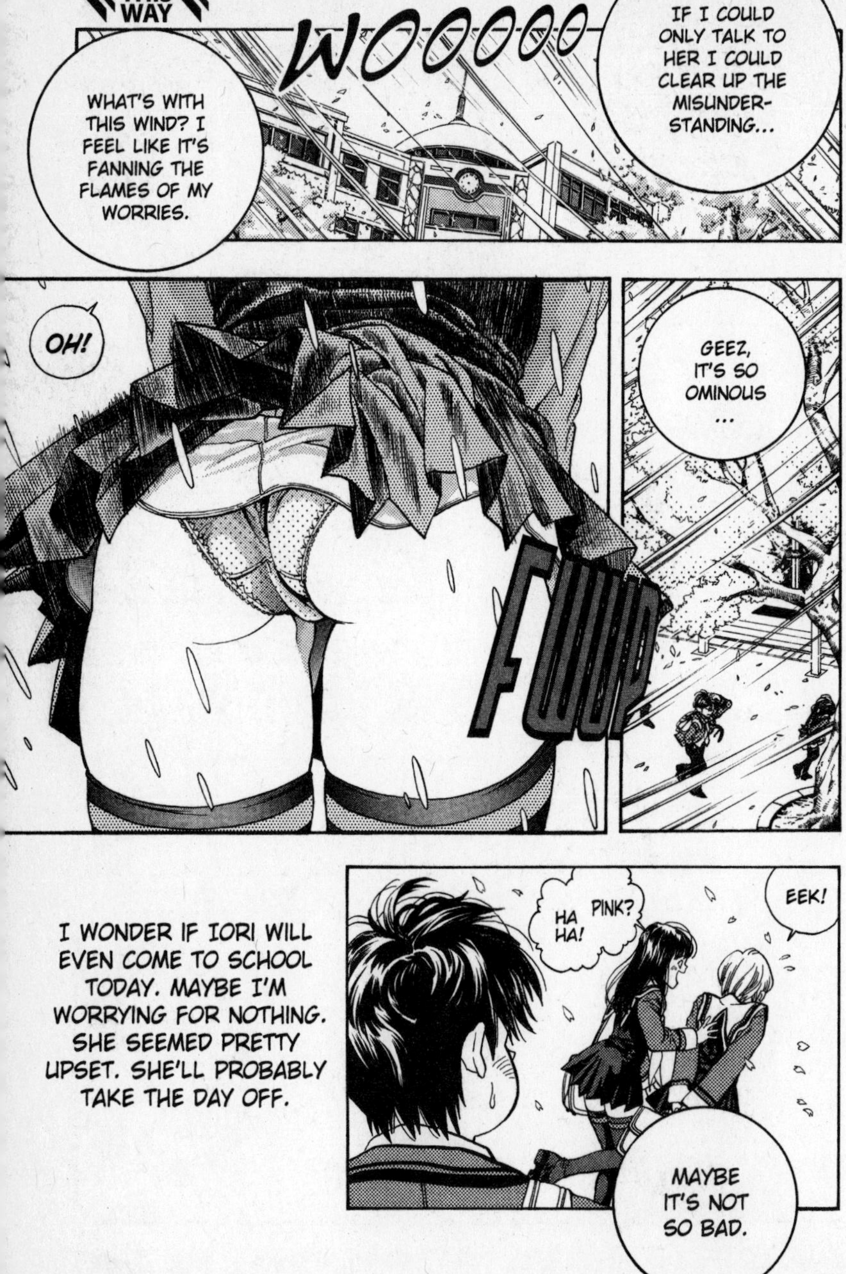
WOOOOO
IF I COULD ONLY TALK TO HER I COULD CLEAR UP THE MISUNDER-STANDING...
WHAT'S WITH THIS WIND? I FEEL LIKE IT'S FANNING THE FLAMES OF MY WORRIES.
GEEZ, IT'S SO OMINOUS ...
OH!
FWUP
EEK!
PINK?
HA HA!
I WONDER IF IORI WILL EVEN COME TO SCHOOL TODAY. MAYBE I'M WORRYING FOR NOTHING. SHE SEEMED PRETTY UPSET. SHE'LL PROBABLY TAKE THE DAY OFF.
MAYBE IT'S NOT SO BAD.

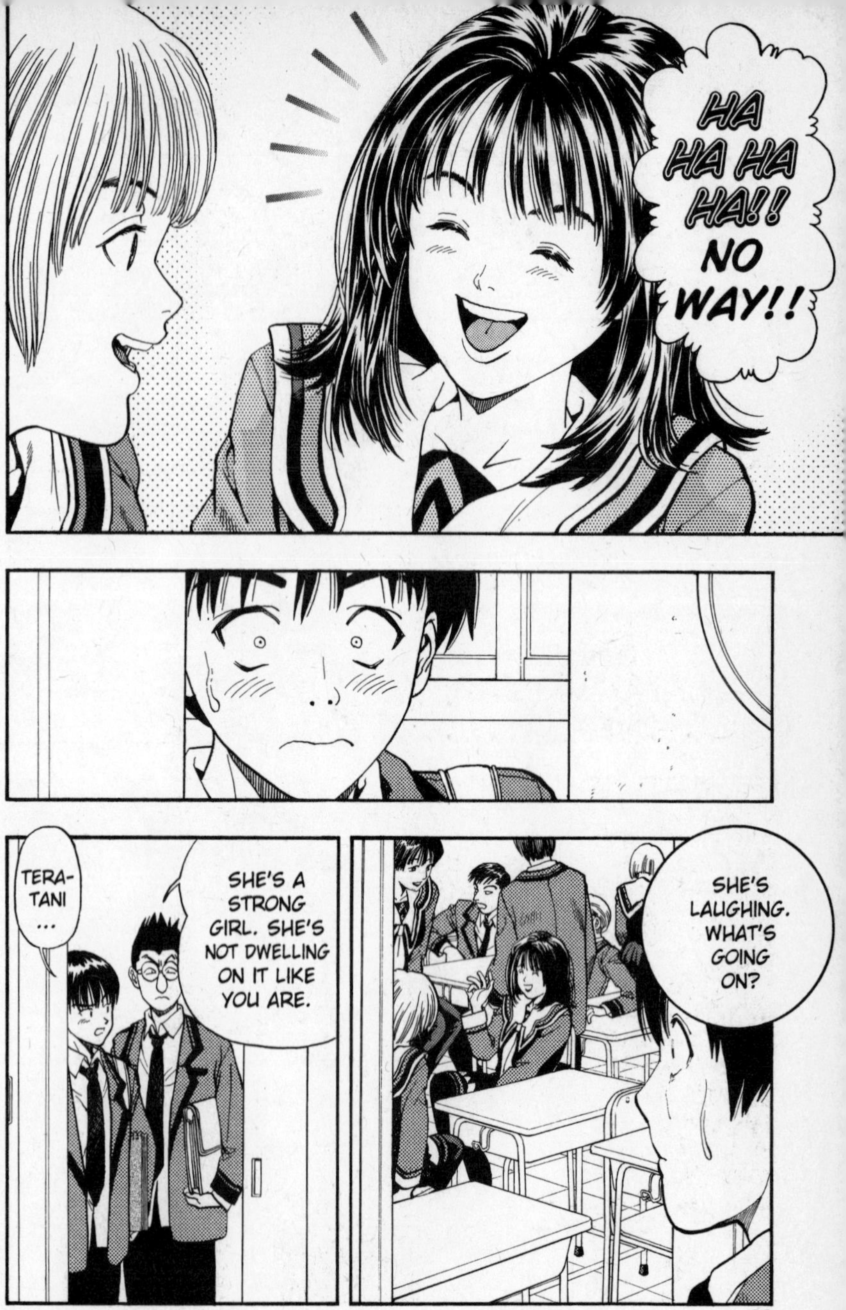
HA HA HA HA HA!! NO WAY!!
SHE'S LAUGHING. WHAT'S GOING ON?
SHE'S A STRONG GIRL. SHE'S NOT DWELLING ON IT LIKE YOU ARE.
TERA-TANI ...

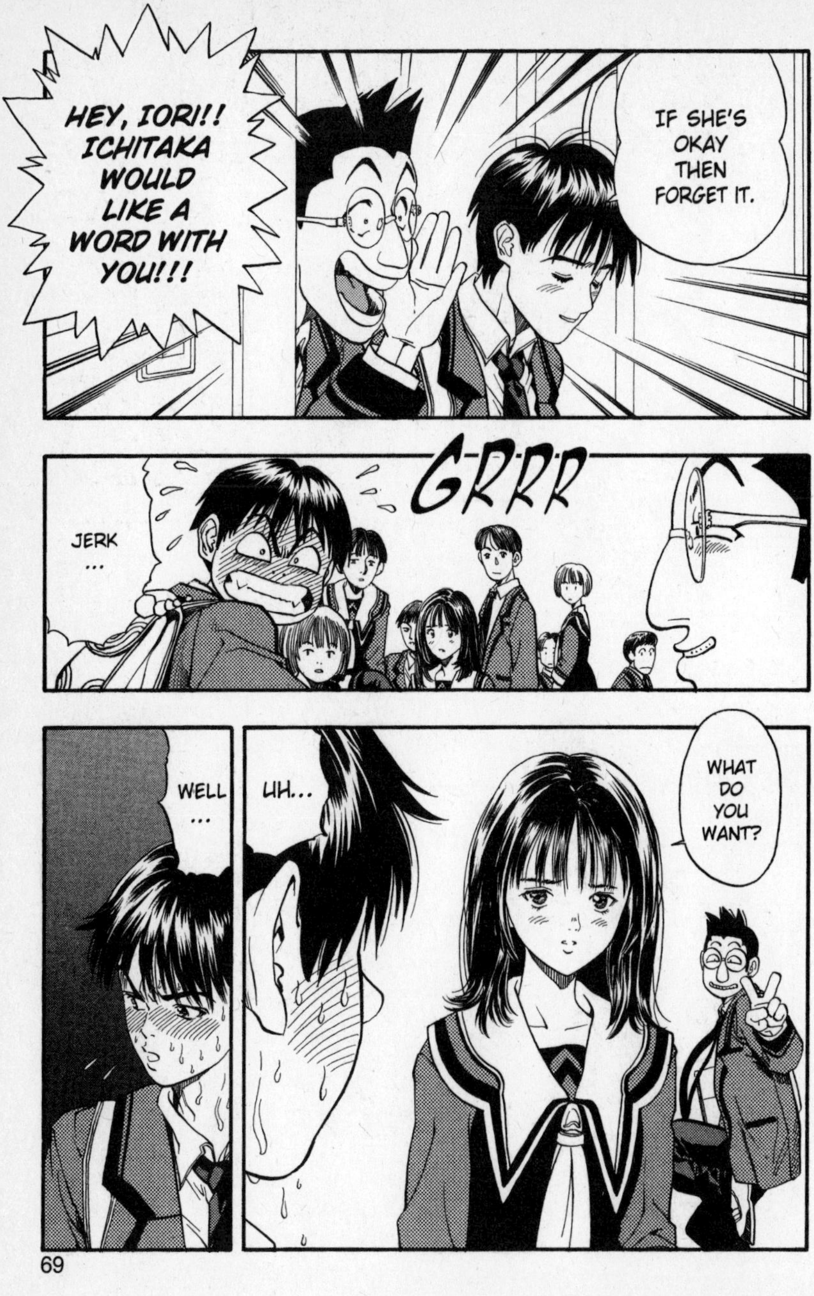
IF SHE'S OKAY THEN FORGET IT.
HEY, IORI!! ICHITAKA WOULD LIKE A WORD WITH YOU!!!
GRRR
JERK ...
WHAT DO YOU WANT?
UH...
WELL ...

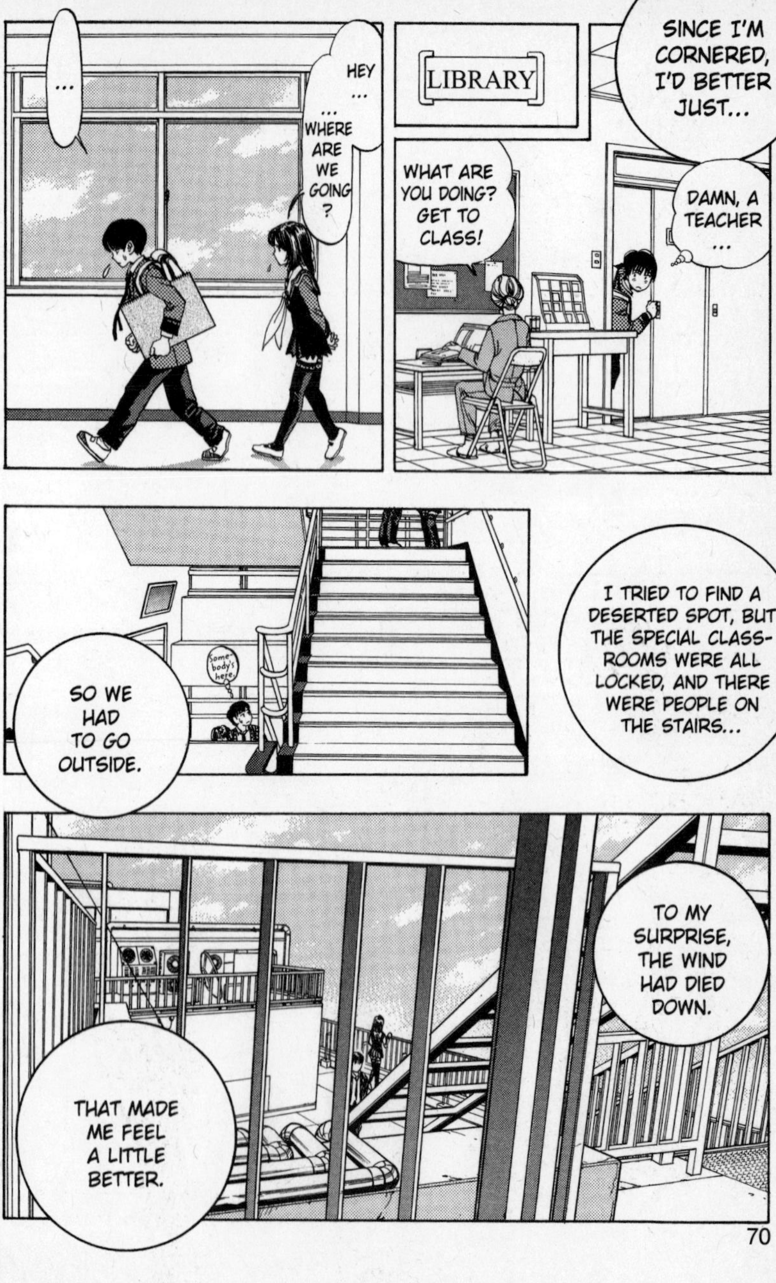
SINCE I'M CORNERED, I'D BETTER JUST...
LIBRARY
DAMN, A TEACHER ...
WHAT ARE YOU DOING? GET TO CLASS!
HEY ... ... WHERE ARE WE GOING ?
...
I TRIED TO FIND A DESERTED SPOT, BUT THE SPECIAL CLASS-ROOMS WERE ALL LOCKED, AND THERE WERE PEOPLE ON THE STAIRS...
Some-body's here.
SO WE HAD TO GO OUTSIDE.
TO MY SURPRISE, THE WIND HAD DIED DOWN.
THAT MADE ME FEEL A LITTLE BETTER.

READ THIS WAY

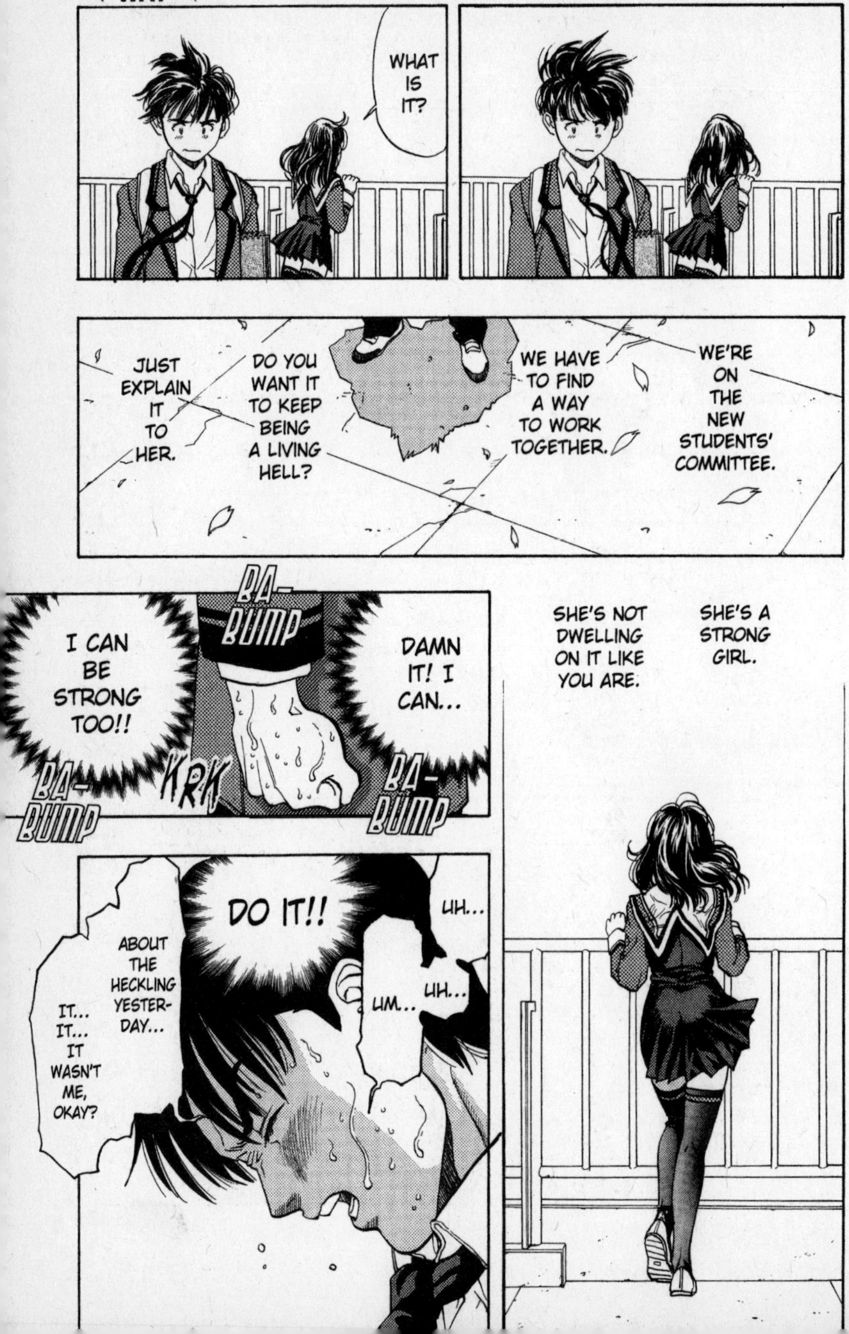
WHAT IS IT?
WE'RE ON THE NEW STUDENTS' COMMITTEE.
WE HAVE TO FIND A WAY TO WORK TOGETHER.
DO YOU WANT IT TO KEEP BEING A LIVING HELL?
JUST EXPLAIN IT TO HER.
SHE'S A STRONG GIRL.
SHE'S NOT DWELLING ON IT LIKE YOU ARE.
BA-BUMP
DAMN IT! I CAN...
BA-BUMP
KRK
I CAN BE STRONG TOO!!
BA-BUMP
DO IT!!
UH...
UH...
UM...
ABOUT THE HECKLING YESTERDAY...
IT... IT... IT WASN'T ME, OKAY?

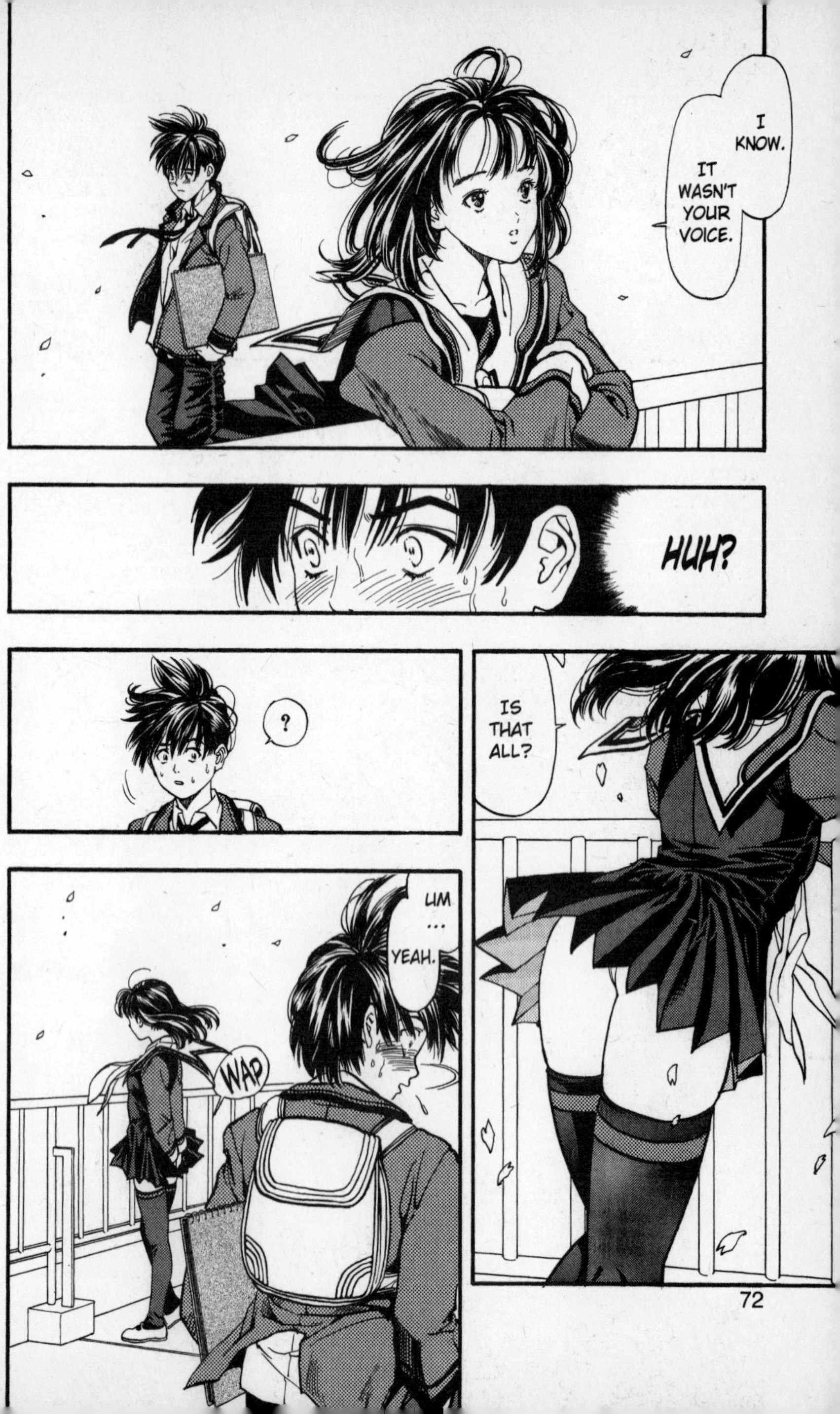
I KNOW.
IT WASN'T YOUR VOICE.
HUH?
IS THAT ALL?
?
UM ... YEAH.
WAP

READ THIS WAY

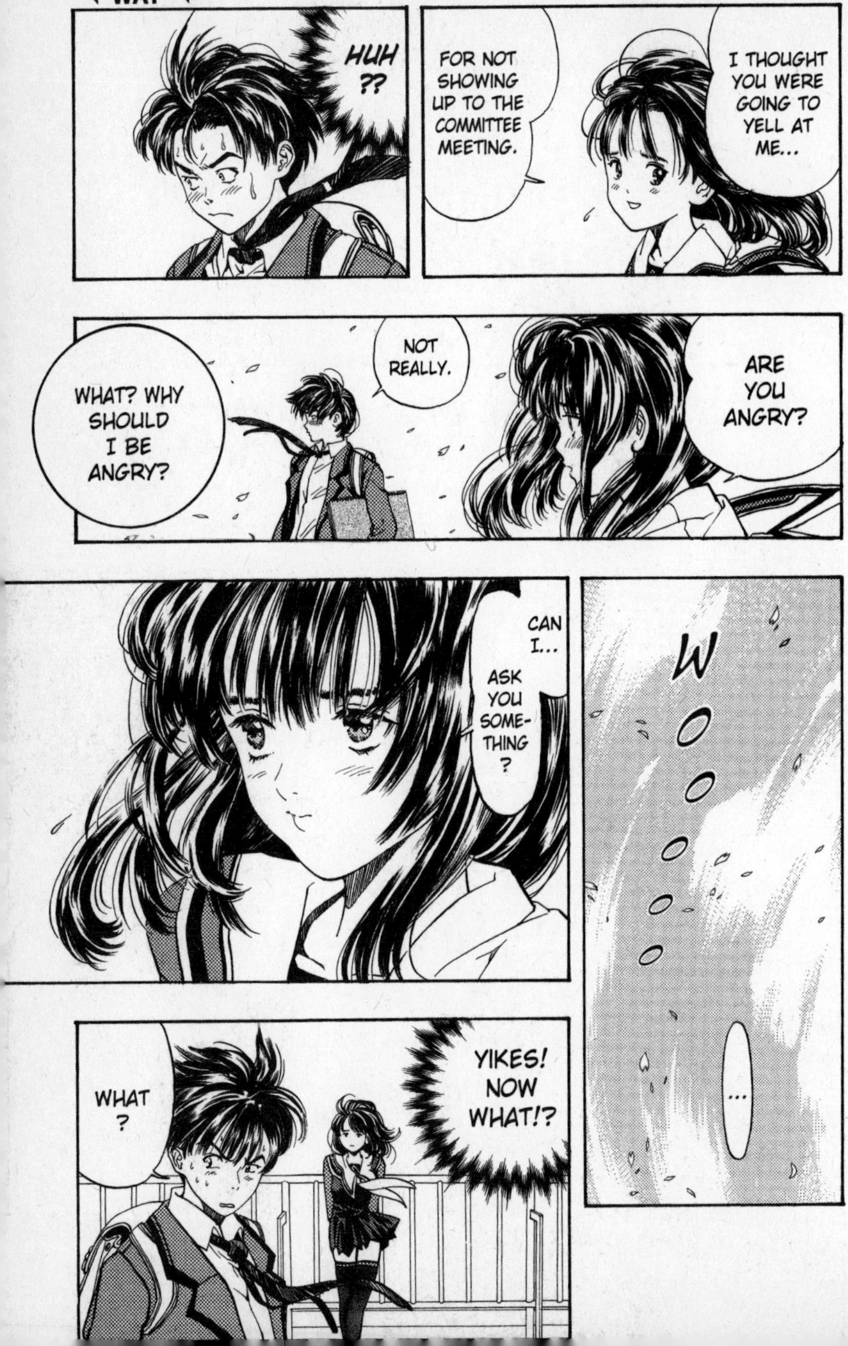
I THOUGHT YOU WERE GOING TO YELL AT ME...
FOR NOT SHOWING UP TO THE COMMITTEE MEETING.
HUH ??
ARE YOU ANGRY?
NOT REALLY.
WHAT? WHY SHOULD I BE ANGRY?
WOOOOOOO
...
CAN I... ASK YOU SOME-THING?
YIKES! NOW WHAT!?
WHAT ?

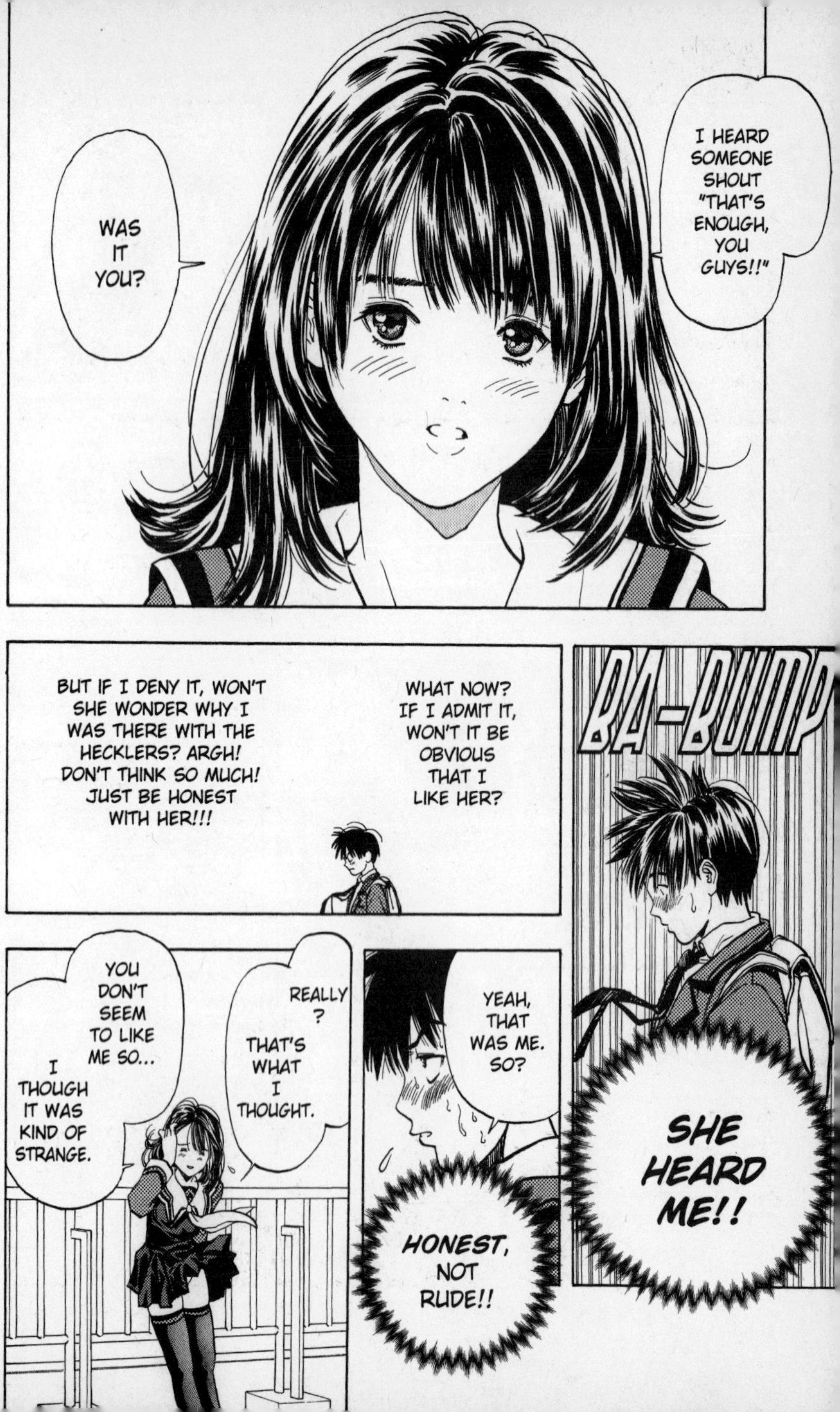
I HEARD SOMEONE SHOUT "THAT'S ENOUGH, YOU GUYS!!"
WAS IT YOU?
BA-BUMP
SHE HEARD ME!!
WHAT NOW? IF I ADMIT IT, WON'T IT BE OBVIOUS THAT I LIKE HER?
BUT IF I DENY IT, WON'T SHE WONDER WHY I WAS THERE WITH THE HECKLERS? ARGH! DON'T THINK SO MUCH! JUST BE HONEST WITH HER!!!
YEAH, THAT WAS ME. SO?
HONEST, NOT RUDE!!
REALLY?
THAT'S WHAT I THOUGHT.
YOU DON'T SEEM TO LIKE ME SO...
I THOUGH IT WAS KIND OF STRANGE.

READ THIS WAY

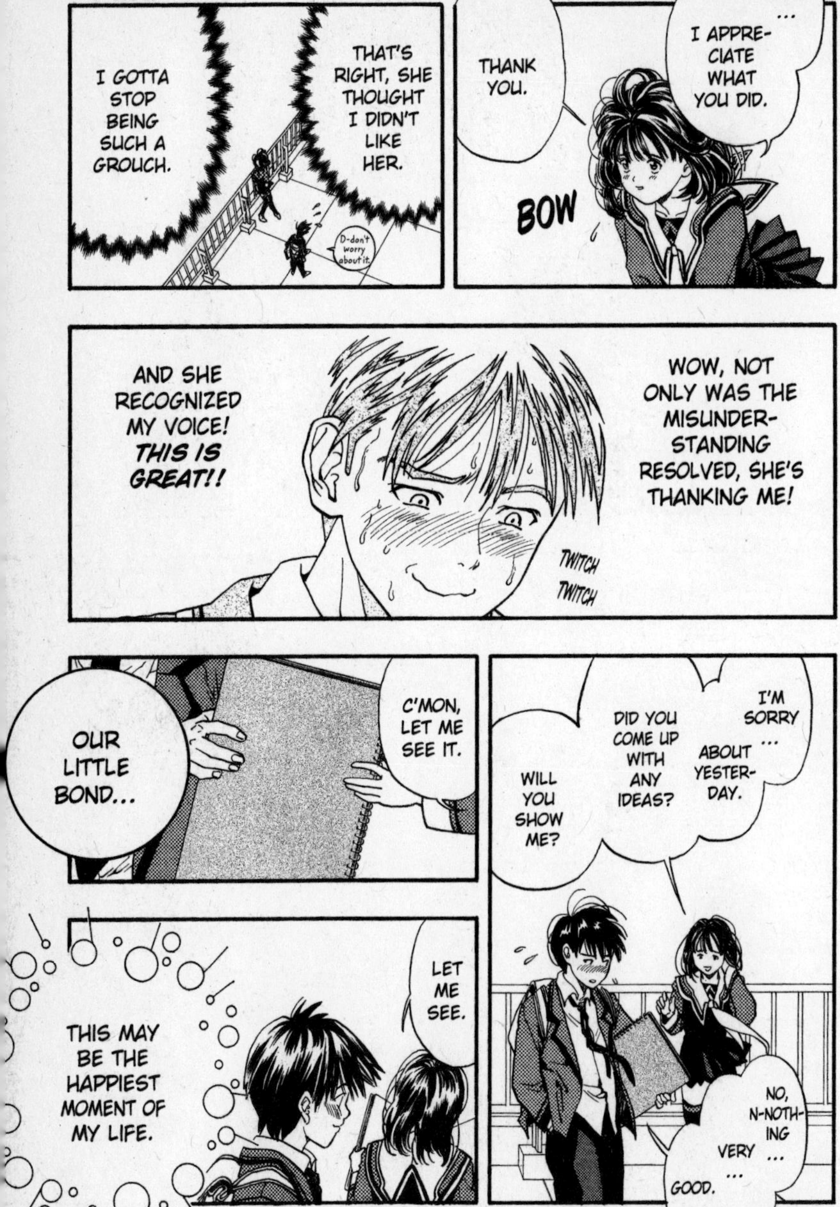
WELL ... I APPRE-CIATE WHAT YOU DID.
THANK YOU.
BOW
THAT'S RIGHT, SHE THOUGHT I DIDN'T LIKE HER.
I GOTTA STOP BEING SUCH A GROUCH.
D-don't worry about it.
WOW, NOT ONLY WAS THE MISUNDER-STANDING RESOLVED, SHE'S THANKING ME!
AND SHE RECOGNIZED MY VOICE! THIS IS GREAT!!
TWITCH TWITCH
I'M SORRY ... ABOUT YESTER-DAY.
DID YOU COME UP WITH ANY IDEAS?
WILL YOU SHOW ME?
NO, N-NOTH-ING ... VERY ... GOOD.
C'MON, LET ME SEE IT.
OUR LITTLE BOND...
LET ME SEE.
THIS MAY BE THE HAPPIEST MOMENT OF MY LIFE.

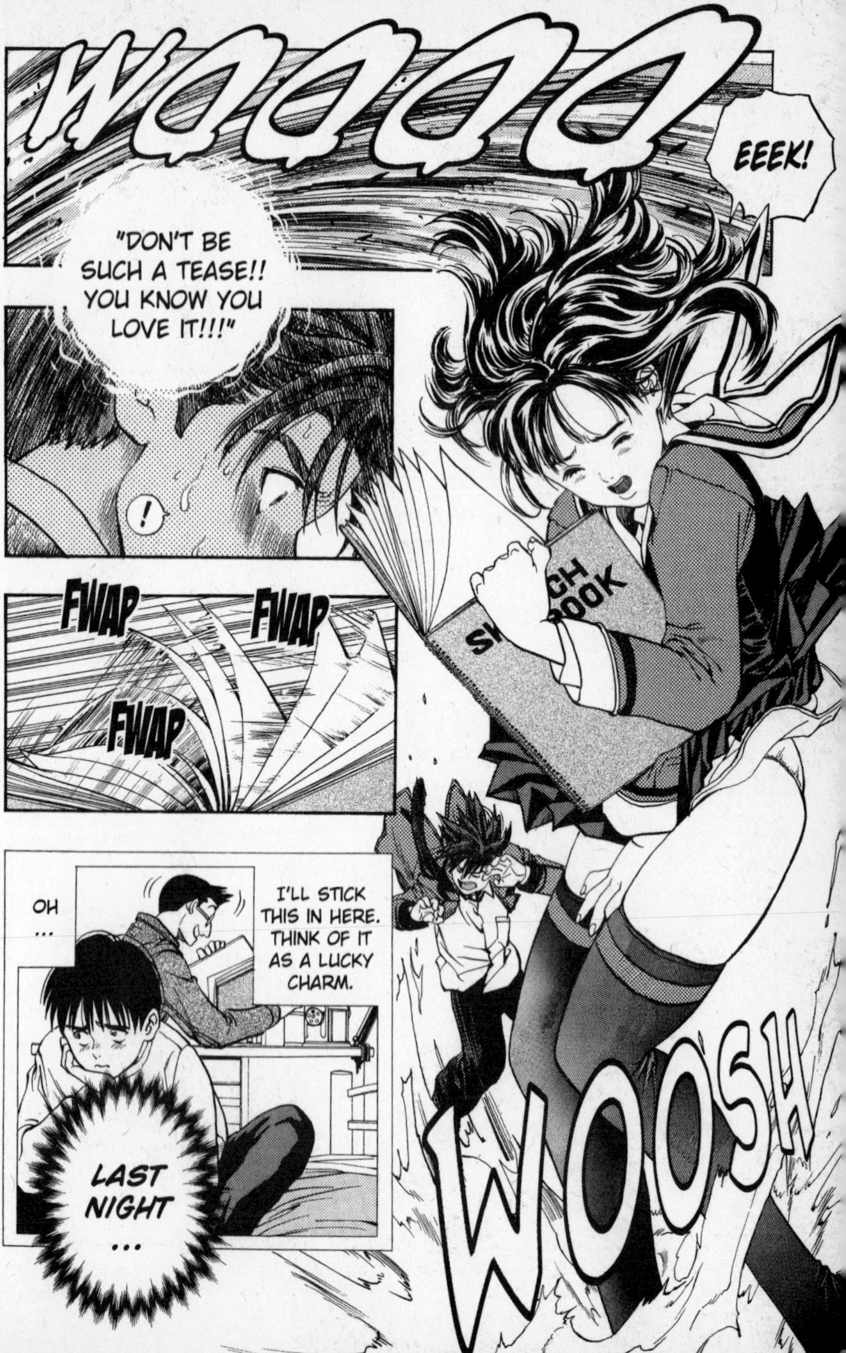
WOOOOO
EEEK!
WOOSH
"DON'T BE SUCH A TEASE!! YOU KNOW YOU LOVE IT!!!"
!
FWAP
FWAP
FWAP
I'LL STICK THIS IN HERE. THINK OF IT AS A LUCKY CHARM.
OH ...
LAST NIGHT ...

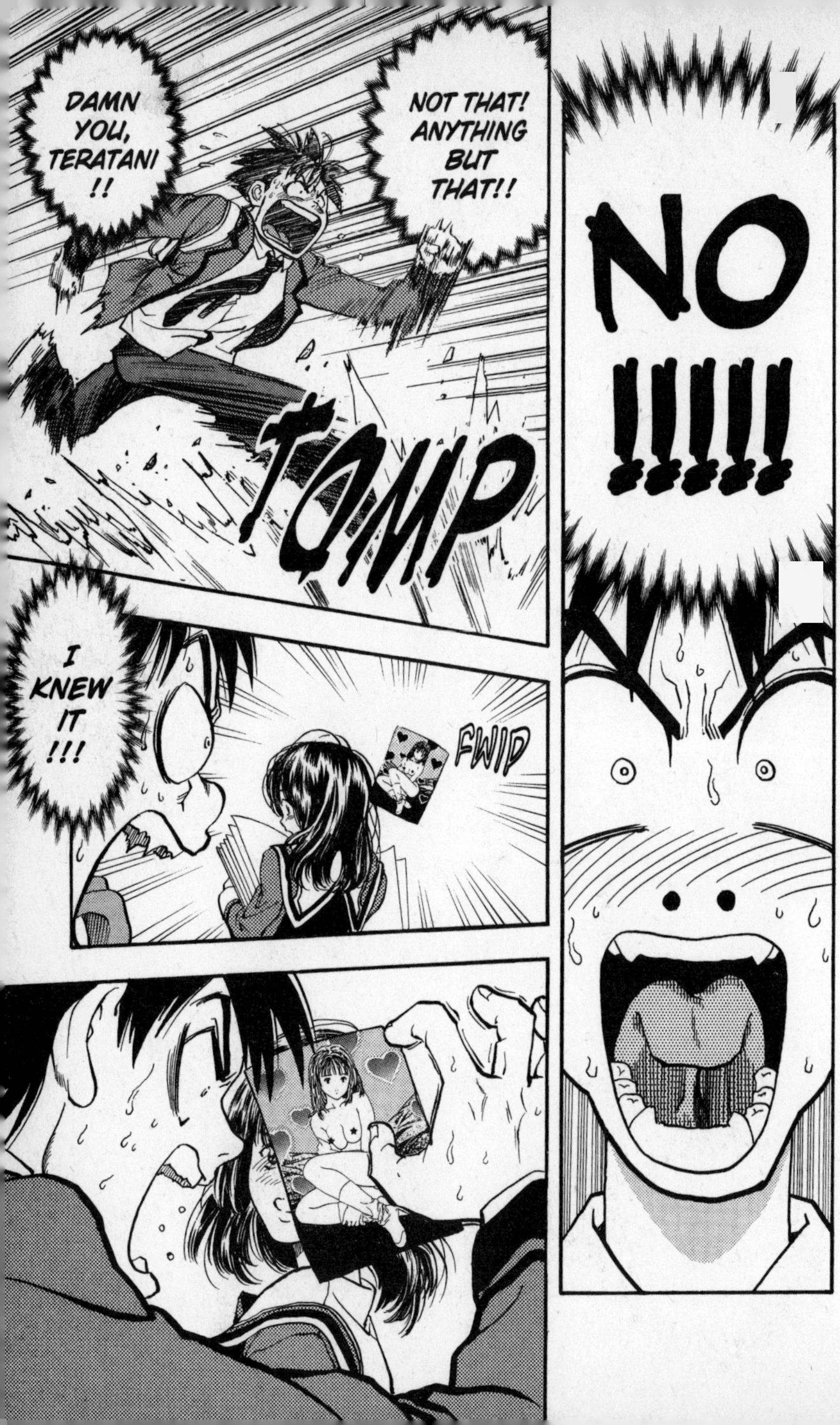
NO !!!!!!
NOT THAT! ANYTHING BUT THAT!!
DAMN YOU, TERATANI !!
TOMP
FWIP
I KNEW IT !!!

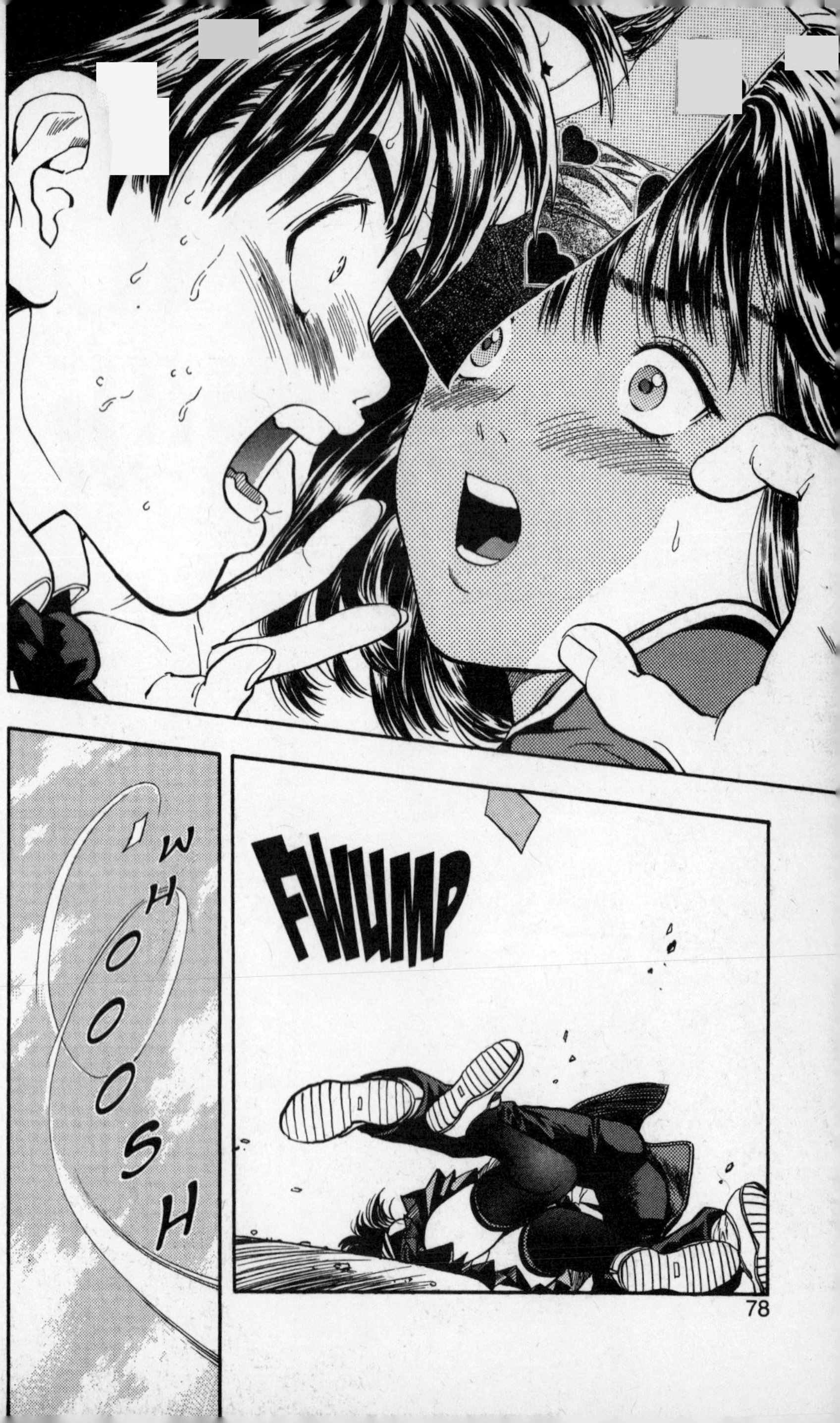
FWUMP
WHOOOSH

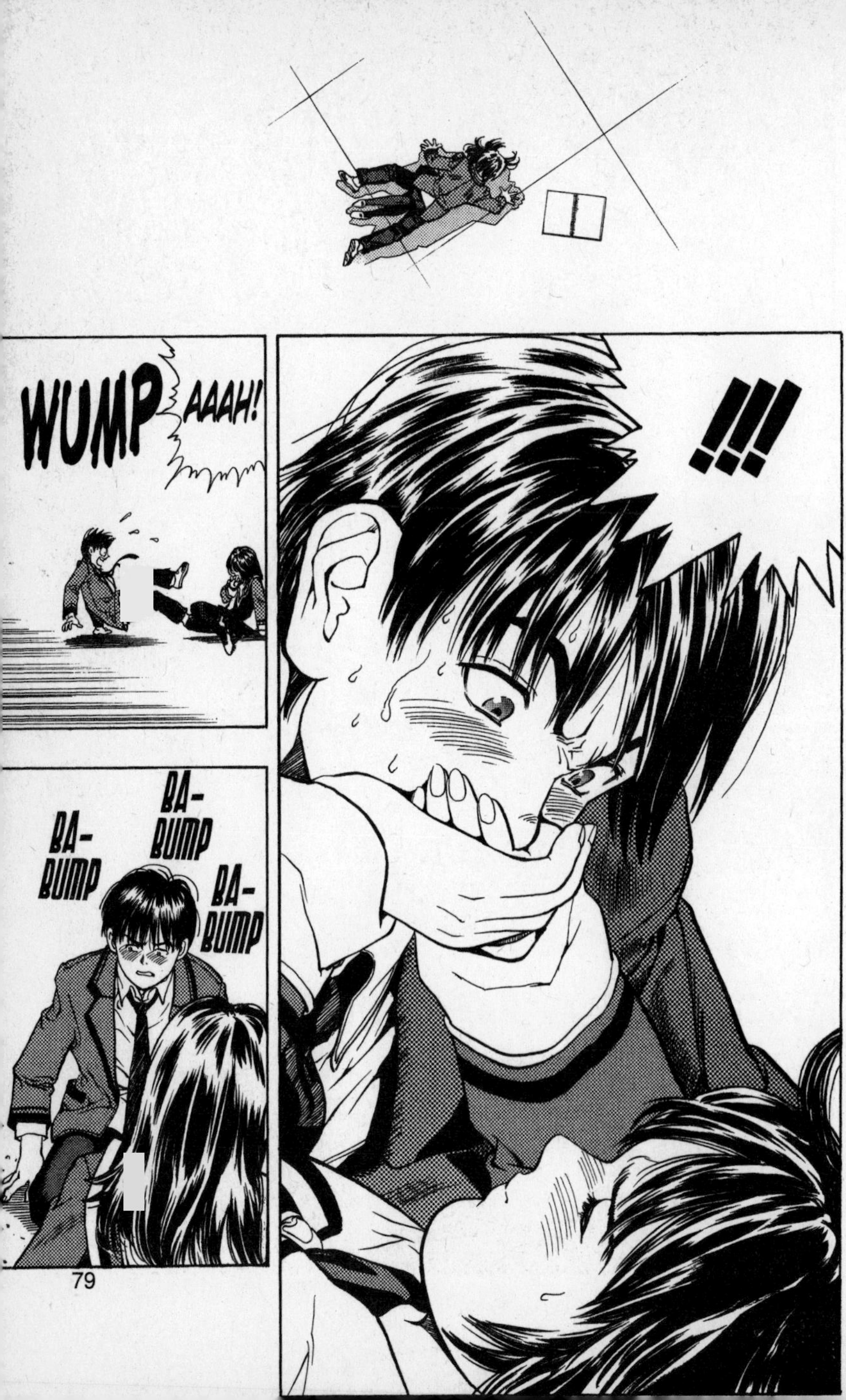
!!!
WUMP
AAAH!
BA-BUMP
BA-BUMP
BA-BUMP

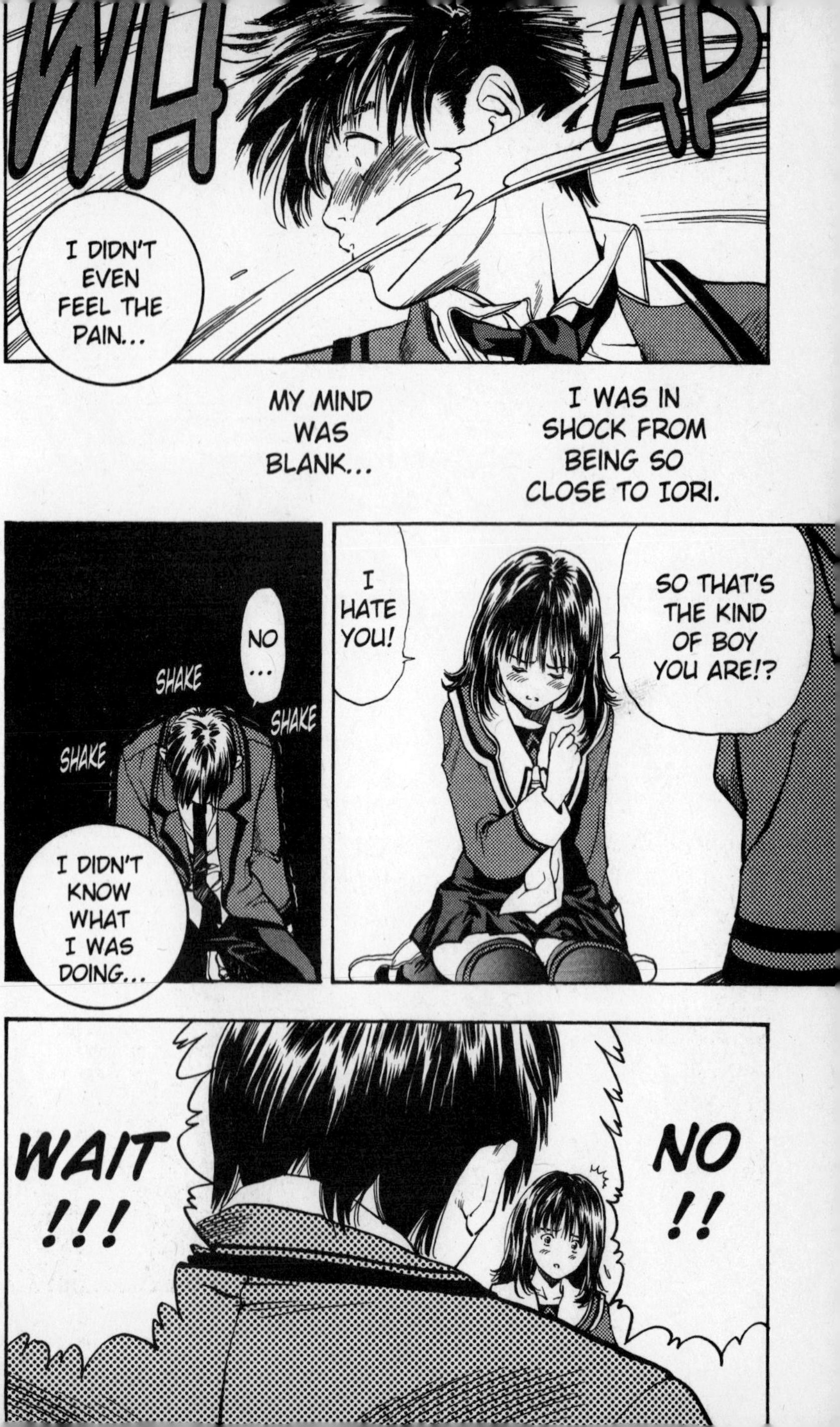
WHAP
I DIDN'T EVEN FEEL THE PAIN...
I WAS IN SHOCK FROM BEING SO CLOSE TO IORI.
MY MIND WAS BLANK...
SO THAT'S THE KIND OF BOY YOU ARE!?
I HATE YOU!
NO ...
SHAKE
SHAKE
SHAKE
I DIDN'T KNOW WHAT I WAS DOING...
NO !!
WAIT !!!

READ THIS WAY

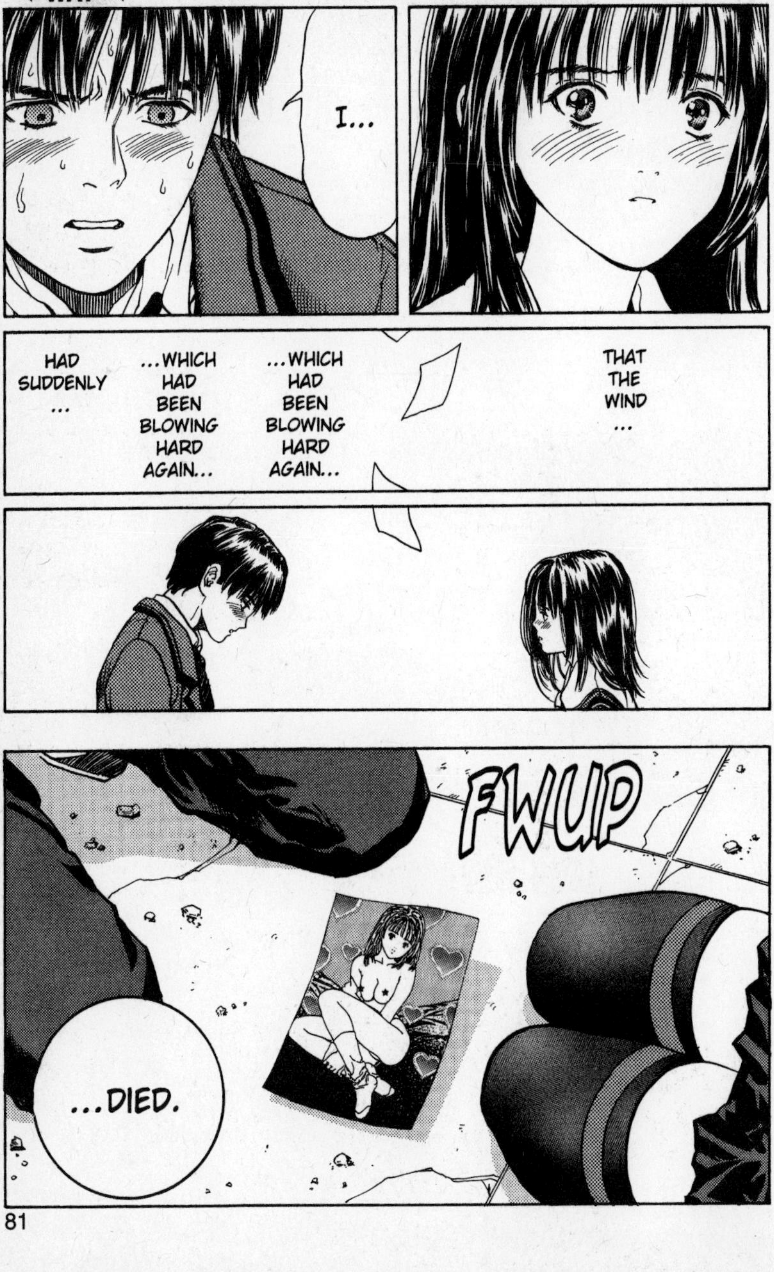
I...
THAT THE WIND ...
...WHICH HAD BEEN BLOWING HARD AGAIN...
...WHICH HAD BEEN BLOWING HARD AGAIN...
HAD SUDDENLY ...
FWUP
...DIED.

Chapter 3:
Eyes in the Shadows

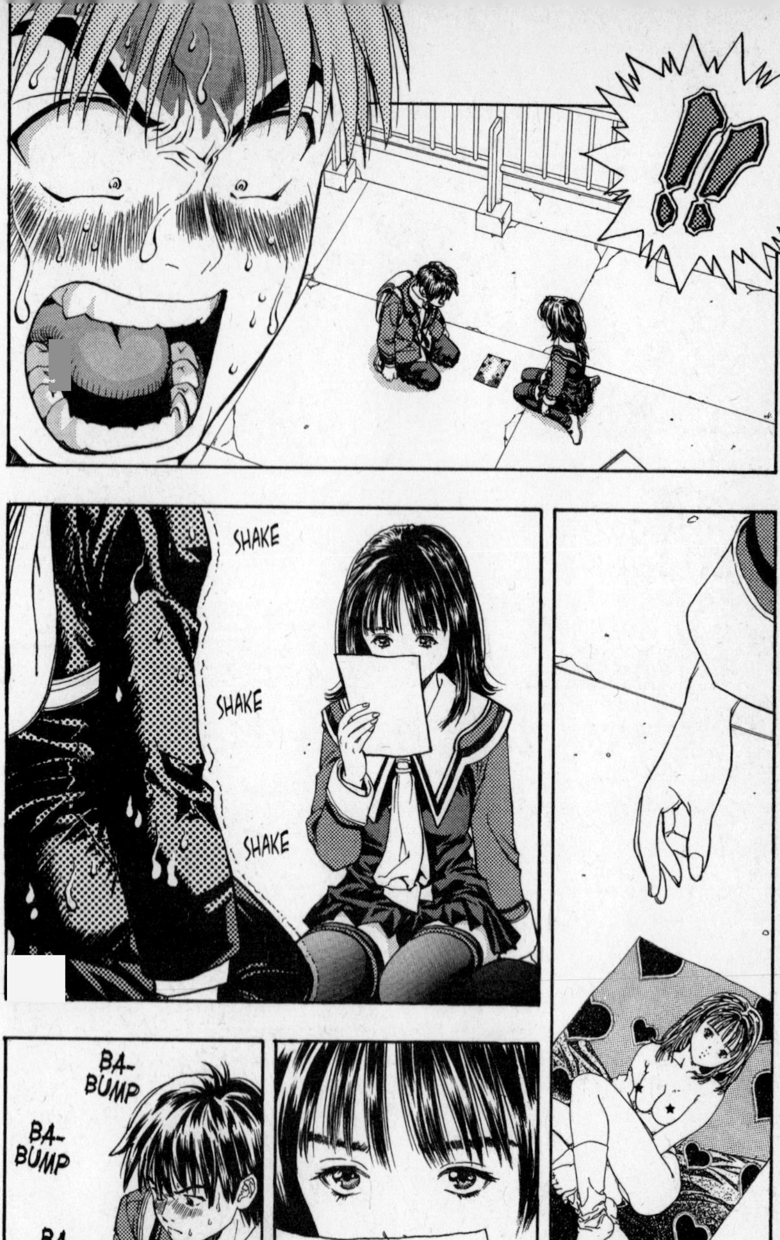
!!
SHAKE
SHAKE
SHAKE
BA-BUMP
BA-BUMP
BA-BUMP

READ THIS WAY

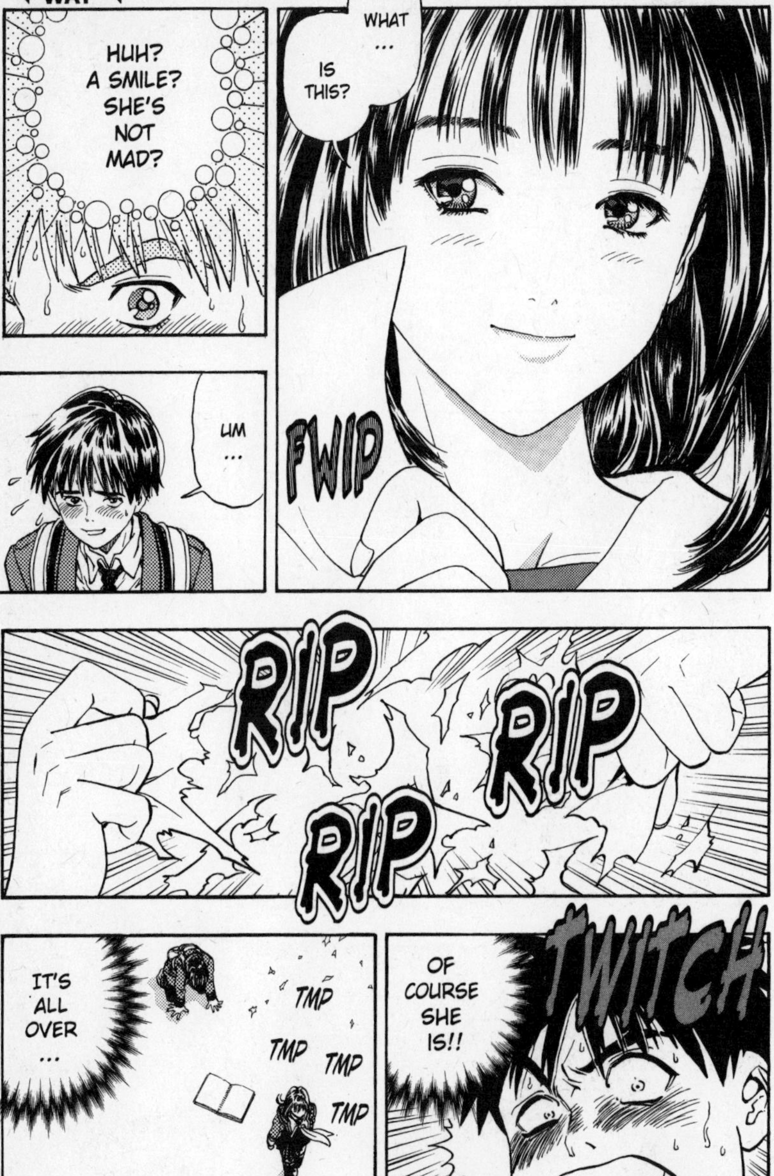

WHAT ... IS THIS?
FWIP
HUH? A SMILE? SHE'S NOT MAD?
UM ...
RIP
RIP
RIP
TWITCH
OF COURSE SHE IS!!
TMP
TMP
TMP
TMP
IT'S ALL OVER ...

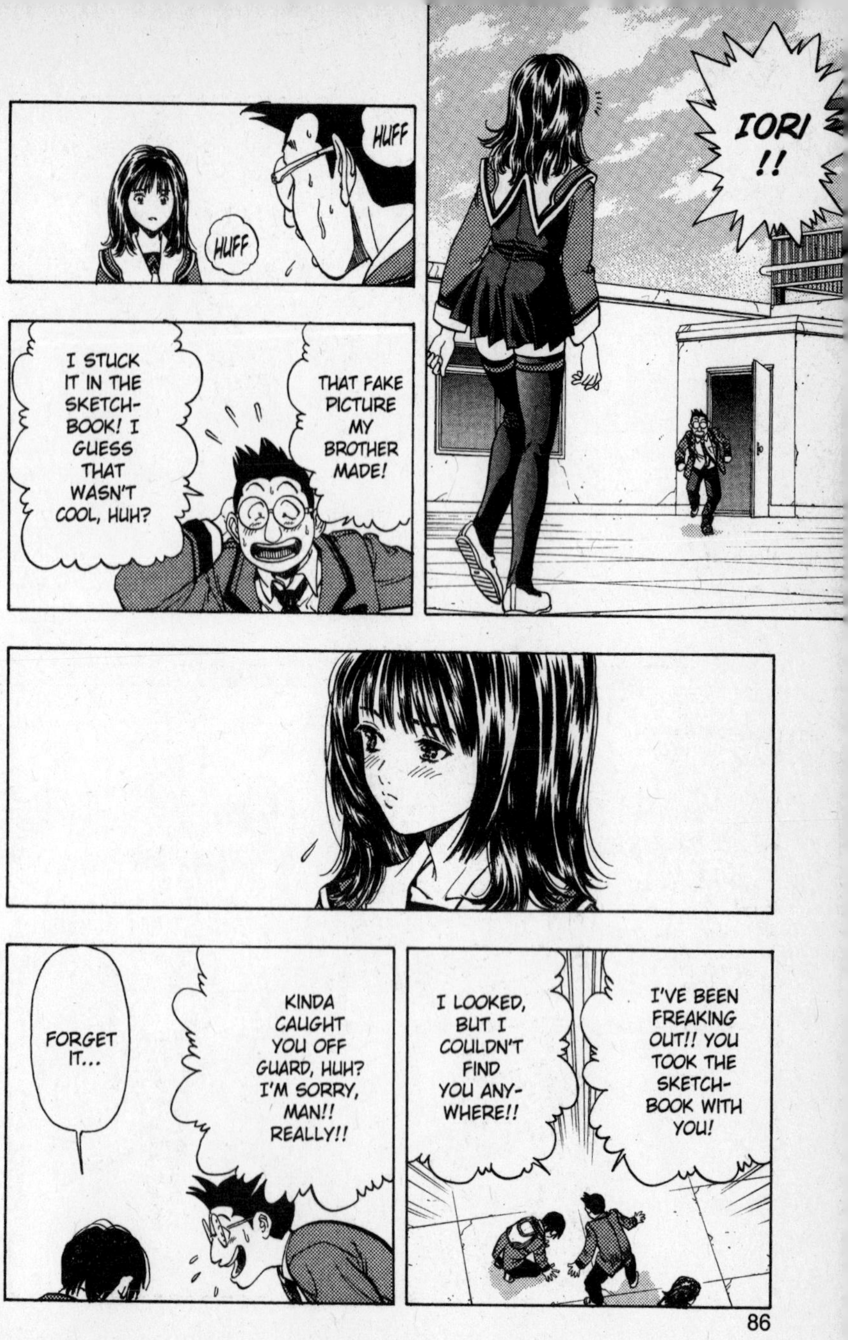
IORI!!
HUFF
HUFF
THAT FAKE PICTURE MY BROTHER MADE!
I STUCK IT IN THE SKETCH-BOOK! I GUESS THAT WASN'T COOL, HUH?
I'VE BEEN FREAKING OUT!! YOU TOOK THE SKETCH-BOOK WITH YOU!
I LOOKED, BUT I COULDN'T FIND YOU ANY-WHERE!!
KINDA CAUGHT YOU OFF GUARD, HUH? I'M SORRY, MAN!! REALLY!!
FORGET IT...

READ THIS WAY

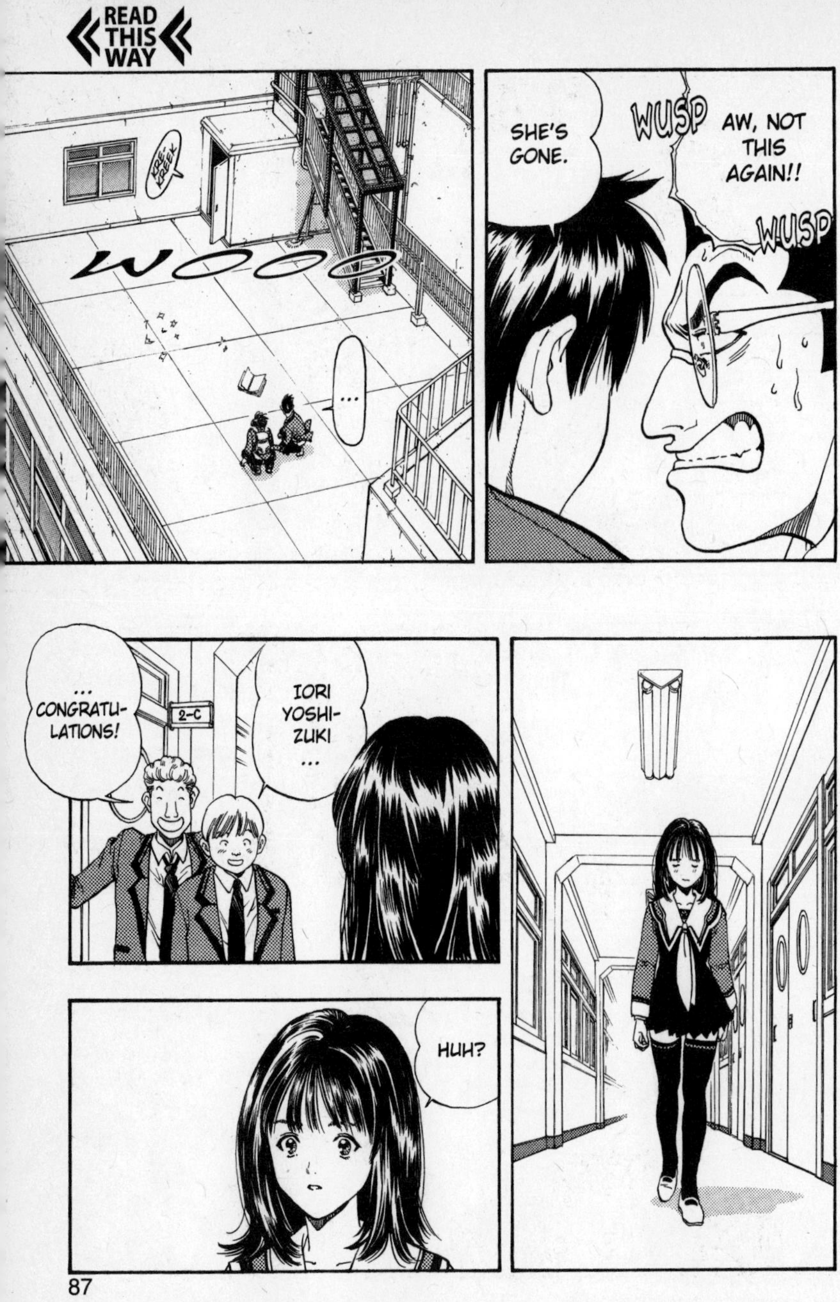

WUSP
AW, NOT THIS AGAIN!!
WUSP
SHE'S GONE.
KRE-KREEK
WOOO
...
IORI YOSHI-ZUKI ...
... CONGRATU-LATIONS!
HUH?

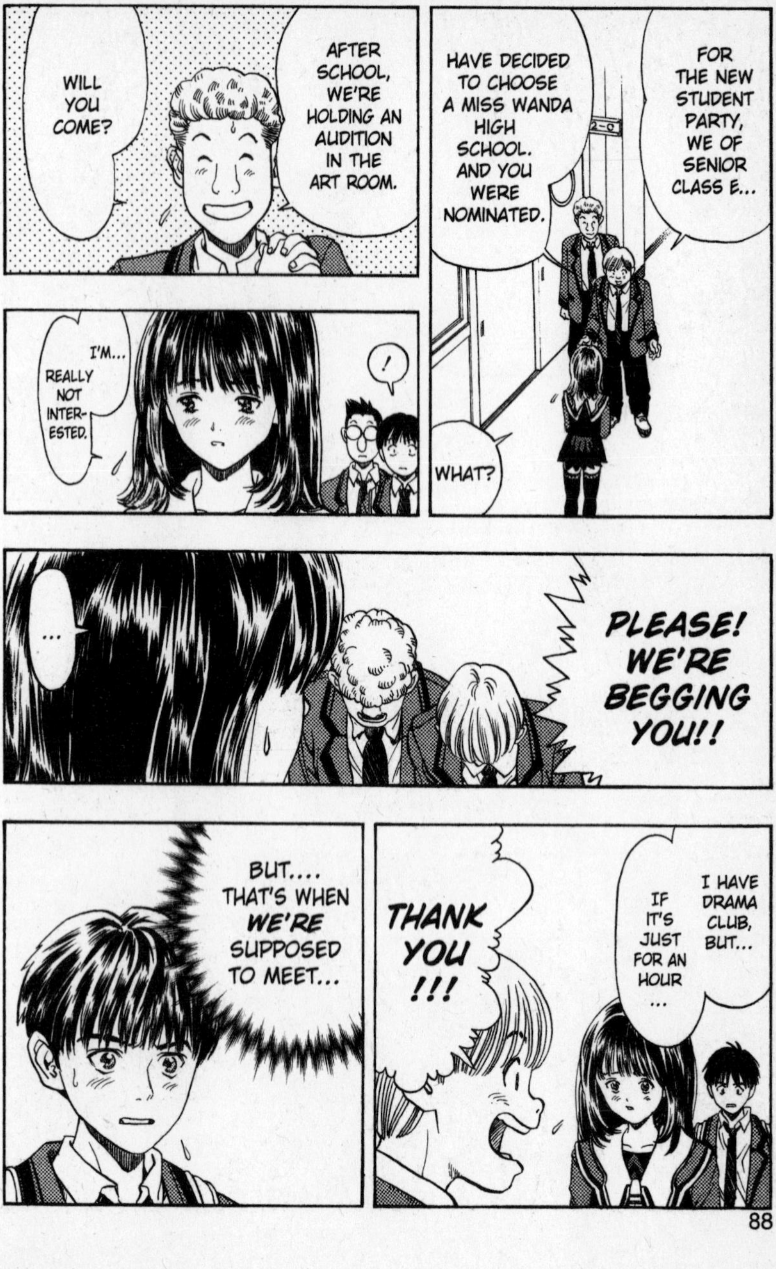
FOR THE NEW STUDENT PARTY, WE OF SENIOR CLASS E...
HAVE DECIDED TO CHOOSE A MISS WANDA HIGH SCHOOL. AND YOU WERE NOMINATED.
WHAT?
AFTER SCHOOL, WE'RE HOLDING AN AUDITION IN THE ART ROOM.
WILL YOU COME?
!
I'M... REALLY NOT INTER-ESTED.
PLEASE! WE'RE BEGGING YOU!!
...
I HAVE DRAMA CLUB, BUT...
IF IT'S JUST FOR AN HOUR ...
THANK YOU !!!
BUT.... THAT'S WHEN WE'RE SUPPOSED TO MEET...

READ THIS WAY

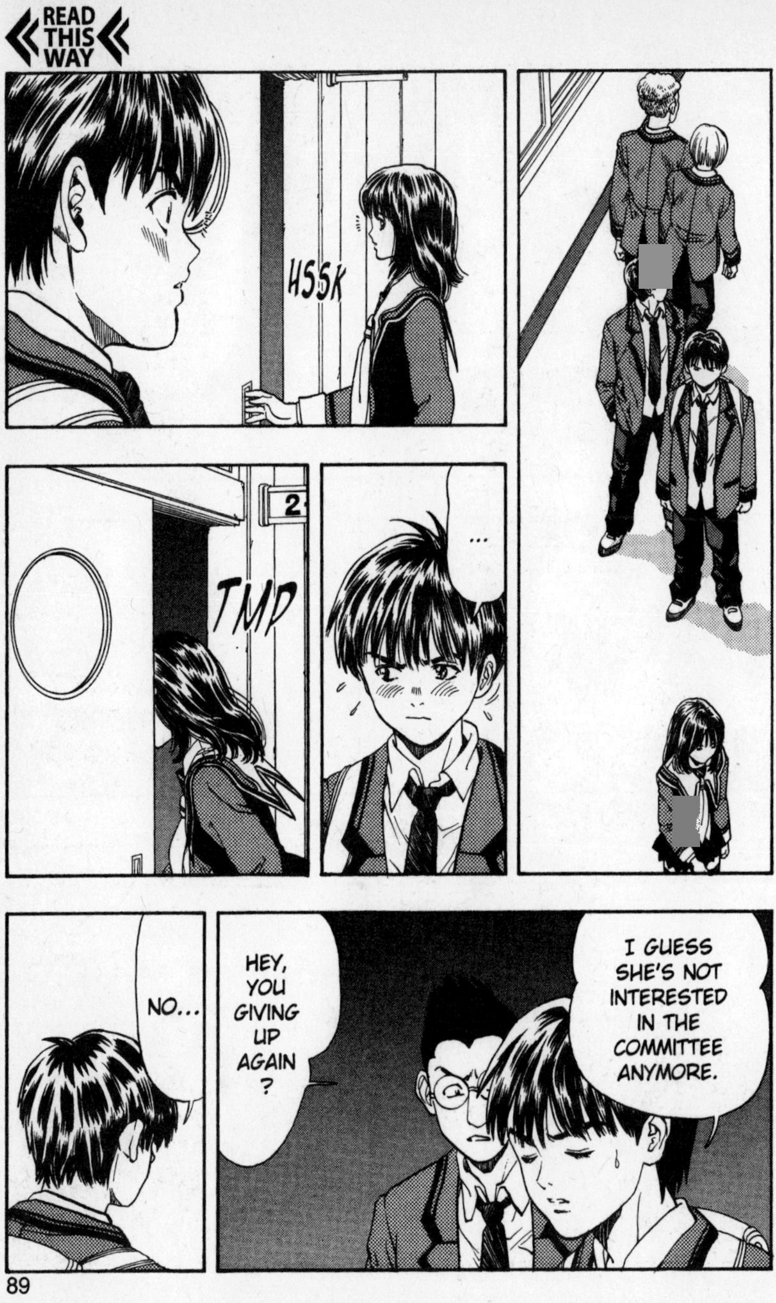

HSSK
...
TMP
I GUESS SHE'S NOT INTERESTED IN THE COMMITTEE ANYMORE.
HEY, YOU GIVING UP AGAIN?
NO...

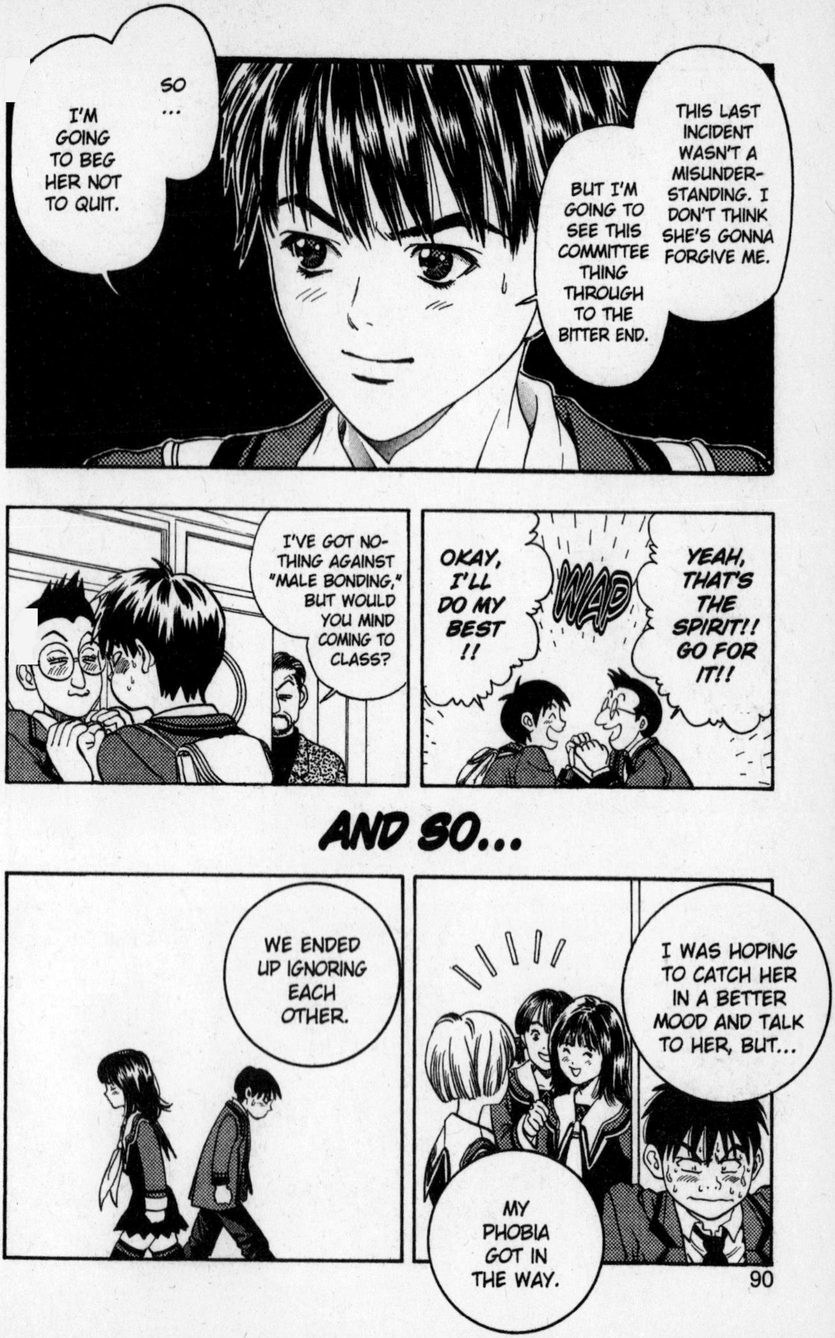
THIS LAST INCIDENT WASN'T A MISUNDER-STANDING. I DON'T THINK SHE'S GONNA FORGIVE ME.
BUT I'M GOING TO SEE THIS COMMITTEE THING THROUGH TO THE BITTER END.
SO ...
I'M GOING TO BEG HER NOT TO QUIT.
YEAH, THAT'S THE SPIRIT!! GO FOR IT!!
WAP
OKAY, I'LL DO MY BEST!!
I'VE GOT NO-THING AGAINST "MALE BONDING," BUT WOULD YOU MIND COMING TO CLASS?
AND SO...
I WAS HOPING TO CATCH HER IN A BETTER MOOD AND TALK TO HER, BUT...
MY PHOBIA GOT IN THE WAY.
WE ENDED UP IGNORING EACH OTHER.

READ THIS WAY

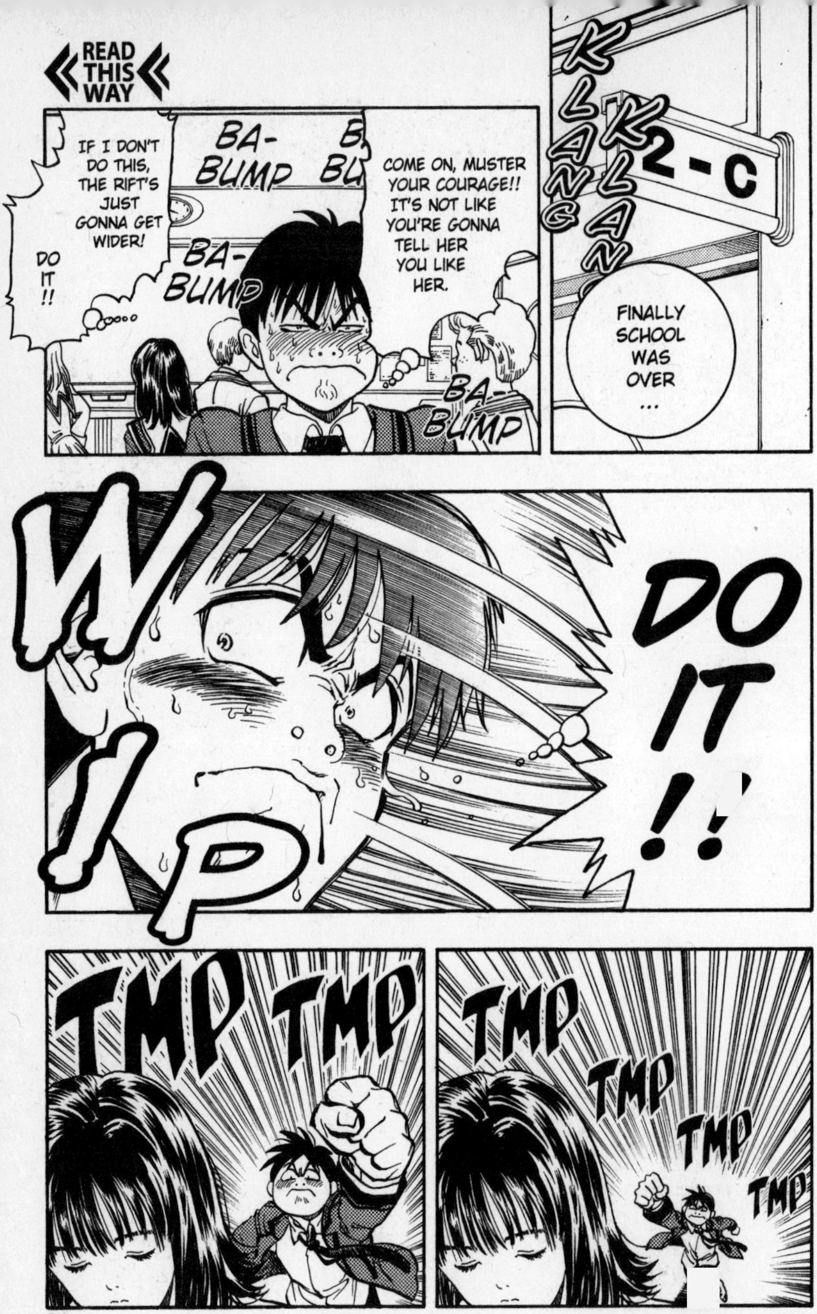
KLANG
KLANG
2-C
FINALLY SCHOOL WAS OVER...
BA-BUMP
COME ON, MUSTER YOUR COURAGE!! IT'S NOT LIKE YOU'RE GONNA TELL HER YOU LIKE HER.
BA-BUMP
IF I DON'T DO THIS, THE RIFT'S JUST GONNA GET WIDER!
DO IT!!
BA-BUMP
BA-BUMP
DO IT!!
WHIP
TMP
TMP
TMP
TMP
TMP TMP

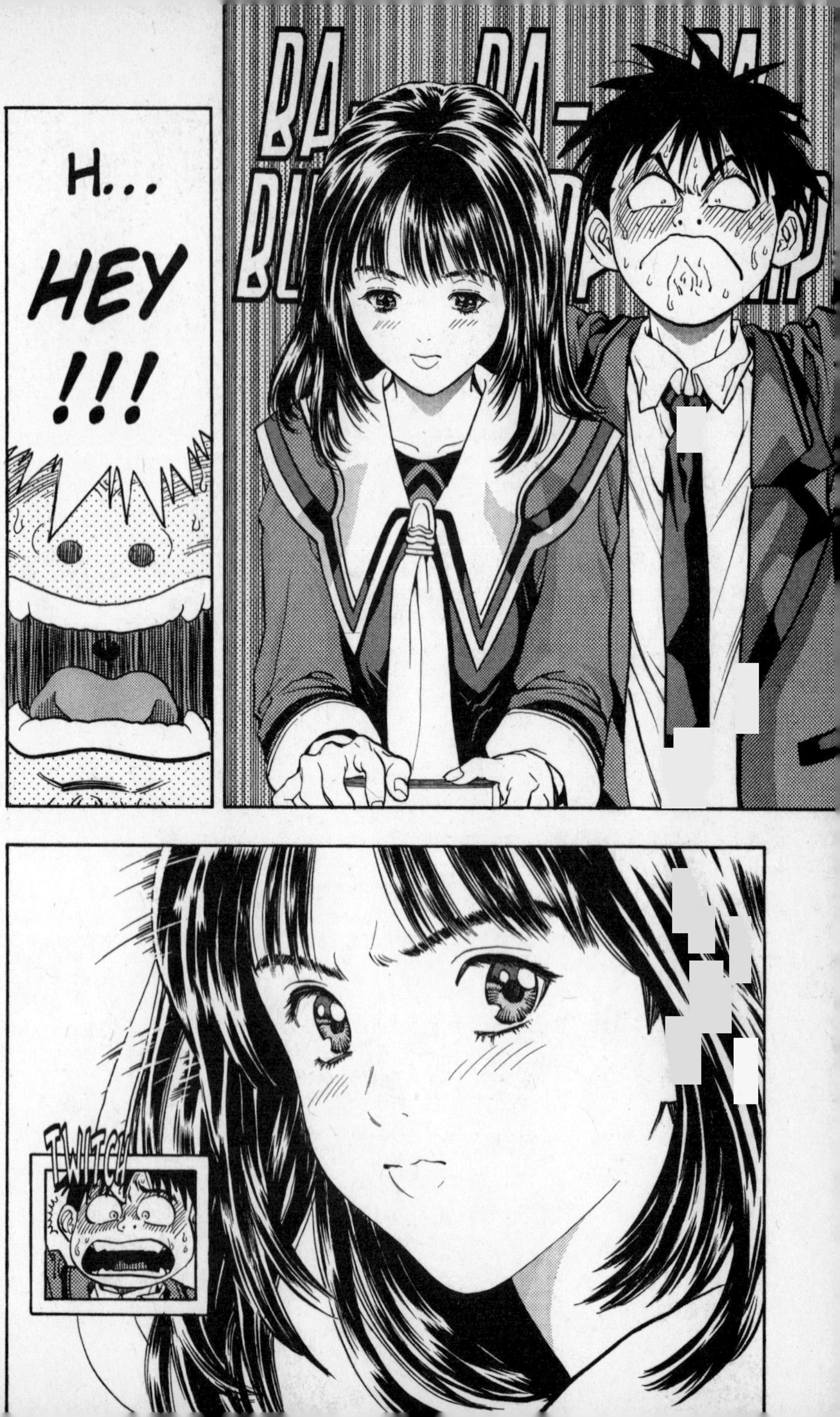
H... HEY !!!
TWITCH

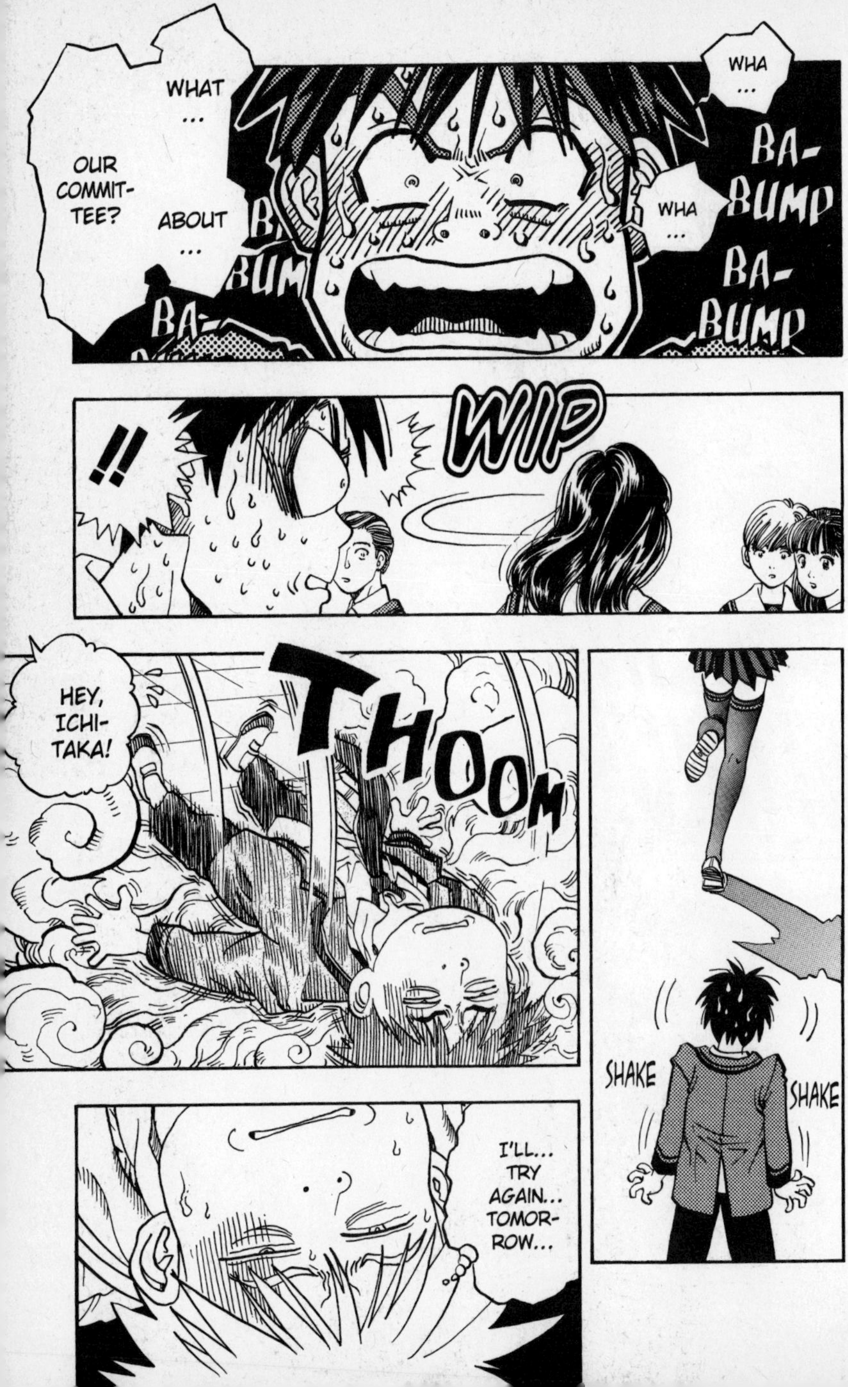
WHA ...
BA-BUMP BA-BUMP
WHA ...
WHAT ... ABOUT ... OUR COMMIT-TEE?
WIP
!!
SHAKE SHAKE
HEY, ICHI-TAKA!
THOOM
I'LL... TRY AGAIN... TOMOR-ROW...

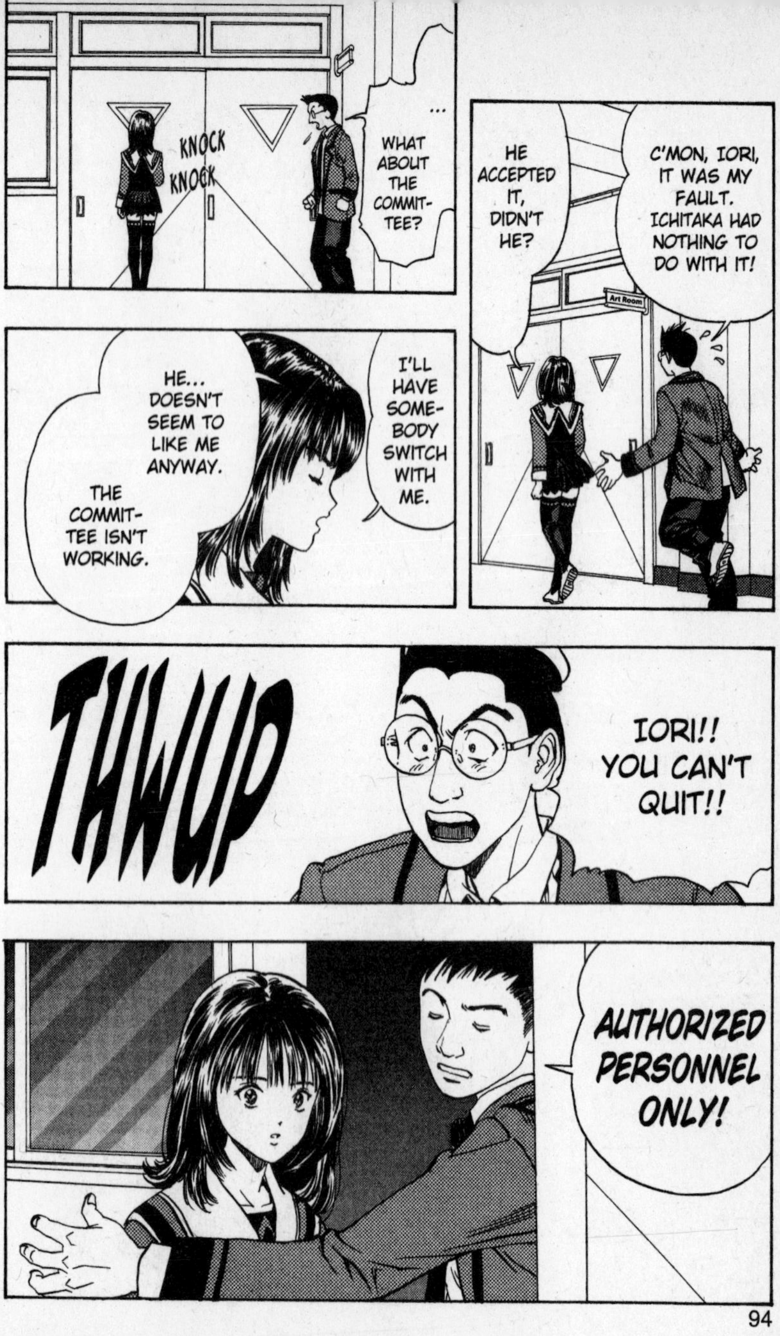
C'MON, IORI, IT WAS MY FAULT. ICHITAKA HAD NOTHING TO DO WITH IT!
HE ACCEPTED IT, DIDN'T HE?
Art Room
...
WHAT ABOUT THE COMMIT-TEE?
KNOCK KNOCK
I'LL HAVE SOME-BODY SWITCH WITH ME.
HE... DOESN'T SEEM TO LIKE ME ANYWAY.
THE COMMIT-TEE ISN'T WORKING.
IORI!! YOU CAN'T QUIT!!
THWUP
AUTHORIZED PERSONNEL ONLY!

READ THIS WAY

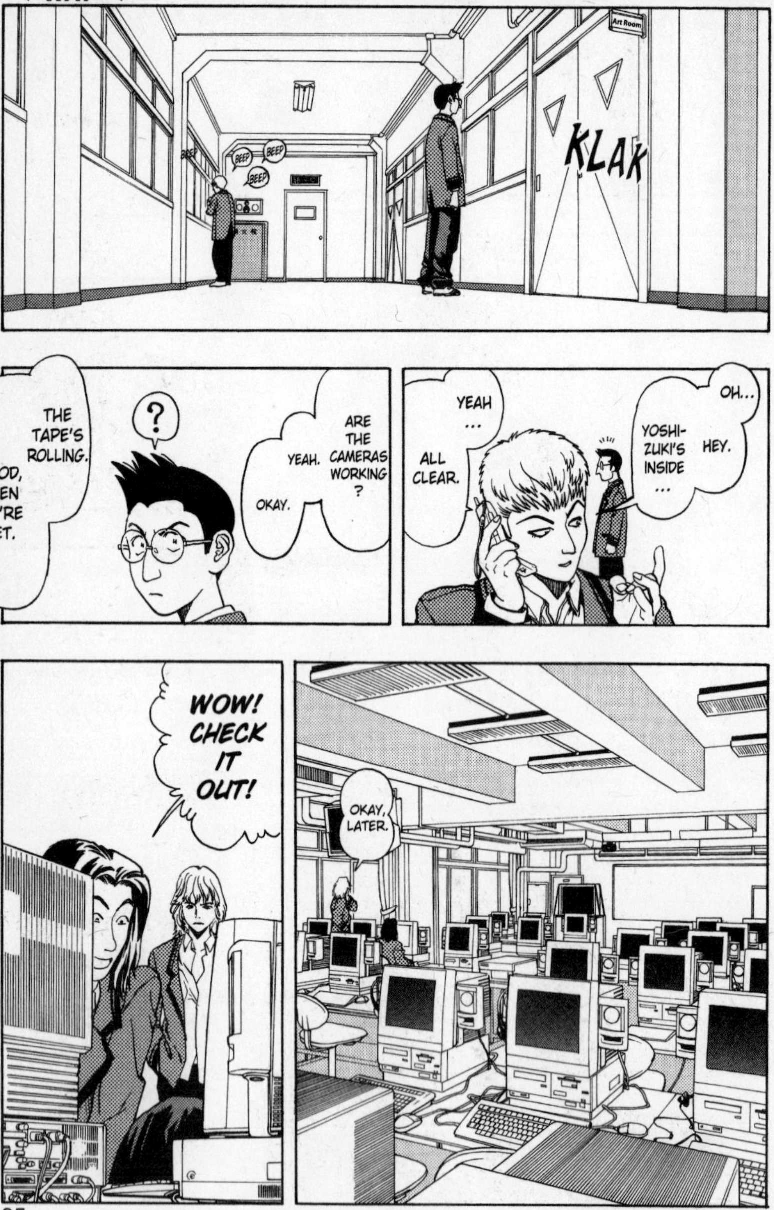
Art Room
KLAK
BEEP
BEEP
BEEP
BEEP
OH... HEY.
YOSHI-ZUKI'S INSIDE ...
YEAH ... ALL CLEAR.
ARE THE CAMERAS WORKING?
YEAH.
OKAY.
?
THE TAPE'S ROLLING.
GOOD, THEN WE'RE SET.
OKAY, LATER.
WOW! CHECK IT OUT!

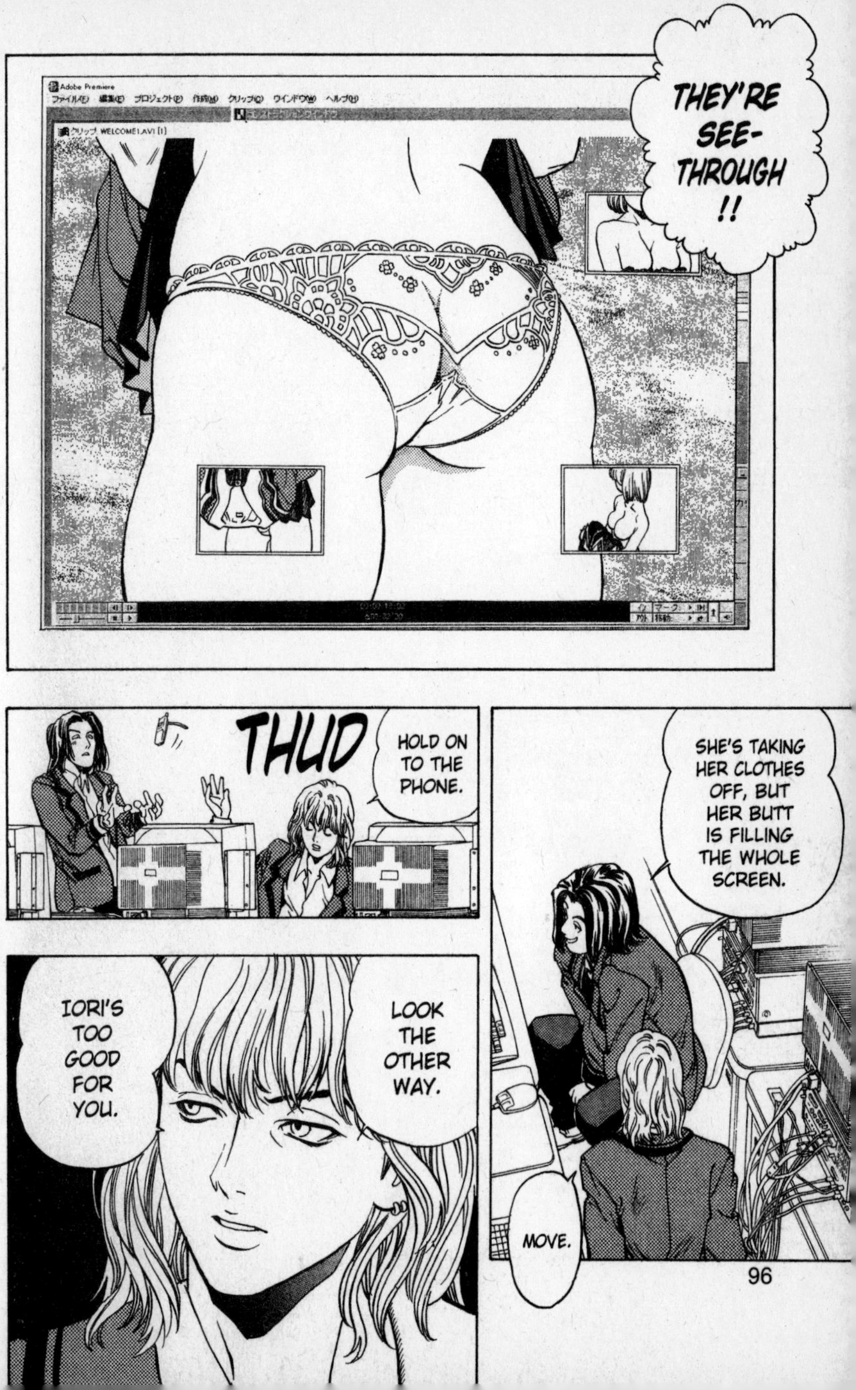
Adobe Premiere
WELCOME1.AVI [1]
THEY'RE SEE-THROUGH!!
SHE'S TAKING HER CLOTHES OFF, BUT HER BUTT IS FILLING THE WHOLE SCREEN.
MOVE.
THUD
HOLD ON TO THE PHONE.
LOOK THE OTHER WAY.
IORI'S TOO GOOD FOR YOU.

READ THIS WAY

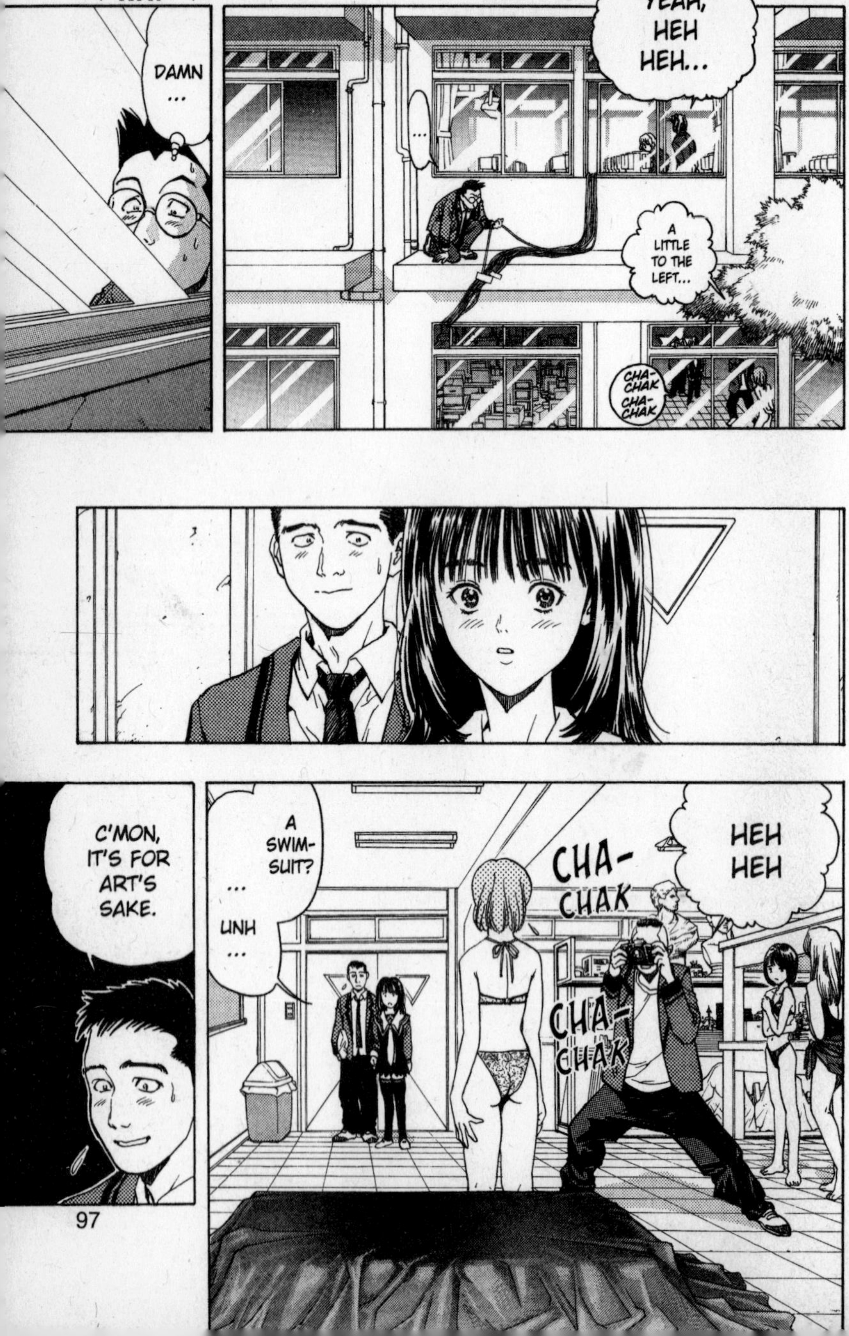
YEAH, HEH HEH...
...
A LITTLE TO THE LEFT...
CHA-CHAK CHA-CHAK
DAMN ...
HEH HEH
CHA-CHAK
CHA-CHAK
A SWIM-SUIT? ... UNH ...
C'MON, IT'S FOR ART'S SAKE.

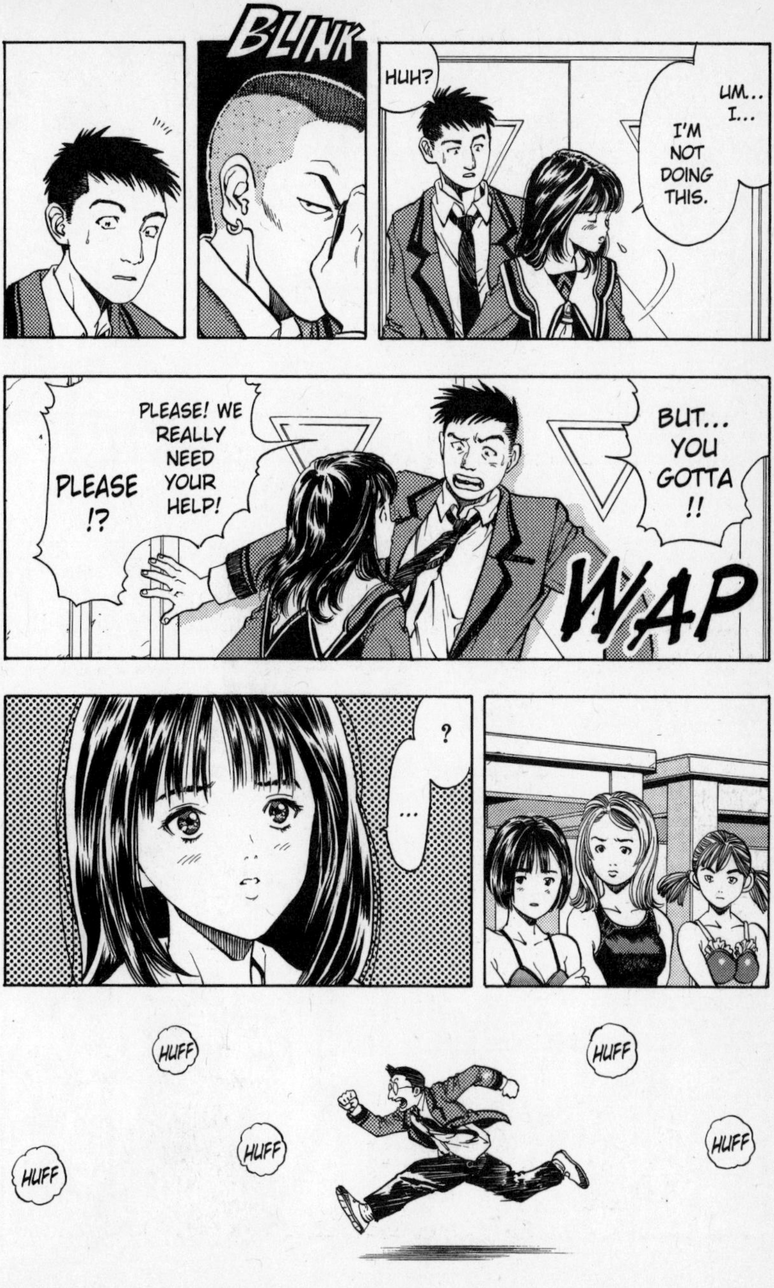
UM... I...
I'M NOT DOING THIS.
HUH?
BLINK
BUT... YOU GOTTA !!
WAP
PLEASE! WE REALLY NEED YOUR HELP!
PLEASE !?
?
...
HUFF
HUFF
HUFF
HUFF
HUFF

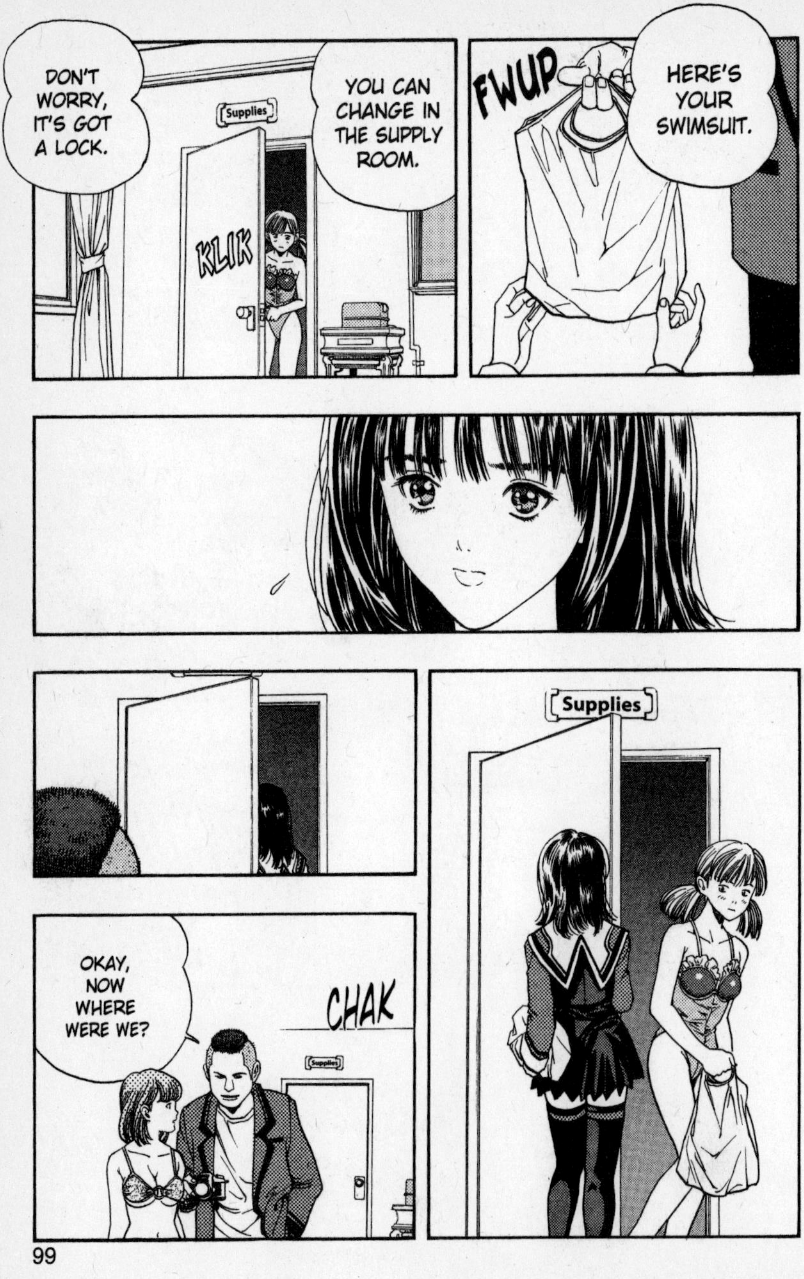
HERE'S YOUR SWIMSUIT.
FWUP
YOU CAN CHANGE IN THE SUPPLY ROOM.
DON'T WORRY, IT'S GOT A LOCK.
Supplies
KLIK
Supplies
OKAY, NOW WHERE WERE WE?
CHAK
Supplies

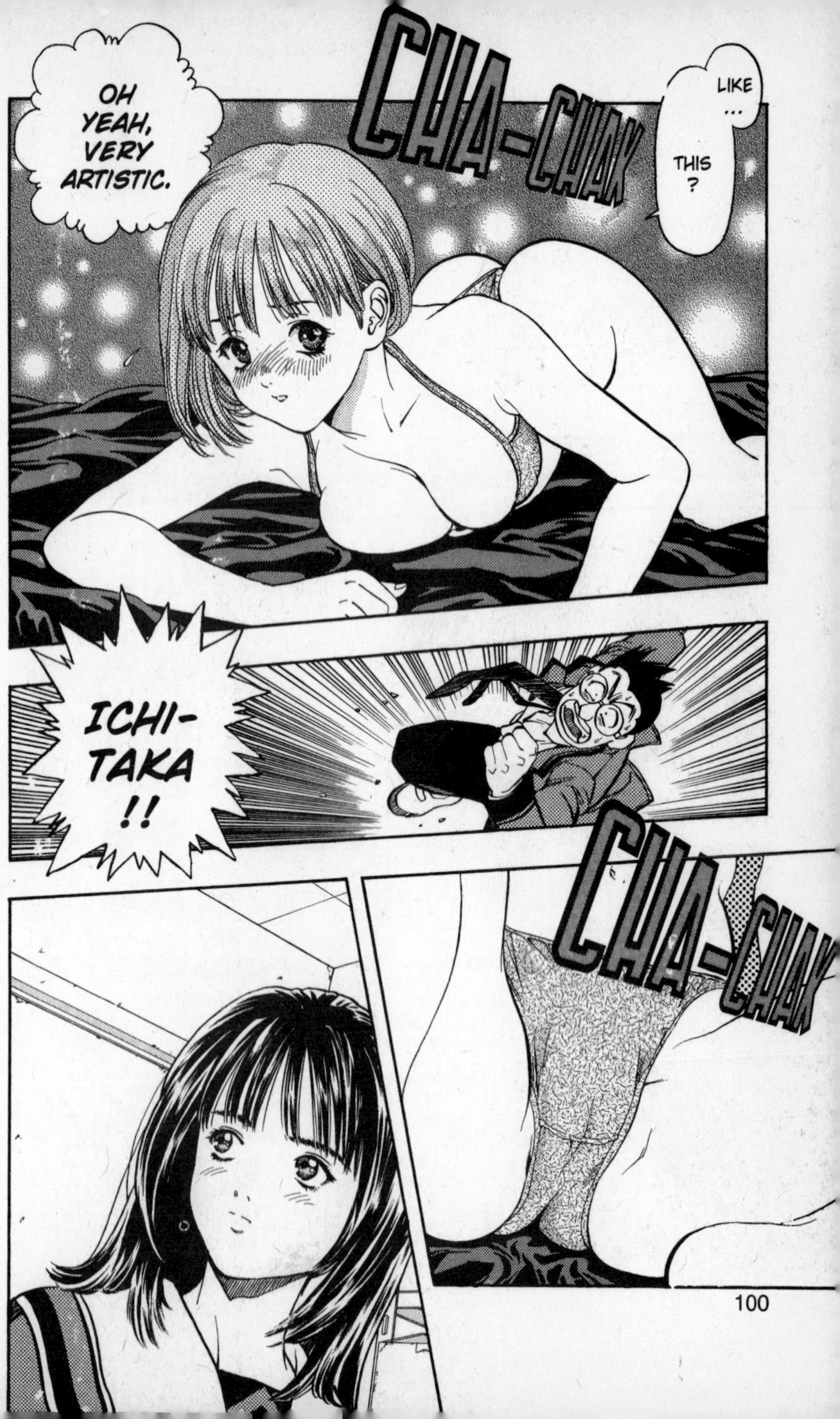
LIKE ... THIS ?
CHA-CHAK
OH YEAH, VERY ARTISTIC.
ICHI-TAKA !!
CHA-CHAK

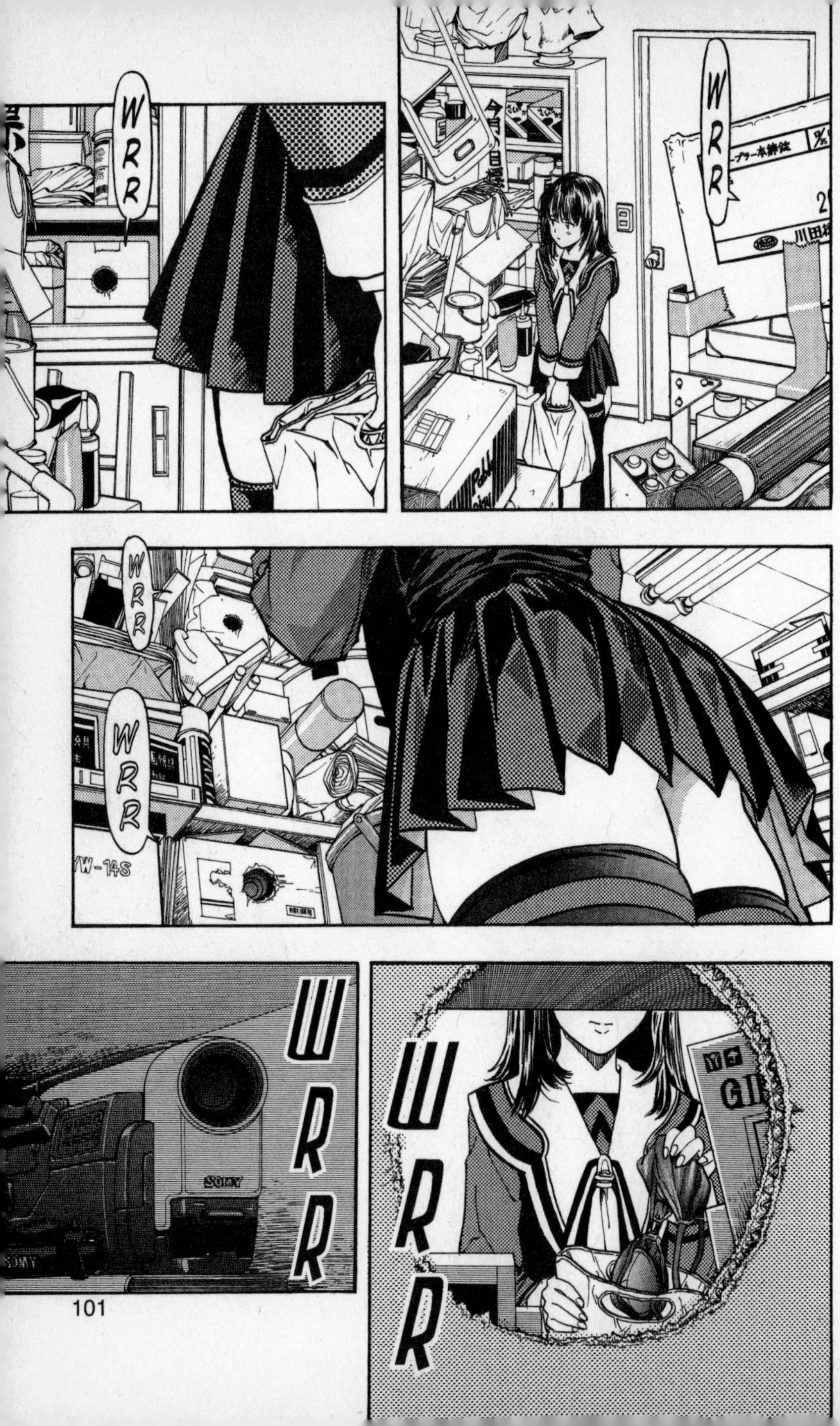
WRR
WRR
WRR
WRR
WRRR
WRR

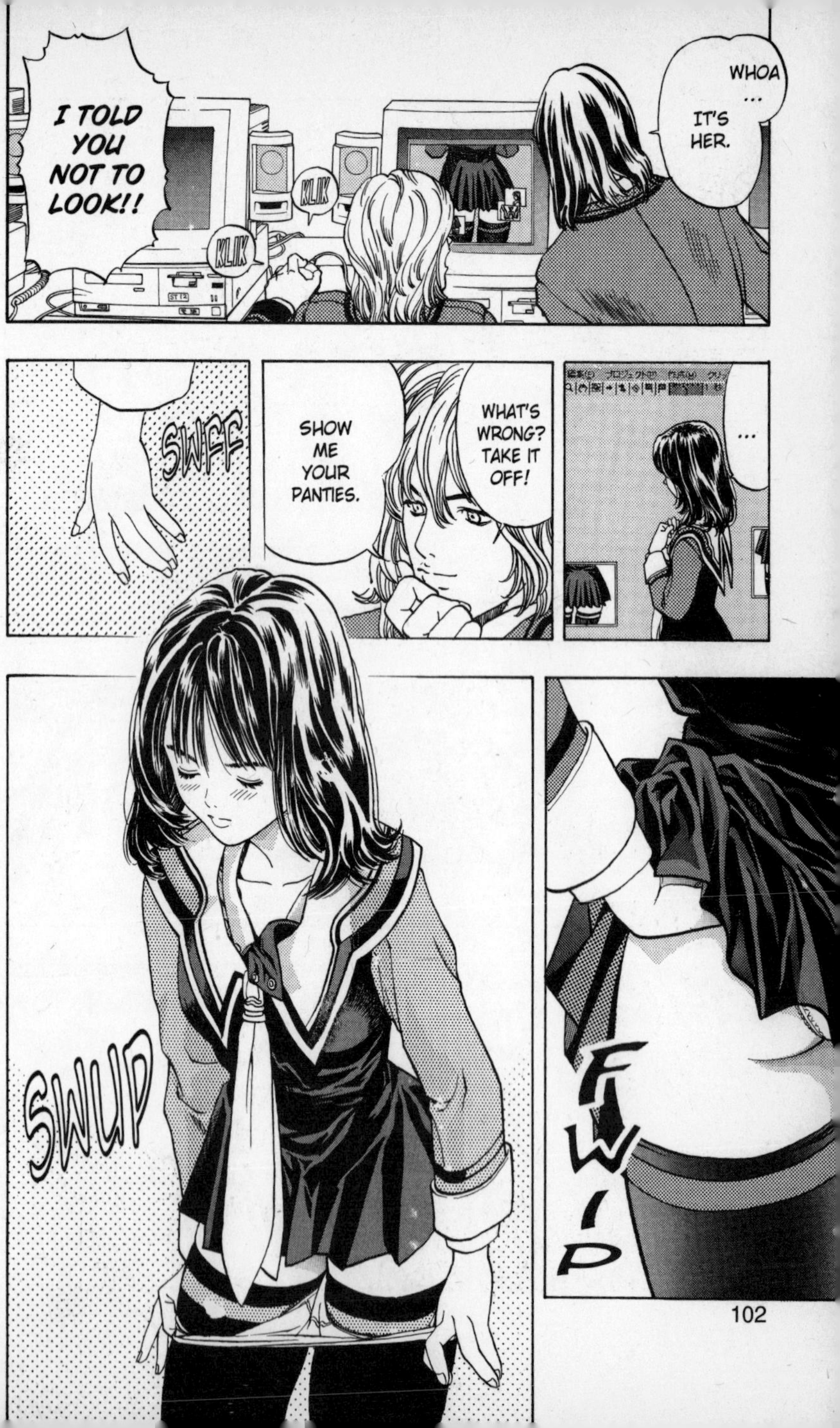
WHOA ...
IT'S HER.
I TOLD YOU NOT TO LOOK!!
KLIK
KLIK
...
WHAT'S WRONG? TAKE IT OFF!
SHOW ME YOUR PANTIES.
SWFF
FWIP
SWUP

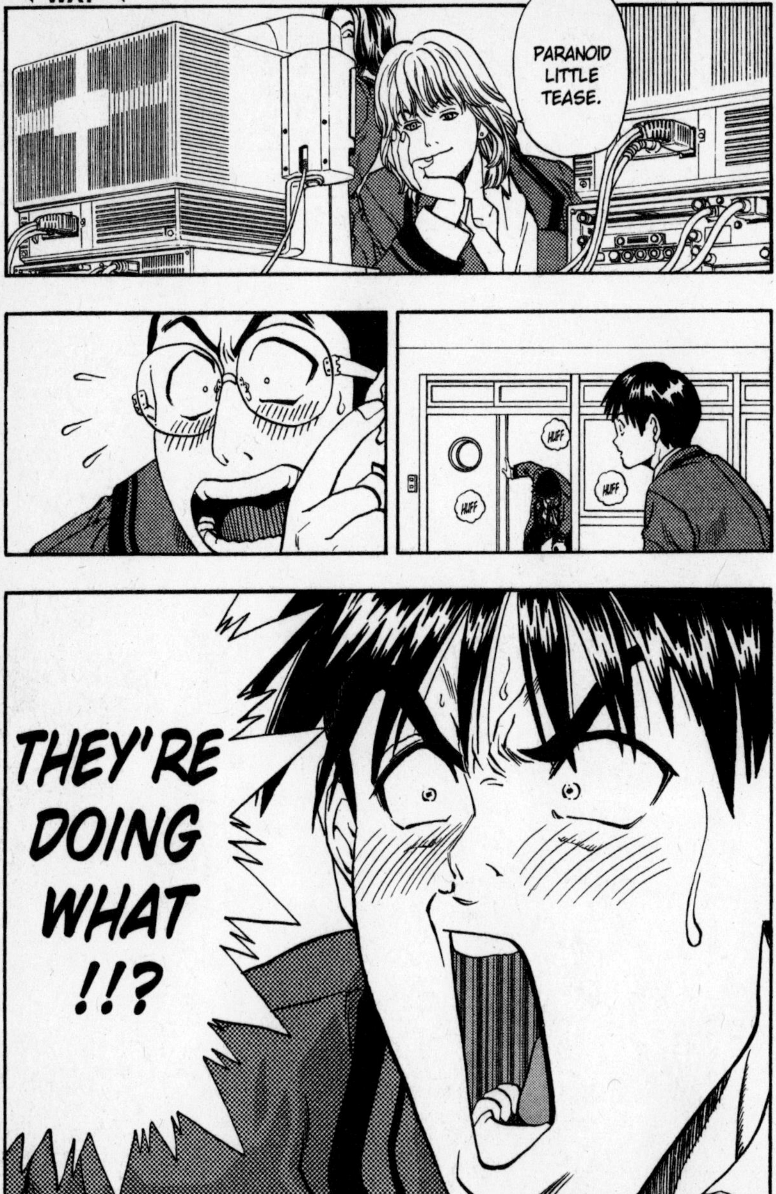
PARANOID LITTLE TEASE.
HUFF
HUFF
HUFF
THEY'RE DOING WHAT !!?

I"s
アイズ

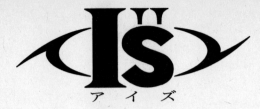

Chapter 4: Timid No More

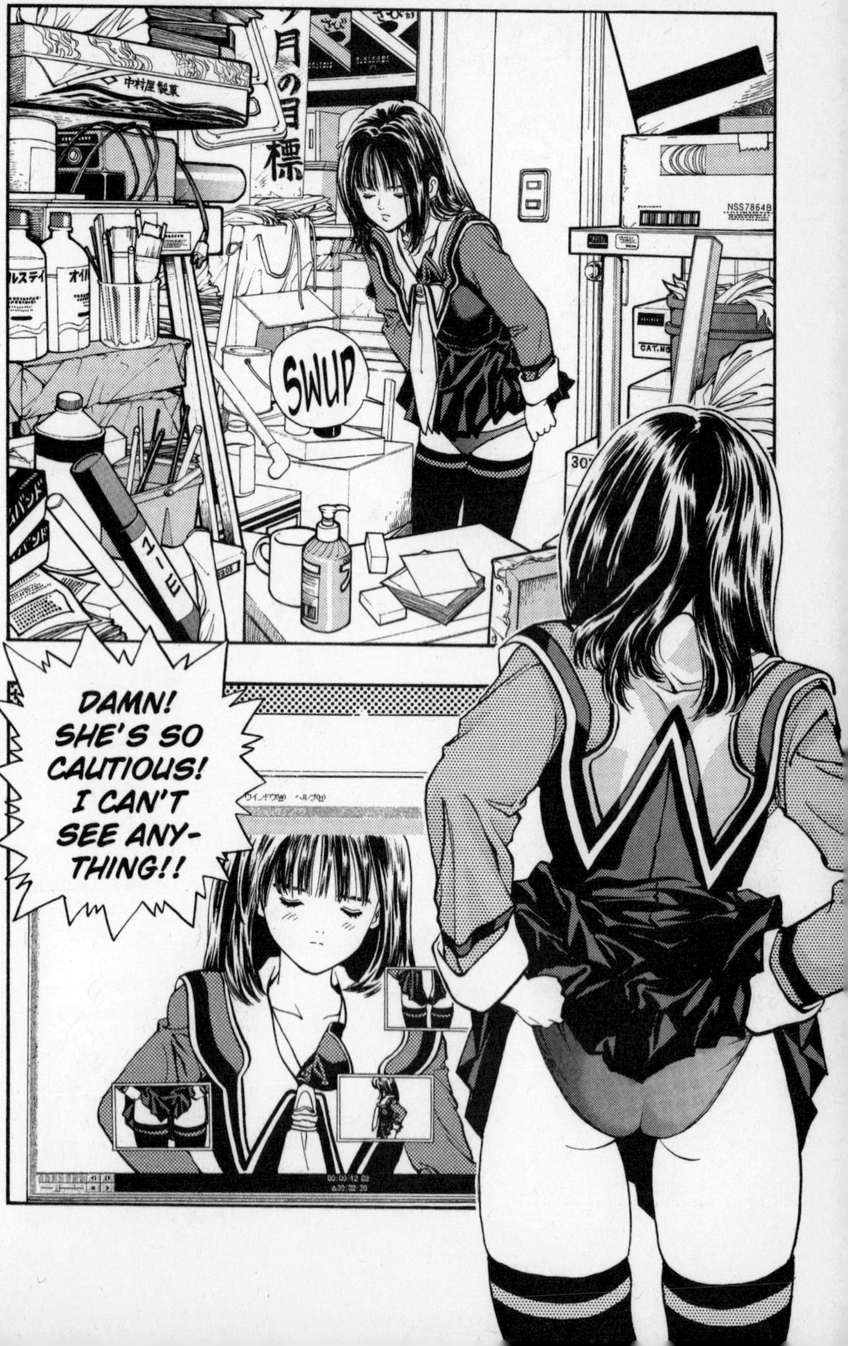
SWUP
DAMN! SHE'S SO CAUTIOUS! I CAN'T SEE ANY-THING!!

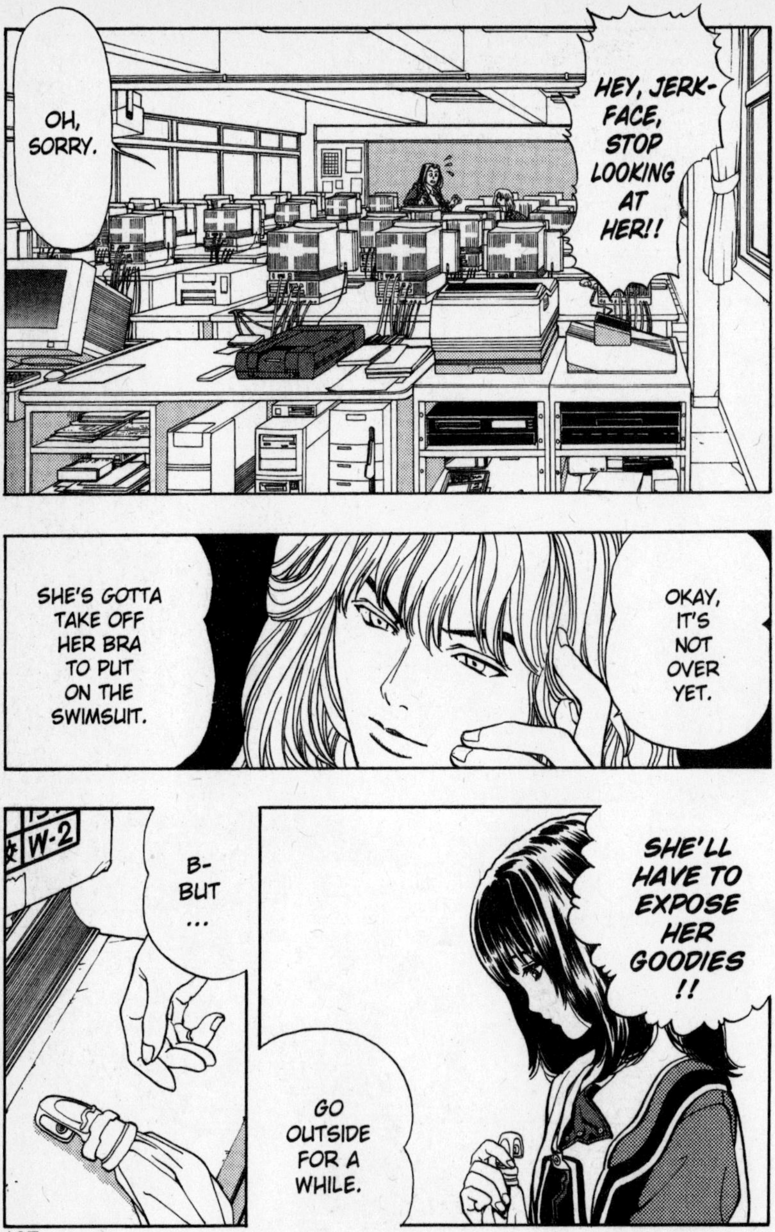
HEY, JERK-FACE, STOP LOOKING AT HER!!
OH, SORRY.
OKAY, IT'S NOT OVER YET.
SHE'S GOTTA TAKE OFF HER BRA TO PUT ON THE SWIMSUIT.
SHE'LL HAVE TO EXPOSE HER GOODIES !!
GO OUTSIDE FOR A WHILE.
W-2
B-BUT ...

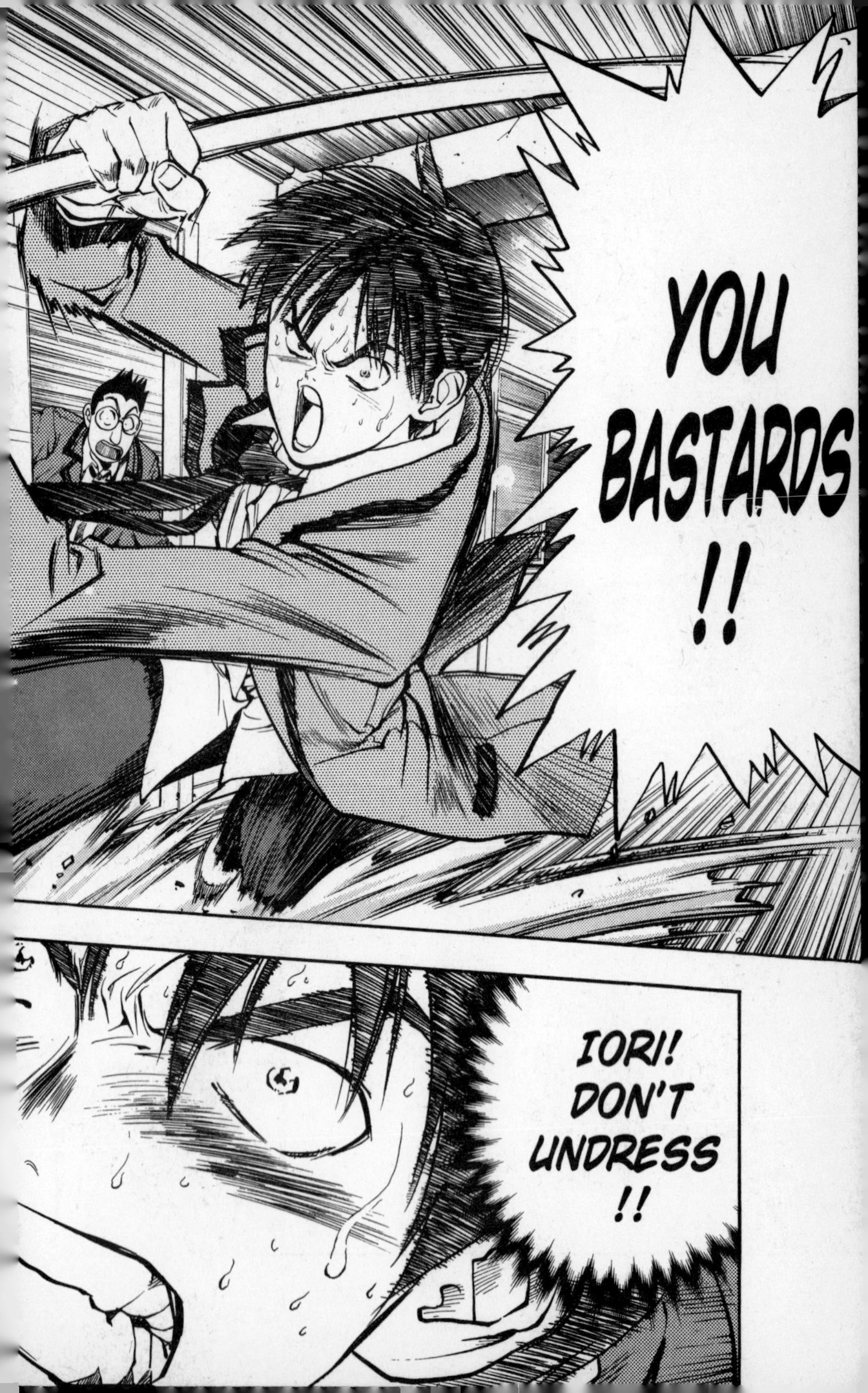
YOU BASTARDS !!
IORI! DON'T UNDRESS !!

READ THIS WAY

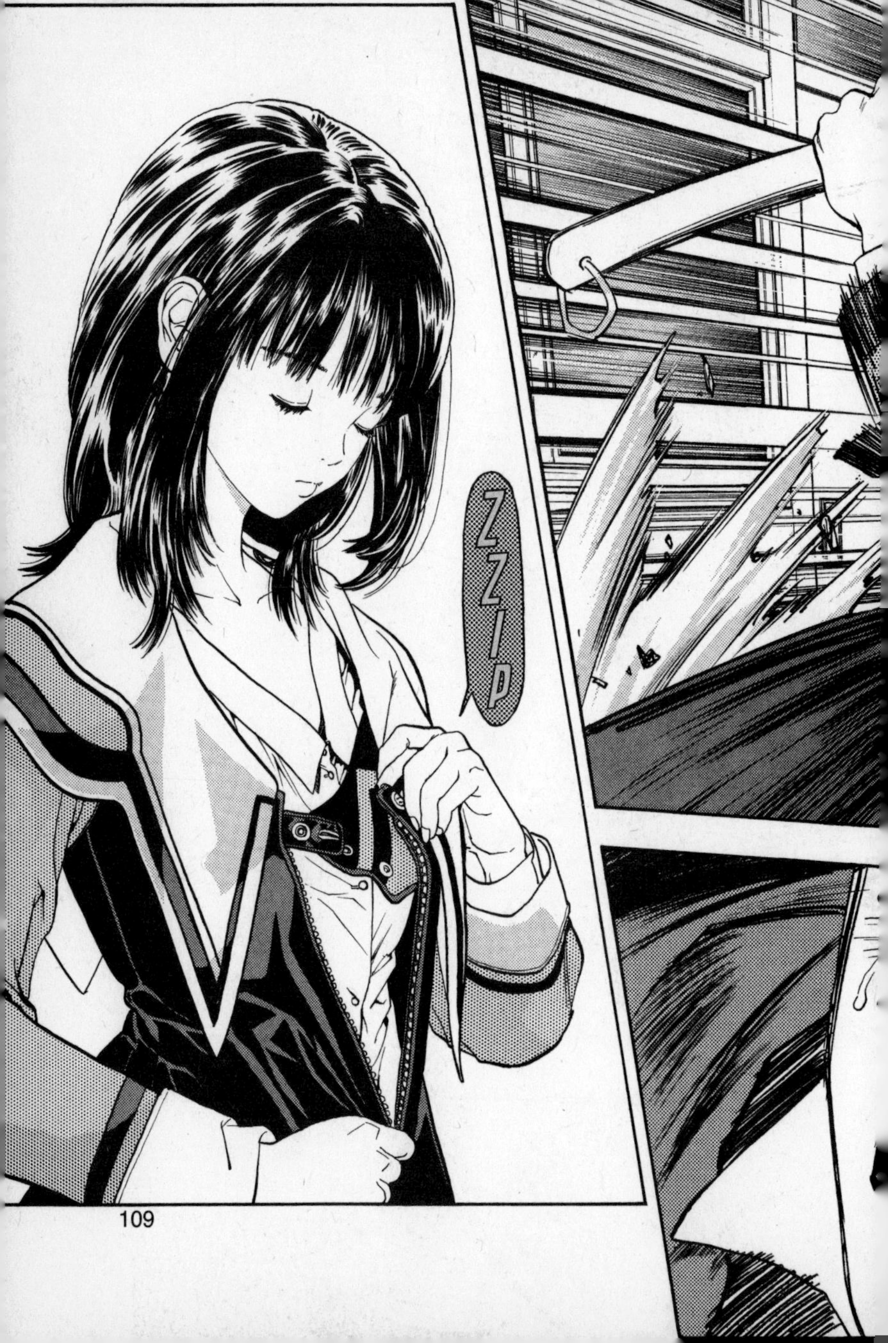
ZZIP

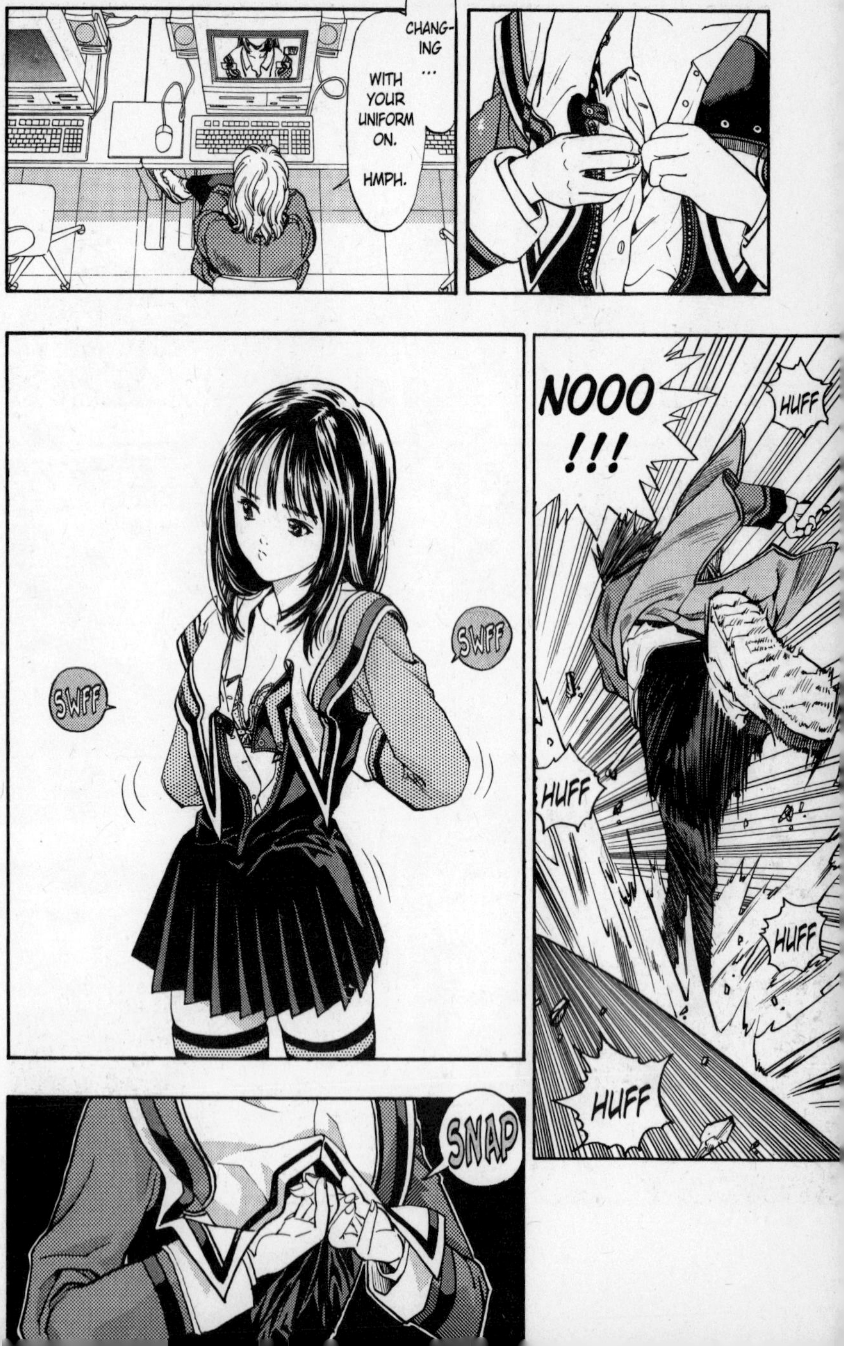
CHANG-ING ... WITH YOUR UNIFORM ON.
HMPH.
NOOO!!!
HUFF
HUFF
HUFF
HUFF
SWFF
SWFF
SNAP

READ THIS WAY

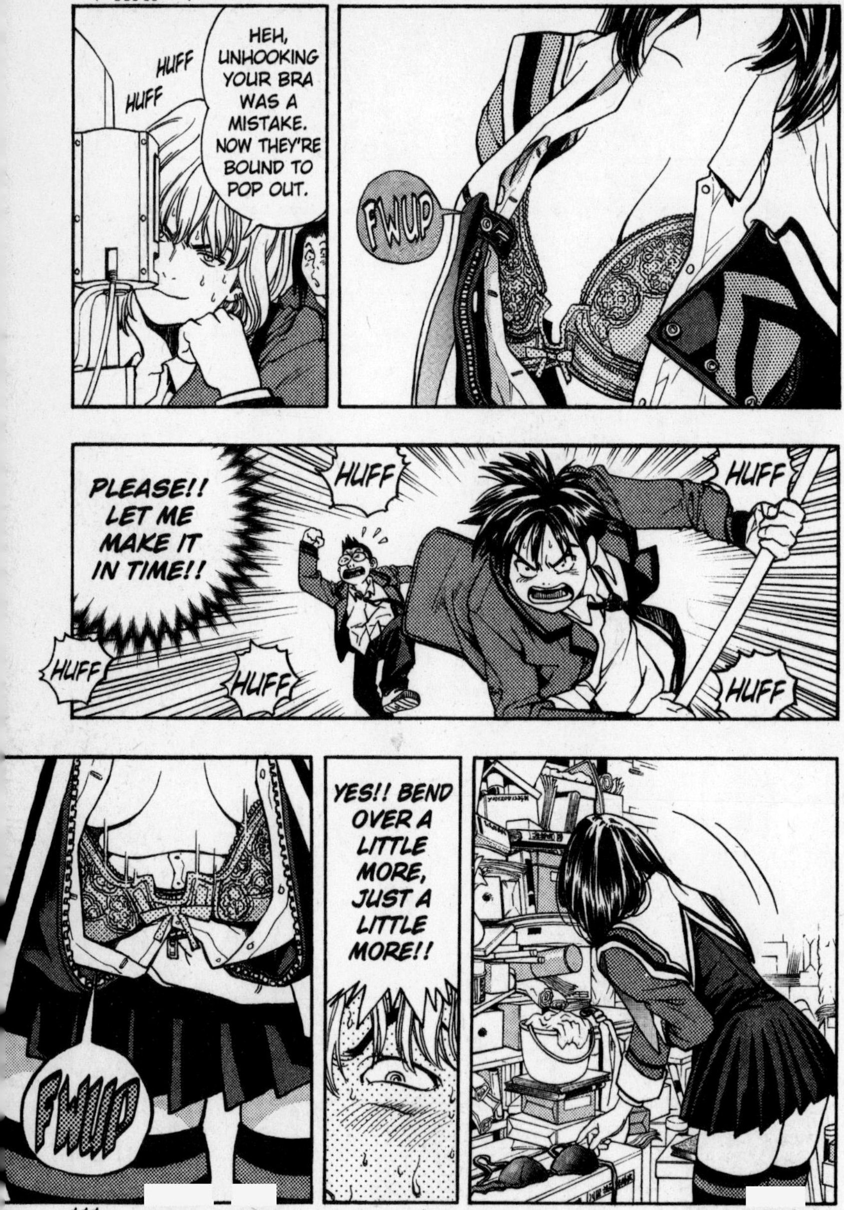
FWUP
HUFF
HUFF
HEH, UNHOOKING YOUR BRA WAS A MISTAKE. NOW THEY'RE BOUND TO POP OUT.
HUFF
HUFF
HUFF
PLEASE!! LET ME MAKE IT IN TIME!!
HUFF
HUFF
YES!! BEND OVER A LITTLE MORE, JUST A LITTLE MORE!!
FWUP

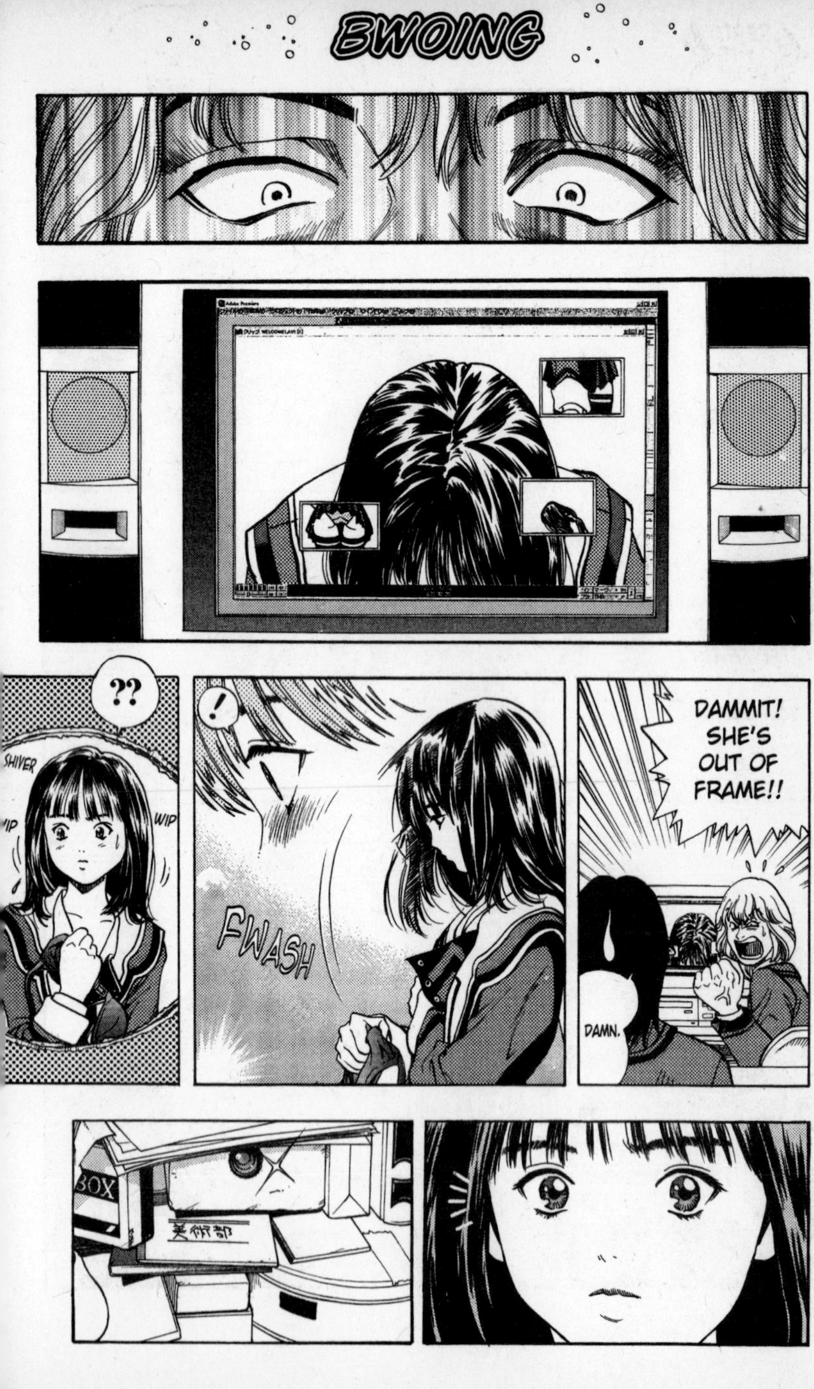
BWOING
DAMMIT! SHE'S OUT OF FRAME!!
DAMN.
!
FWASH
??
SHIVER
WIP
WIP

READ THIS WAY

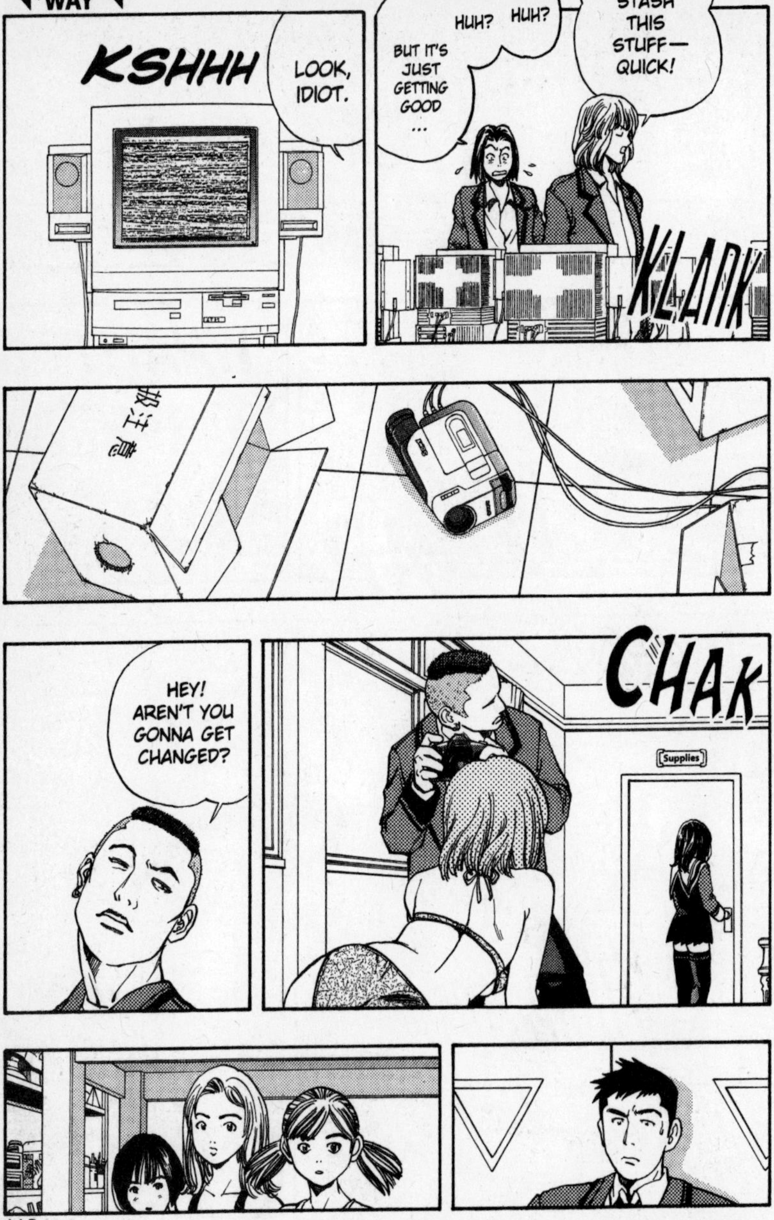
LET'S STASH THIS STUFF— QUICK!
HUH? HUH?
BUT IT'S JUST GETTING GOOD ...
KLANK
LOOK, IDIOT.
KSHHH
般注意
CHAK
Supplies
HEY! AREN'T YOU GONNA GET CHANGED?

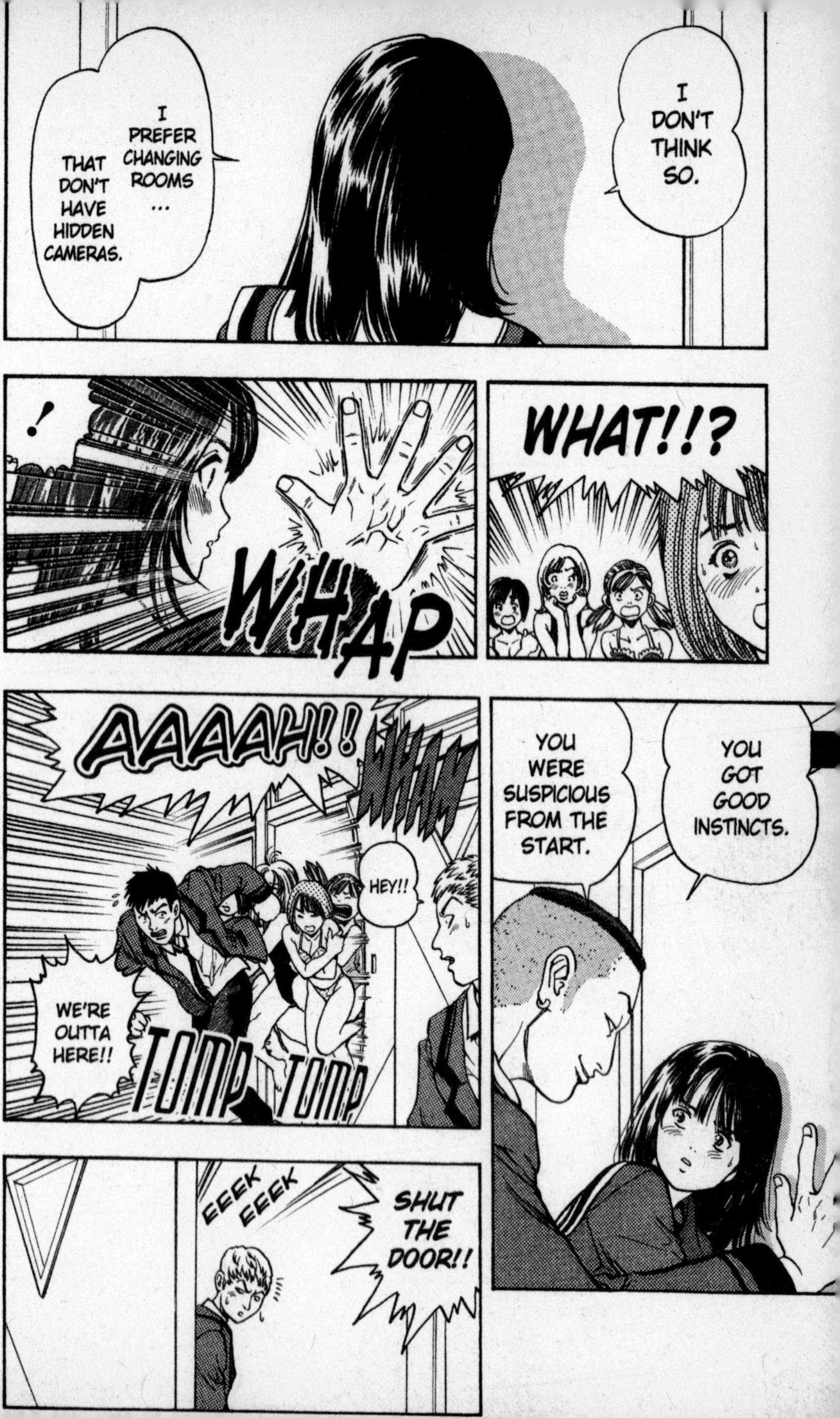
I DON'T THINK SO.
I PREFER CHANGING ROOMS ...
THAT DON'T HAVE HIDDEN CAMERAS.
WHAT!!?
!
WHAP
YOU GOT GOOD INSTINCTS.
YOU WERE SUSPICIOUS FROM THE START.
AAAAH!!
HEY!!
WE'RE OUTTA HERE!!
TOMP TOMP
SHUT THE DOOR!!
EEEK EEEK

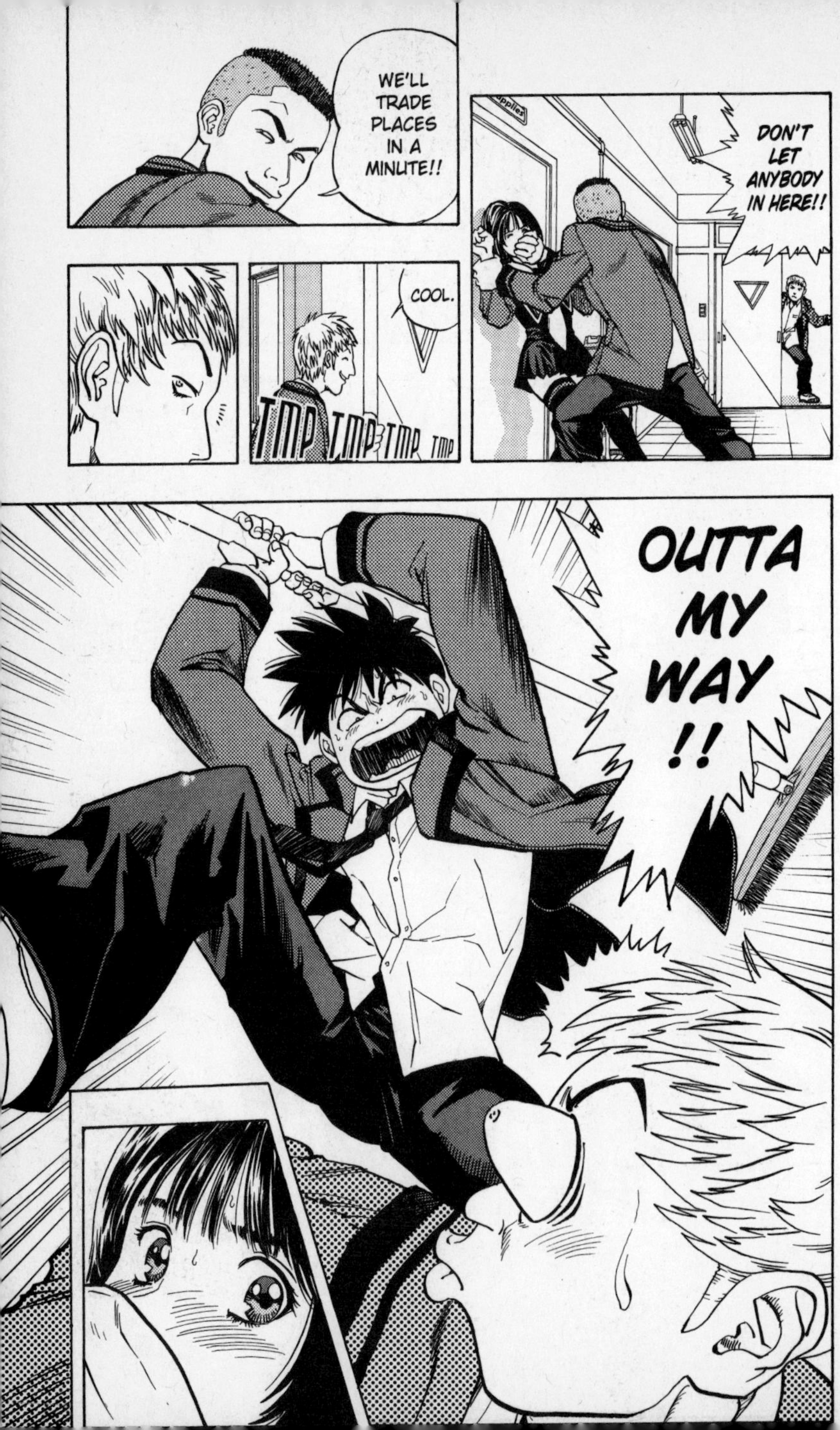
DON'T LET ANYBODY IN HERE!!
WE'LL TRADE PLACES IN A MINUTE!!
COOL.
TMP TMP TMP TMP
OUTTA MY WAY!!

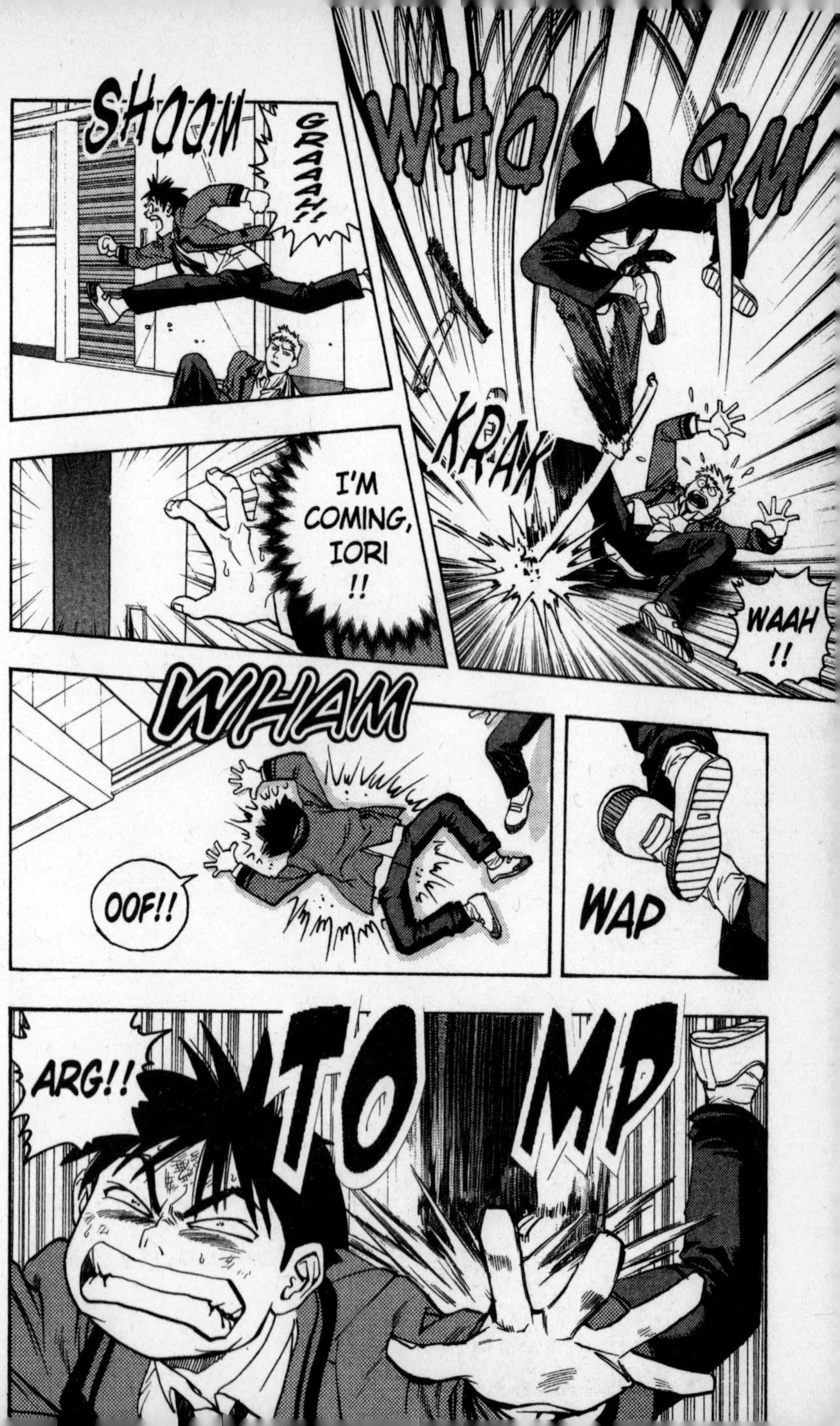

WHOOM
KRAK
WAAH!!
SHOOM
GRAAAAH!!
I'M COMING, IORI!!
WAP
WHAM
OOF!!
TOMP
ARG!!

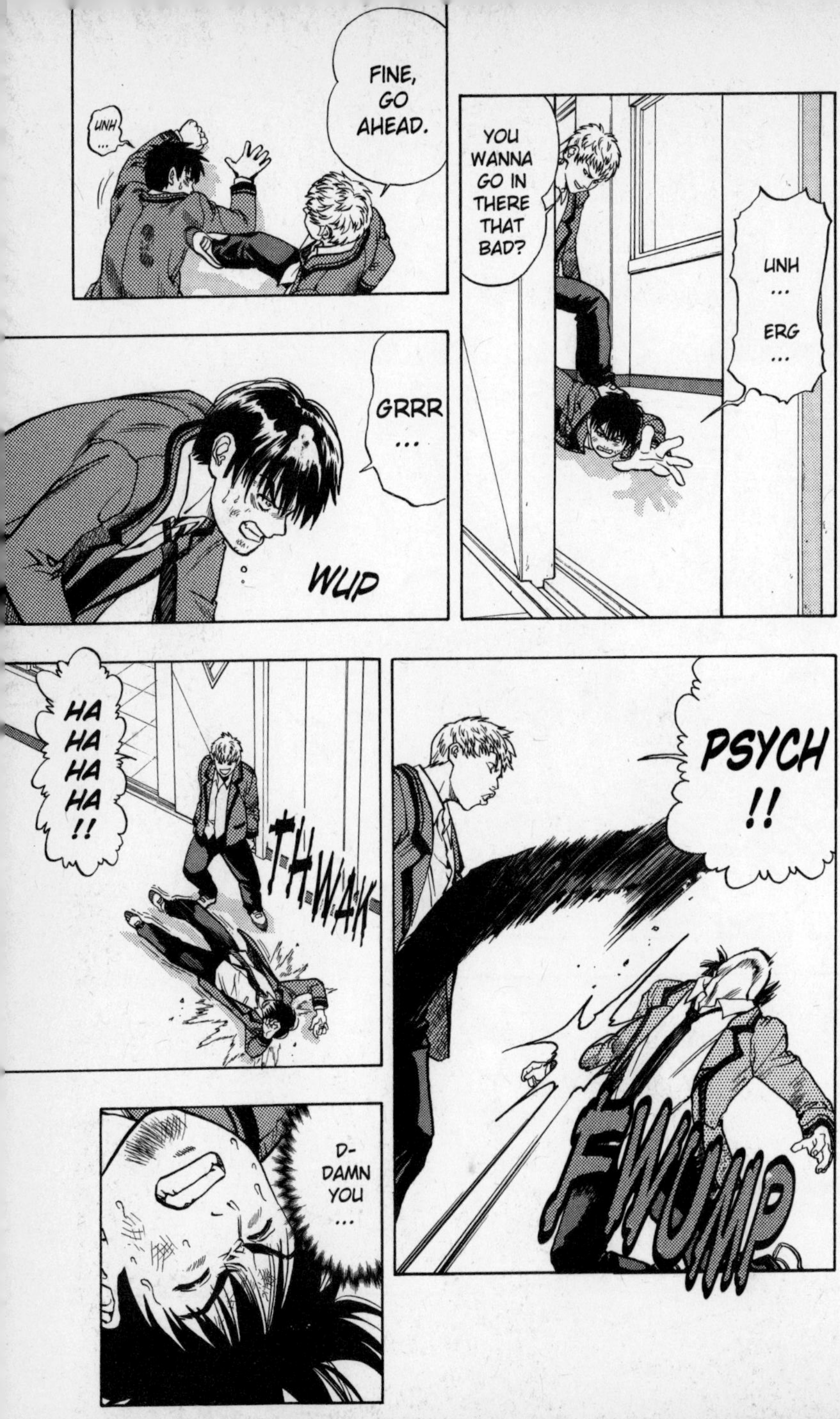
YOU WANNA GO IN THERE THAT BAD?
UNH ... ERG ...
FINE, GO AHEAD.
UNH ...
GRRR ...
WUP
PSYCH !!
FWUMP
HA HA HA HA !!
THWAK
D-DAMN YOU ...

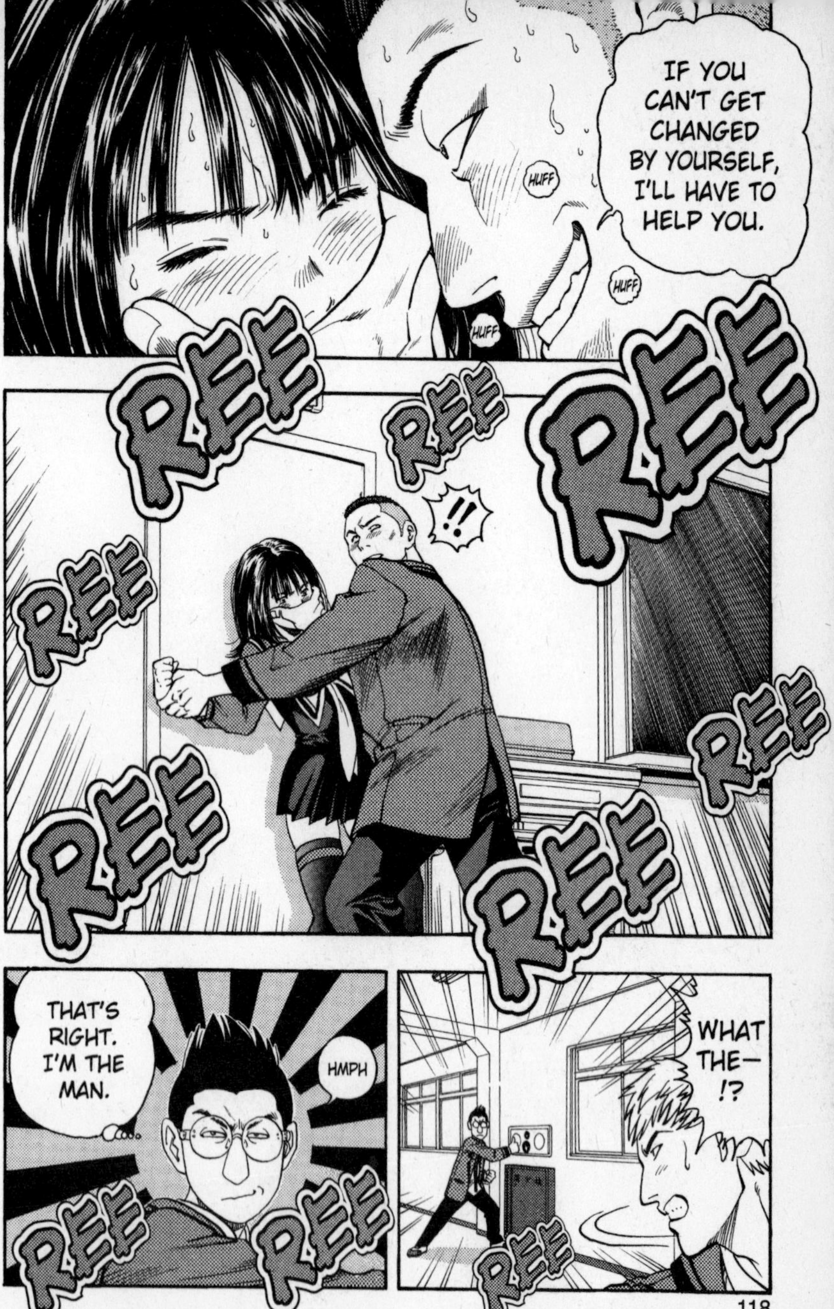
IF YOU CAN'T GET CHANGED BY YOURSELF, I'LL HAVE TO HELP YOU.
HUFF
HUFF
HUFF
REE
REE
REE
!!
REE
REE
REE
REE
WHAT THE— !?
REE
THAT'S RIGHT. I'M THE MAN.
HMPH
REE
REE

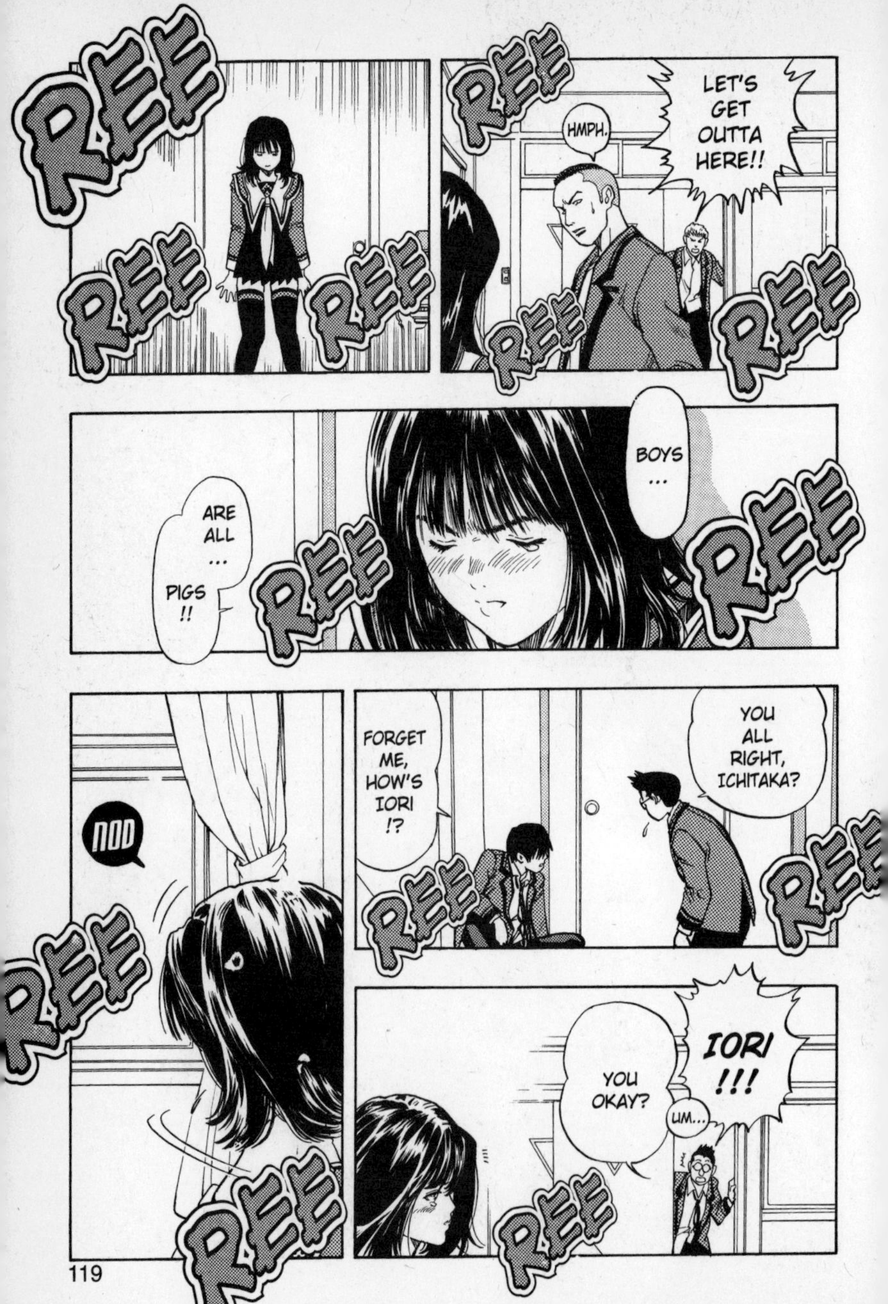
REE
HMPH.
LET'S GET OUTTA HERE!!
REE
REE
REE
REE
REE
BOYS ...
REE
ARE ALL ... PIGS !!
REE
YOU ALL RIGHT, ICHITAKA?
FORGET ME, HOW'S IORI !?
REE
REE
IORI !!!
YOU OKAY?
UM...
REE
NOD
REE
REE

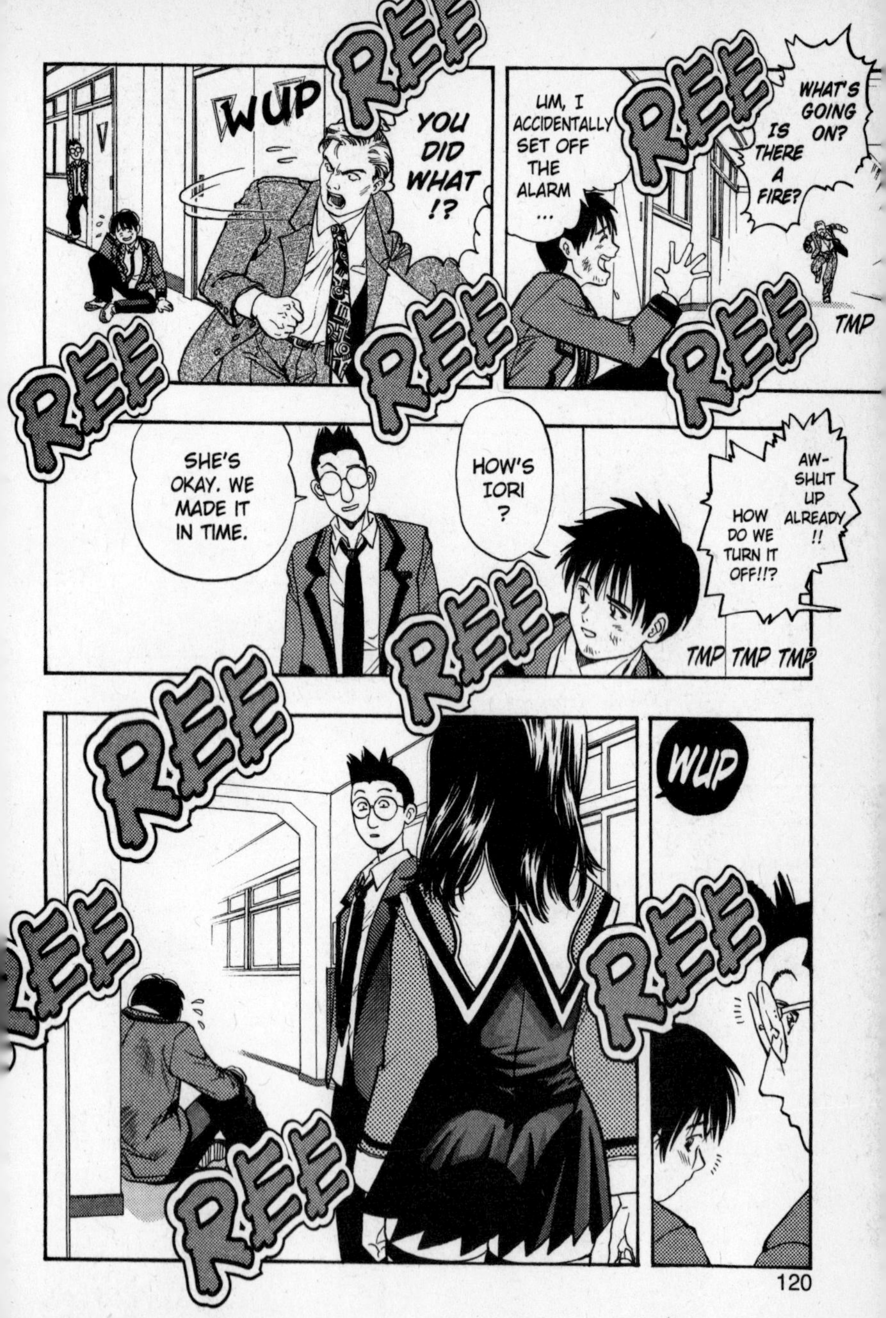
WHAT'S GOING ON?
IS THERE A FIRE?
REE
UM, I ACCIDENTALLY SET OFF THE ALARM ...
TMP
REE
REE
YOU DID WHAT!?
WUP
REE
REE
AW-SHUT UP ALREADY!!
HOW DO WE TURN IT OFF!!?
TMP TMP TMP
HOW'S IORI?
REE
SHE'S OKAY. WE MADE IT IN TIME.
WUP
REE
REE
REE
REE

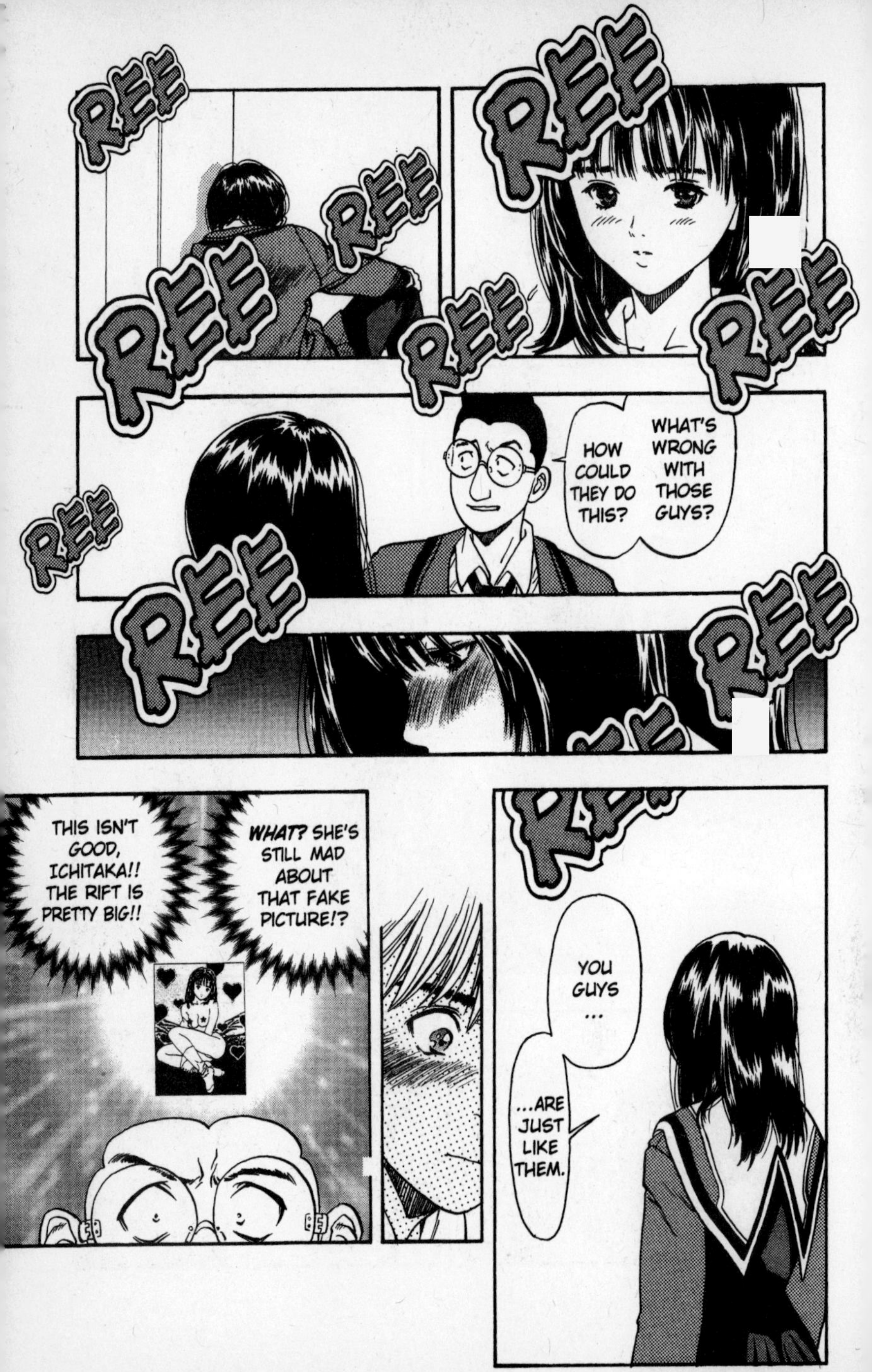
REE
REE
REE
REE
REE
REE
WHAT'S WRONG WITH THOSE GUYS?
HOW COULD THEY DO THIS?
REE
REE
REE
YOU GUYS...
...ARE JUST LIKE THEM.
WHAT? SHE'S STILL MAD ABOUT THAT FAKE PICTURE!?
THIS ISN'T GOOD, ICHITAKA!! THE RIFT IS PRETTY BIG!!

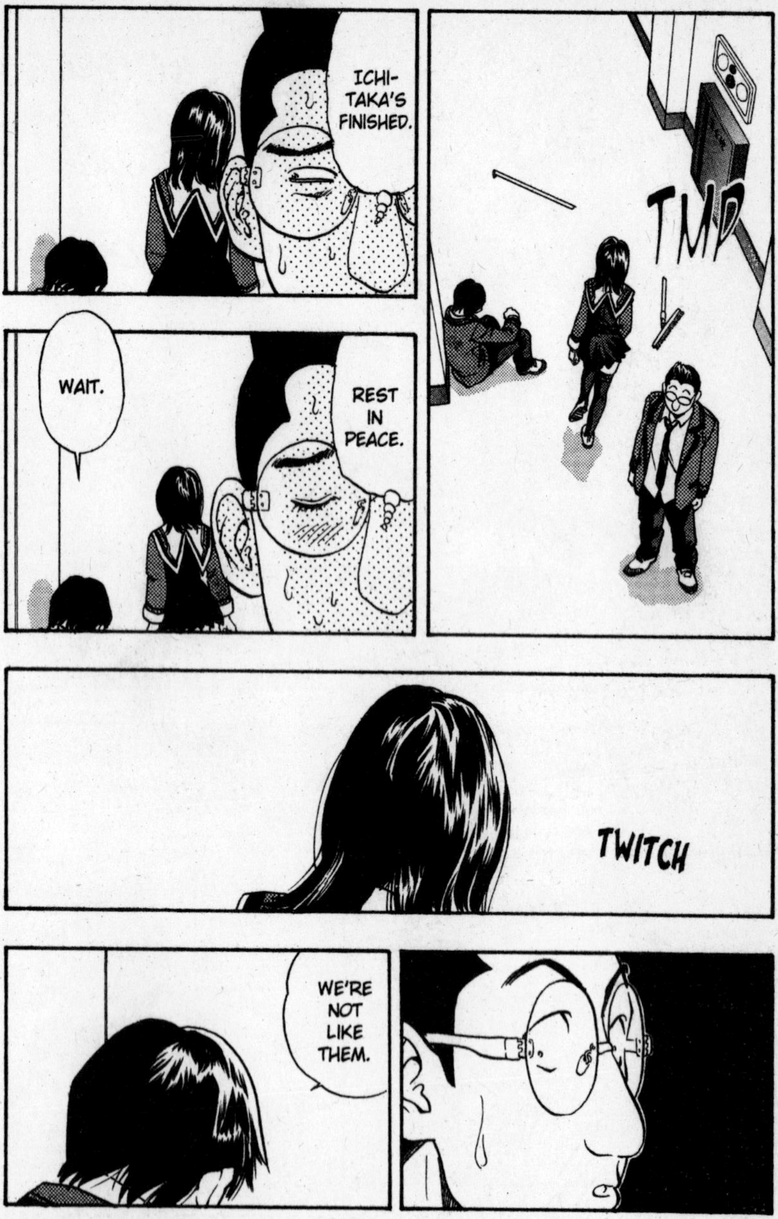
TMP
ICHI-TAKA'S FINISHED.
REST IN PEACE.
WAIT.
TWITCH
WE'RE NOT LIKE THEM.

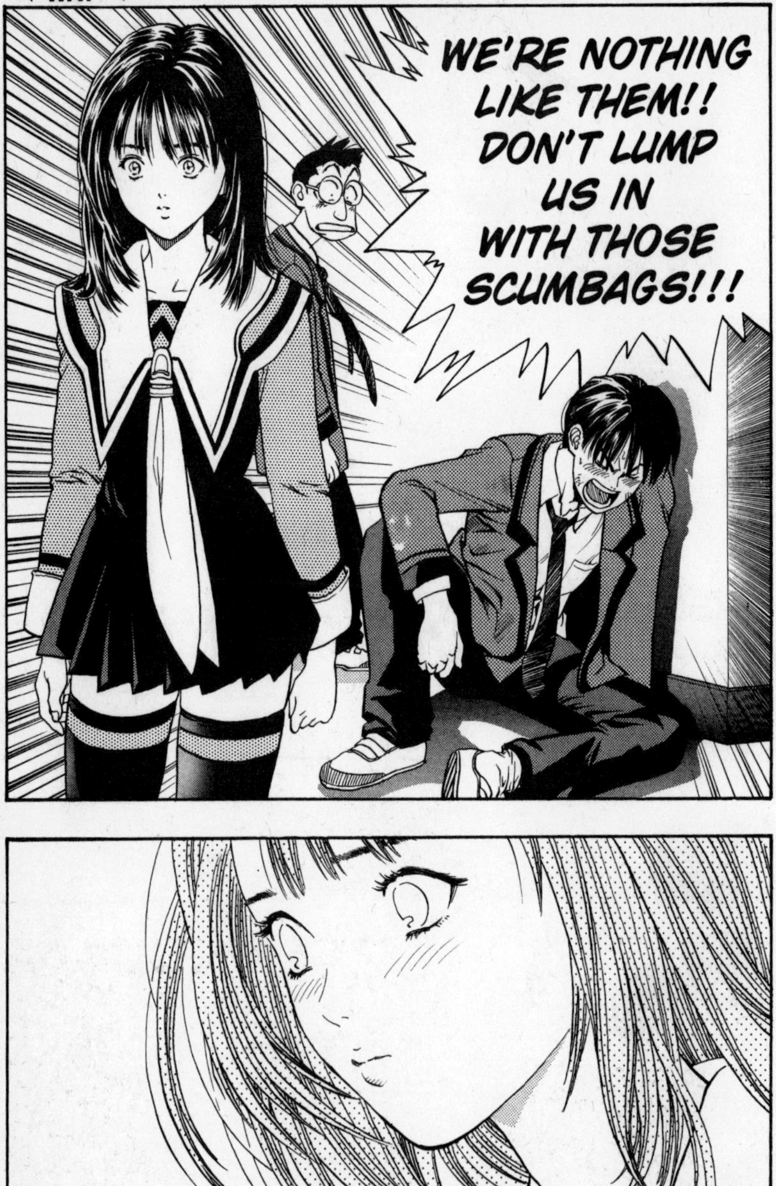
WE'RE NOTHING LIKE THEM!! DON'T LUMP US IN WITH THOSE SCUMBAGS!!!

Chapter 5:
Spanning the Rift

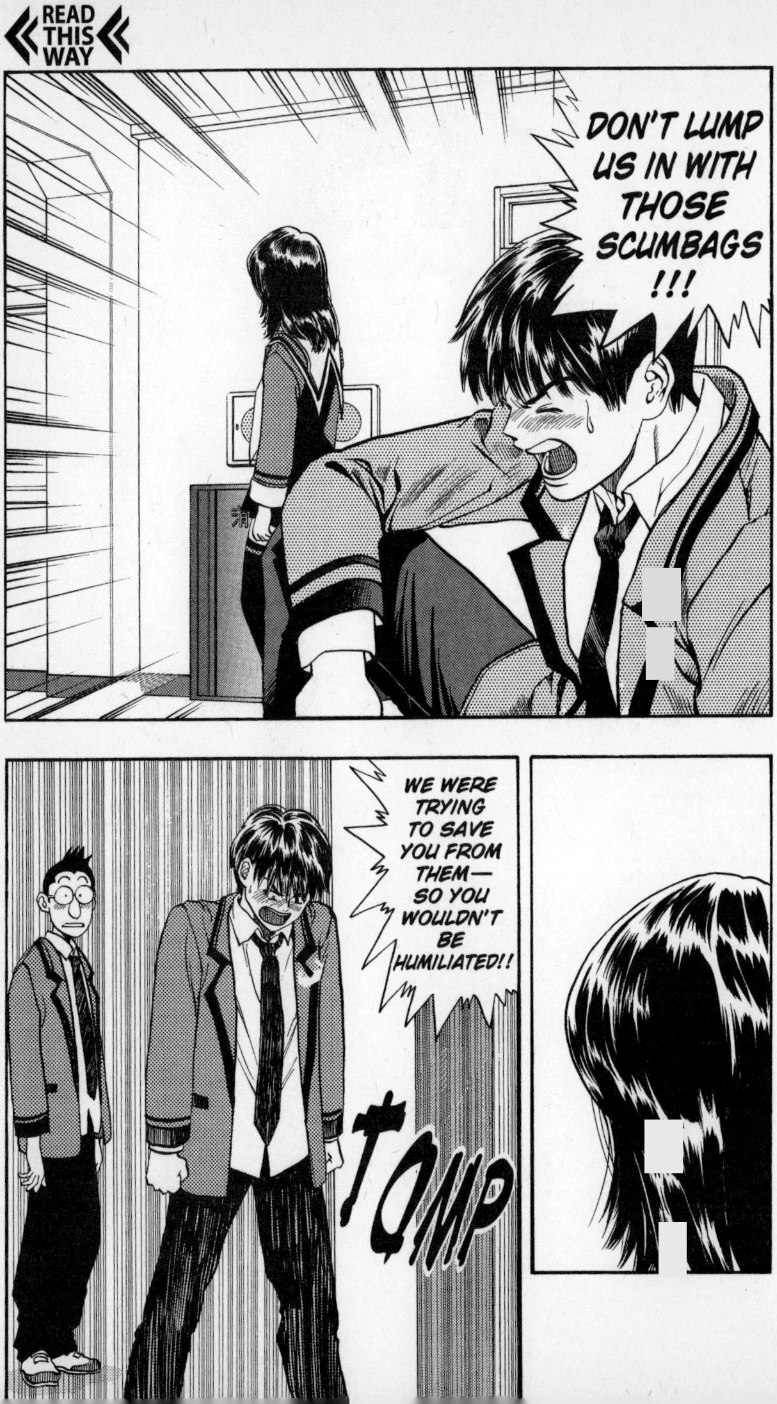
READ THIS WAY
DON'T LUMP US IN WITH THOSE SCUMBAGS!!!
WE WERE TRYING TO SAVE YOU FROM THEM—SO YOU WOULDN'T BE HUMILIATED!!
TOMP

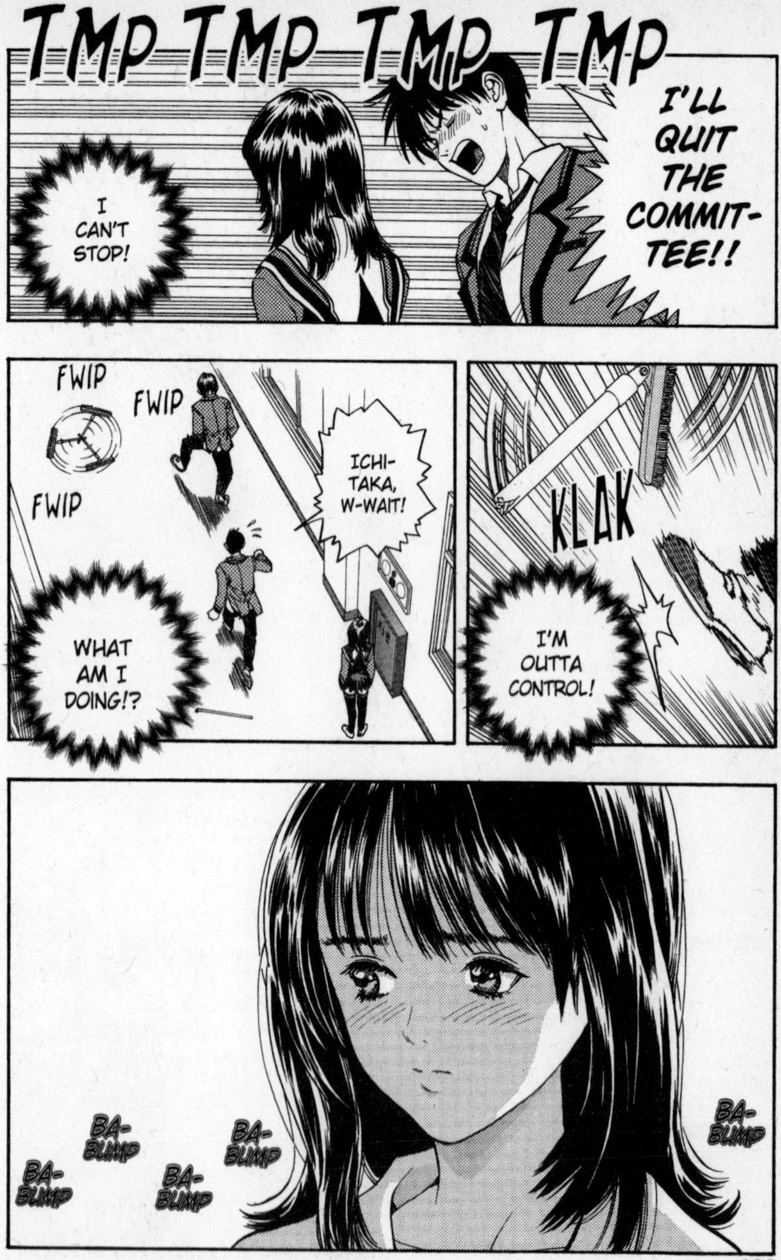
TMP TMP TMP TMP
I'LL QUIT THE COMMIT-TEE!!
I CAN'T STOP!
KLAK
I'M OUTTA CONTROL!
ICHI-TAKA, W-WAIT!
FWIP
FWIP
FWIP
WHAT AM I DOING!?
BA-BUMP
BA-BUMP
BA-BUMP
BA-BUMP
BA-BUMP

READ THIS WAY

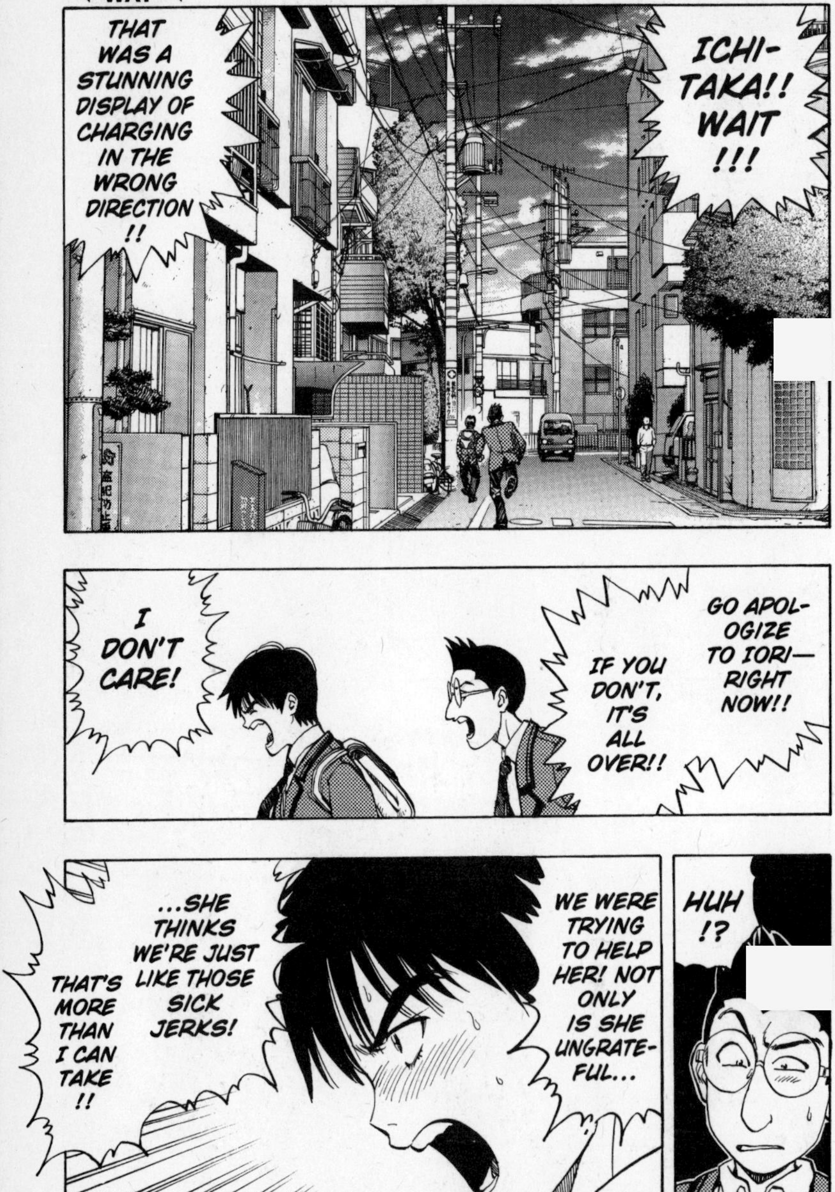
ICHI-TAKA!! WAIT!!!
THAT WAS A STUNNING DISPLAY OF CHARGING IN THE WRONG DIRECTION!!
GO APOLOGIZE TO IORI— RIGHT NOW!!
IF YOU DON'T, IT'S ALL OVER!!
I DON'T CARE!
HUH!?
WE WERE TRYING TO HELP HER! NOT ONLY IS SHE UNGRATEFUL...
...SHE THINKS WE'RE JUST LIKE THOSE SICK JERKS!
THAT'S MORE THAN I CAN TAKE!!

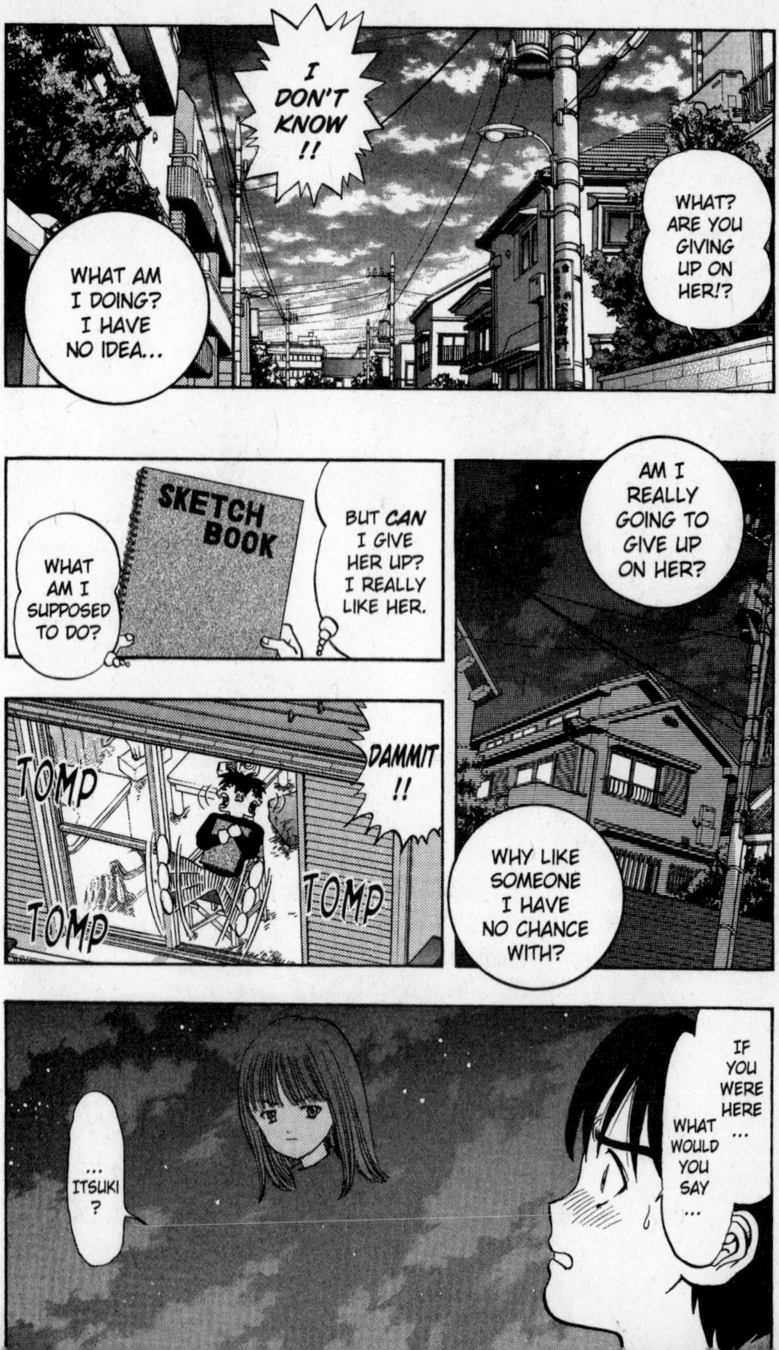
WHAT? ARE YOU GIVING UP ON HER!?
I DON'T KNOW!!
WHAT AM I DOING? I HAVE NO IDEA...
AM I REALLY GOING TO GIVE UP ON HER?
WHY LIKE SOMEONE I HAVE NO CHANCE WITH?
BUT CAN I GIVE HER UP? I REALLY LIKE HER.
SKETCH BOOK
WHAT AM I SUPPOSED TO DO?
DAMMIT!!
TOMP
TOMP
TOMP
IF YOU WERE HERE...
WHAT WOULD YOU SAY...
...ITSUKI?

READ THIS WAY

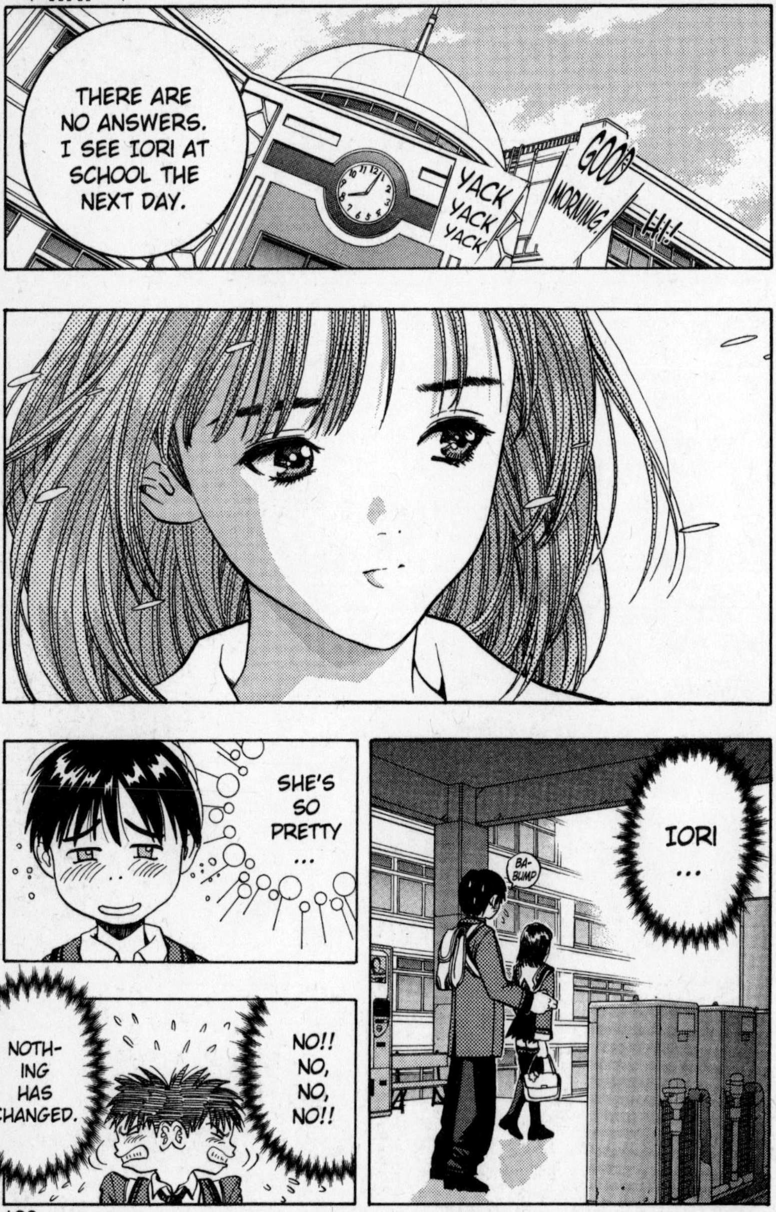
GOOD MORNING.
YACK YACK YACK
HI!!
THERE ARE NO ANSWERS. I SEE IORI AT SCHOOL THE NEXT DAY.
IORI ...
BA-BUMP
SHE'S SO PRETTY ...
NO!! NO, NO, NO!!
NOTHING HAS CHANGED.

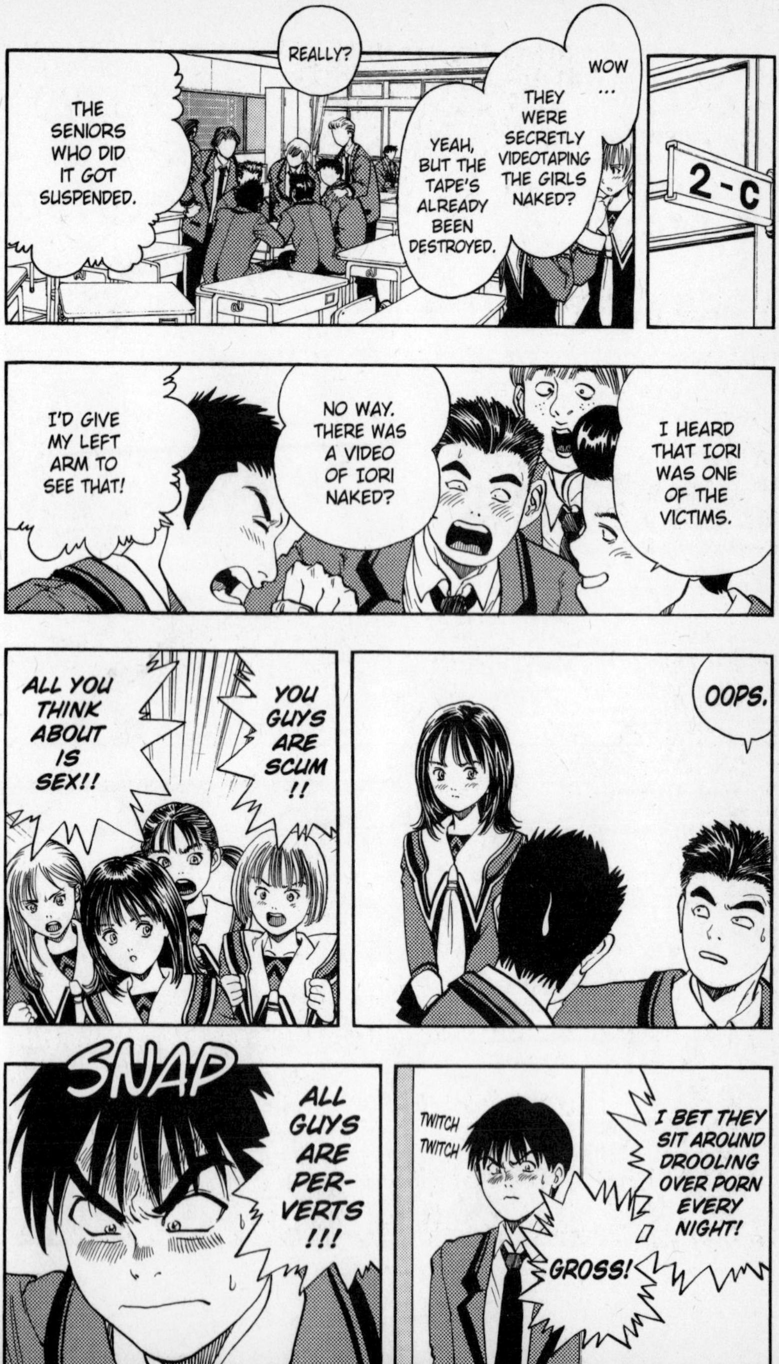
2-C
WOW ...
THEY WERE SECRETLY VIDEOTAPING THE GIRLS NAKED?
REALLY?
YEAH, BUT THE TAPE'S ALREADY BEEN DESTROYED.
THE SENIORS WHO DID IT GOT SUSPENDED.
I HEARD THAT IORI WAS ONE OF THE VICTIMS.
NO WAY. THERE WAS A VIDEO OF IORI NAKED?
I'D GIVE MY LEFT ARM TO SEE THAT!
OOPS.
YOU GUYS ARE SCUM!!
ALL YOU THINK ABOUT IS SEX!!
I BET THEY SIT AROUND DROOLING OVER PORN EVERY NIGHT!
TWITCH TWITCH
GROSS!
SNAP
ALL GUYS ARE PER-VERTS!!!

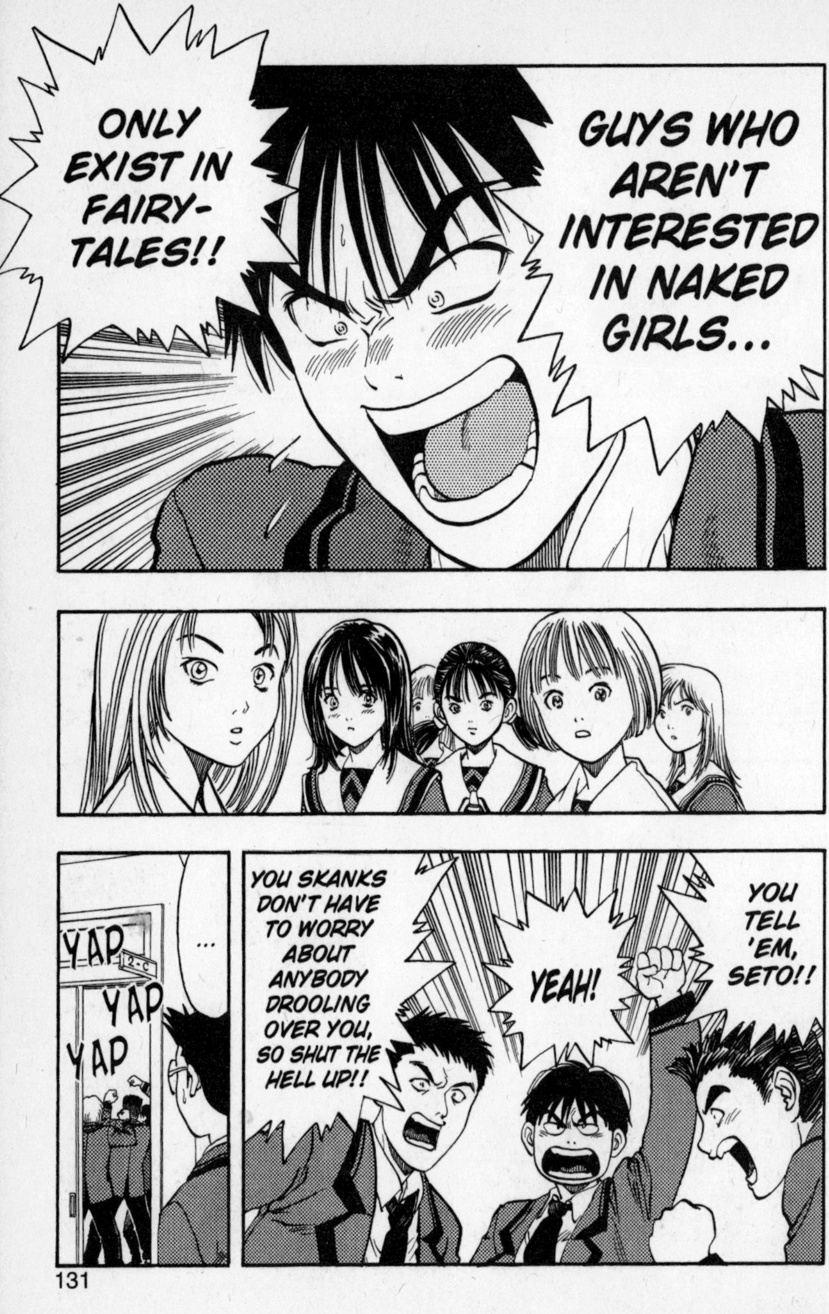

GUYS WHO AREN'T INTERESTED IN NAKED GIRLS...
ONLY EXIST IN FAIRY-TALES!!
YOU TELL 'EM, SETO!!
YOU SKANKS DON'T HAVE TO WORRY ABOUT ANYBODY DROOLING OVER YOU, SO SHUT THE HELL UP!!
YEAH!
...
YAP
2-C
YAP
YAP

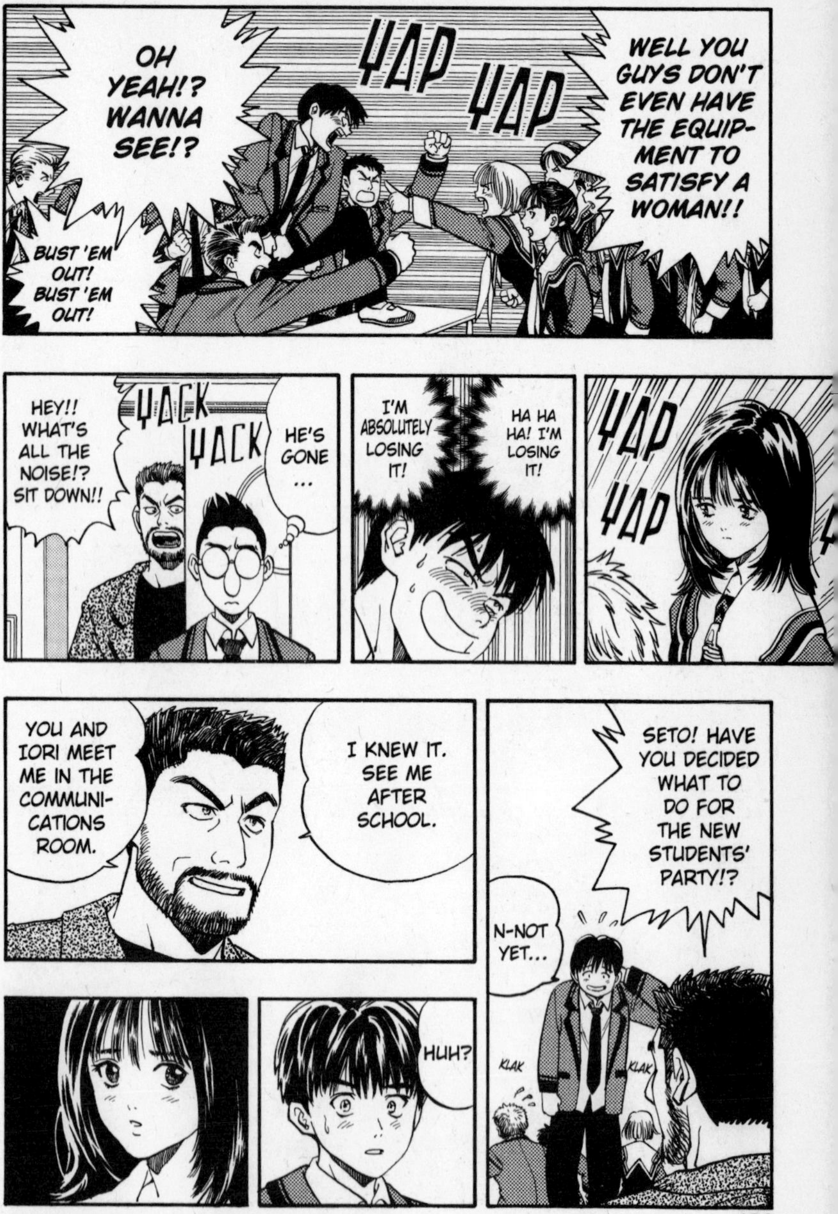
WELL YOU GUYS DON'T EVEN HAVE THE EQUIP-MENT TO SATISFY A WOMAN!!
YAP YAP
OH YEAH!? WANNA SEE!?
BUST 'EM OUT! BUST 'EM OUT!
YAP YAP
HA HA HA! I'M LOSING IT!
I'M ABSOLUTELY LOSING IT!
HE'S GONE ...
YACK YACK
HEY!! WHAT'S ALL THE NOISE!? SIT DOWN!!
SETO! HAVE YOU DECIDED WHAT TO DO FOR THE NEW STUDENTS' PARTY!?
N-NOT YET...
KLAK
KLAK
I KNEW IT. SEE ME AFTER SCHOOL.
YOU AND IORI MEET ME IN THE COMMUNI-CATIONS ROOM.
HUH?

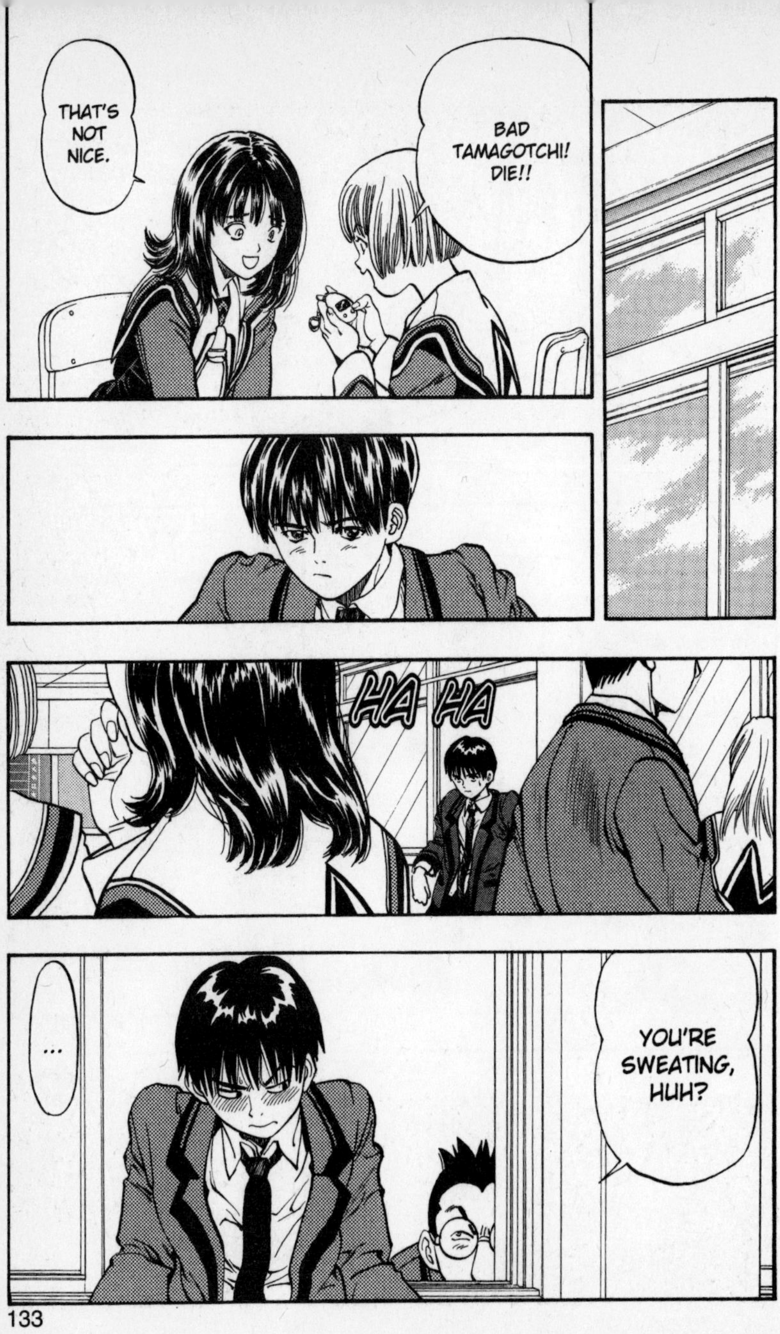
BAD TAMAGOTCHI! DIE!!
THAT'S NOT NICE.
HA HA
YOU'RE SWEATING, HUH?
...

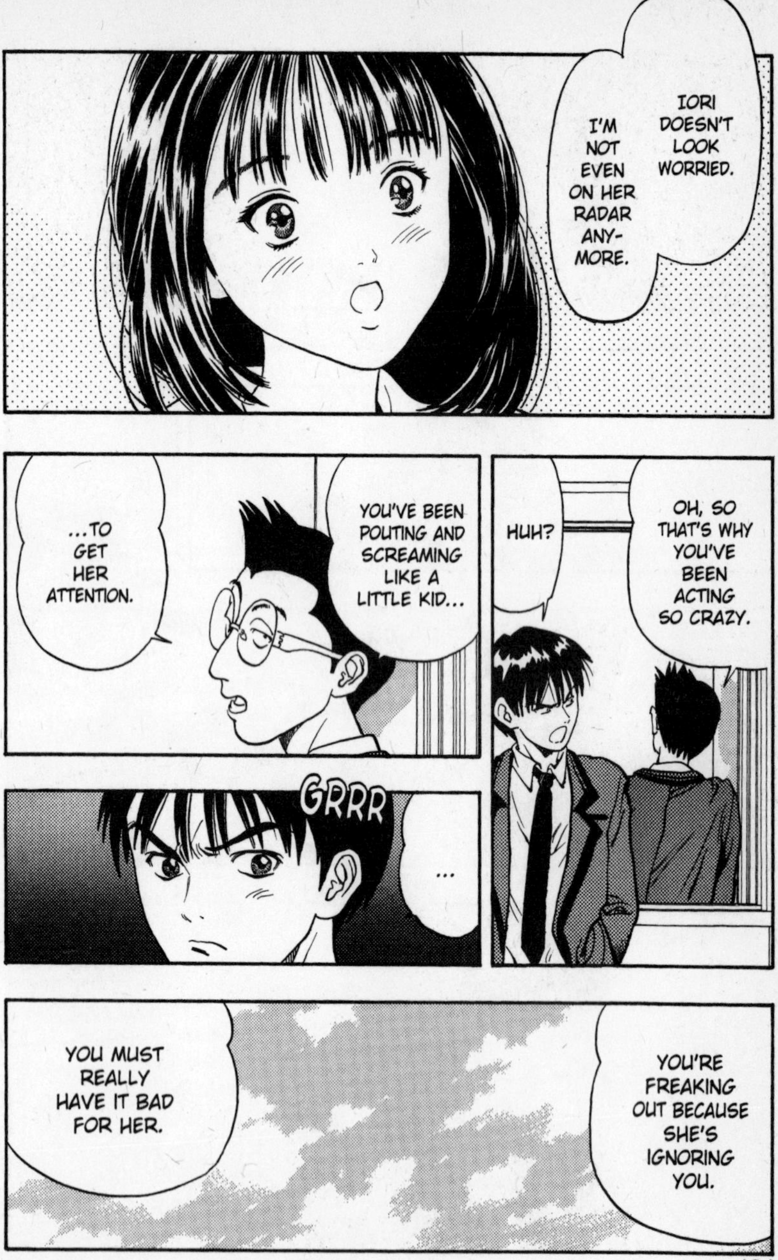
IORI DOESN'T LOOK WORRIED.
I'M NOT EVEN ON HER RADAR ANYMORE.
OH, SO THAT'S WHY YOU'VE BEEN ACTING SO CRAZY.
HUH?
YOU'VE BEEN POUTING AND SCREAMING LIKE A LITTLE KID...
...TO GET HER ATTENTION.
GRRR
...
YOU'RE FREAKING OUT BECAUSE SHE'S IGNORING YOU.
YOU MUST REALLY HAVE IT BAD FOR HER.

READ THIS WAY

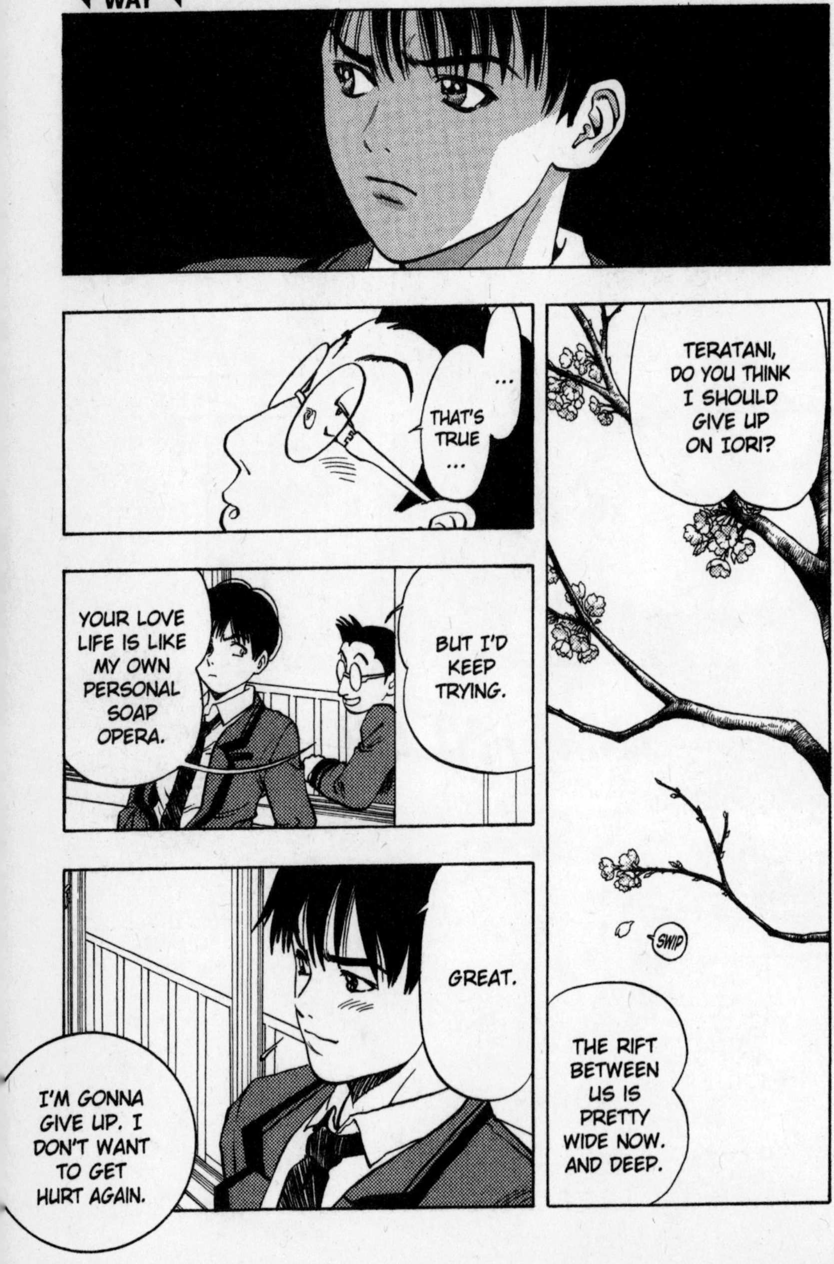

TERATANI, DO YOU THINK I SHOULD GIVE UP ON IORI?
SWIP
THE RIFT BETWEEN US IS PRETTY WIDE NOW. AND DEEP.
...
THAT'S TRUE ...
BUT I'D KEEP TRYING.
YOUR LOVE LIFE IS LIKE MY OWN PERSONAL SOAP OPERA.
GREAT.
I'M GONNA GIVE UP. I DON'T WANT TO GET HURT AGAIN.

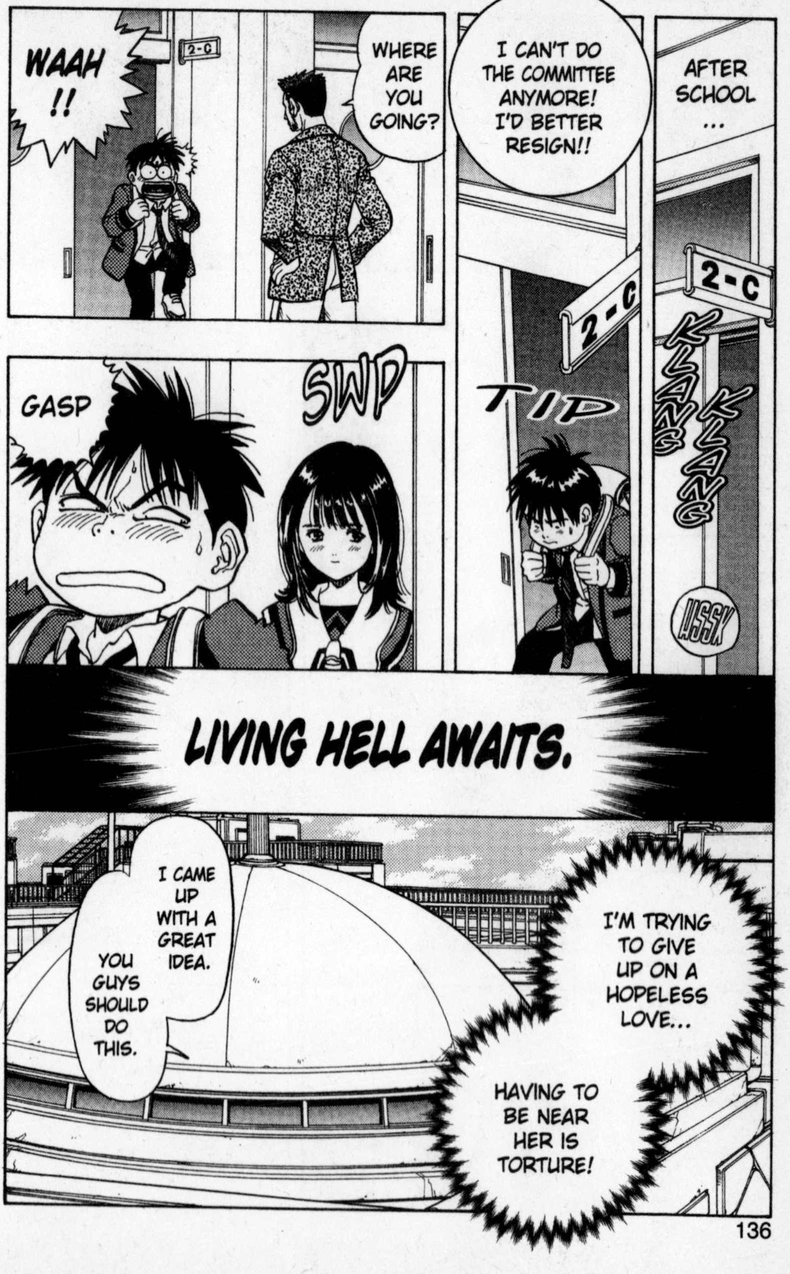
AFTER SCHOOL ...
KLANG KLANG
HSSK
I CAN'T DO THE COMMITTEE ANYMORE! I'D BETTER RESIGN!!
TIP
WHERE ARE YOU GOING?
WAAH !!
SWP
GASP
LIVING HELL AWAITS.
I'M TRYING TO GIVE UP ON A HOPELESS LOVE...
HAVING TO BE NEAR HER IS TORTURE!
I CAME UP WITH A GREAT IDEA.
YOU GUYS SHOULD DO THIS.

READ THIS WAY

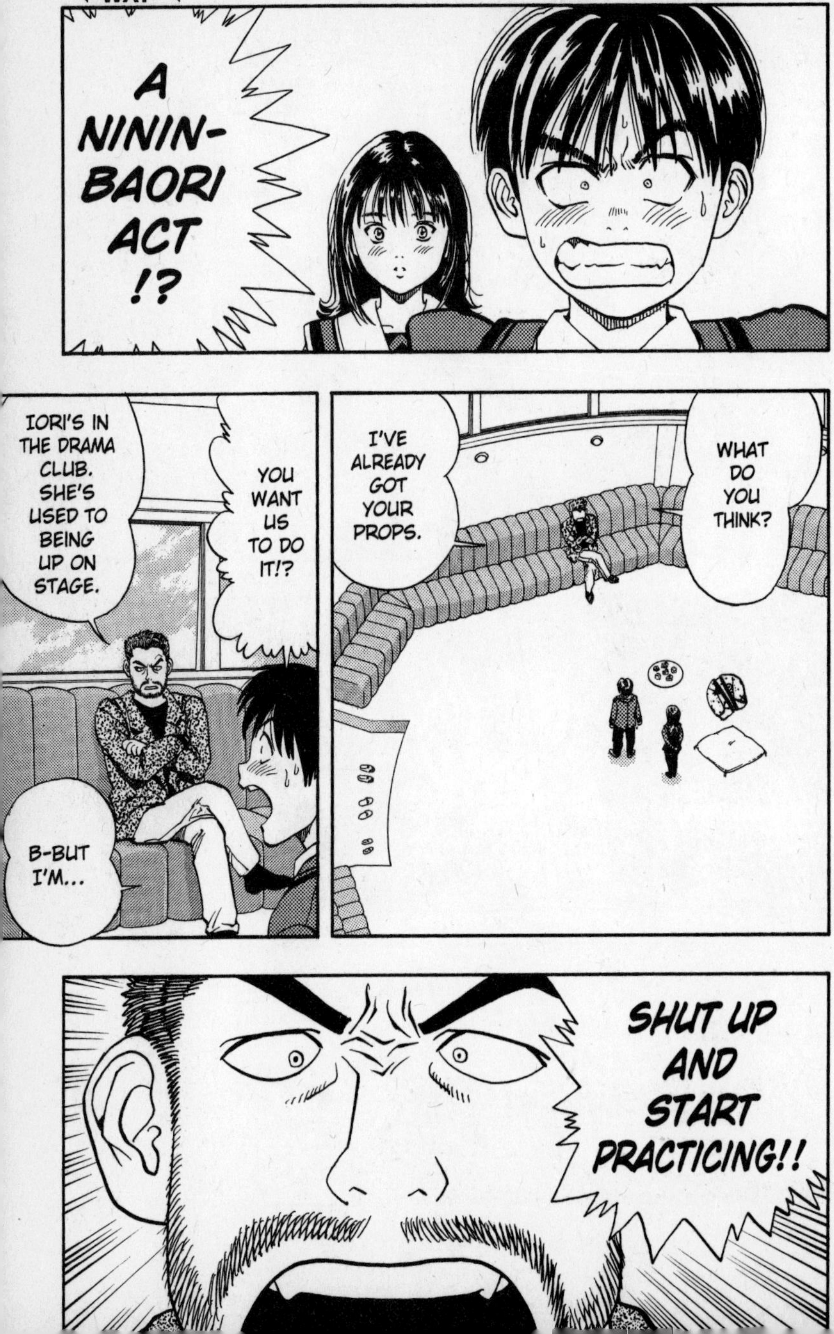
A NININ-BAORI ACT !?
WHAT DO YOU THINK?
I'VE ALREADY GOT YOUR PROPS.
YOU WANT US TO DO IT!?
IORI'S IN THE DRAMA CLUB. SHE'S USED TO BEING UP ON STAGE.
B-BUT I'M...
SHUT UP AND START PRACTICING!!

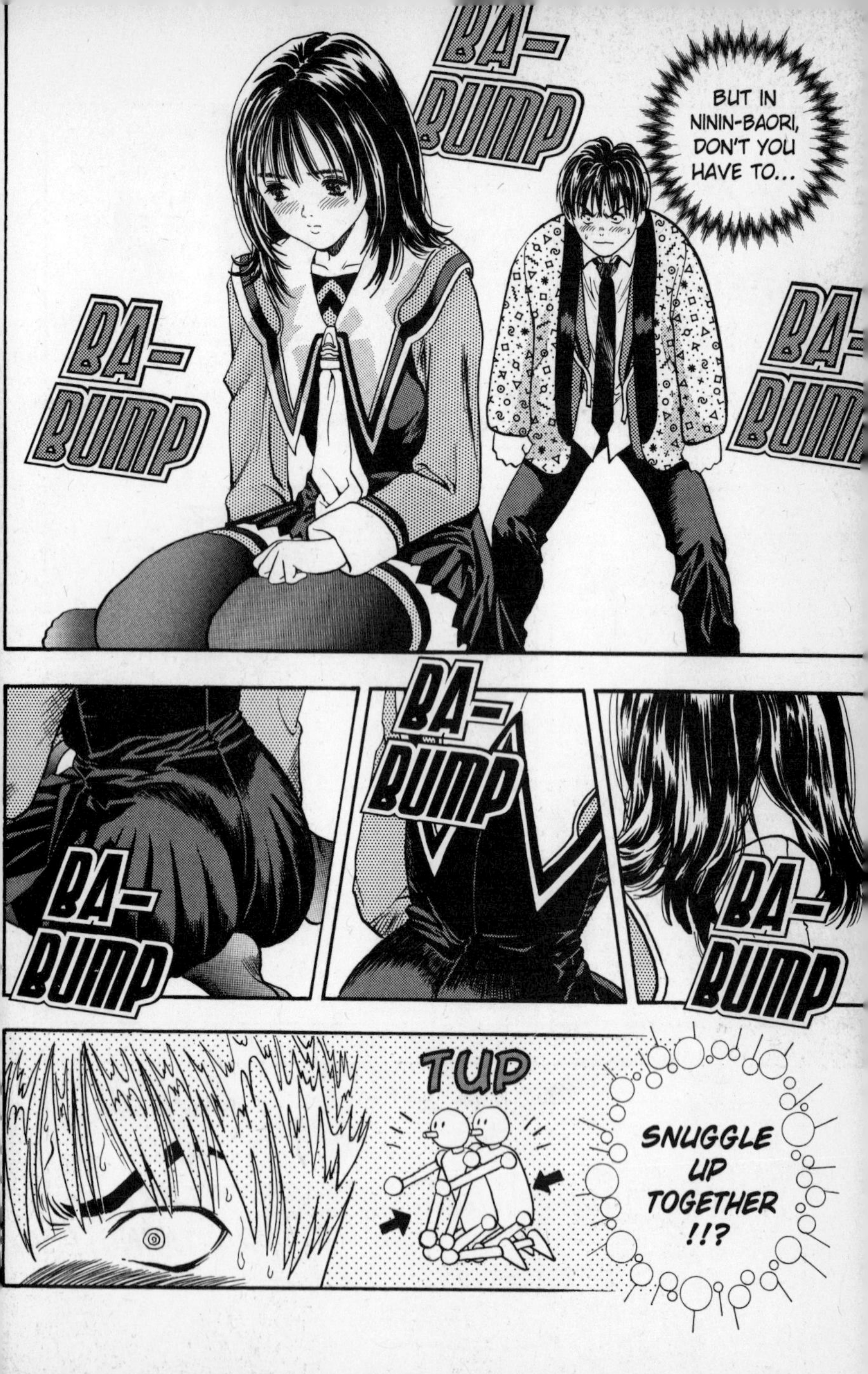
BA-BUMP
BUT IN NININ-BAORI, DON'T YOU HAVE TO...
BA-BUM
BA-BUMP
BA-BUMP
BA-BUMP
BA-BUMP
SNUGGLE UP TOGETHER !!?
TUP

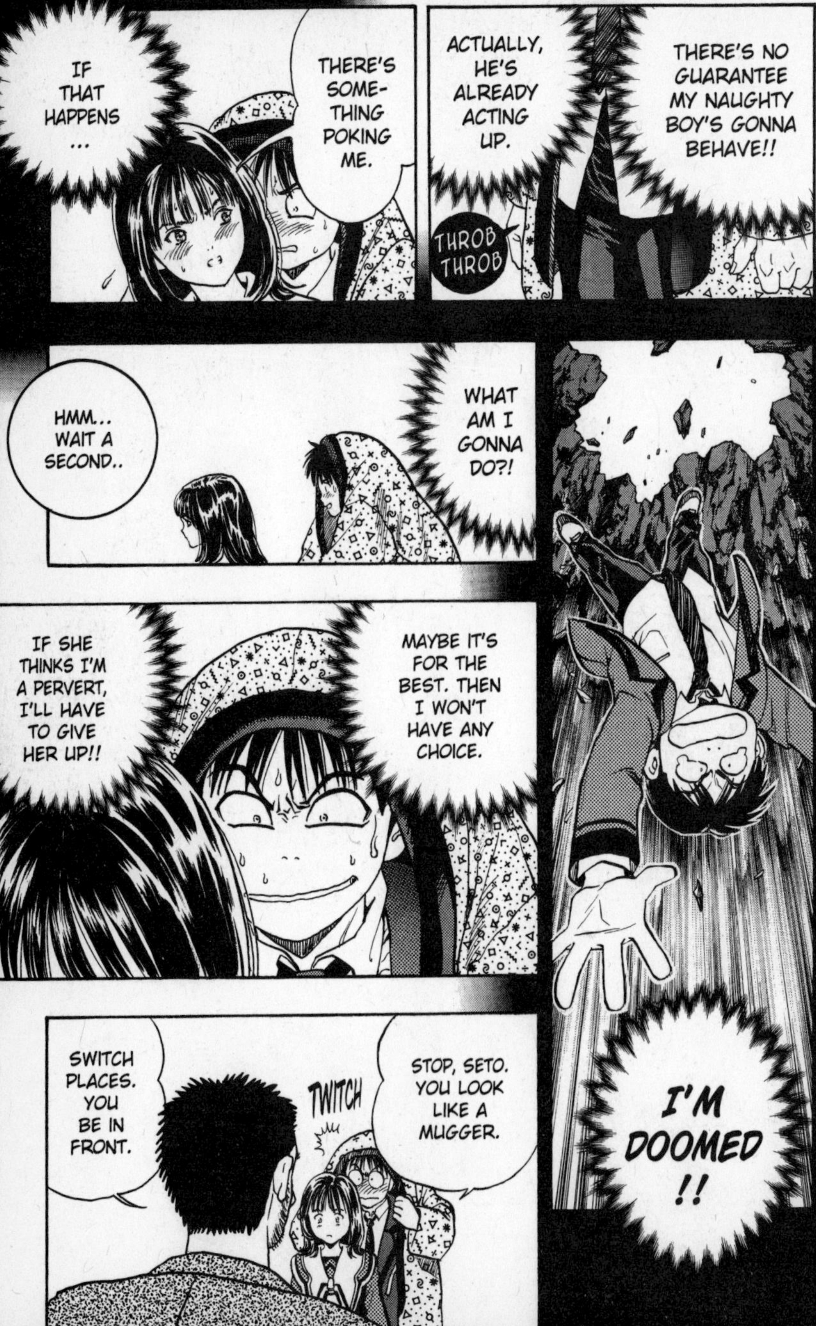
THERE'S NO GUARANTEE MY NAUGHTY BOY'S GONNA BEHAVE!!
ACTUALLY, HE'S ALREADY ACTING UP.
THROB THROB
THERE'S SOME-THING POKING ME.
IF THAT HAPPENS ...
I'M DOOMED !!
WHAT AM I GONNA DO?!
HMM... WAIT A SECOND..
MAYBE IT'S FOR THE BEST. THEN I WON'T HAVE ANY CHOICE.
IF SHE THINKS I'M A PERVERT, I'LL HAVE TO GIVE HER UP!!
STOP, SETO. YOU LOOK LIKE A MUGGER.
TWITCH
SWITCH PLACES. YOU BE IN FRONT.

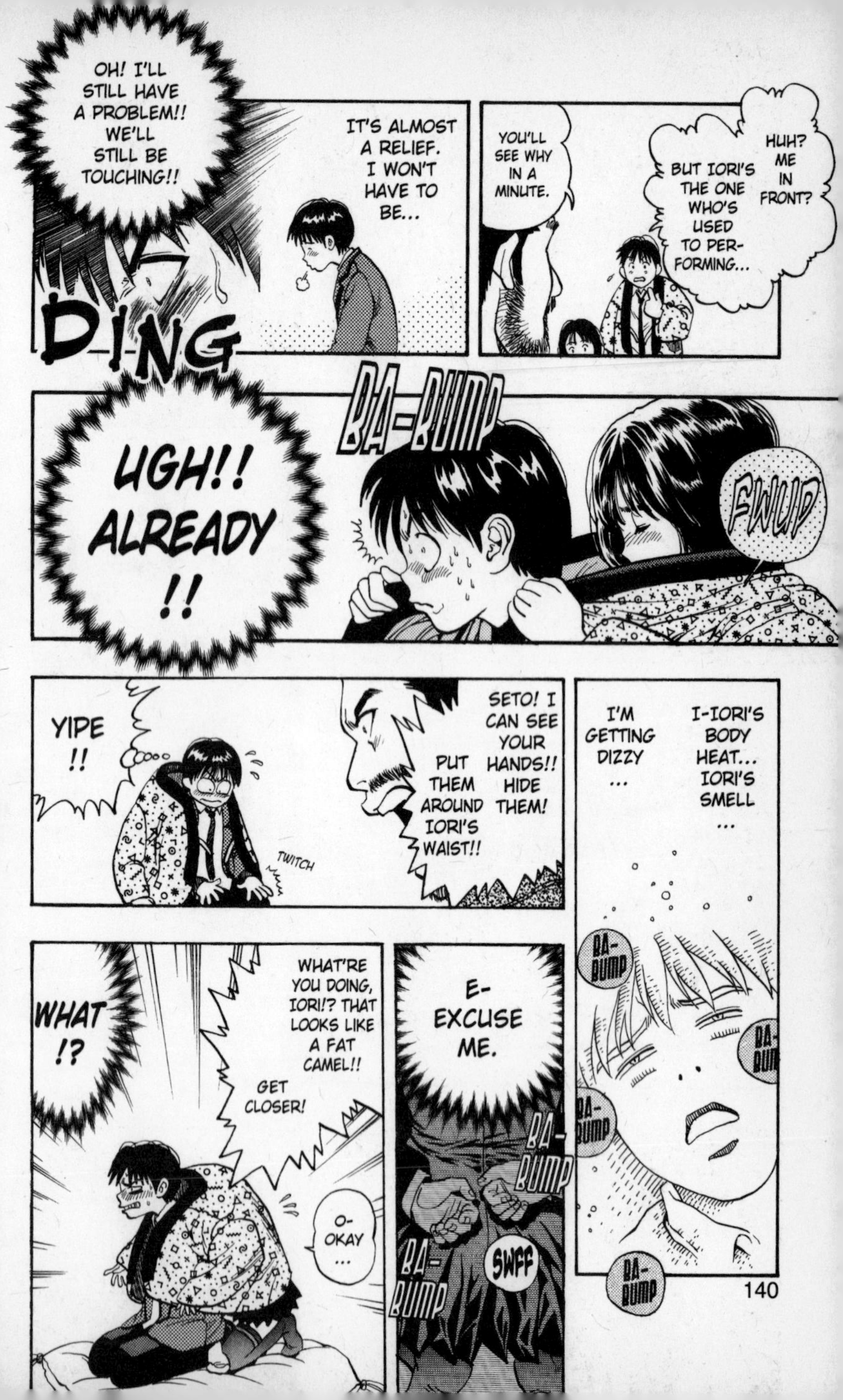
HUH? ME IN FRONT?
BUT IORI'S THE ONE WHO'S USED TO PER-FORMING...
YOU'LL SEE WHY IN A MINUTE.
IT'S ALMOST A RELIEF. I WON'T HAVE TO BE...
OH! I'LL STILL HAVE A PROBLEM!! WE'LL STILL BE TOUCHING!!
DING
FWUP
BA-BUMP
UGH!! ALREADY !!
I-IORI'S BODY HEAT... IORI'S SMELL ...
I'M GETTING DIZZY ...
BA-BUMP
BA-BUMP
BA-BUMP
BA-BUMP
SETO! I CAN SEE YOUR HANDS!! HIDE THEM!
PUT THEM AROUND IORI'S WAIST!!
YIPE !!
TWITCH
E-EXCUSE ME.
BA-BUMP
SWFF
BA-BUMP
WHAT'RE YOU DOING, IORI!? THAT LOOKS LIKE A FAT CAMEL!!
GET CLOSER!
WHAT !?
O-OKAY ...

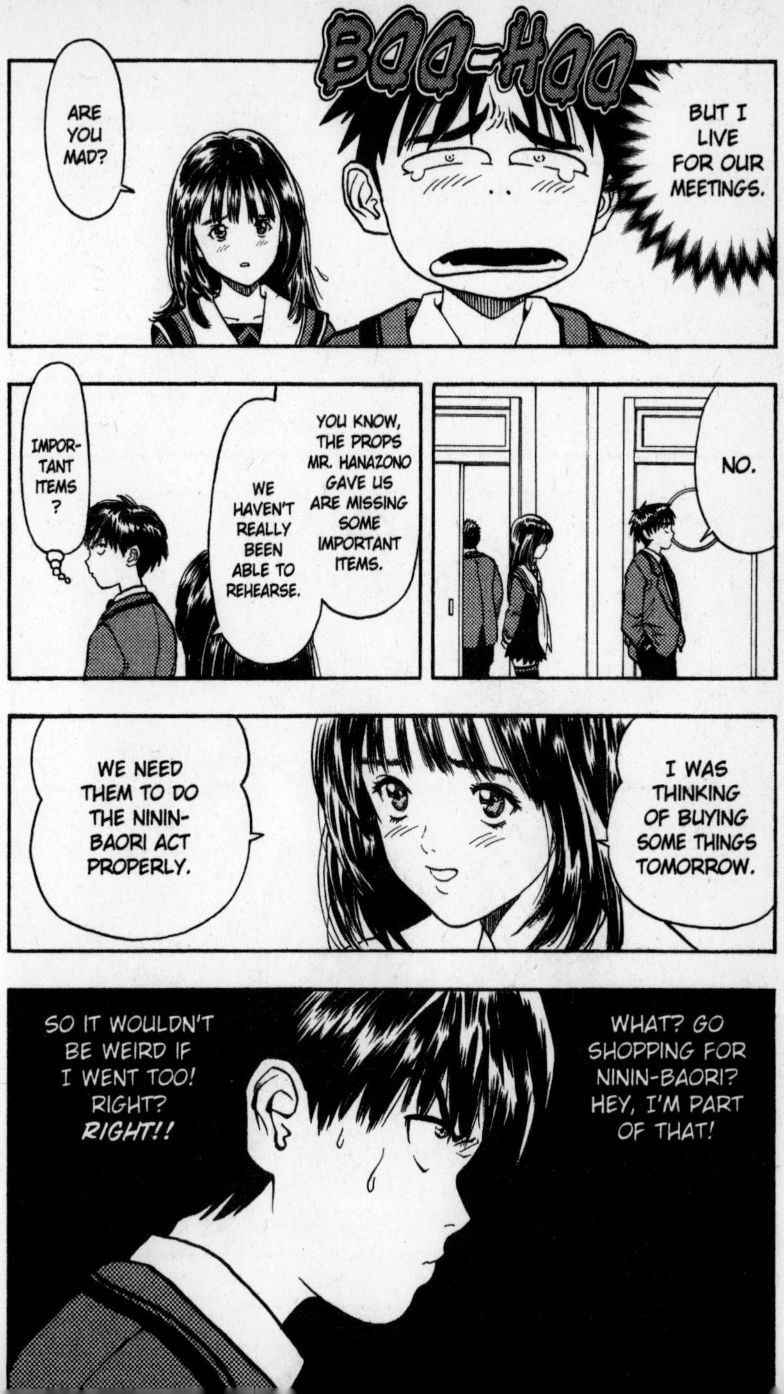
BOO-HOO
BUT I LIVE FOR OUR MEETINGS.
ARE YOU MAD?
NO.
YOU KNOW, THE PROPS MR. HANAZONO GAVE US ARE MISSING SOME IMPORTANT ITEMS.
WE HAVEN'T REALLY BEEN ABLE TO REHEARSE.
IMPOR-TANT ITEMS?
I WAS THINKING OF BUYING SOME THINGS TOMORROW.
WE NEED THEM TO DO THE NININ-BAORI ACT PROPERLY.
WHAT? GO SHOPPING FOR NININ-BAORI? HEY, I'M PART OF THAT!
SO IT WOULDN'T BE WEIRD IF I WENT TOO! RIGHT? *RIGHT!!*

READ THIS WAY

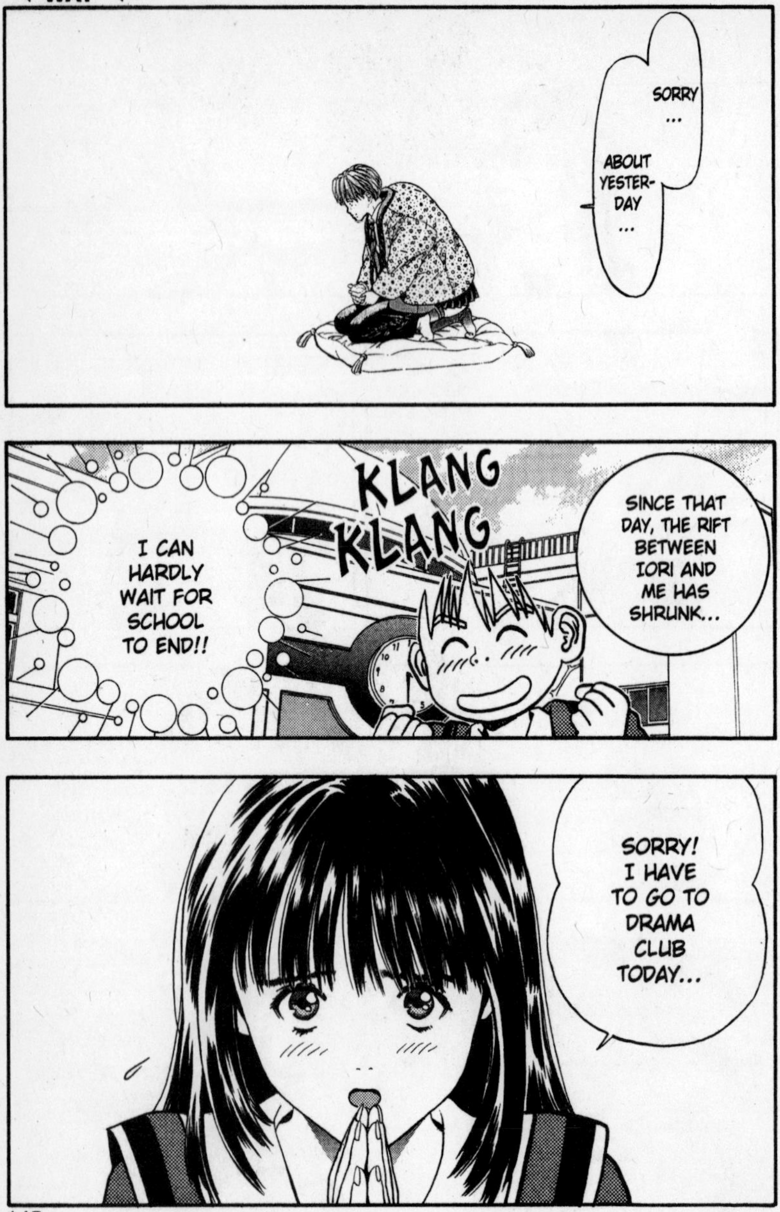
SORRY ... ABOUT YESTER-DAY ...
SINCE THAT DAY, THE RIFT BETWEEN IORI AND ME HAS SHRUNK...
KLANG KLANG
I CAN HARDLY WAIT FOR SCHOOL TO END!!
SORRY! I HAVE TO GO TO DRAMA CLUB TODAY...

Chapter 6:
Wildest Dreams

READ THIS WAY

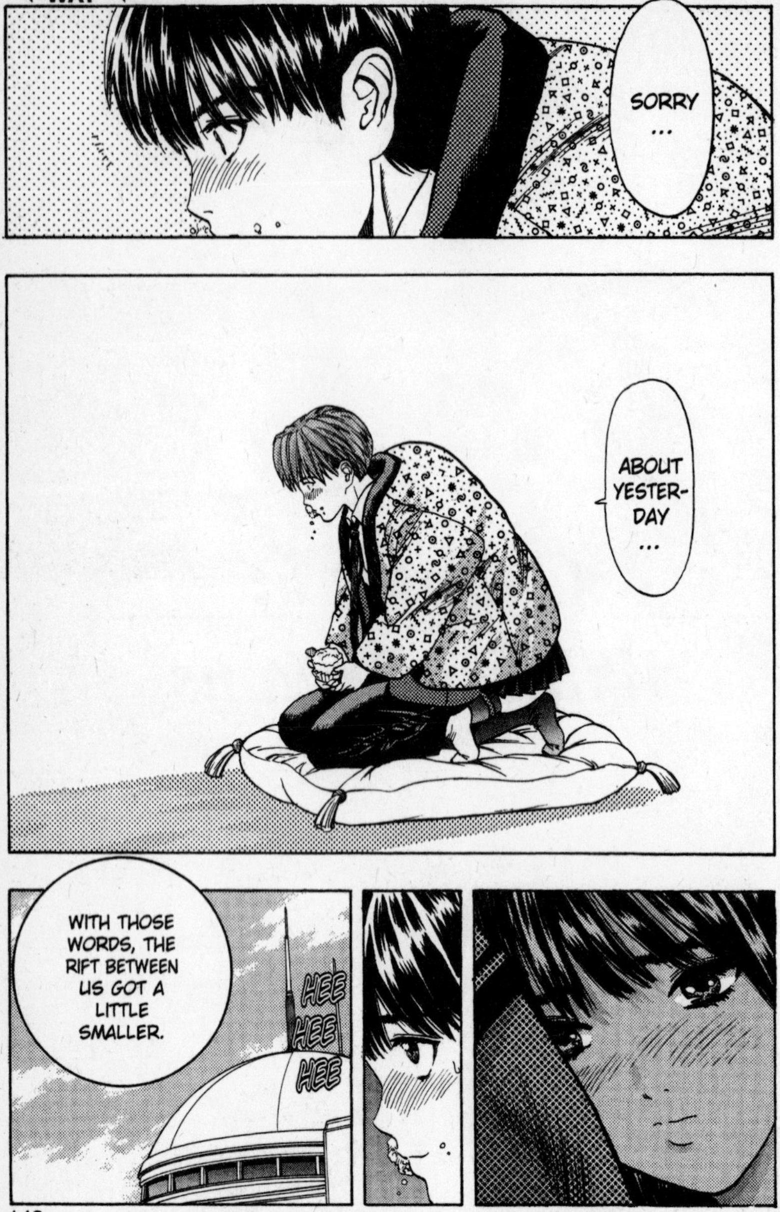
SORRY ...
ABOUT YESTER-DAY ...
WITH THOSE WORDS, THE RIFT BETWEEN US GOT A LITTLE SMALLER.
HEE HEE HEE

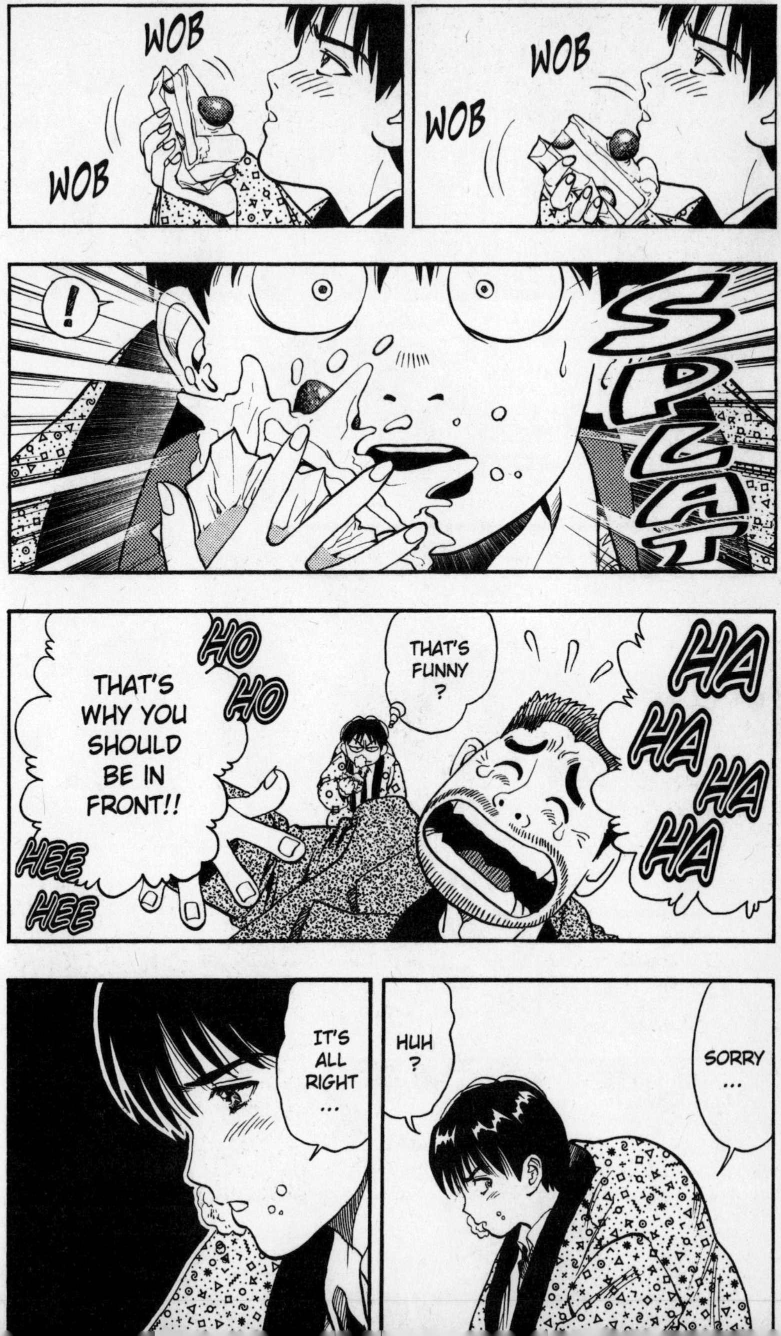
WOB
WOB
WOB
WOB
SPLAT
!
HA HA HA HA HA
THAT'S FUNNY ?
HO HO
THAT'S WHY YOU SHOULD BE IN FRONT!!
HEE HEE
SORRY ...
HUH ?
IT'S ALL RIGHT ...

READ THIS WAY

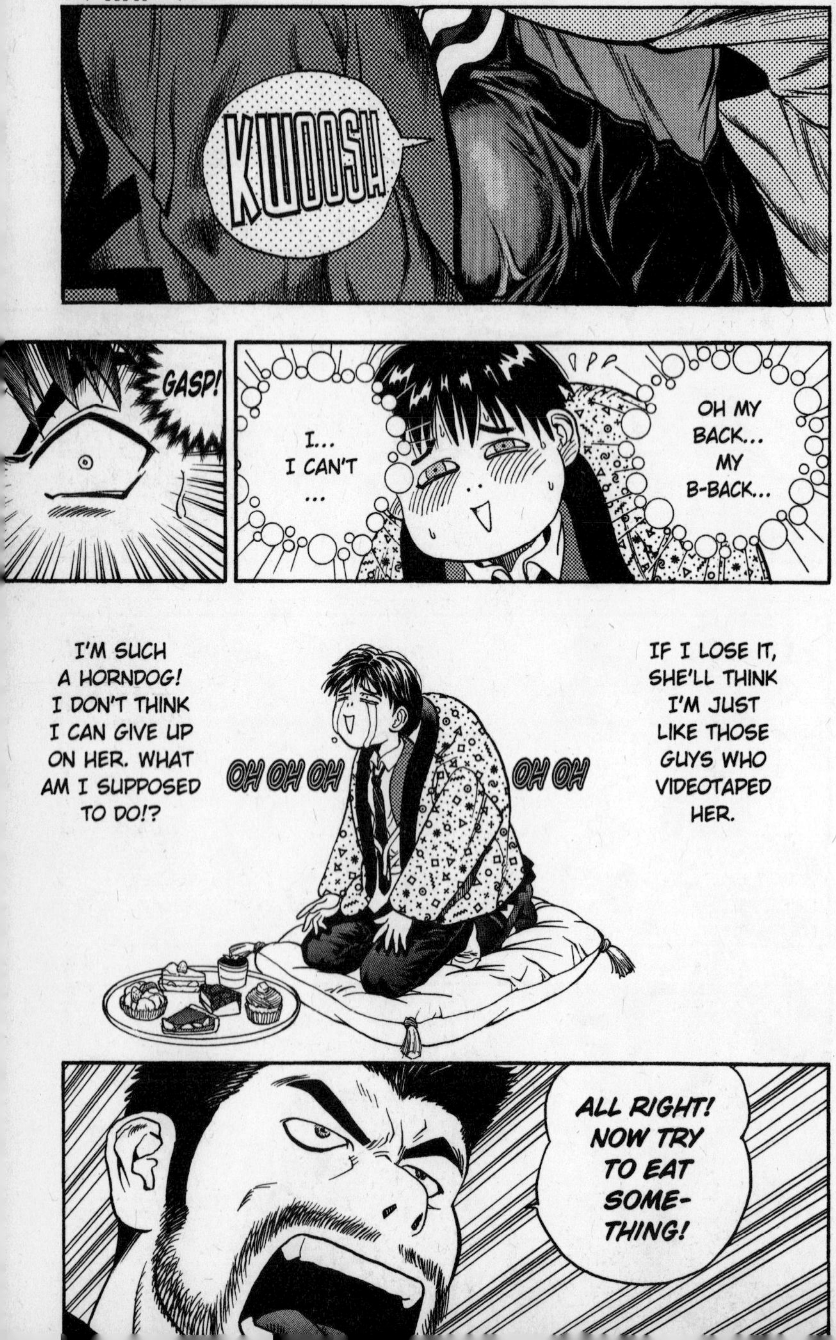
KWOOSH
OH MY BACK... MY B-BACK...
I... I CAN'T ...
GASP!
IF I LOSE IT, SHE'LL THINK I'M JUST LIKE THOSE GUYS WHO VIDEOTAPED HER.
OH OH
OH OH OH
I'M SUCH A HORNDOG! I DON'T THINK I CAN GIVE UP ON HER. WHAT AM I SUPPOSED TO DO!?
ALL RIGHT! NOW TRY TO EAT SOME-THING!

READ THIS WAY

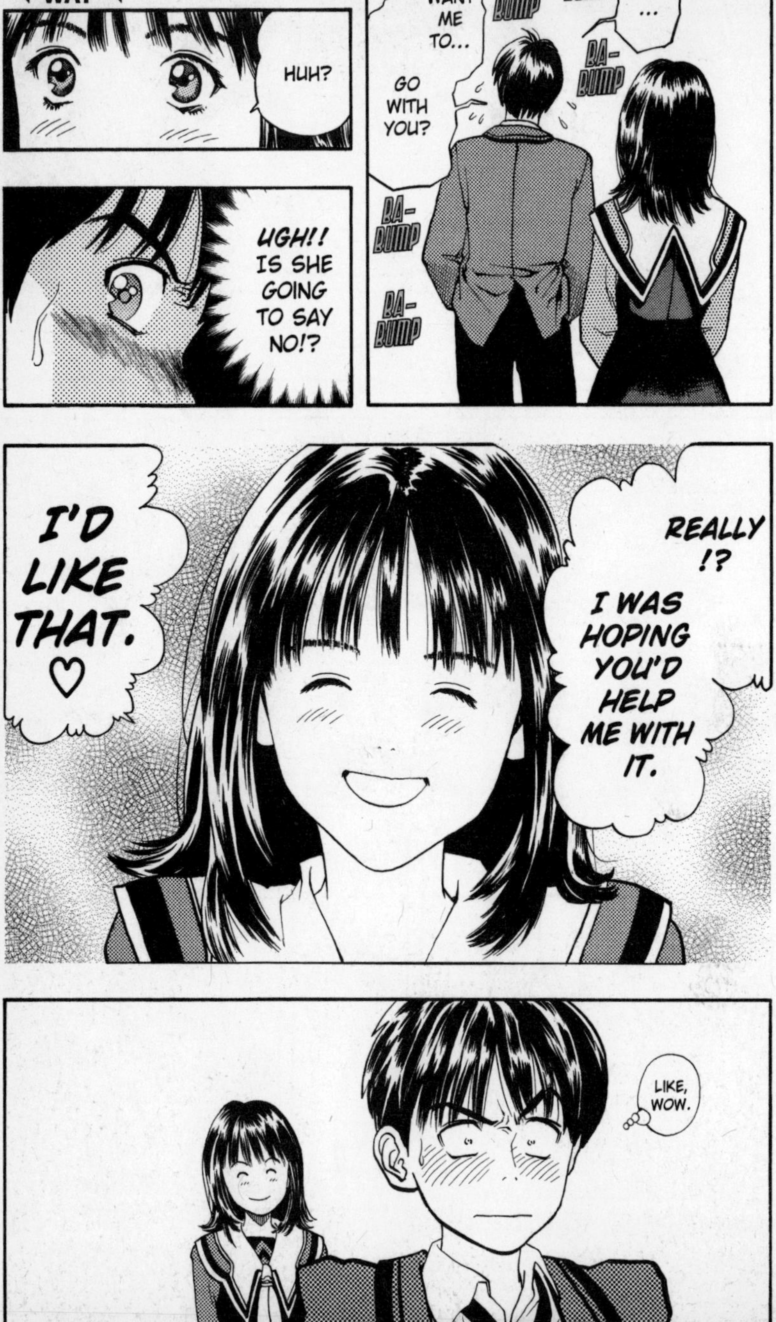

WA ...
BA-BUMP
BA-BUMP
WANT ME TO... GO WITH YOU?
BA-BUMP
BA-BUMP
BA-BUMP
HUH?
UGH!! IS SHE GOING TO SAY NO!?
REALLY!? I WAS HOPING YOU'D HELP ME WITH IT.
I'D LIKE THAT. ♡
LIKE, WOW.

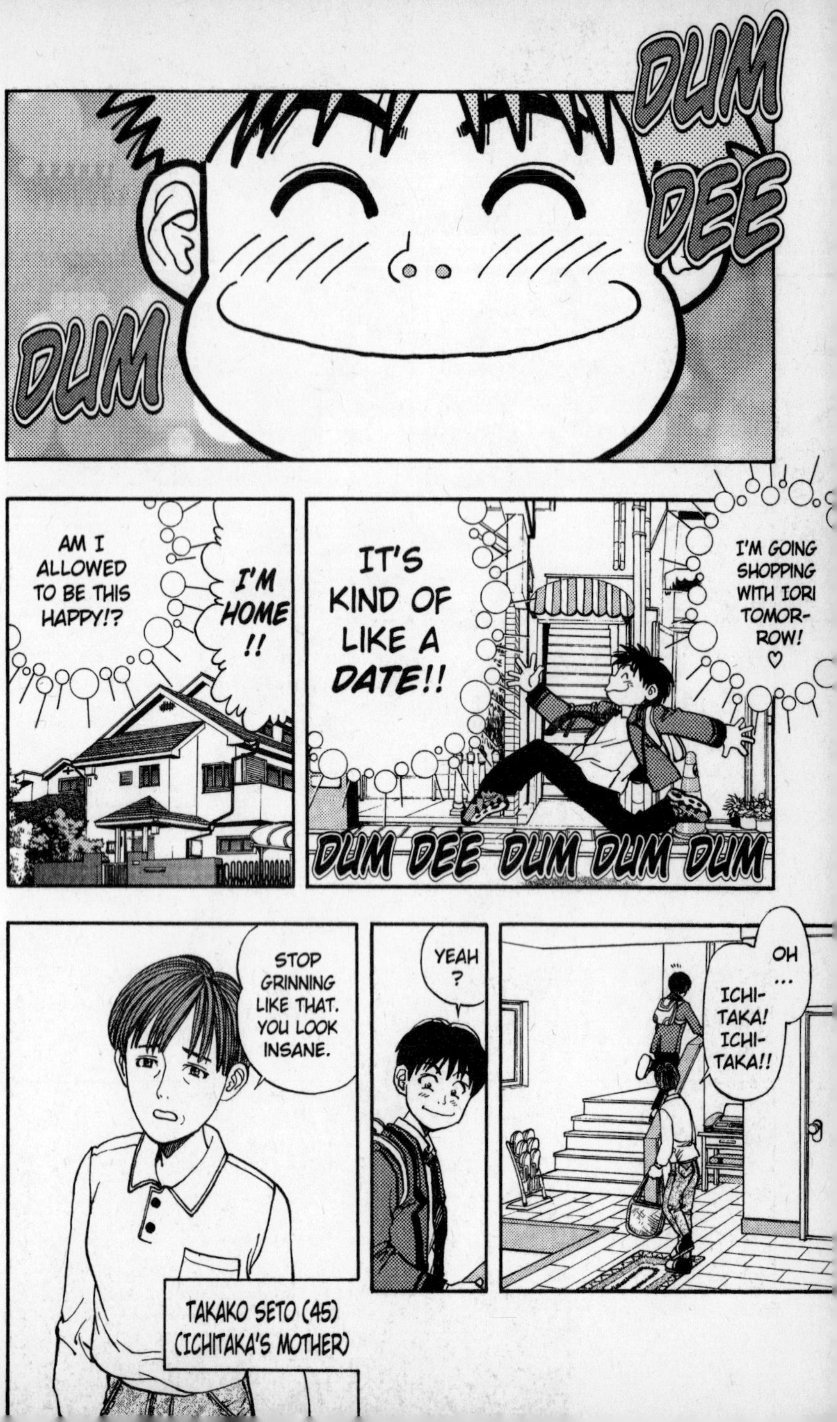
DUM DEE
DUM
I'M GOING SHOPPING WITH IORI TOMOR-ROW! ♡
IT'S KIND OF LIKE A DATE!!
DUM DEE DUM DUM DUM
I'M HOME !!
AM I ALLOWED TO BE THIS HAPPY!?
OH ... ICHI-TAKA! ICHI-TAKA!!
YEAH ?
STOP GRINNING LIKE THAT. YOU LOOK INSANE.
TAKAKO SETO (45) (ICHITAKA'S MOTHER)

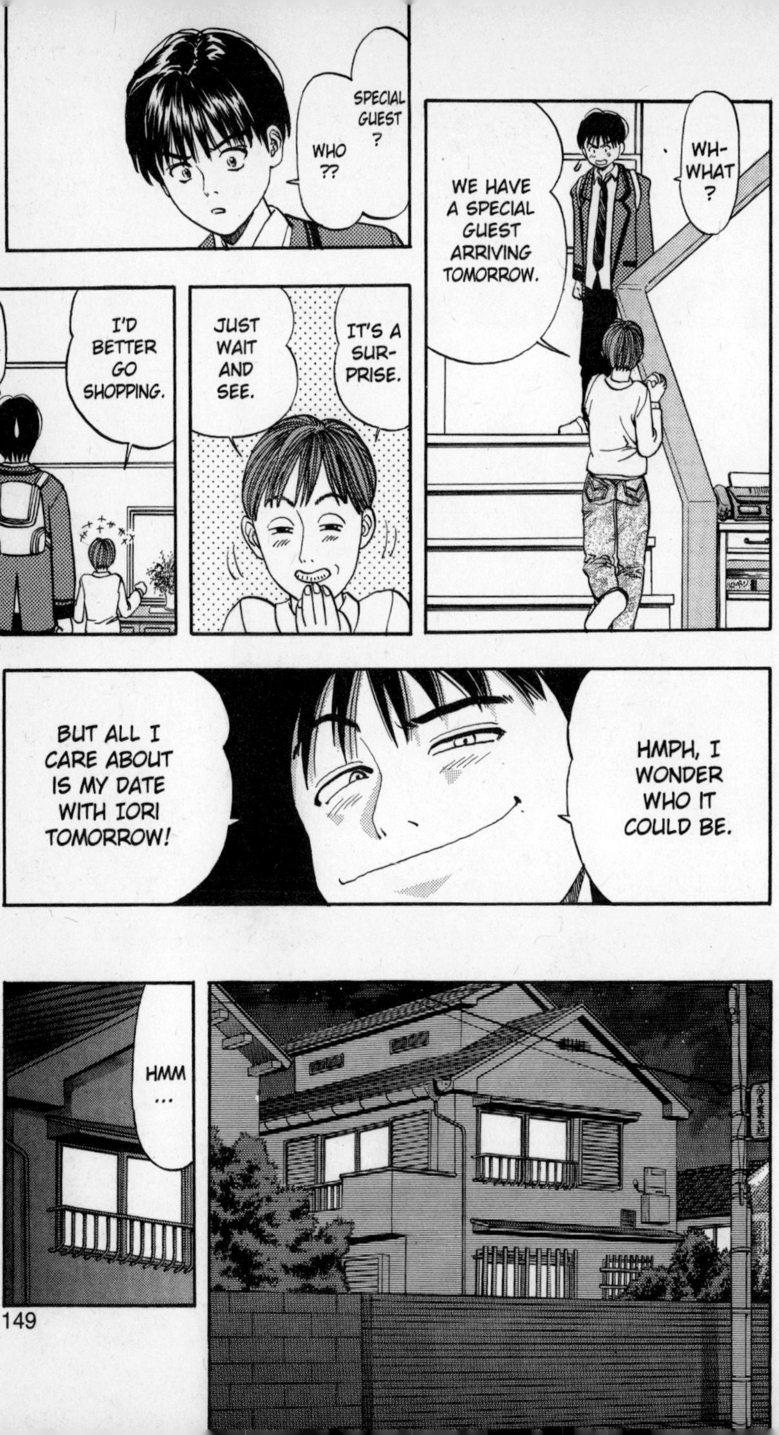
WH-WHAT?
WE HAVE A SPECIAL GUEST ARRIVING TOMORROW.
SPECIAL GUEST?
WHO??
IT'S A SURPRISE.
JUST WAIT AND SEE.
I'D BETTER GO SHOPPING.
...
HMPH, I WONDER WHO IT COULD BE.
BUT ALL I CARE ABOUT IS MY DATE WITH IORI TOMORROW!
HMM...

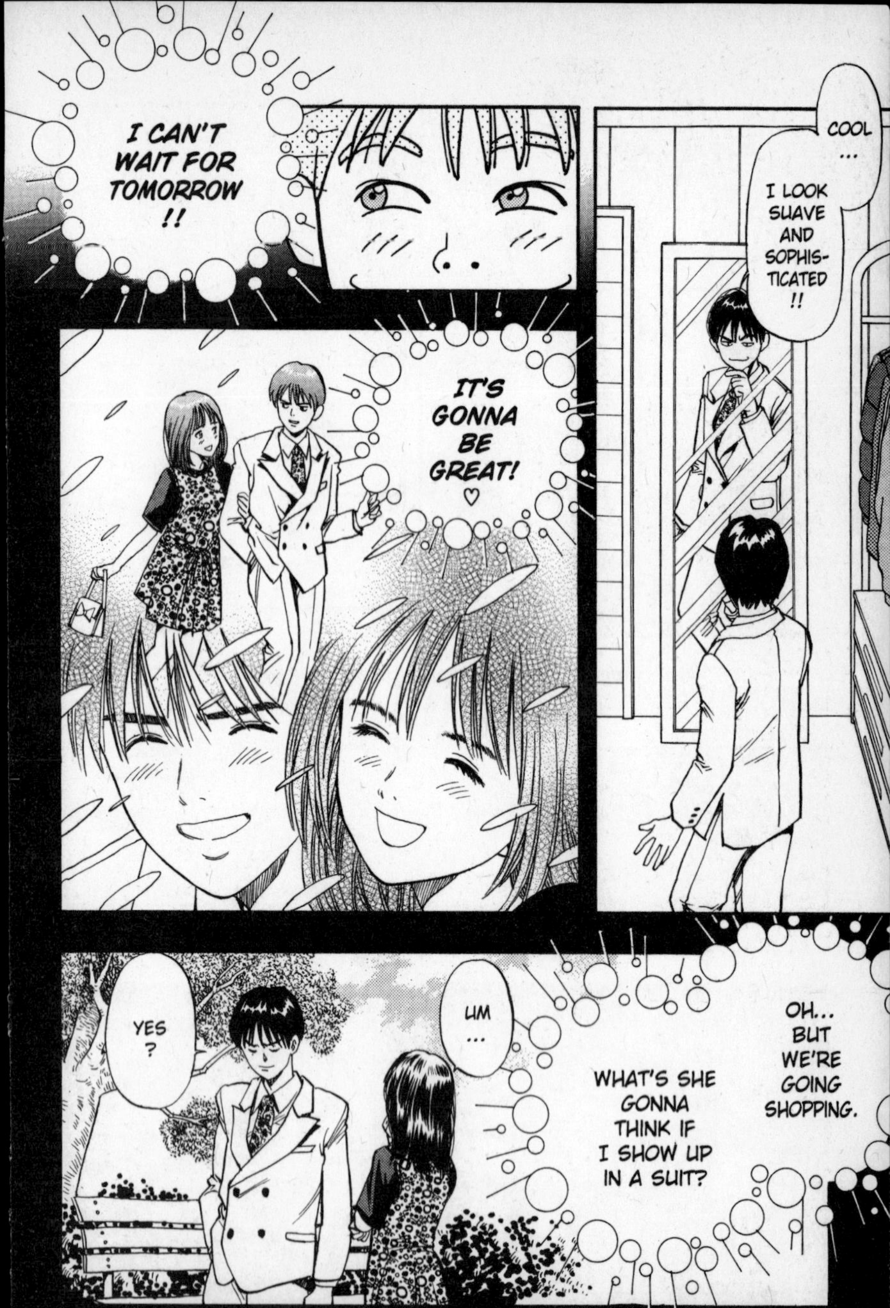
COOL ...
I LOOK SUAVE AND SOPHIS-TICATED !!
I CAN'T WAIT FOR TOMORROW !!
IT'S GONNA BE GREAT! ♡
OH... BUT WE'RE GOING SHOPPING.
WHAT'S SHE GONNA THINK IF I SHOW UP IN A SUIT?
UM ...
YES ?

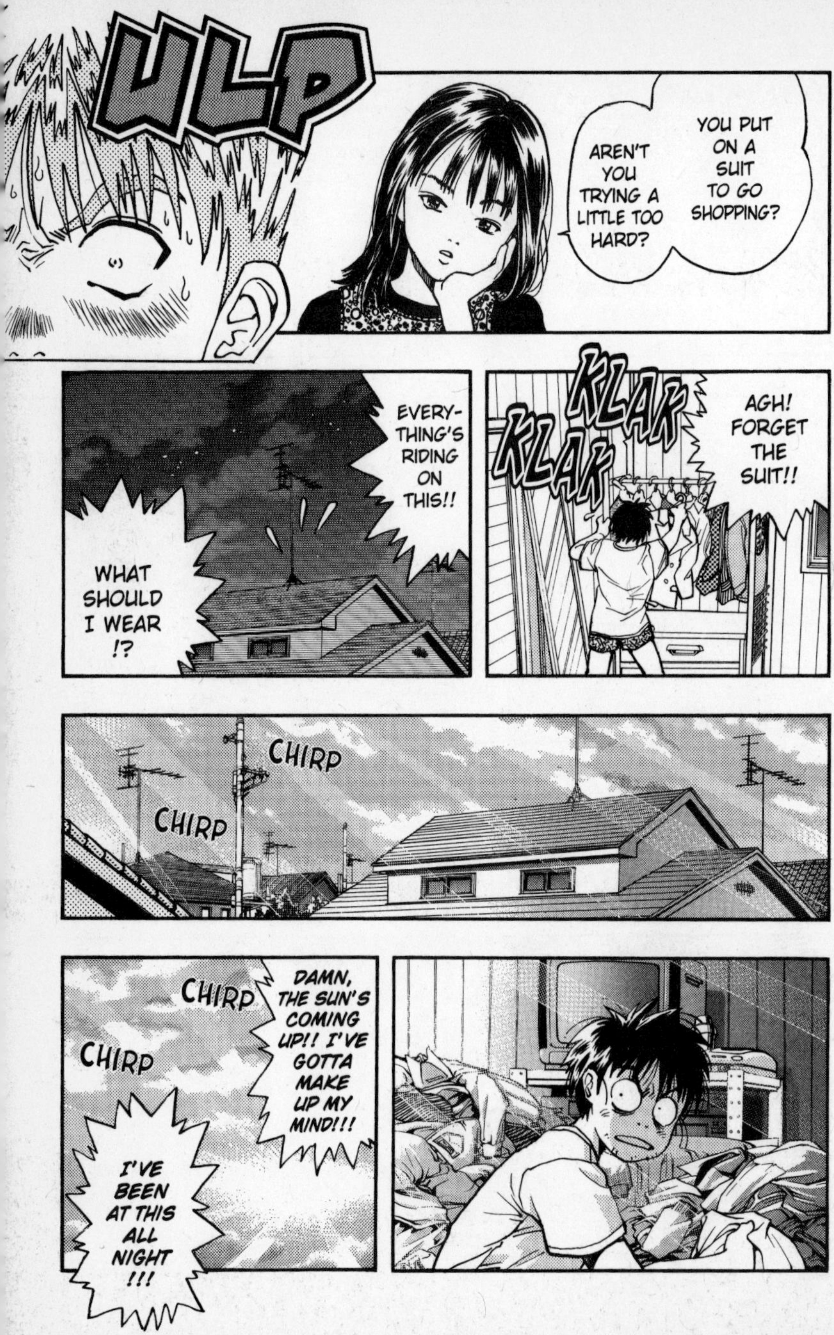
YOU PUT ON A SUIT TO GO SHOPPING?
AREN'T YOU TRYING A LITTLE TOO HARD?
ULP
KLAK
KLAK
AGH! FORGET THE SUIT!!
EVERY-THING'S RIDING ON THIS!!
WHAT SHOULD I WEAR !?
CHIRP
CHIRP
DAMN, THE SUN'S COMING UP!! I'VE GOTTA MAKE UP MY MIND!!!
CHIRP
CHIRP
I'VE BEEN AT THIS ALL NIGHT !!!

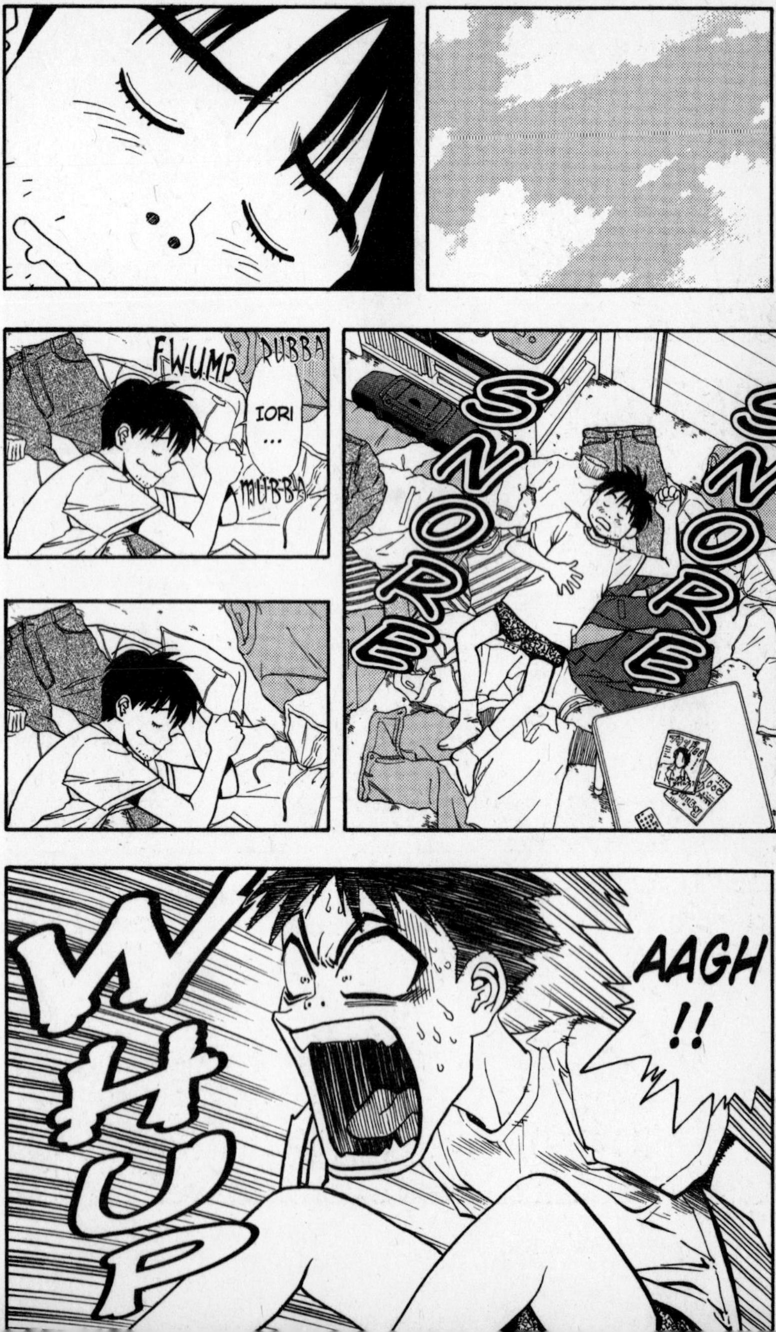
SNORE
SNORE
DUBBA
FWUMP
IORI...
MUBBA
AAGH!!
WHUP

READ THIS WAY

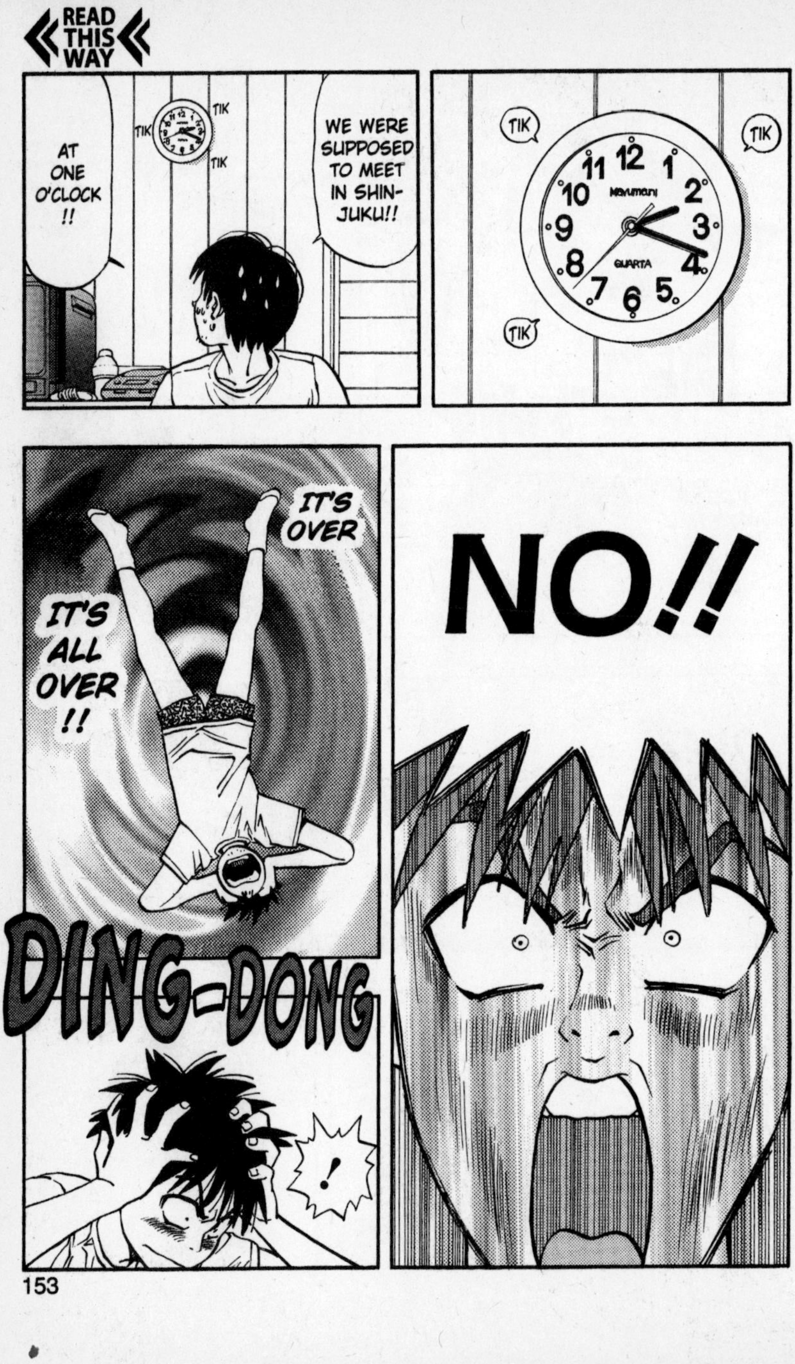

TIK
TIK
TIK
WE WERE SUPPOSED TO MEET IN SHIN-JUKU!!
TIK
TIK
TIK
AT ONE O'CLOCK !!
NO!!
IT'S OVER
IT'S ALL OVER !!
DING-DONG
!

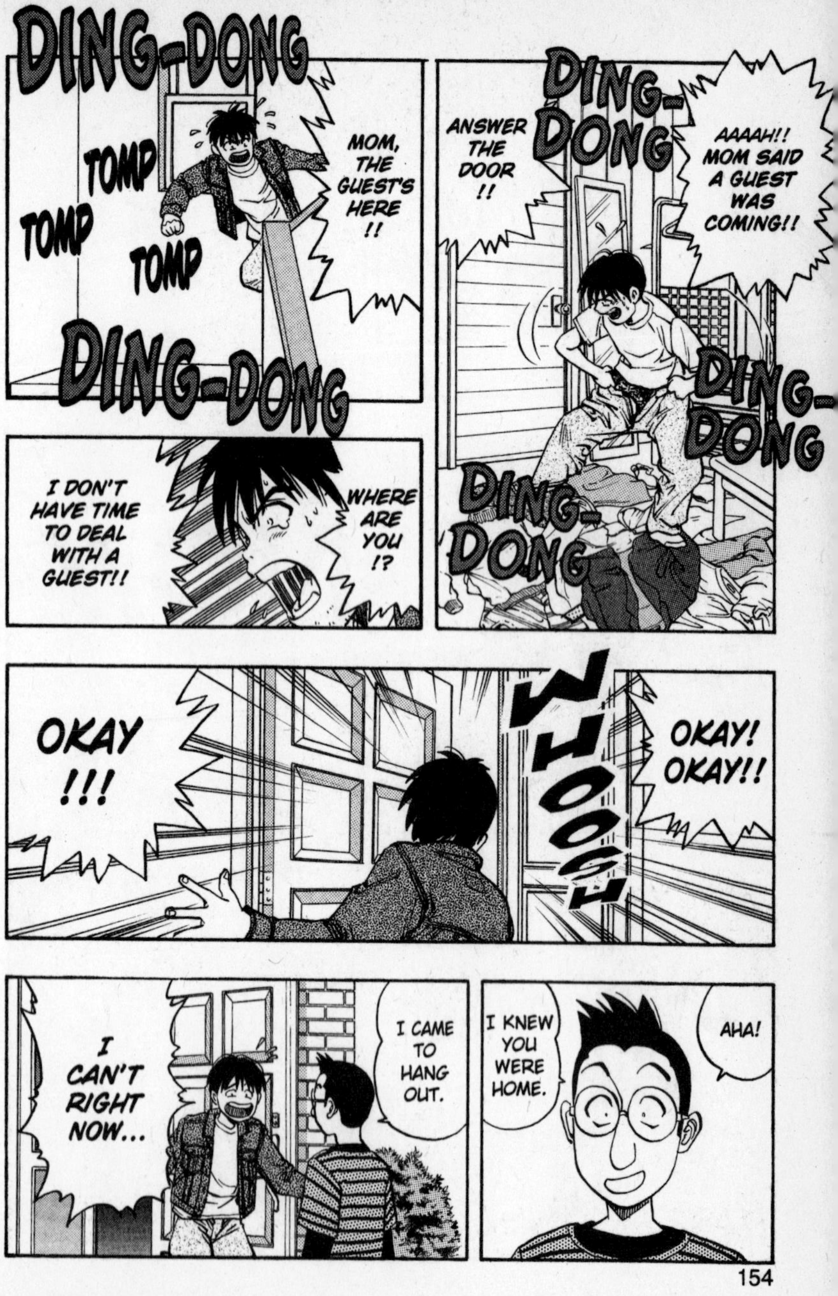

DING-DONG
AAAAH!! MOM SAID A GUEST WAS COMING!!
ANSWER THE DOOR!!
DING-DONG
DING-DONG
DING-DONG
MOM, THE GUEST'S HERE!!
TOMP
TOMP
TOMP
DING-DONG
DING-DONG
WHERE ARE YOU!?
I DON'T HAVE TIME TO DEAL WITH A GUEST!!
OKAY! OKAY!!
WHOOSH
OKAY!!!
AHA!
I KNEW YOU WERE HOME.
I CAME TO HANG OUT.
I CAN'T RIGHT NOW...

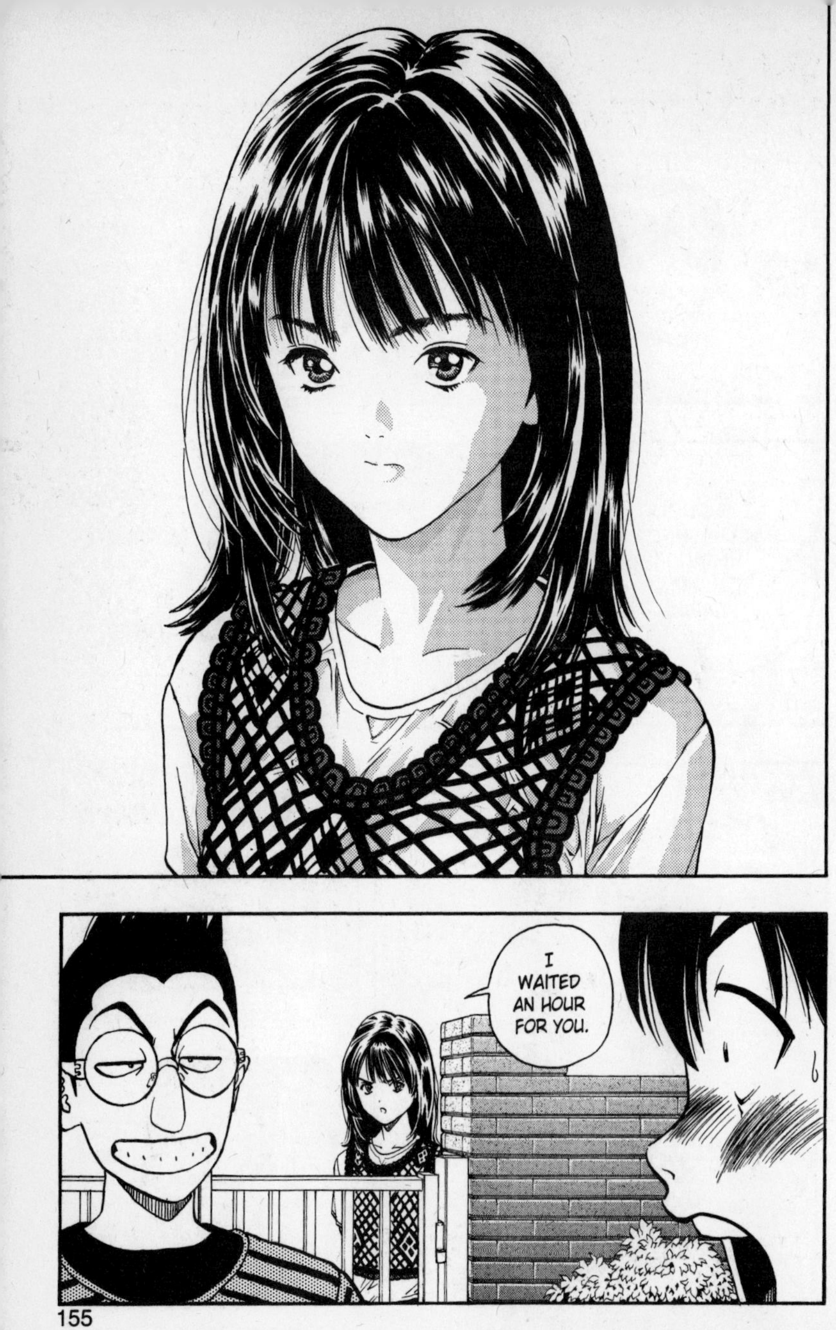
I WAITED AN HOUR FOR YOU.

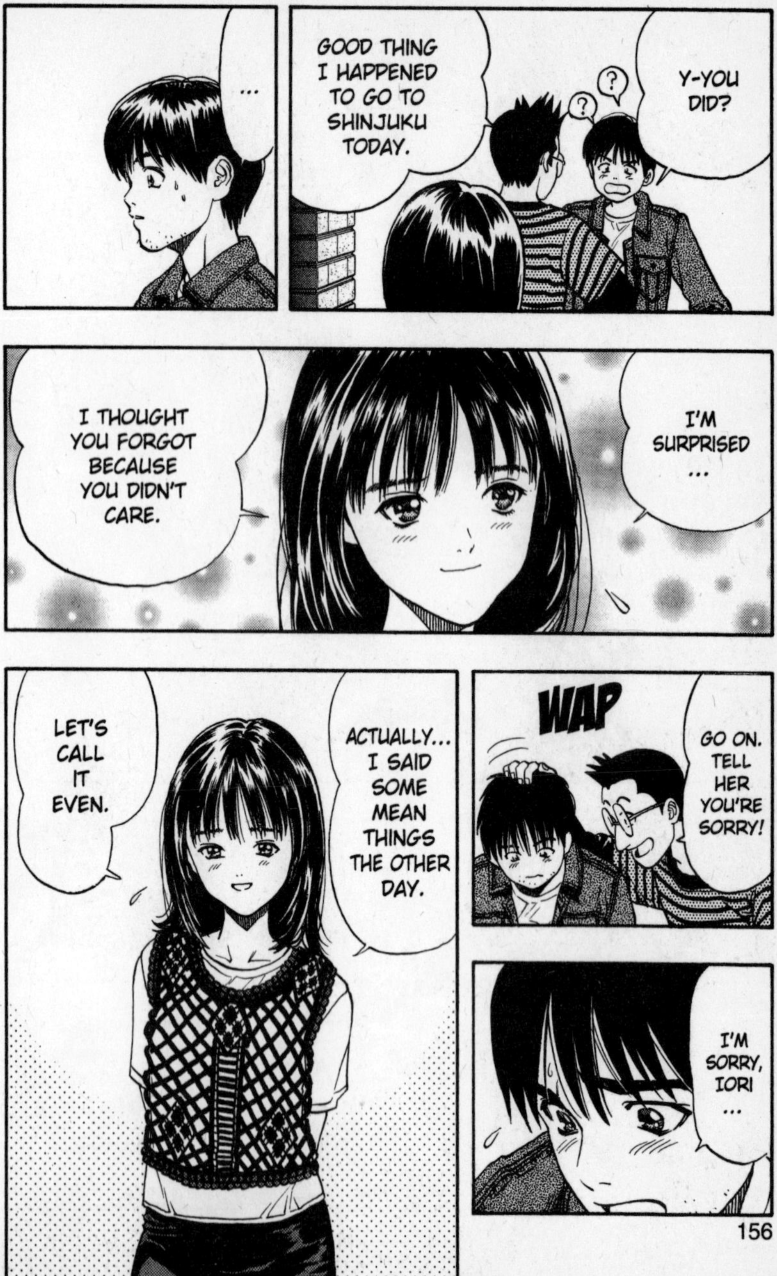
Y-YOU DID?
GOOD THING I HAPPENED TO GO TO SHINJUKU TODAY.
...
I'M SURPRISED ...
I THOUGHT YOU FORGOT BECAUSE YOU DIDN'T CARE.
WAP
GO ON. TELL HER YOU'RE SORRY!
I'M SORRY, IORI ...
ACTUALLY... I SAID SOME MEAN THINGS THE OTHER DAY.
LET'S CALL IT EVEN.

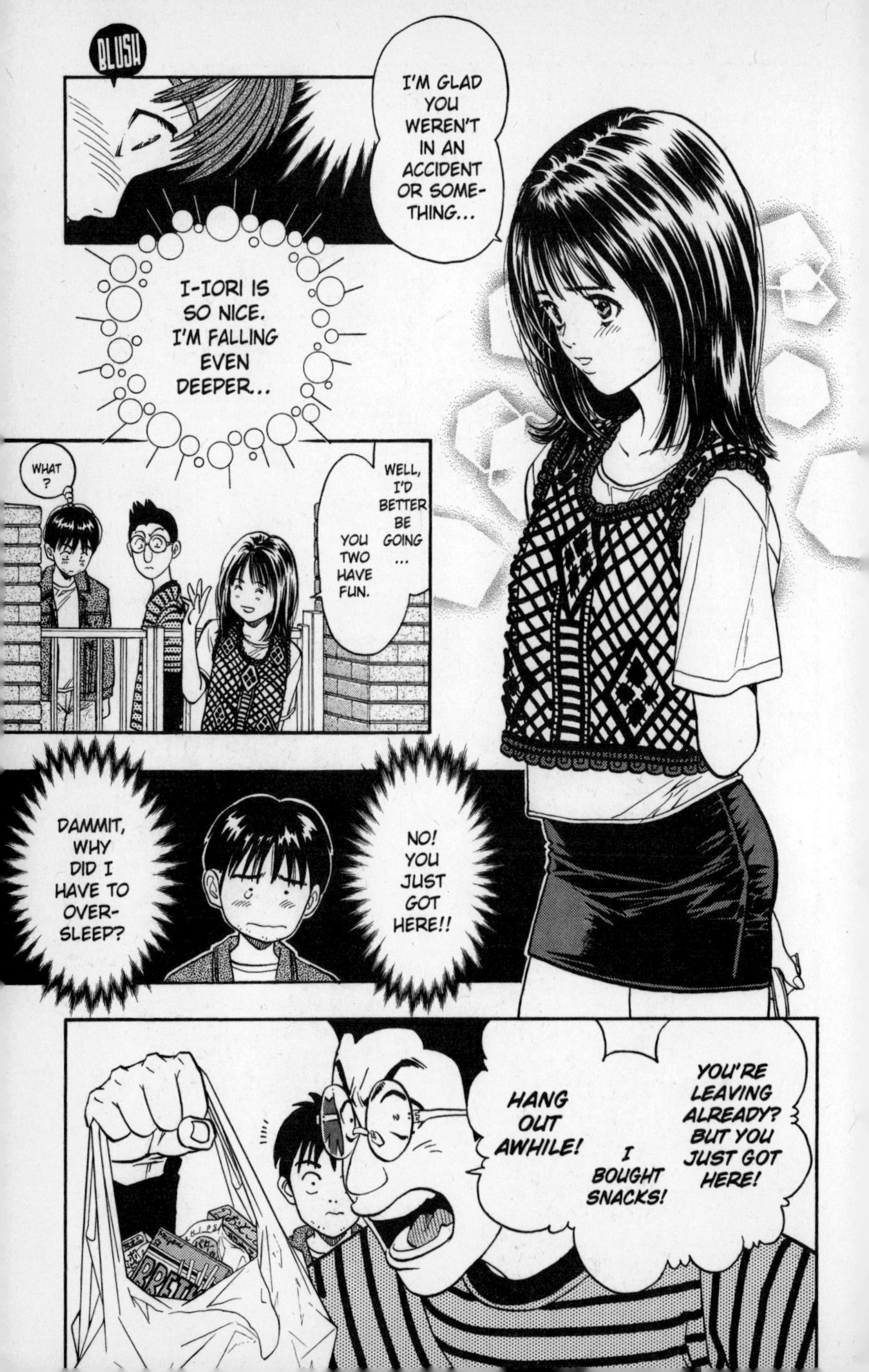
I'M GLAD YOU WEREN'T IN AN ACCIDENT OR SOME-THING...
BLUSH
I-IORI IS SO NICE. I'M FALLING EVEN DEEPER...
WELL, I'D BETTER BE GOING...
YOU TWO HAVE FUN.
WHAT?
NO! YOU JUST GOT HERE!!
DAMMIT, WHY DID I HAVE TO OVER-SLEEP?
YOU'RE LEAVING ALREADY? BUT YOU JUST GOT HERE!
I BOUGHT SNACKS!
HANG OUT AWHILE!

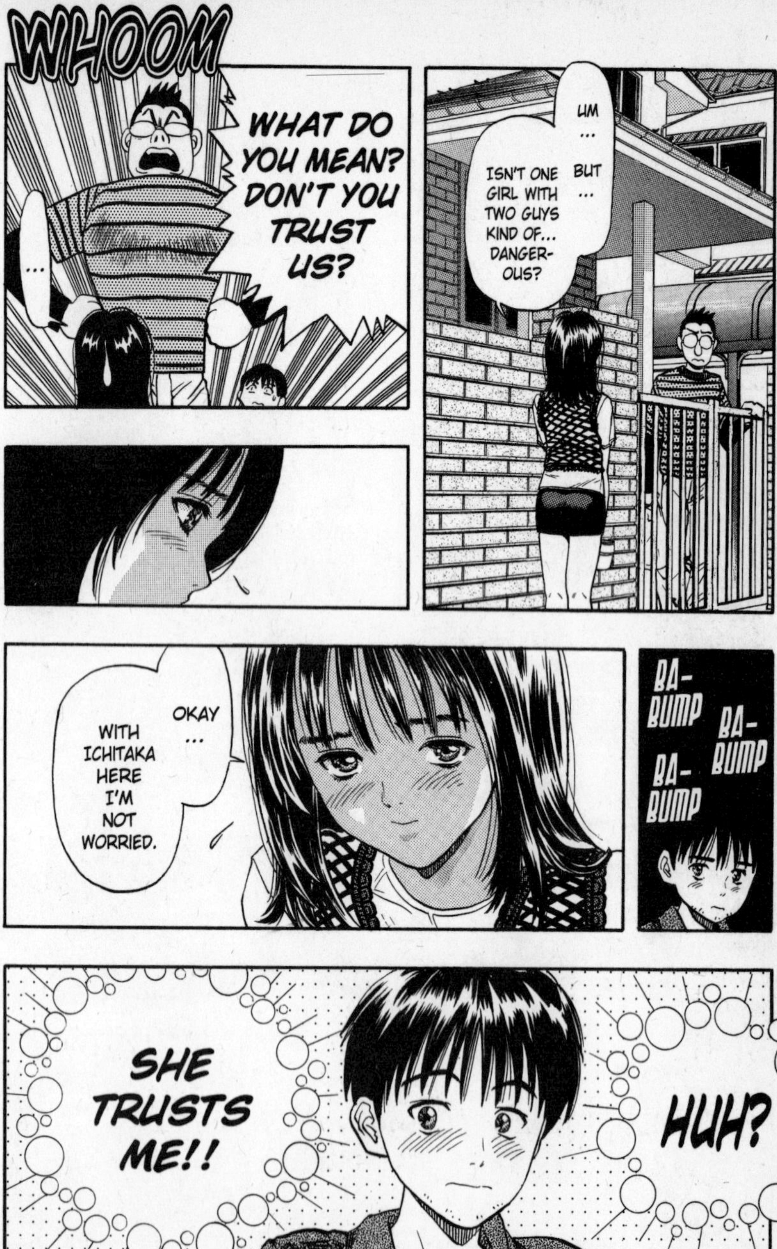
UM ... BUT ...
ISN'T ONE GIRL WITH TWO GUYS KIND OF... DANGER-OUS?
WHOOM
WHAT DO YOU MEAN? DON'T YOU TRUST US?
...
BA-BUMP BA-BUMP BA-BUMP
OKAY ...
WITH ICHITAKA HERE I'M NOT WORRIED.
HUH?
SHE TRUSTS ME!!

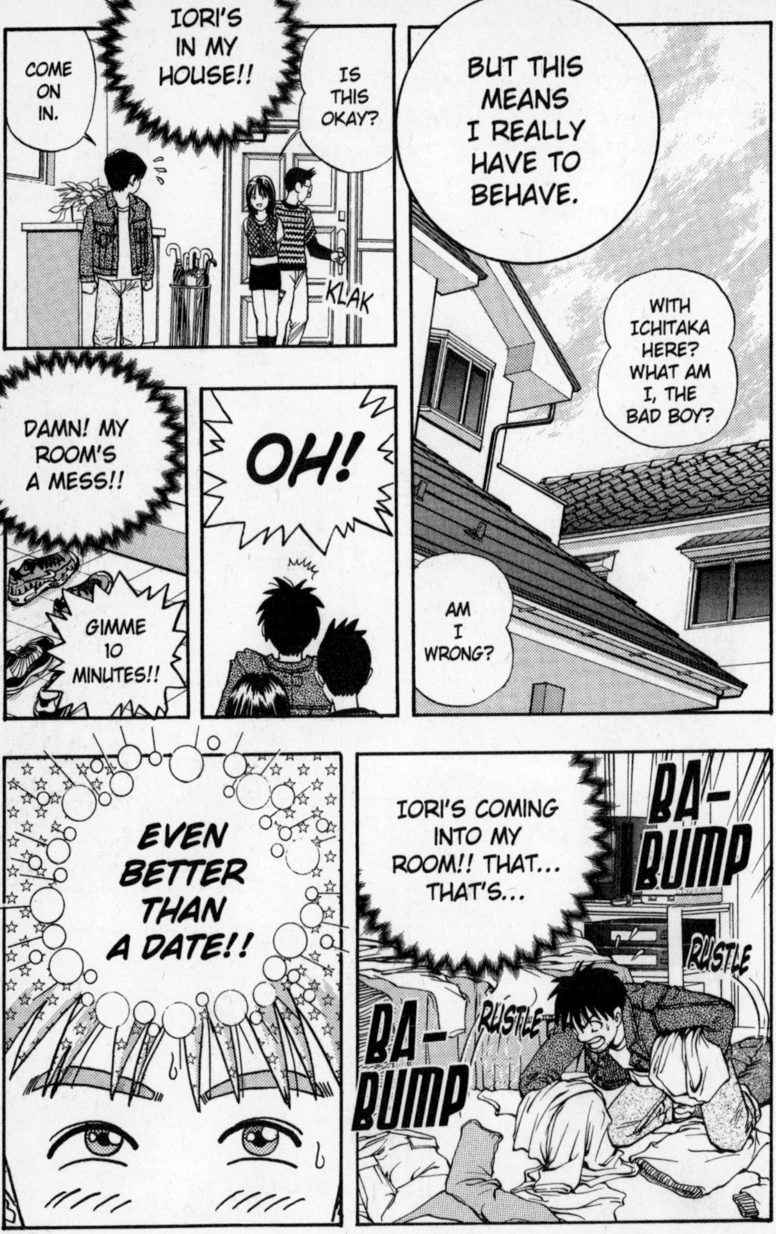
BUT THIS MEANS I REALLY HAVE TO BEHAVE.
WITH ICHITAKA HERE? WHAT AM I, THE BAD BOY?
AM I WRONG?
IS THIS OKAY?
IORI'S IN MY HOUSE!!
COME ON IN.
KLAK
OH!
DAMN! MY ROOM'S A MESS!!
GIMME 10 MINUTES!!
BA-BUMP
IORI'S COMING INTO MY ROOM!! THAT... THAT'S...
RUSTLE
RUSTLE
BA-BUMP
EVEN BETTER THAN A DATE!!

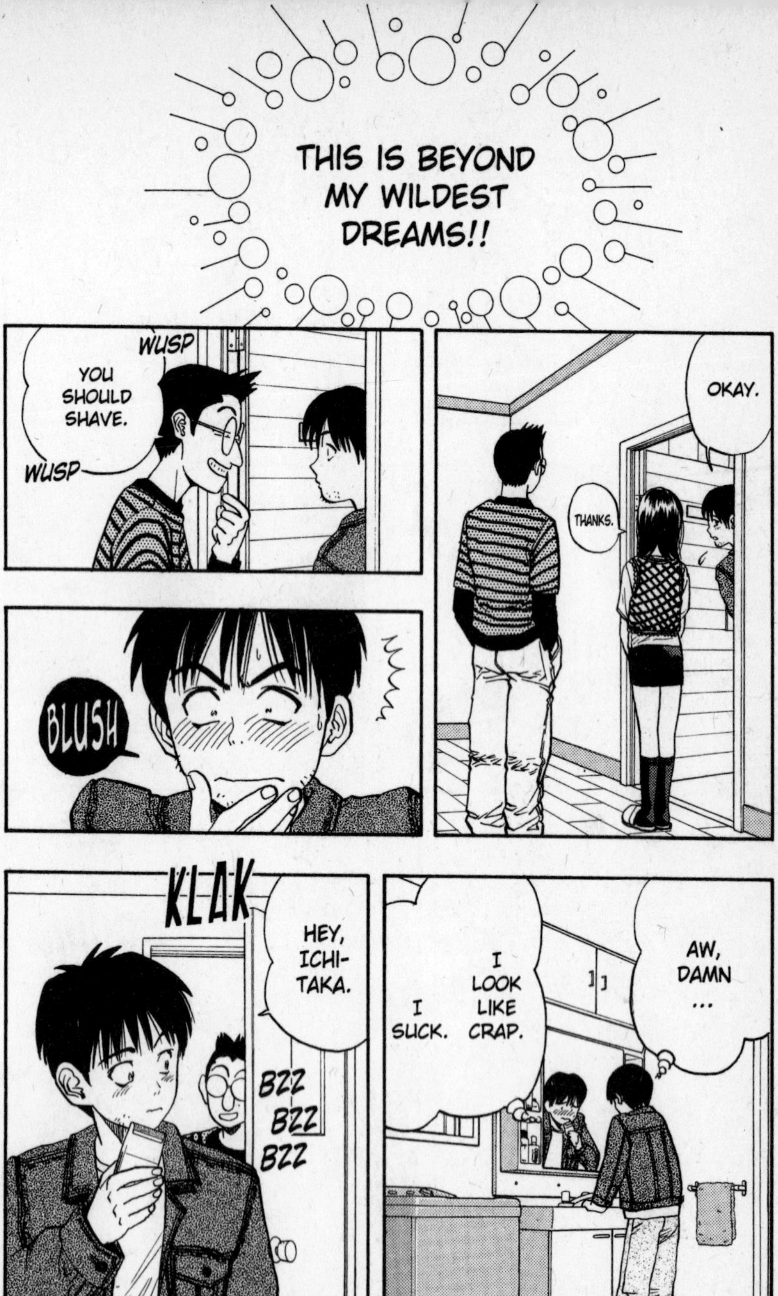
THIS IS BEYOND MY WILDEST DREAMS!!
OKAY.
THANKS.
WUSP
YOU SHOULD SHAVE.
WUSP
BLUSH
AW, DAMN ...
I LOOK LIKE CRAP.
I SUCK.
KLAK
HEY, ICHI-TAKA.
BZZ BZZ BZZ

READ THIS WAY

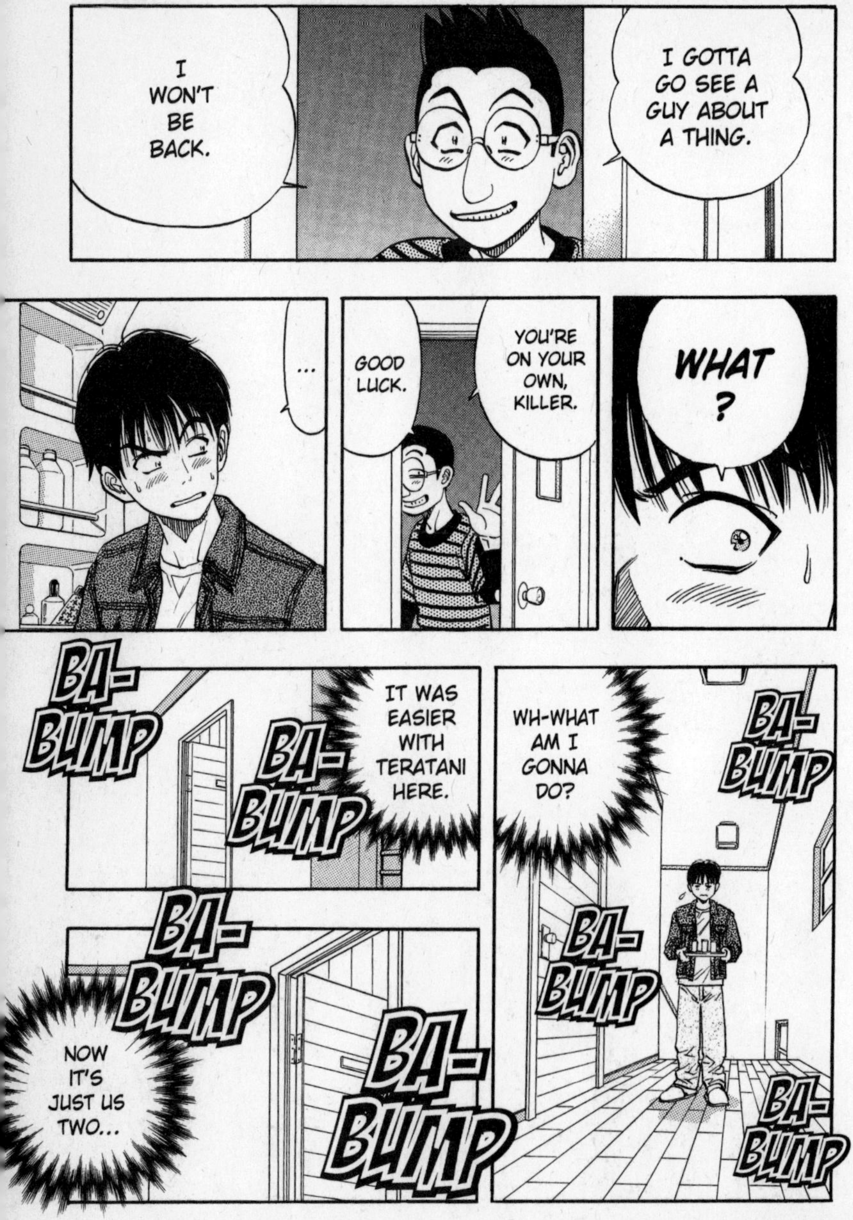
I GOTTA GO SEE A GUY ABOUT A THING.
I WON'T BE BACK.
WHAT?
YOU'RE ON YOUR OWN, KILLER.
GOOD LUCK.
...
BA-BUMP
WH-WHAT AM I GONNA DO?
BA-BUMP
BA-BUMP
IT WAS EASIER WITH TERATANI HERE.
BA-BUMP
BA-BUMP
BA-BUMP
NOW IT'S JUST US TWO...
BA-BUMP

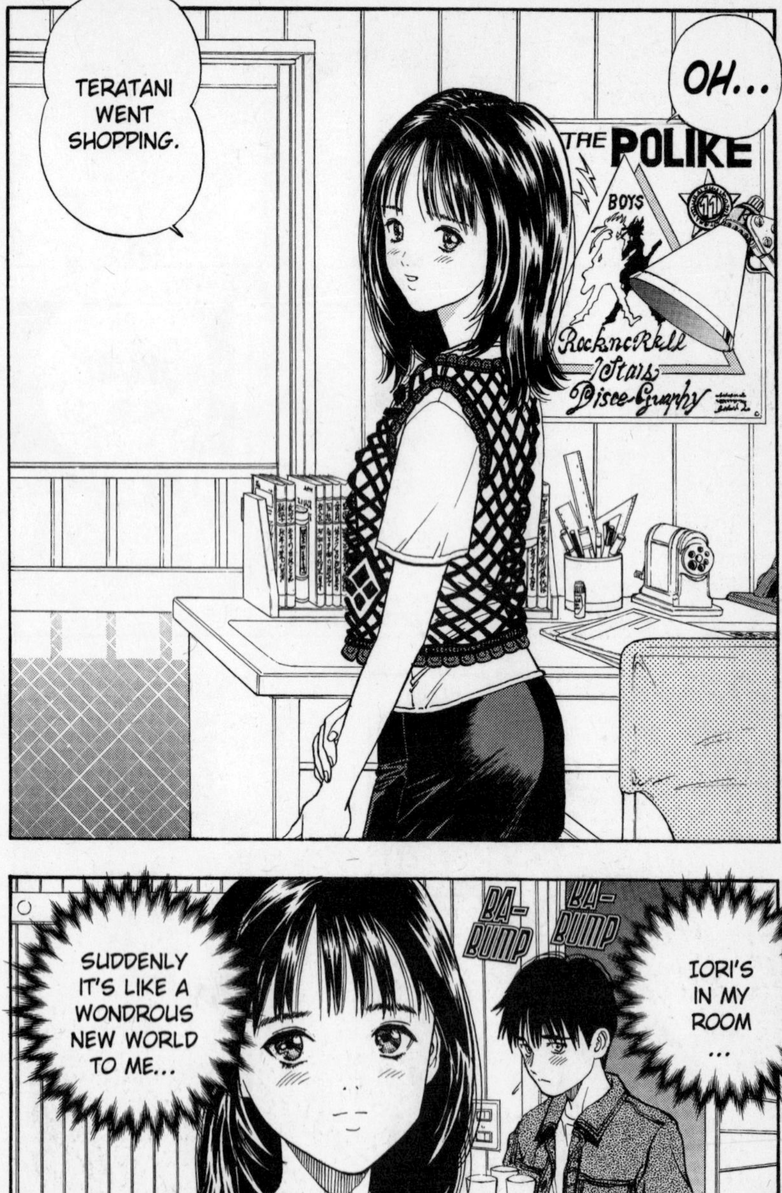
OH...
TERATANI WENT SHOPPING.
THE POLIKE
BOYS
IORI'S IN MY ROOM ...
BA-BUMP
BA-BUMP
SUDDENLY IT'S LIKE A WONDROUS NEW WORLD TO ME...

READ THIS WAY

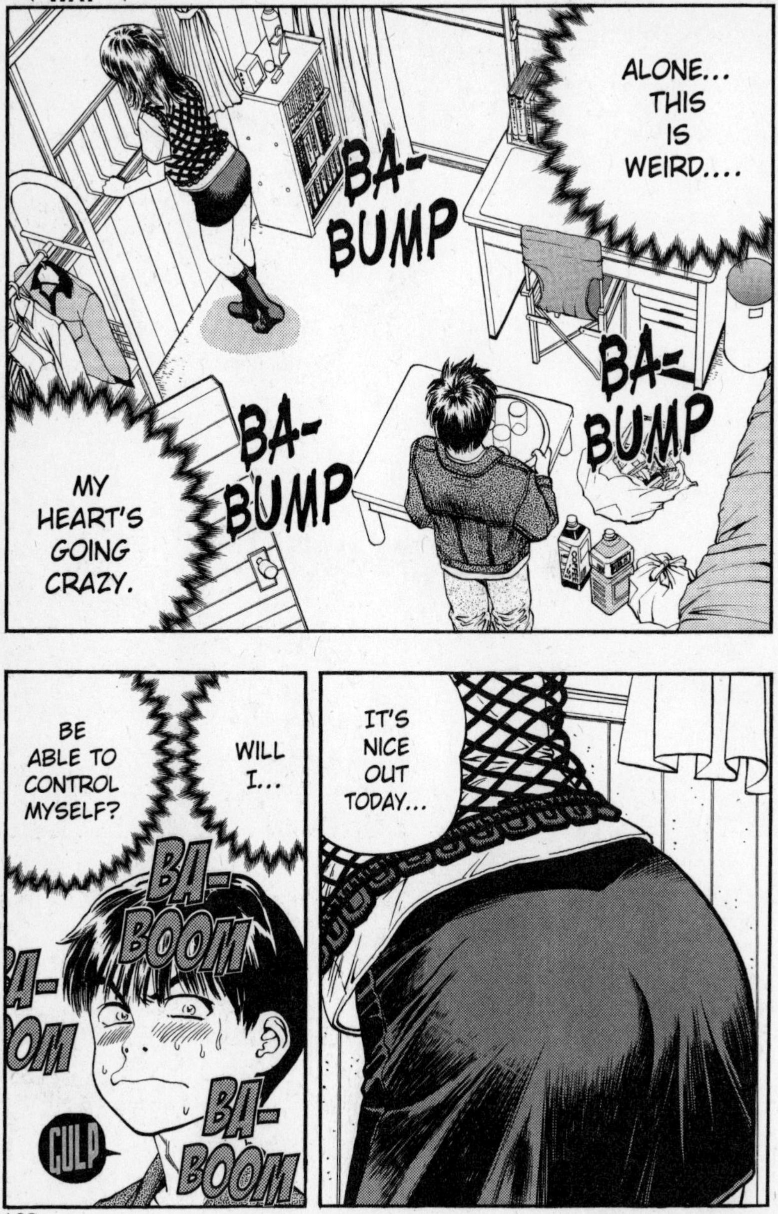

ALONE... THIS IS WEIRD....
BA-BUMP
BA-BUMP
BA-BUMP
MY HEART'S GOING CRAZY.
IT'S NICE OUT TODAY...
WILL I...
BE ABLE TO CONTROL MYSELF?
BA-BOOM
BA-BOOM
GULP
BA-BOOM

I"s

アイズ

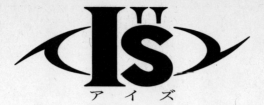

Chapter 7: Adrenaline

READ THIS WAY

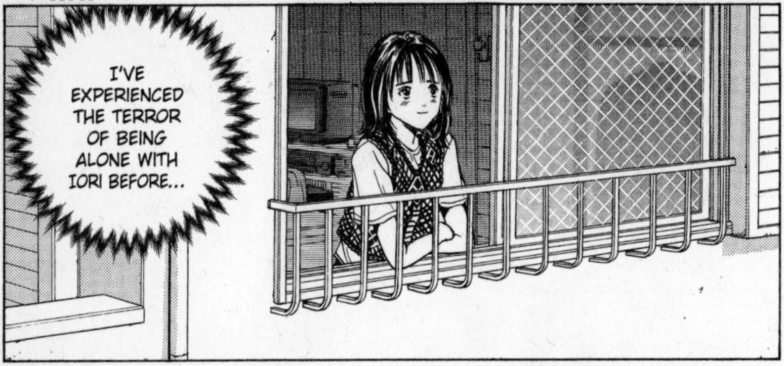
I'VE EXPERIENCED THE TERROR OF BEING ALONE WITH IORI BEFORE...

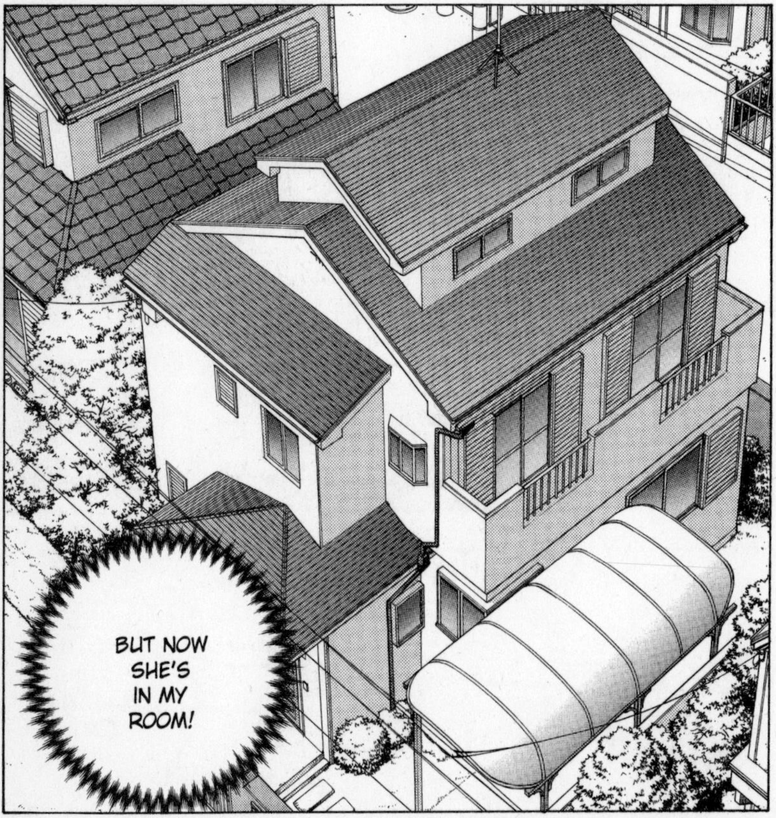
BUT NOW SHE'S IN MY ROOM!

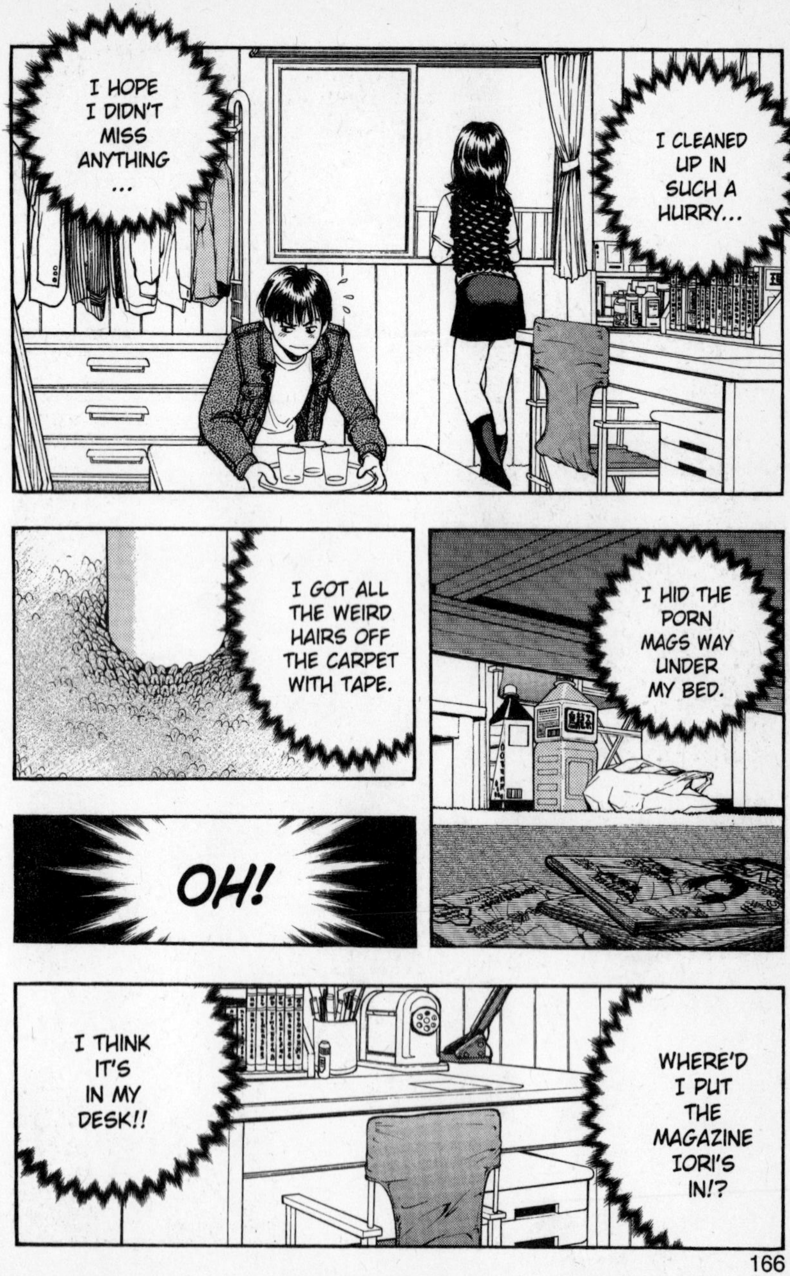
I CLEANED UP IN SUCH A HURRY...
I HOPE I DIDN'T MISS ANYTHING ...
I HID THE PORN MAGS WAY UNDER MY BED.
I GOT ALL THE WEIRD HAIRS OFF THE CARPET WITH TAPE.
OH!
WHERE'D I PUT THE MAGAZINE IORI'S IN!?
I THINK IT'S IN MY DESK!!

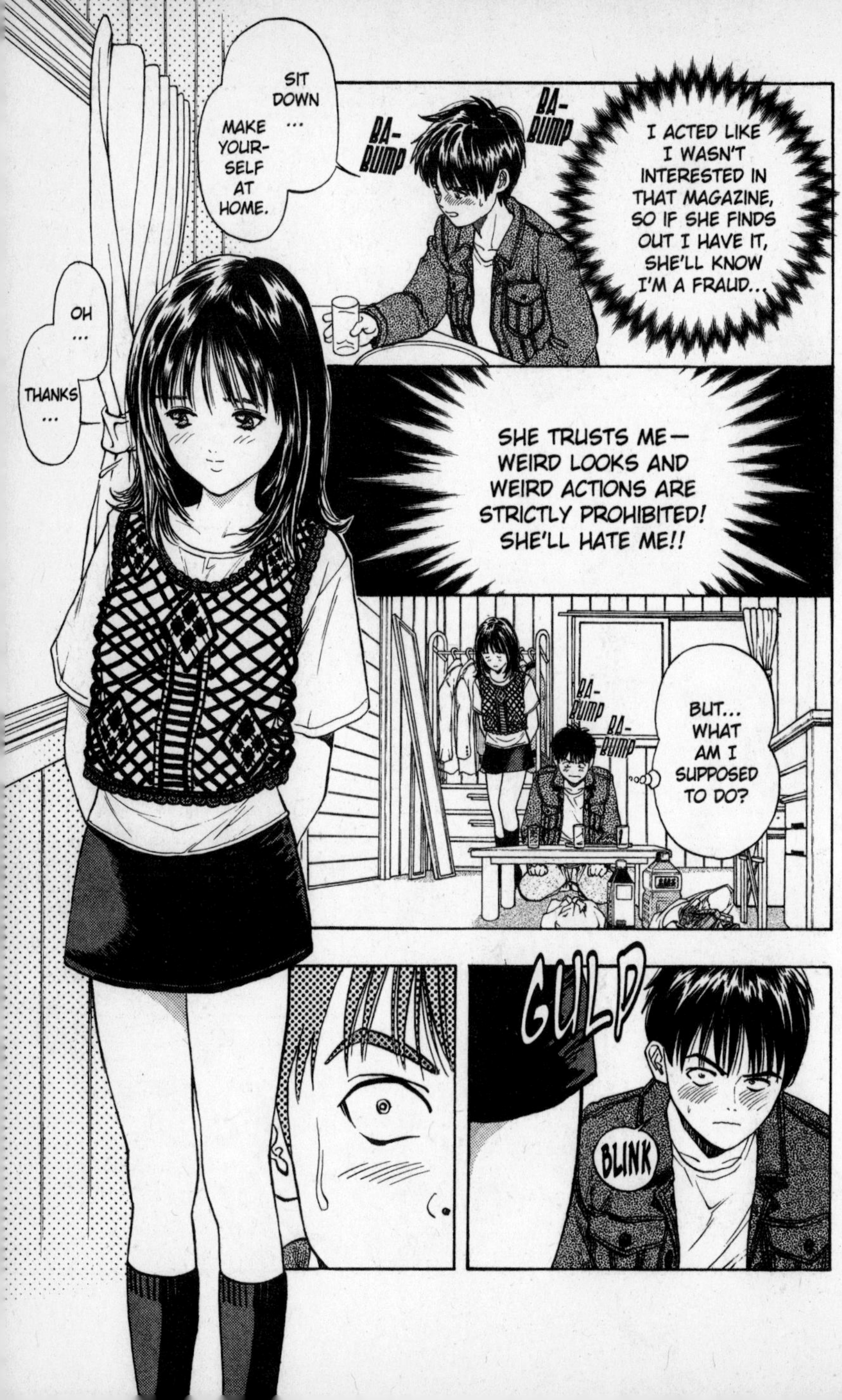
BA-BUMP
BA-BUMP
I ACTED LIKE I WASN'T INTERESTED IN THAT MAGAZINE, SO IF SHE FINDS OUT I HAVE IT, SHE'LL KNOW I'M A FRAUD...
SIT DOWN ... MAKE YOURSELF AT HOME.
SHE TRUSTS ME— WEIRD LOOKS AND WEIRD ACTIONS ARE STRICTLY PROHIBITED! SHE'LL HATE ME!!
BUT... WHAT AM I SUPPOSED TO DO?
BA-BUMP
BA-BUMP
GULP
BLINK
OH ... THANKS ...

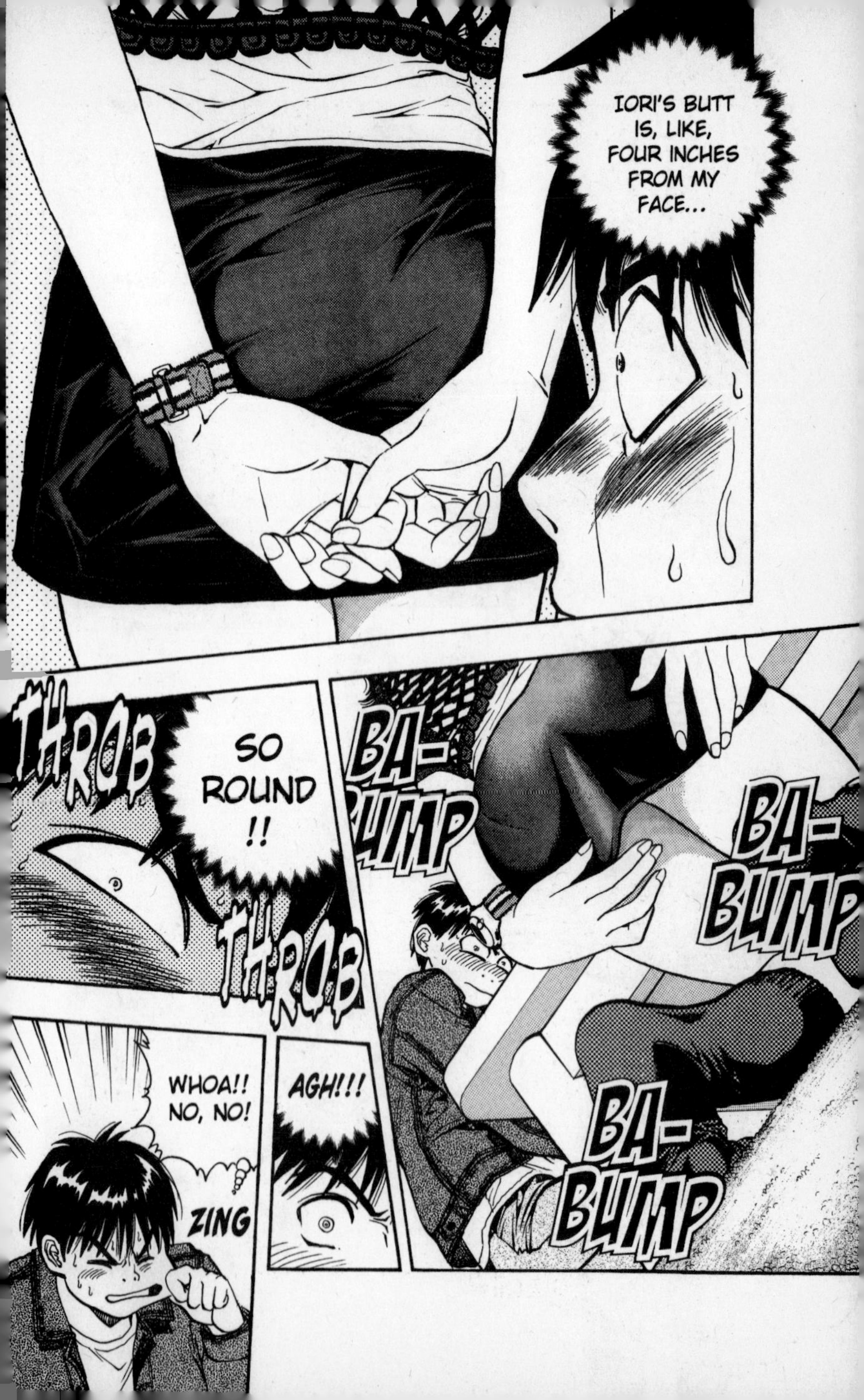
IORI'S BUTT IS, LIKE, FOUR INCHES FROM MY FACE...
BA-BUMP
BA-BUMP
BA-BUMP
SO ROUND !!
THROB
THROB
AGH!!!
WHOA!! NO, NO!
ZING

READ THIS WAY

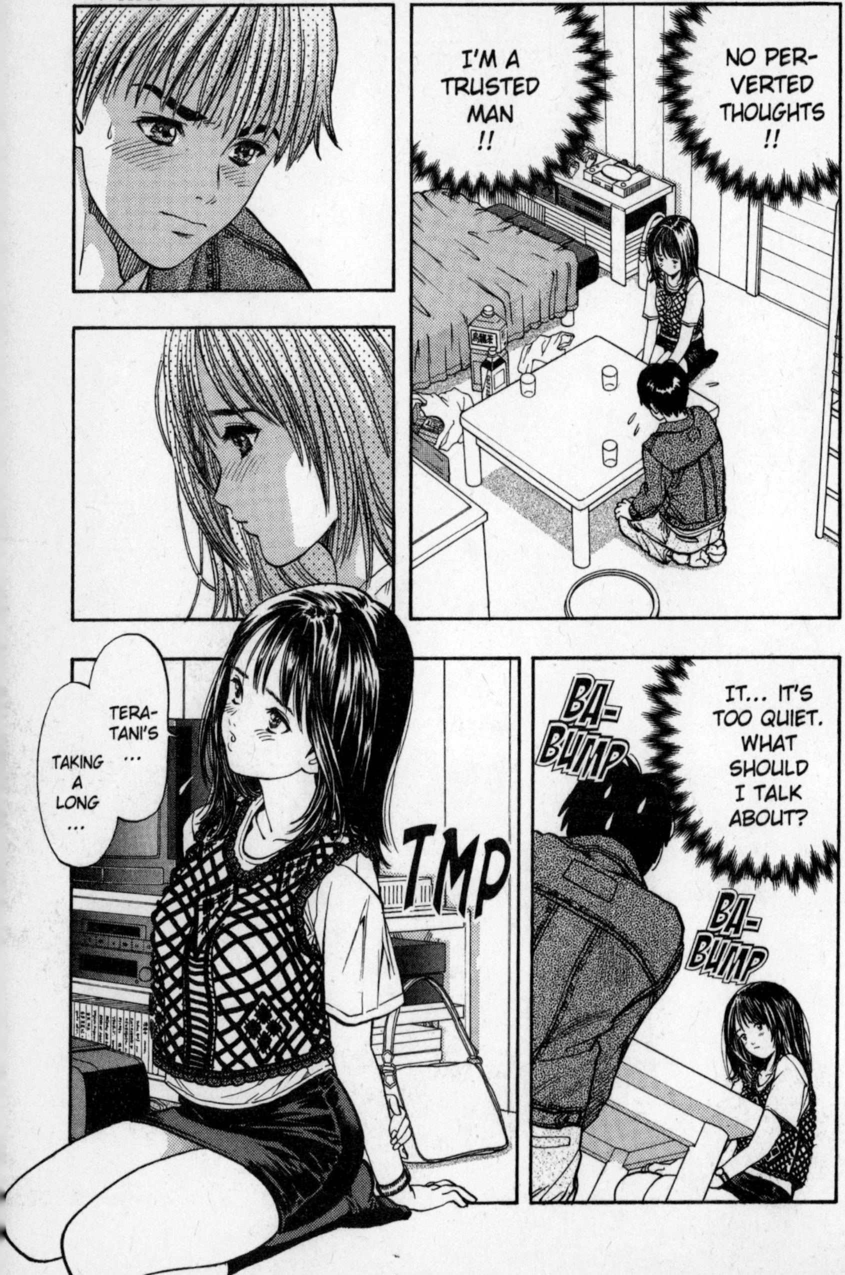
NO PER-VERTED THOUGHTS !!
I'M A TRUSTED MAN !!
IT... IT'S TOO QUIET. WHAT SHOULD I TALK ABOUT?
BA-BUMP
BA-BUMP
TMP
TERA-TANI'S ... TAKING A LONG ...

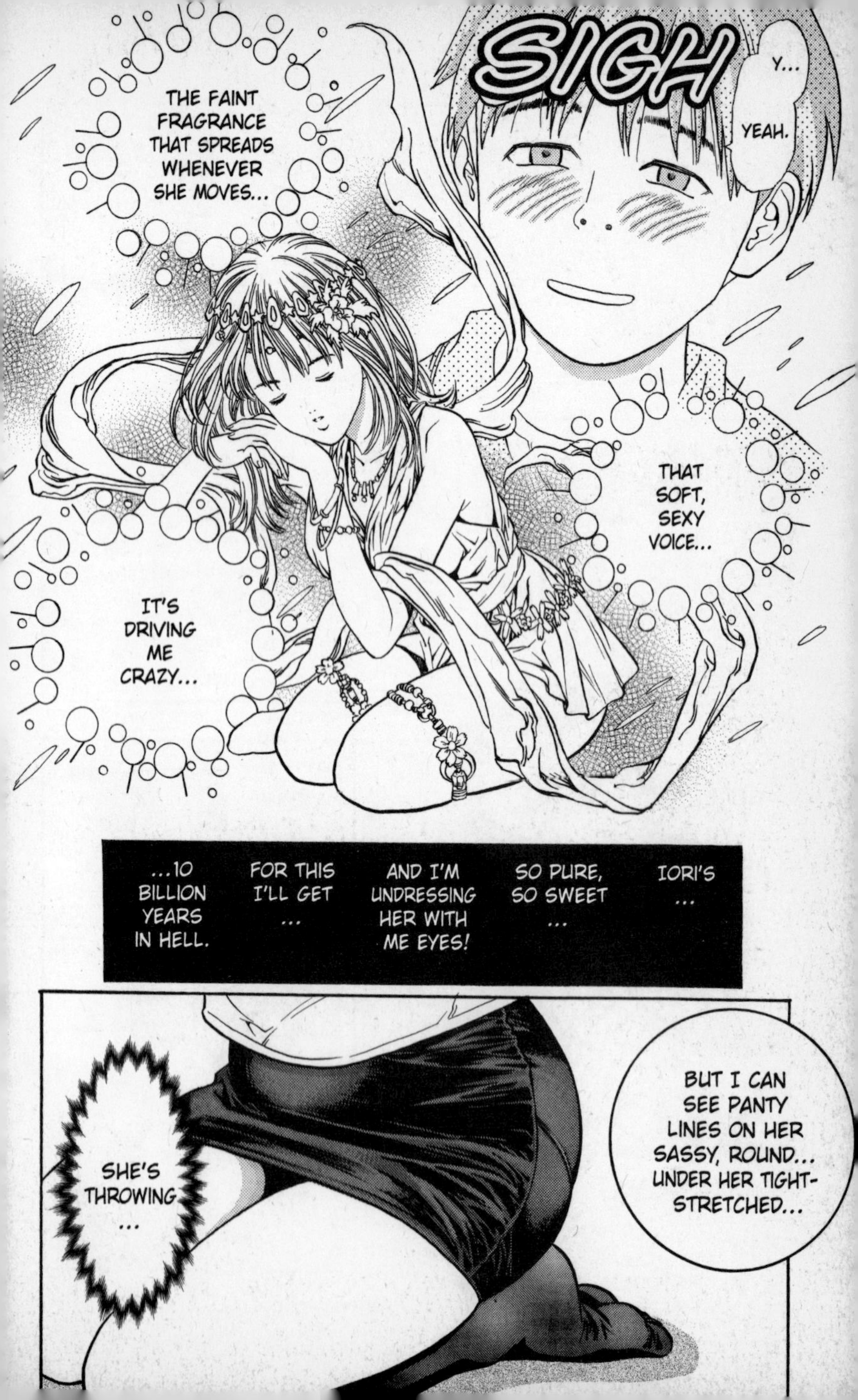
SIGH
Y... YEAH.
THE FAINT FRAGRANCE THAT SPREADS WHENEVER SHE MOVES...
THAT SOFT, SEXY VOICE...
IT'S DRIVING ME CRAZY...
IORI'S...
SO PURE, SO SWEET...
AND I'M UNDRESSING HER WITH ME EYES!
FOR THIS I'LL GET...
...10 BILLION YEARS IN HELL.
BUT I CAN SEE PANTY LINES ON HER SASSY, ROUND... UNDER HER TIGHT-STRETCHED...
SHE'S THROWING...

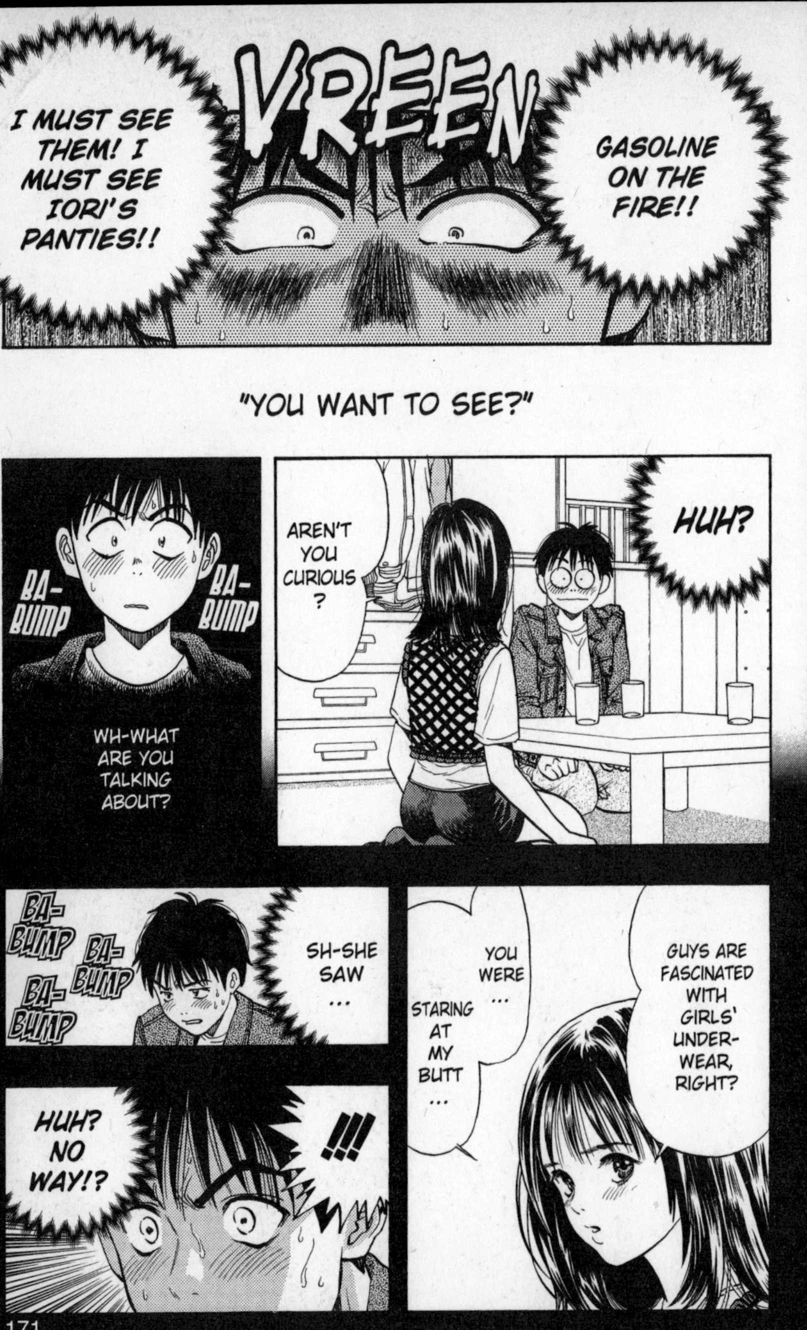
GASOLINE ON THE FIRE!!
VREEN
I MUST SEE THEM! I MUST SEE IORI'S PANTIES!!
"YOU WANT TO SEE?"
HUH?
AREN'T YOU CURIOUS?
BA-BUMP BA-BUMP
WH-WHAT ARE YOU TALKING ABOUT?
GUYS ARE FASCINATED WITH GIRLS' UNDER-WEAR, RIGHT?
YOU WERE ...
STARING AT MY BUTT ...
SH-SHE SAW ...
BA-BUMP BA-BUMP BA-BUMP
!!!
HUH? NO WAY!?

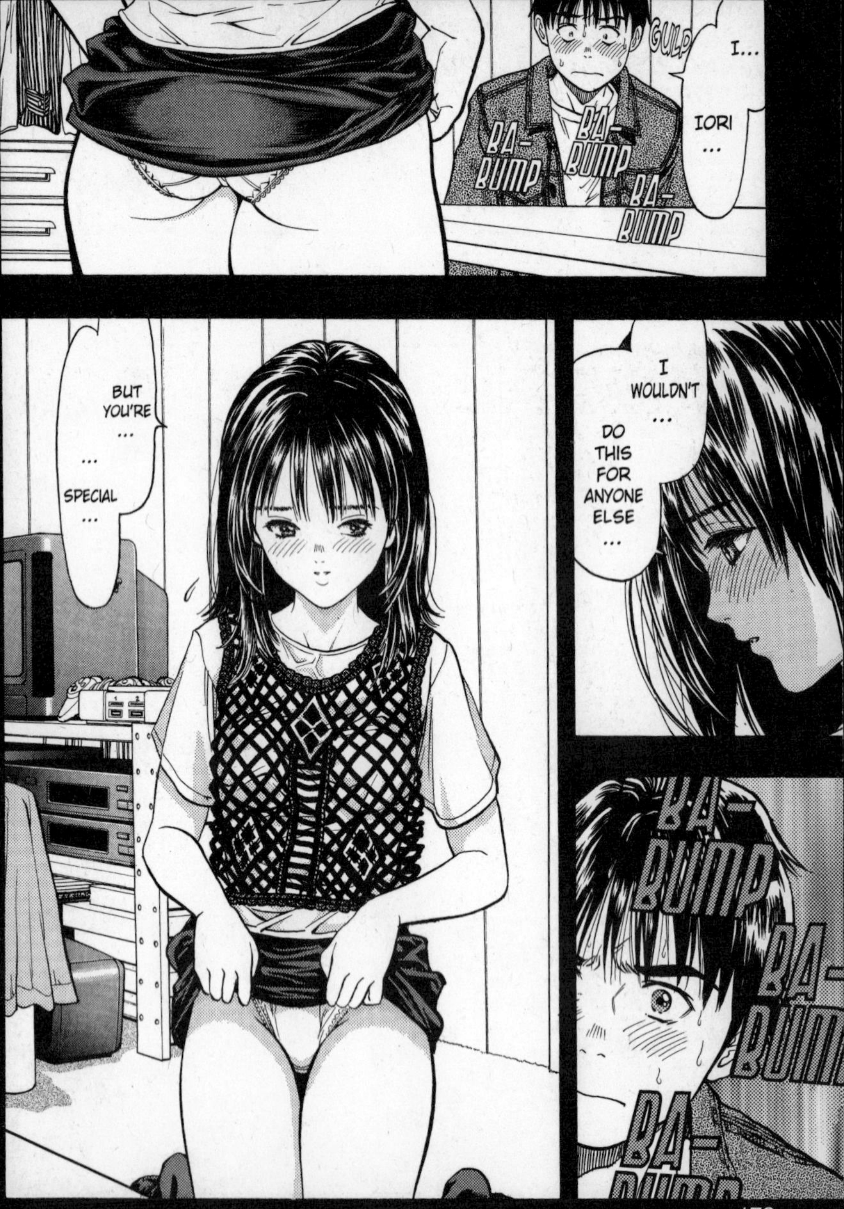
I...
GULP
IORI ...
BA-BUMP
BA-BUMP
BA-BUMP
BA-BUMP
I WOULDN'T ... DO THIS FOR ANYONE ELSE ...
BA-BUMP
BA-
BA-
BUT YOU'RE ... ... SPECIAL ...

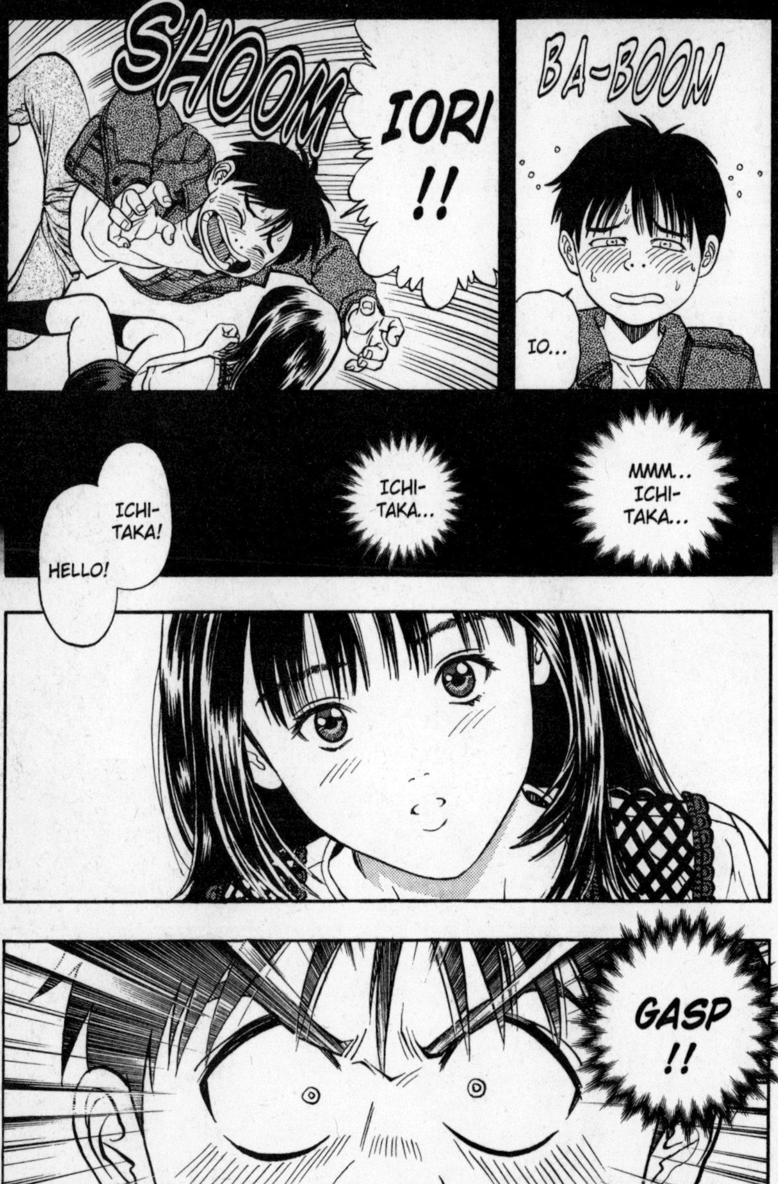
BA-BOOM
IO...
SHOOM
IORI !!
MMM... ICHI-TAKA...
ICHI-TAKA...
ICHI-TAKA!
HELLO!
GASP !!

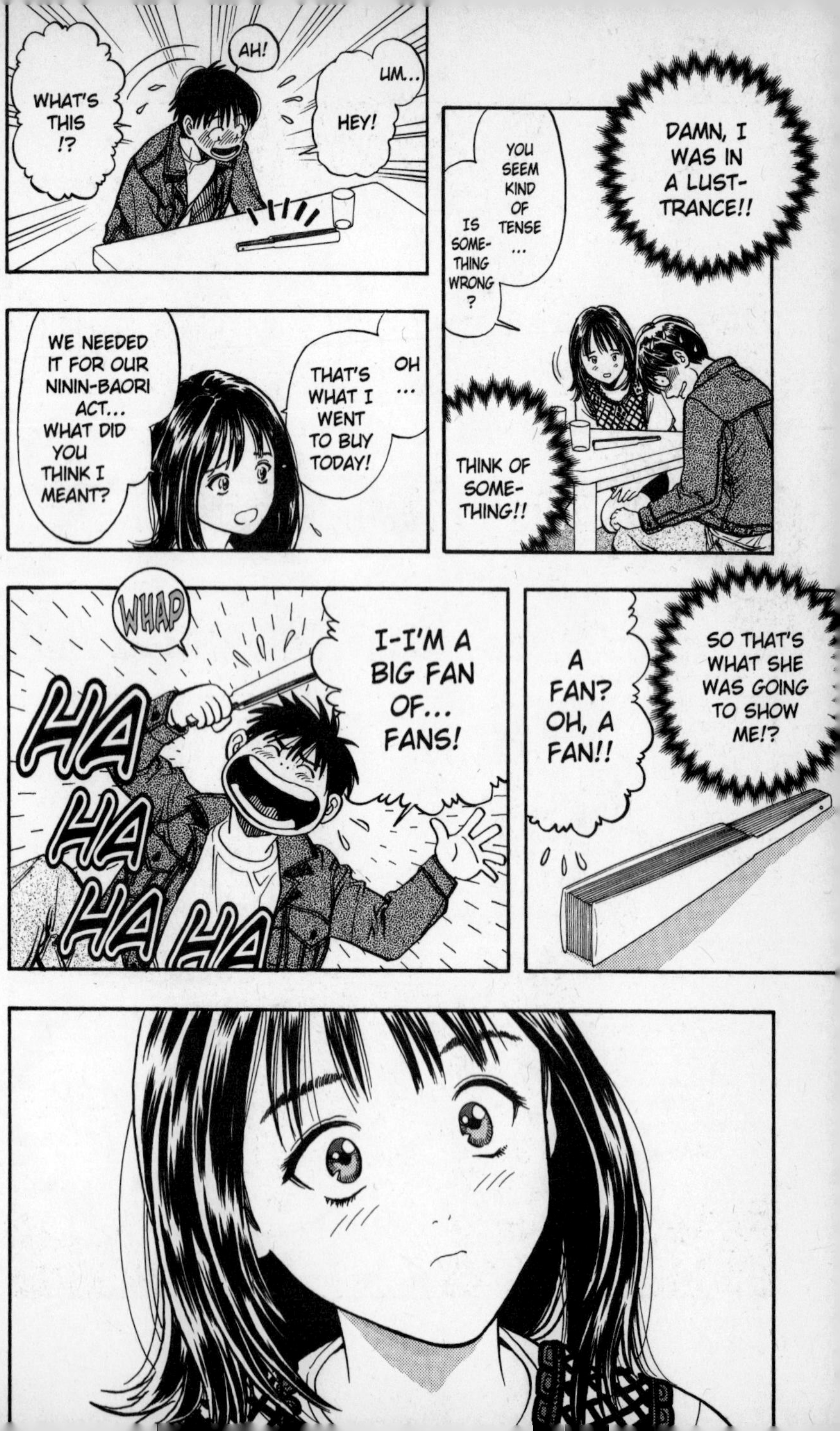
UM...
HEY!
AH!
WHAT'S THIS !?
DAMN, I WAS IN A LUST-TRANCE!!
YOU SEEM KIND OF TENSE ...
IS SOMETHING WRONG ?
THINK OF SOMETHING!!
OH ...
THAT'S WHAT I WENT TO BUY TODAY!
WE NEEDED IT FOR OUR NININ-BAORI ACT... WHAT DID YOU THINK I MEANT?
SO THAT'S WHAT SHE WAS GOING TO SHOW ME!?
A FAN? OH, A FAN!!
I-I'M A BIG FAN OF... FANS!
WHAP
HA HA HA HA

READ THIS WAY

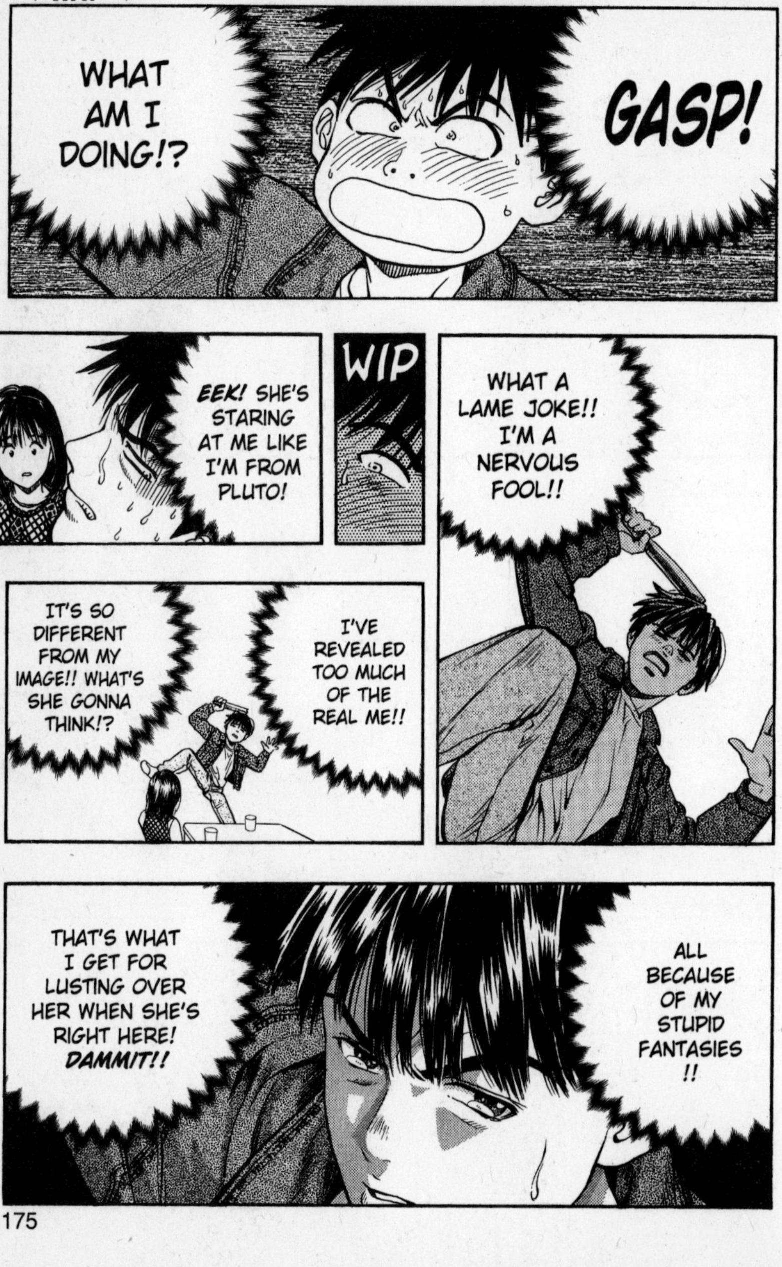

GASP!
WHAT AM I DOING!?
WHAT A LAME JOKE!! I'M A NERVOUS FOOL!!
WIP
EEK! SHE'S STARING AT ME LIKE I'M FROM PLUTO!
I'VE REVEALED TOO MUCH OF THE REAL ME!!
IT'S SO DIFFERENT FROM MY IMAGE!! WHAT'S SHE GONNA THINK!?
ALL BECAUSE OF MY STUPID FANTASIES !!
THAT'S WHAT I GET FOR LUSTING OVER HER WHEN SHE'S RIGHT HERE! DAMMIT!!

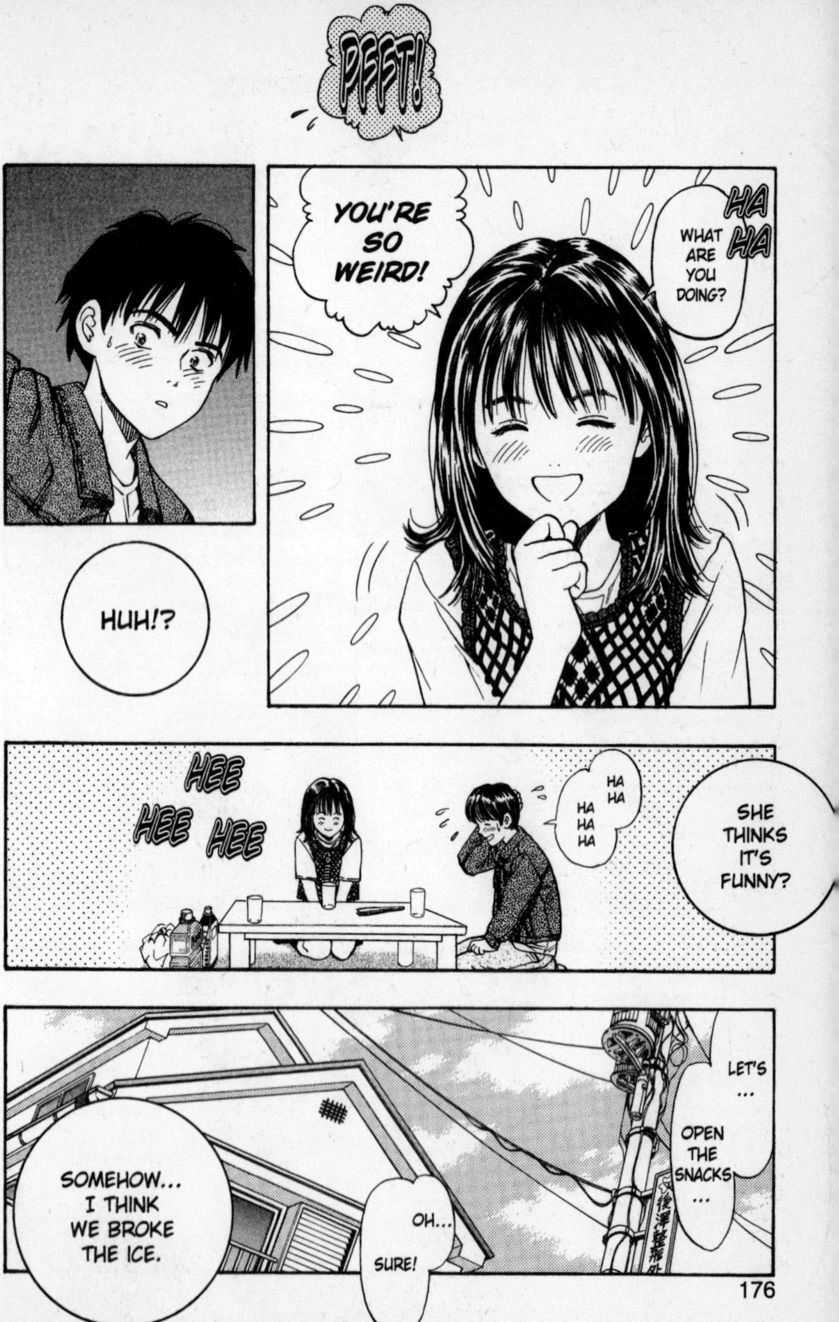
PFFT!
HA HA
WHAT ARE YOU DOING?
YOU'RE SO WEIRD!
HUH!?
SHE THINKS IT'S FUNNY?
HA HA HA HA HA
HEE HEE HEE
LET'S ... OPEN THE SNACKS ...
OH... SURE!
SOMEHOW... I THINK WE BROKE THE ICE.

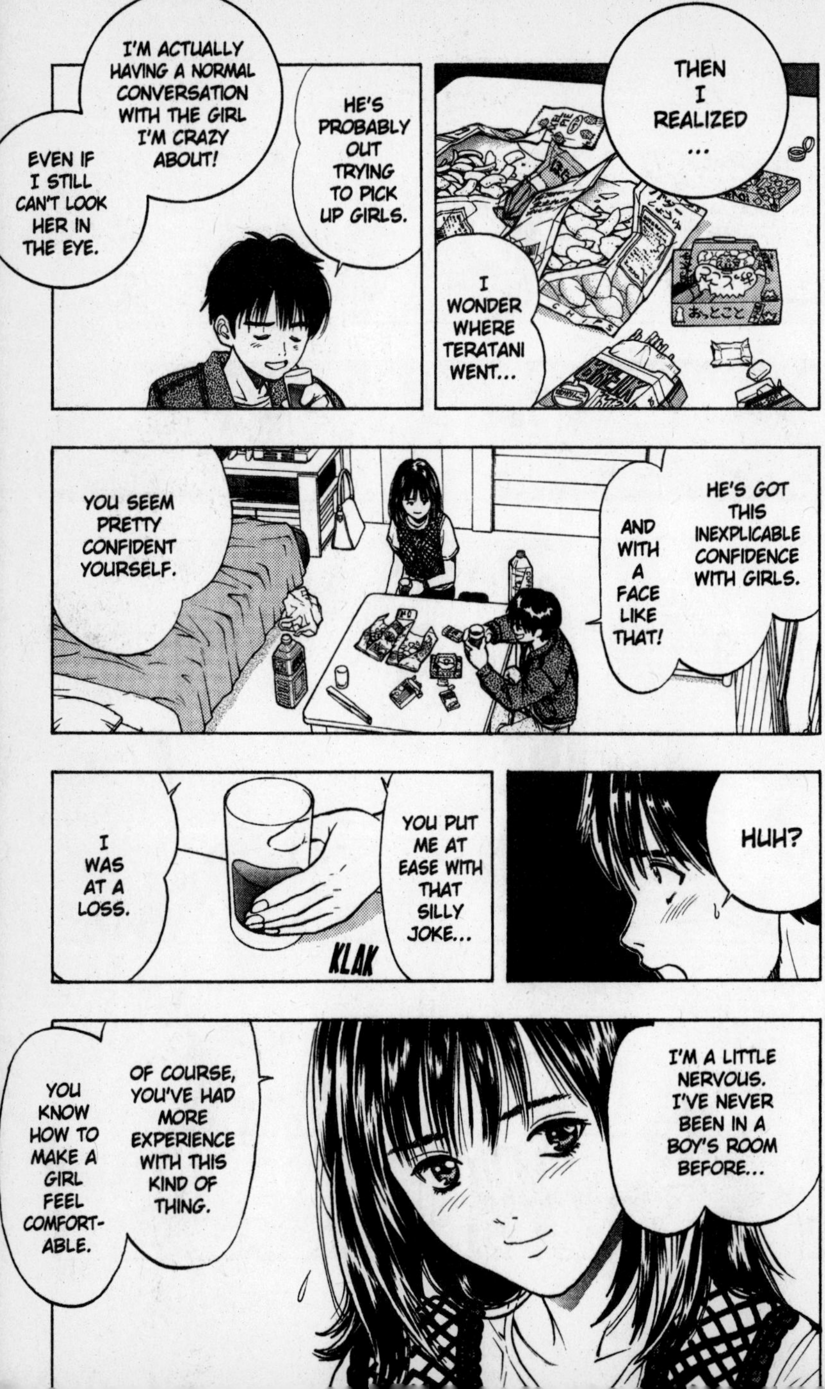
THEN I REALIZED...
I WONDER WHERE TERATANI WENT...
HE'S PROBABLY OUT TRYING TO PICK UP GIRLS.
I'M ACTUALLY HAVING A NORMAL CONVERSATION WITH THE GIRL I'M CRAZY ABOUT!
EVEN IF I STILL CAN'T LOOK HER IN THE EYE.
HE'S GOT THIS INEXPLICABLE CONFIDENCE WITH GIRLS.
AND WITH A FACE LIKE THAT!
YOU SEEM PRETTY CONFIDENT YOURSELF.
HUH?
YOU PUT ME AT EASE WITH THAT SILLY JOKE...
KLAK
I WAS AT A LOSS.
I'M A LITTLE NERVOUS. I'VE NEVER BEEN IN A BOY'S ROOM BEFORE...
OF COURSE, YOU'VE HAD MORE EXPERIENCE WITH THIS KIND OF THING.
YOU KNOW HOW TO MAKE A GIRL FEEL COMFORTABLE.

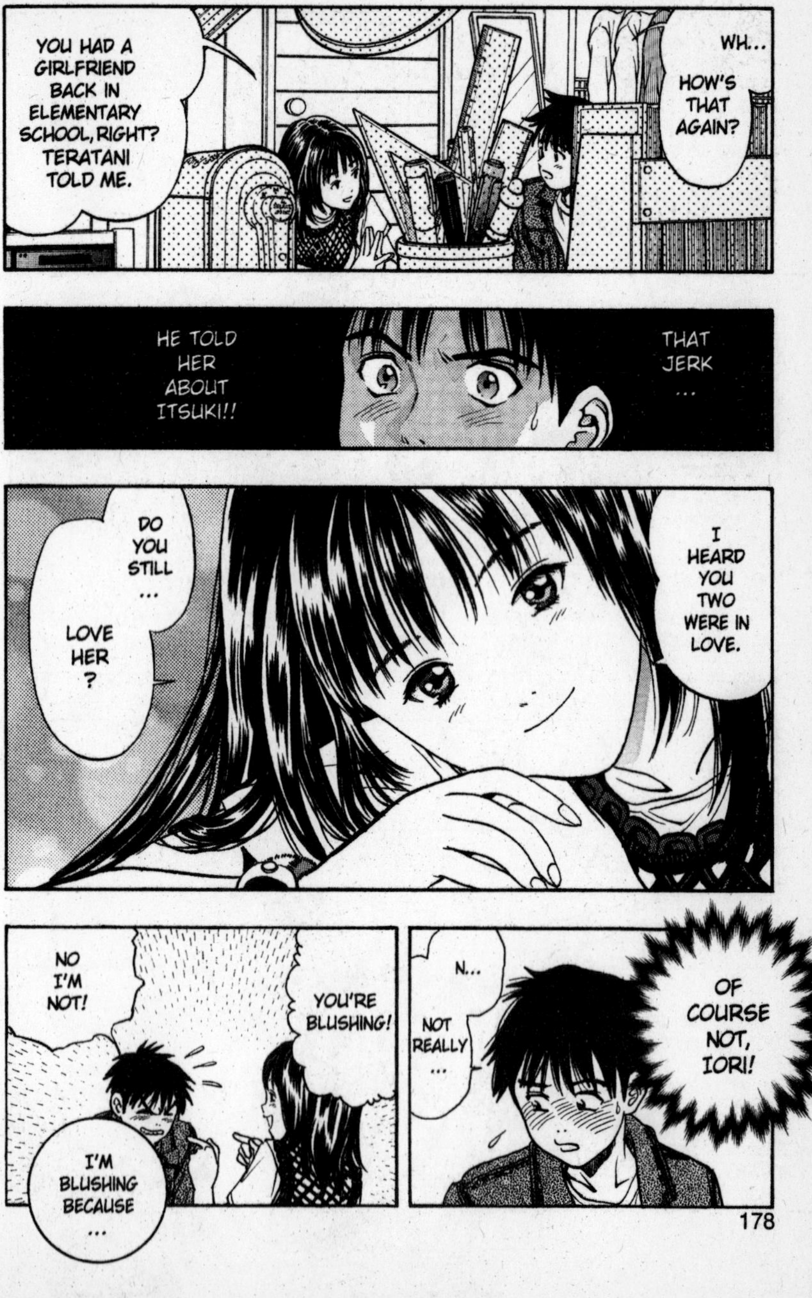
WH... HOW'S THAT AGAIN?
YOU HAD A GIRLFRIEND BACK IN ELEMENTARY SCHOOL, RIGHT? TERATANI TOLD ME.
THAT JERK ...
HE TOLD HER ABOUT ITSUKI!!
I HEARD YOU TWO WERE IN LOVE.
DO YOU STILL ... LOVE HER ?
OF COURSE NOT, IORI!
N... NOT REALLY ...
YOU'RE BLUSHING!
NO I'M NOT!
I'M BLUSHING BECAUSE ...

READ THIS WAY

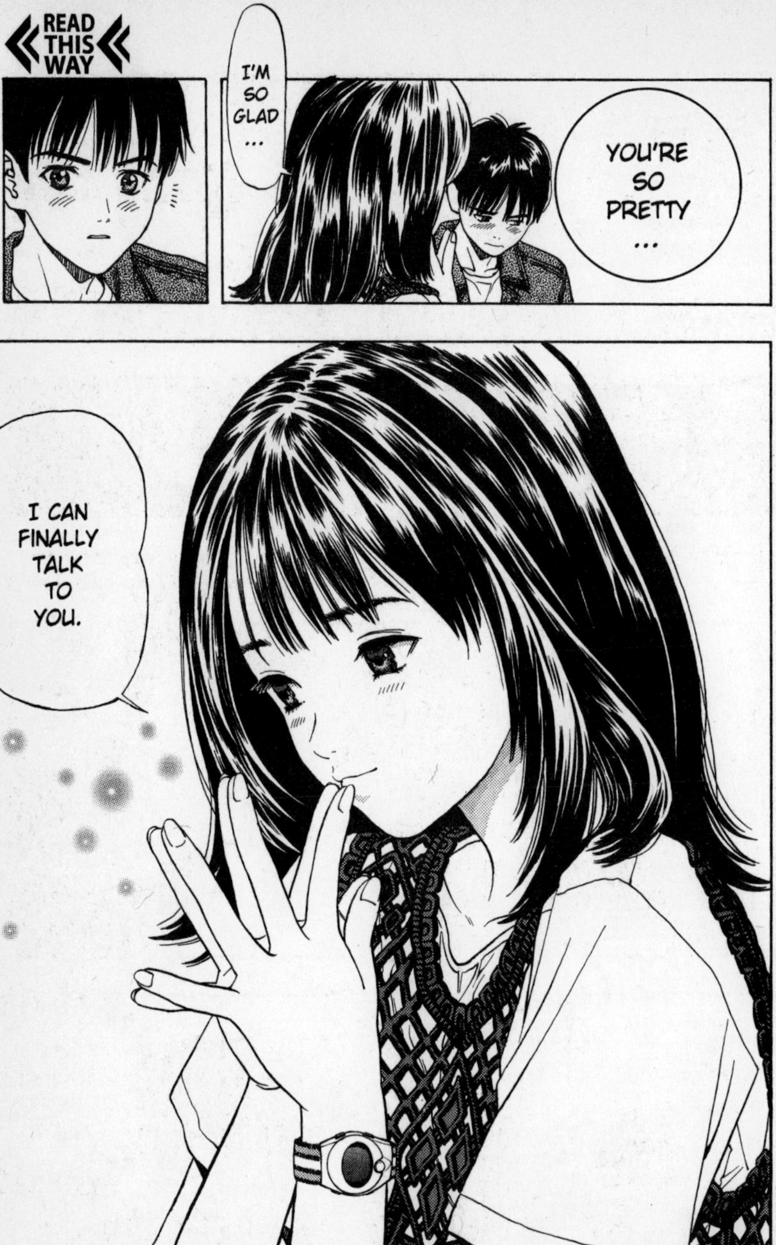
YOU'RE SO PRETTY ...
I'M SO GLAD ...
I CAN FINALLY TALK TO YOU.

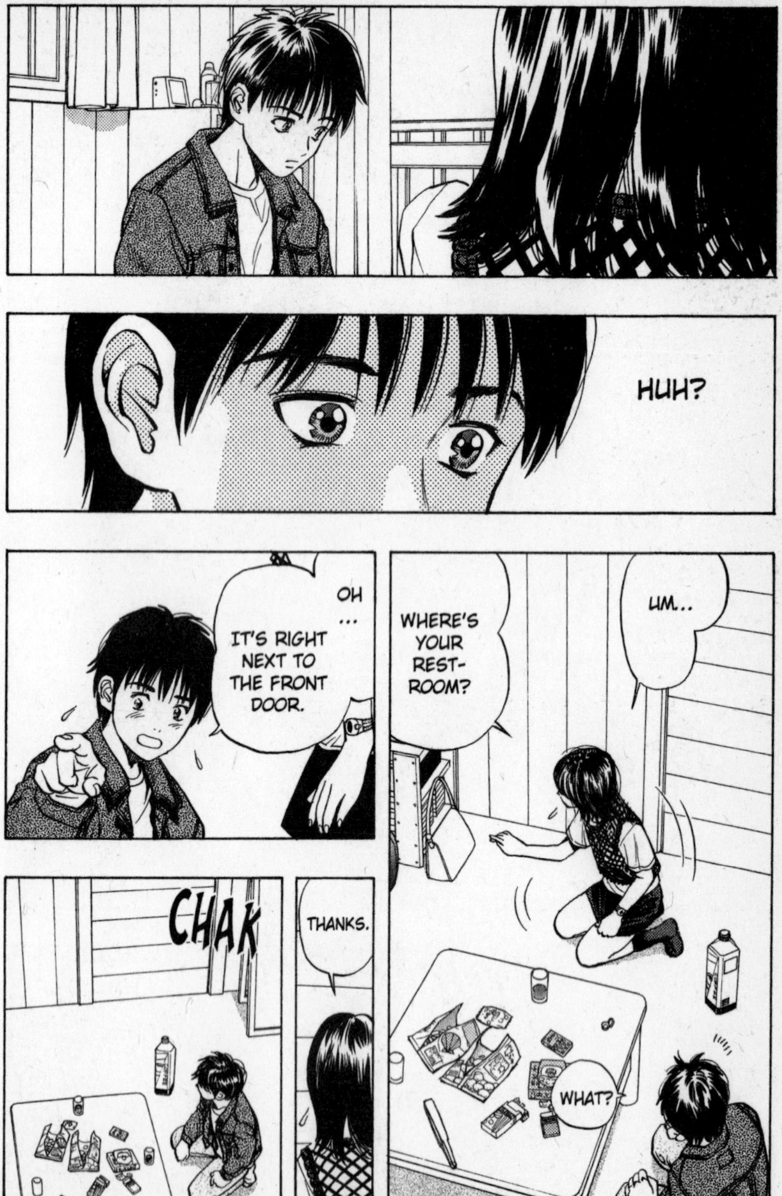
HUH?
UM...
WHERE'S YOUR REST-ROOM?
WHAT?
OH ... IT'S RIGHT NEXT TO THE FRONT DOOR.
THANKS.
CHAK

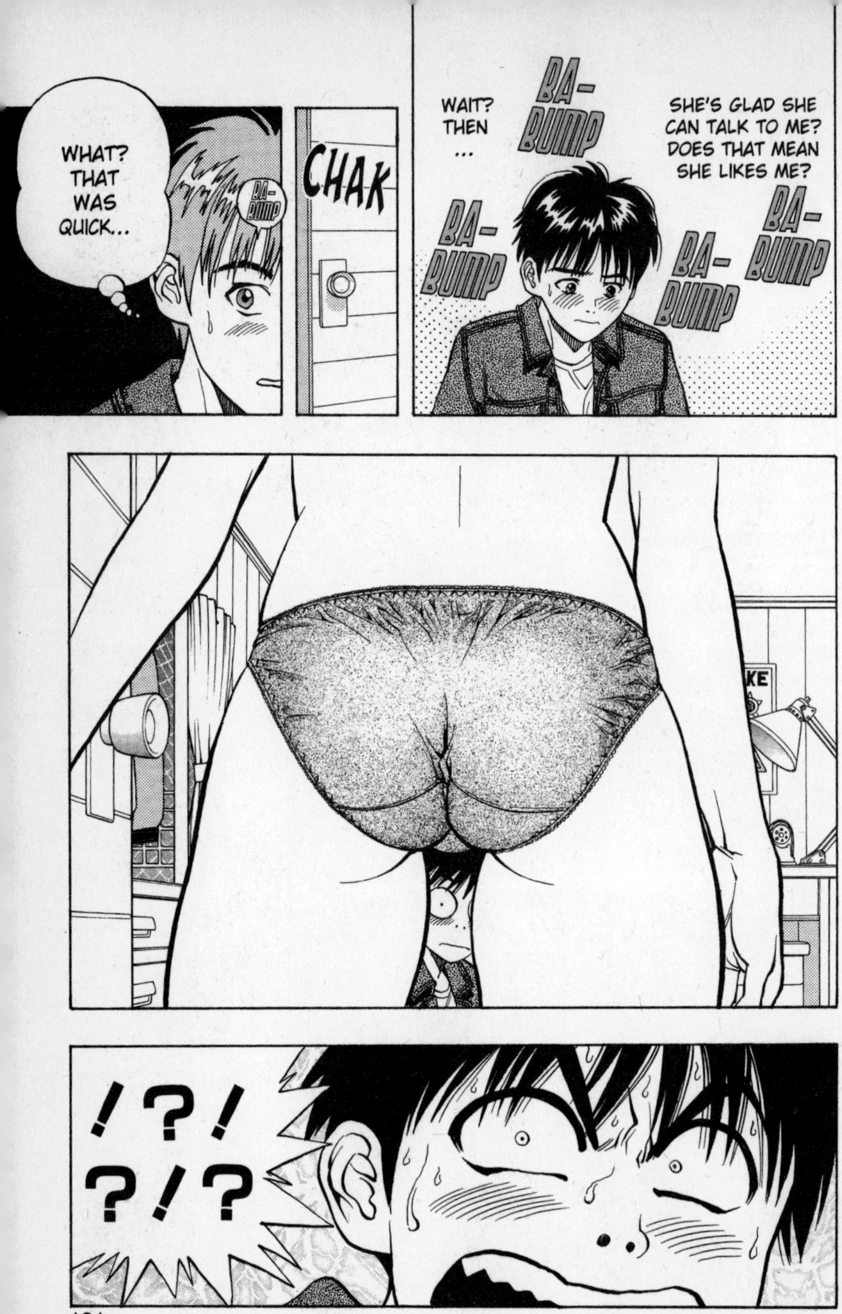
SHE'S GLAD SHE CAN TALK TO ME? DOES THAT MEAN SHE LIKES ME?
BA-BUMP
BA-BUMP
BA-BUMP
WAIT? THEN ...
BA-BUMP
CHAK
BA-BUMP
WHAT? THAT WAS QUICK...
!?!
?!?

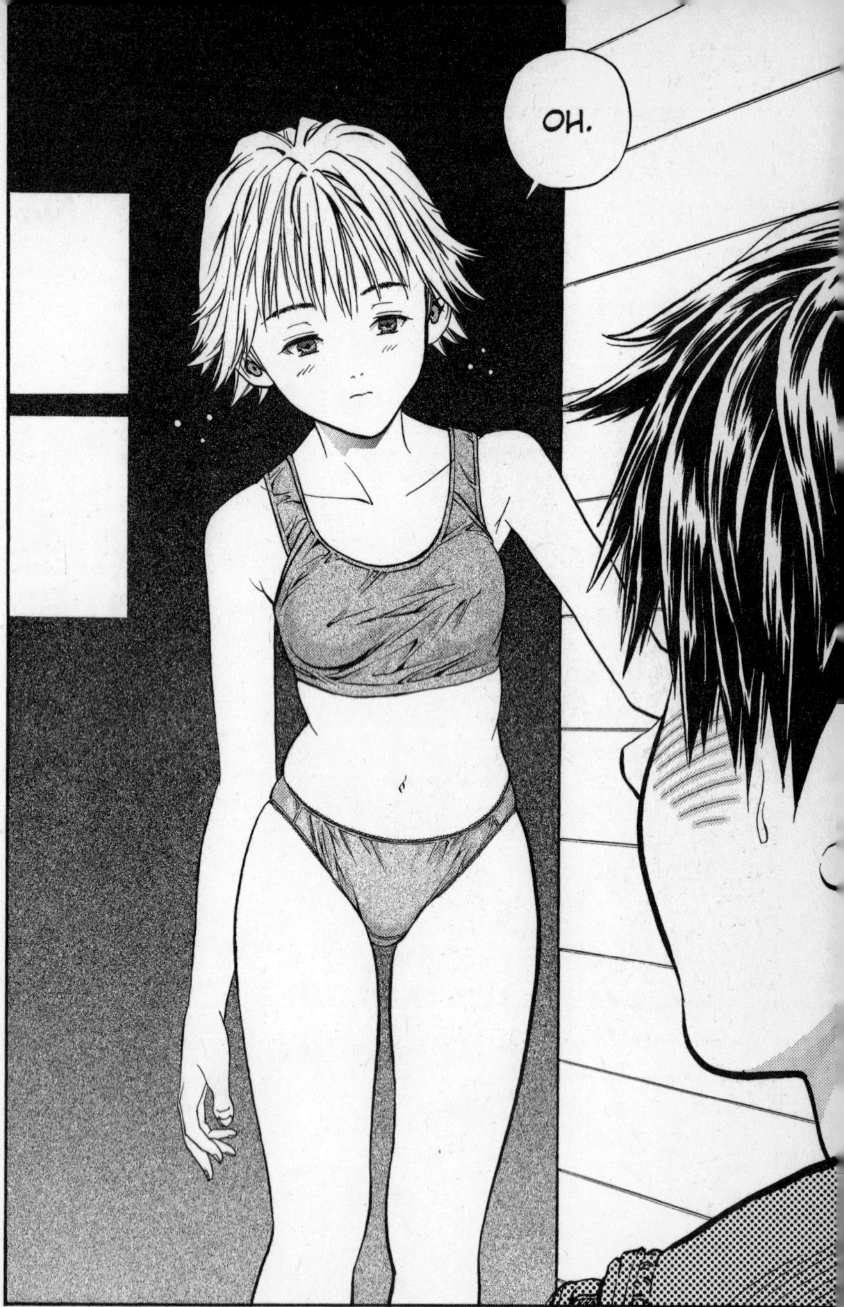
OH.

READ THIS WAY

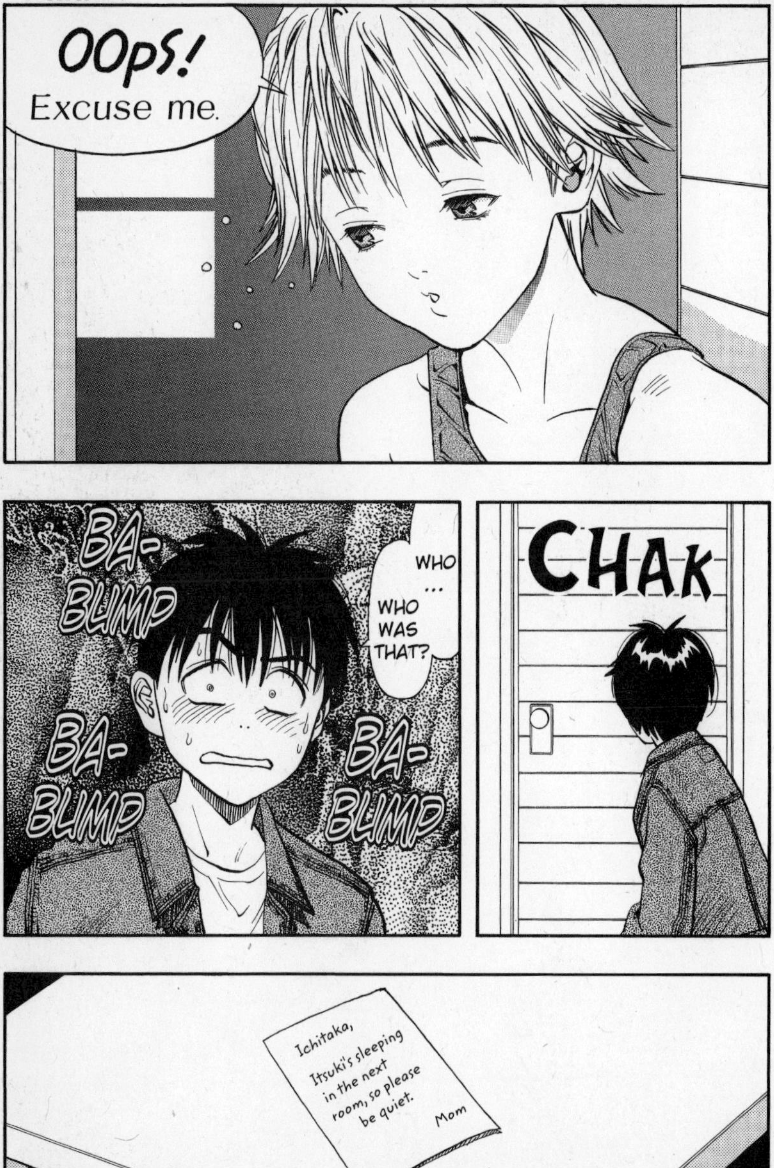
OOPS!
Excuse me.
CHAK
WHO ... WHO WAS THAT?
BA-BUMP
BA-BUMP
BA-BUMP
Ichitaka,
Itsuki's sleeping in the next room, so please be quiet.
Mom

To be continued in Vol. 2!

IS

I's Illustration
Collection

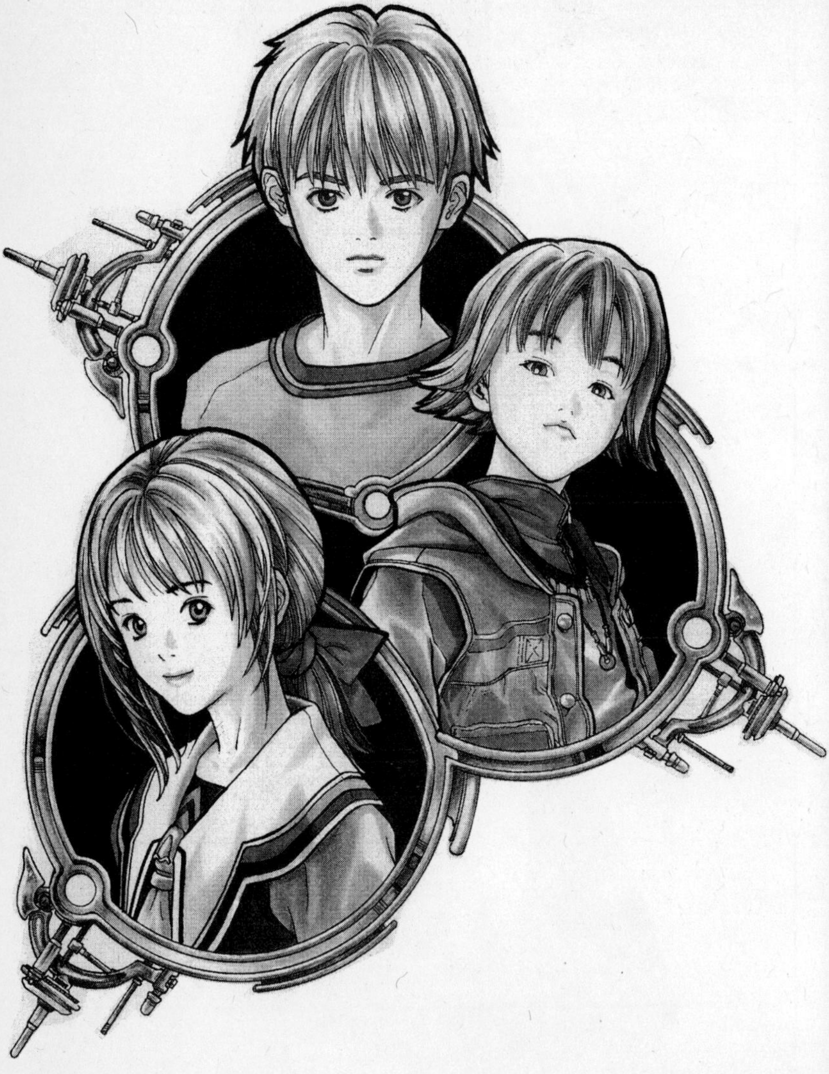

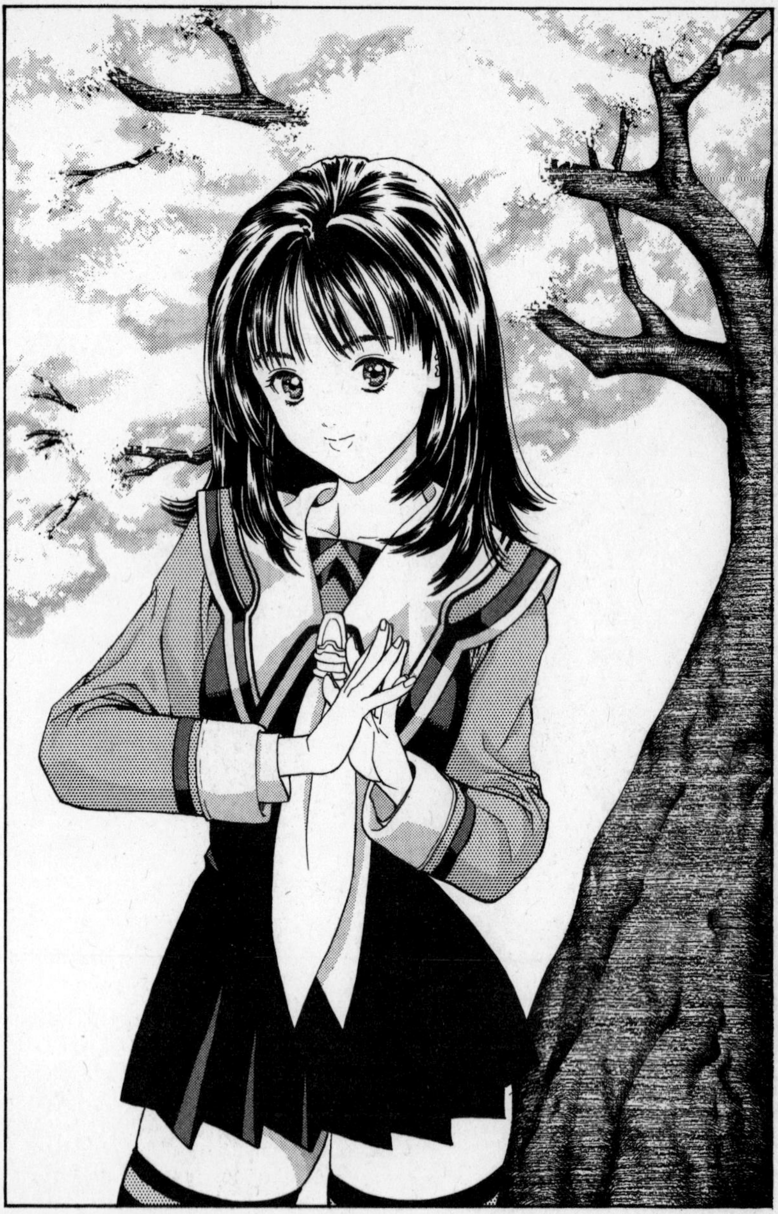

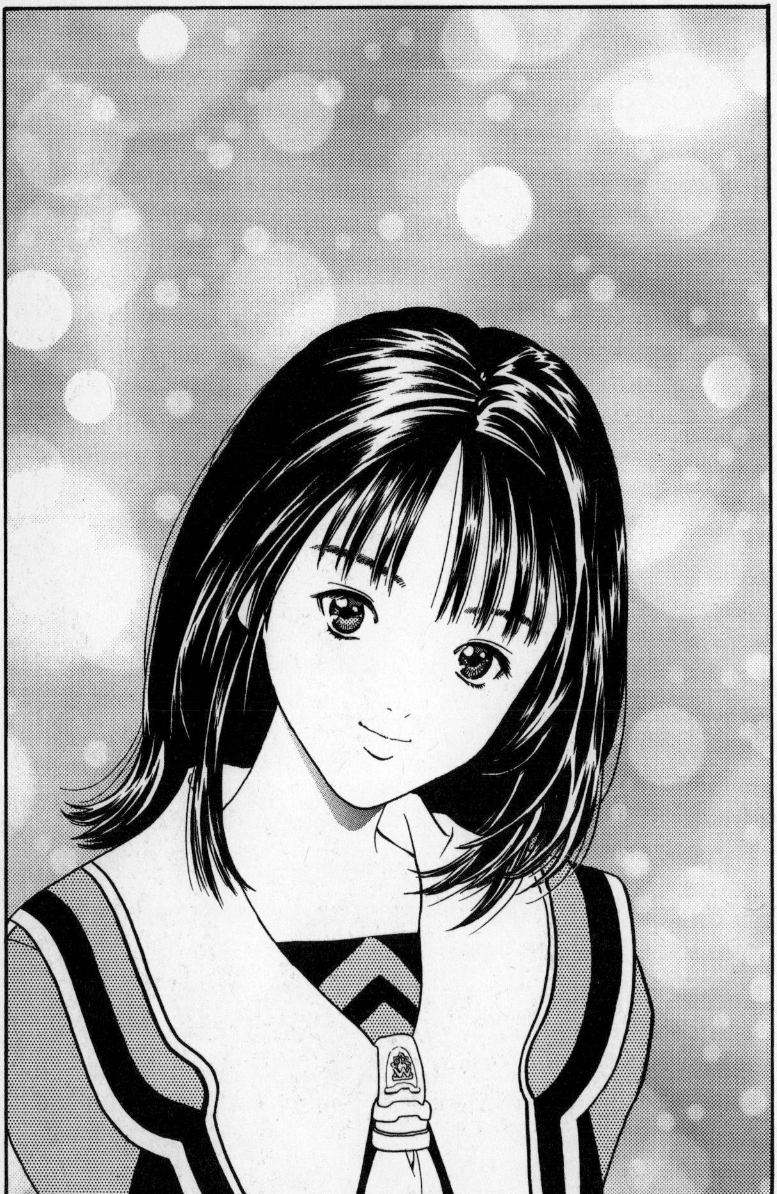

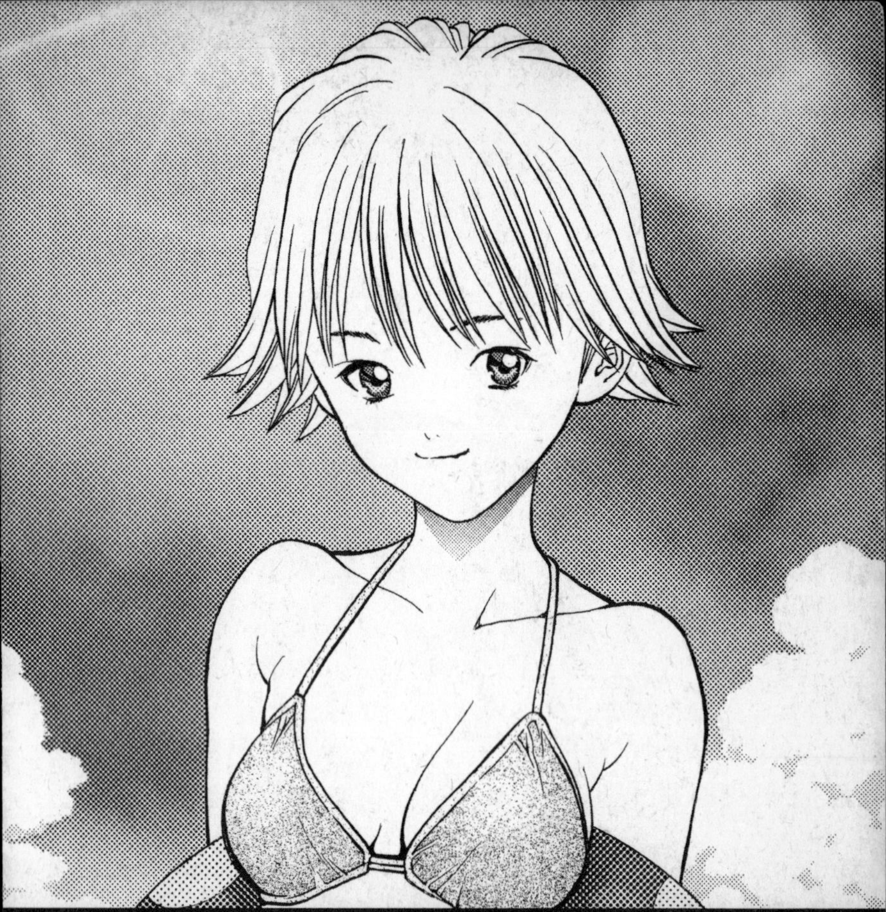

NEXT VOLUME PREVIEW

Ichitaka Seto's never been too successful with the ladies. In fact, his earliest memories are fraught with unrequited love and painful refusals. One girl, however, was always by his side—his childhood friend (and *sort of* girlfriend) Itsuki. But Itsuki moved away, leaving the borderline-loser Ichitaka all alone. Well, not only is she back in his life (and staying at his house), but she's a knock-down, five-alarm, grade-A, three-hoots-and-a-howl hottie! Will this change how Ichitaka feels about Iori, or will he simply try to double his pleasure?

Available now

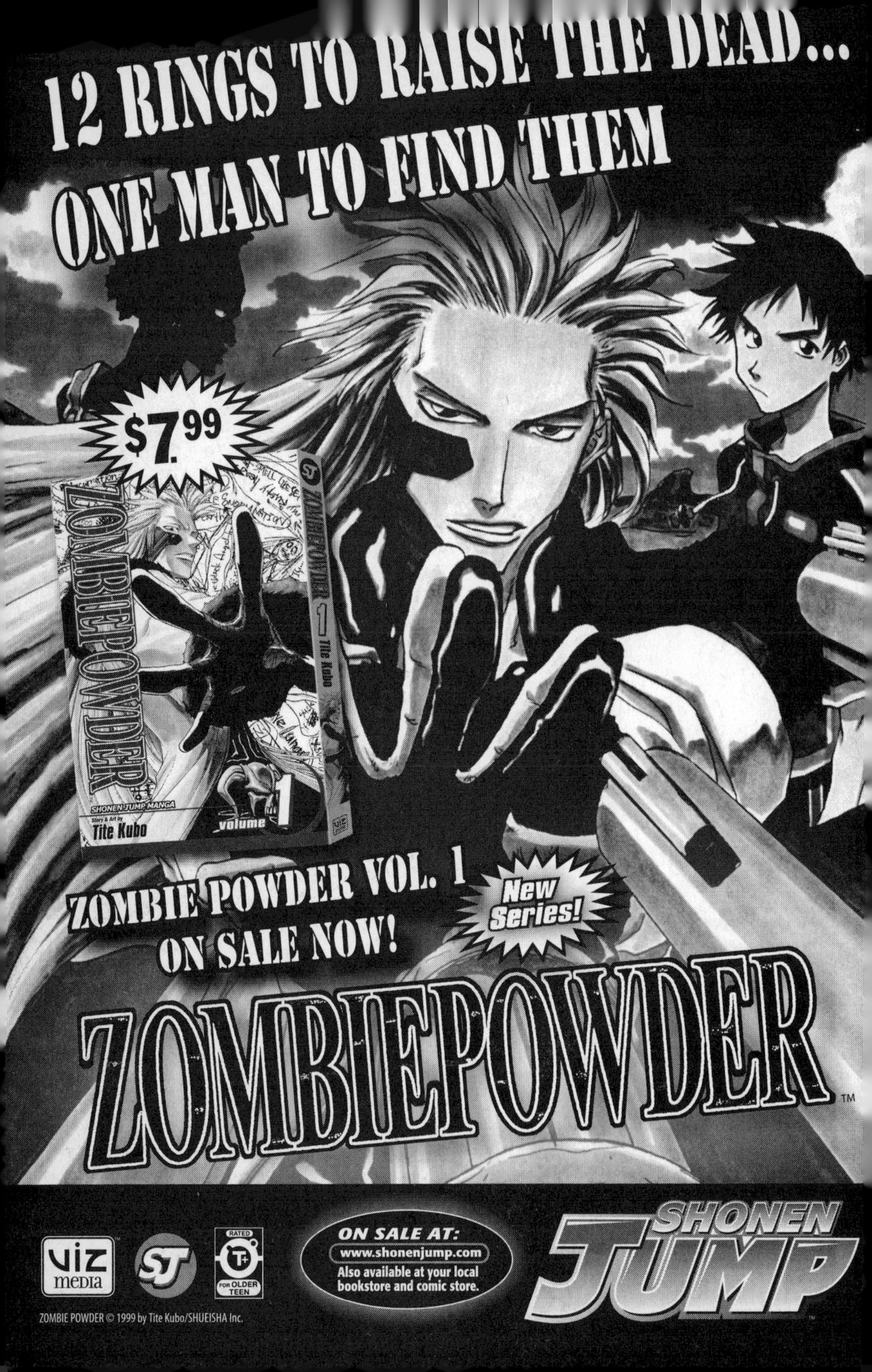
12 RINGS TO RAISE THE DEAD...
ONE MAN TO FIND THEM
$7.99
ZOMBIEPOWDER
SHONEN JUMP MANGA
Story & Art by
Tite Kubo
volume 1
ZOMBIE POWDER VOL. 1
ON SALE NOW!
New Series!
ZOMBIEPOWDER™
viz media
SJ
RATED T+ FOR OLDER TEEN
ON SALE AT:
www.shonenjump.com
Also available at your local bookstore and comic store.
SHONEN JUMP
ZOMBIE POWDER © 1999 by Tite Kubo/SHUEISHA Inc.

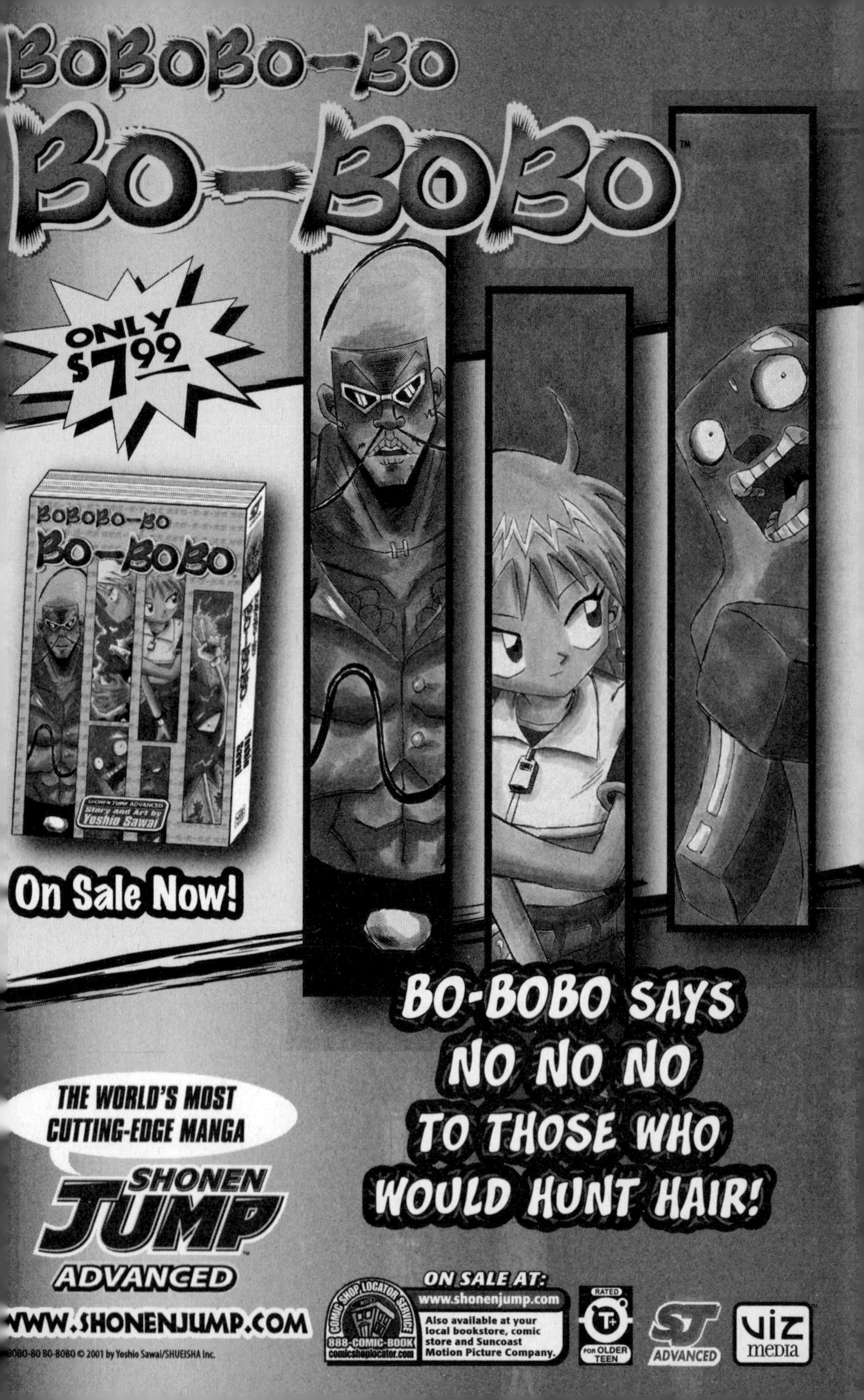

Check us out on the web!

www.shonenjump.com